M000307532

Scorecard Diplomacy

What can the international community do when countries would rather ignore a thorny problem? *Scorecard Diplomacy* shows that, despite lacking traditional force, public grades are potent symbols that can evoke countries' concerns about their reputations and motivate them to address the problem. The book develops an unconventional but careful argument about the growing phenomenon of such ratings and rankings. It supports this by examining the United States' foreign policy on human trafficking using a global survey of NGOs, case studies, thousands of diplomatic cables, media stories, 90 interviews worldwide, and other documents. All of this is gathered together in a format that walks the reader through the mechanisms of scorecard diplomacy, including assessment of the outcomes. *Scorecard Diplomacy* speaks both to those keen to understand the pros and cons of the US policy on human trafficking and to those interested in the central question of influence in international relations.

Judith G. Kelley is the Kevin D. Gorter Professor of Public Policy and Political Science at Duke University as well as the senior associate dean of the Sanford School of Public Policy. She was born and raised in Denmark and has lived in Germany, Ireland, and the United States. She also lived in China during the year before and after the Tiananmen Square massacre. A graduate of Stanford and Harvard's Kennedy School of Government, at Duke she writes on how the international community can promote democracy and human rights. Her last book, *Monitoring Democracy: When International Election Monitoring Works and Why It Often Fails* (2012) won the Chadwick F. Alger Prize for best book about international organization and multilateralism.

Scorecard Diplomacy

Grading States to Influence Their Reputation and Behavior

JUDITH G. KELLEY
Duke University

CAMBRIDGE
UNIVERSITY PRESS

CAMBRIDGE
UNIVERSITY PRESS

University Printing House, Cambridge CB2 8BS, United Kingdom

One Liberty Plaza, 20th Floor, New York, NY 10006, USA

477 Williamstown Road, Port Melbourne, VIC 3207, Australia

4843/24, 2nd Floor, Ansari Road, Daryaganj, Delhi – 110002, India

79 Anson Road, #06-04/06, Singapore 079906

Cambridge University Press is part of the University of Cambridge.

It furthers the University's mission by disseminating knowledge in the pursuit of education, learning, and research at the highest international levels of excellence.

www.cambridge.org
Information on this title: www.cambridge.org/9781107199972
DOI: 10.1017/9781108186100

© Judith G. Kelley 2017

This publication is in copyright. Subject to statutory exception and to the provisions of relevant collective licensing agreements, no reproduction of any part may take place without the written permission of Cambridge University Press.

First published 2017

Printed in the United States of America by Sheridan Books, Inc.

A catalogue record for this publication is available from the British Library.

ISBN 978-1-107-19997-2 Hardback
ISBN 978-1-316-64913-8 Paperback

Cambridge University Press has no responsibility for the persistence or accuracy of URLs for external or third-party Internet Web sites referred to in this publication and does not guarantee that any content on such Web sites is, or will remain, accurate or appropriate.

In memory of my grandmother, Ane Katrine Nielsen
1903–1987

Contents

PART II EFFECTS

Figures

Tables

Preface

This book was conceived the day before Christmas 2011. I had long been interested in the US effort to grade countries on their performance on fighting human trafficking. I thought the problem was horrific and the strategy interesting. When the US Department of State issued its first Trafficking in Persons Report (TIP) in 2001, I was intrigued whether this approach would work. Unfortunately, as a social scientist, I needed data, and data takes time to accumulate. So I waited ... for ten years.

In 2011 I started to study the developments on human trafficking since the report. That day in December in 2011, I was wrapping up a case study of Oman. I had picked this randomly to understand the dynamics of the policy in connection with a project that I was doing with Beth Simmons. That project was primarily statistical, but I always try to do case studies as background for anything statistical I do, even if these never see the light of day. I just need to know how things work on the ground, so I had picked Oman because it was a country I also didn't know much about so thought it would be interesting. I was fairly satisfied with the study I'd written based on conventional sources and was about to wrap it up, when right before I headed home that day I stumbled on one of the newly released quarter-million Wikileaks cables entitled: "Our TIP dispute with Oman." "*Dispute?*" I thought, what dispute? I soon found 78 cables that discussed TIP in Oman and realized that my case study was missing much of the story. That's when I knew I wanted to do many more of these case studies, because the interactions in the cables were so interesting, revealing reactions that scholars normally are not able to observe. I've always been interested in how the international community can promote political reforms in recalcitrant countries. Here was the United States using a novel and provocative approach – issuing grades – and the cables allowed me to look under the hood to see how countries responded. I was hooked. A computer science student helped me figure out how to write an algorithm to extract the cables relevant to human trafficking. The more I read, the more I became convinced that the US policy was on to something. It was clear that many countries cared about their grades and that the diplomacy on this issue was extensive. What was going on? This was when the research project became a book.

Like all books, writing this one has had its ups and down. The subject matter has been trying at times. When I was halfway through writing the book I'd read so many stories of horrific human rights abuses, though I realized naturally that any discomfort I suffered from reading about them paled in comparison to having to experience them. I still find it difficult to grasp that these atrocities take place today and how normal they are in some societies, sometimes even occurring with the consent of families. Then I came across some writing by my paternal grandmother, Ane Katrine Nielsen, who was born in the Danish countryside in 1902. She wrote:

I was sent out to serve the first time when I was only 6 years old, and that was far from pleasant, far away from your home, and only home twice for the whole summer; it was, I suppose, not completely without reason that one shed a few tears when the longings took hold. But time went, and I came home again. As an 8-year old I once again was sent out to serve and had once again a long road to walk to be able to be home a few hours on Sunday afternoon. From when I got the cows out past noon and until they had to come in at night, yes, a child only 8 years old and so alone in getting 8–10 cows out and in.

So we don't have to go so far back before practices like child labor were normal, even in my birth country. That also gives hope, however, that we can change practices around the world within our lifetimes. Criminalizing these behaviors has been the first step, but eradication remains an enormous challenge in a world where human trafficking and forced labor is estimated to be a $150 billion "industry."

I could not have written this book without the financial and institutional support I have received. I was fortunate to get an NSF grant, but it nearly didn't happen, because just after I had received notice, Senator Tom Coburn added an amendment to the bill funding the NSF stipulating that political science grants would be subject to additional review certifying that it was in the national interest. Fortunately, it turned out that this book *is* in the national interest. Thanks to Brian Humes for encouraging me and to the Senate for eventually restoring NSF unfettered funding to political science.

I am particularly grateful to the Smith Richardson Foundation for supporting me as a Strategy & Policy Fellow and to the Josiah Trent Memorial Endowment Fund for additional funding. Duke University and the Sanford School of Public Policy have provided me with a wonderful environment for my research.

Like most authors, I have many people to thank for their support. I have been fortunate to be able to blend my research and teaching and have a lot of students who helped along the way. Thanks to Miguel Guevara Jr., Lena de Santo, Maria Romano, Jan Pachon, Erik Wu, Justine Hong, Nadia Hajji, Elizabeth Reiser, Renata Dinamarco, Ade Olayinka, Elizabeth White, and Megan Ye. Three students in particular stand out: Gloria Dabek and Jessica Van Meir worked on this project for their entire Duke undergraduate career. They both worked on the case studies and Jessica did interviews in several countries. When this book comes out they will just be graduating. I cannot thank them enough for the outstanding work they put in and the companionship they provided along the way. Andrew Heiss, a Duke Ph.D. student, also deserves special praise. A few years before finishing this book I became Senior Associate Dean at the Sanford School of Public Policy. Andrew was nothing short of a wizard. He administered the global NGO survey and helped me continue my research. He kept me sane. He also deserves credit for all the fine figures throughout this book, although all errors remain my own.

I'm also privileged to have terrific colleagues who took the time to read the entire manuscript. In April 2016 I held a book workshop at Duke attended by Layna Mosley, Eddy Malesky, Tim Büthe, Gunther Peck, Bruce Jentleson, Fritz Mayer, Tana Johnson, and Sarah Bermeo. I am grateful to these people for reading the manuscript and spending half a day with me to discuss it. I am also grateful to Paulette Lloyd. Others who were kind enough to read the manuscript in its entirety include Robert Keohane, Peter Katzenstein, Michael Barnett, Karen Alter, and Beth Simmons, plus several anonymous reviewers. Each of these readers made distinct contributions to my revisions and I'm grateful for such tremendous colleagues who don't shy away from offering blunt advice. I am also grateful to Nancy Heiss for skillful editing.

Along the way I've presented work related to the book at multiple venues and appreciate the feedback this provided. These included the International Relations seminar, Stockholm University, the MacMillan International Relations Seminar Series, Yale University, the Bush School of Public Policy, the Cornell IR-Law Seminar, New York University Law School workshop on Global Governance Indicators, University of Pennsylvania Browne Center Seminar, Harvard's John F. Kennedy School of Government, Florida State University Ph.D. Seminar in Human Rights, the Triangle International Relations Seminar, Chapel Hill, NC, Georgetown University International Theory and Research Seminar, the Hauser Colloquium at NYU School of Law, workshop on the tools of international pressure, Yale University, as well as several Duke seminars and multiple presentations at Annual Political Science Association Conferences.

I also want to thank the 90 people who agreed to be interviewed for this book (for a complete list, please see the Methods Appendix), as well as the nearly 500 people who took the time to fill out our NGO survey. I am particularly grateful to John Miller and Mark Lagon, both former US TIP ambassadors, who offered candid insights.

Finally, I want to thank Karin and Lars, who let me make their home my home when I am in Denmark; Michael, who keeps me sane and knows when humor is the only way out; and Liv and Leif, who have matured along with this book and who bring me such pride and joy.

Abbreviations

ASEAN	Association of Southeast Asian Nations
DOJ	US Department of Justice
DOL	US Department of Labor
DOS	US Department of State
EU	European Union
FDI	Foreign Direct Investment
G/TIP	The US Department of State Office to Monitor and Combat Trafficking in Persons. Later renamed J/TIP
IGO	Intergovernmental Organization
ILO	International Labour Organization
IOM	International Organization for Migration
J/TIP	The US Department of State Office to Monitor and Combat Trafficking in Persons. Initially named G/TIP
NGO	Non-Governmental Organization
OECD	Organisation for Economic Co-operation and Development
OPDAT	Overseas Prosecutorial Development, Assistance, and Training, Criminal Division, US Department of Justice
OSCE	Organization for Security and Co-operation in Europe
TIP	Trafficking in Persons
TVPA	Victims of Trafficking and Violence Protection Act
UAE	United Arab Emirates
UN	United Nations
UNHCR	United Nations High Commissioner for Refugees
UNICEF	United Nations Children's Fund
UNODC	United Nations Office on Drugs and Crime
US	United States
USAID	United States Agency for International Development

PART I

THEORY AND PRODUCTION

I

Introduction

It's June 2001 and Israeli officials are in shock over statements by the United States Department of State (DOS). Public Security Minister Uzi Landau has called the DOS information outright "inaccurate,"[1] while somewhat more conciliatory, Mark Regev, the spokesman for the Israeli Embassy in Washington, has stressed that "Israel takes the issues raised very seriously." The Internal Security Minister advisor Hagai Herzl has called an emergency conference on setting the matter as a top policy priority.[2] Those near the key players describe the reaction as "hysteria" and "fireworks."[3] *The Jerusalem Post* has reported that Dan Ben-Eliezer of the Foreign Ministry called the international repercussions for Israel "severe" and added that "steps must be taken to remove Israel from the *unflattering* category [emphasis added]."[4]

What upset and embarrassed Israel so?

Fast forward to June 2005 in Jamaica. United States (US) officials are worried about the silence from Kingston. They worry about the "clock running," and fret that Jamaican officials do not want to be seen as "answering to instructions from Washington."[5] On June 24, after what

---

[1] Gilbert 2001b.
[2] Gilbert 2001a.
[3] Efrat 2012, 204.
[4] Gilbert 2001a.
[5] 05KINGSTON1531. Note that all ID numbers like this refer to a US Department of State Cable. These all follow the format TWO-DIGIT YEAR, EMBASSY CITY, CABLE NUMBER (without commas or spaces). Each ID is unique and sufficient to identify the document following the US Department of State identification system. Most can be brought up with a simple Internet search. They are also all stored in a database that will be made available on the book's resources site (www.cambridge.org/ScorecardDiplomacy).

the embassy characterizes as "sensational media coverage that reported (feigned) surprise and disbelief on the part of many [government] officials,"[6] National Security Minister Peter Phillips finally summons US embassy officials to the Ministry of National Security. They arrive for what turns out to be a 90-minute meeting with 15 Jamaican top officials. The embassy officials later write to Washington describing the meeting's "public ministerial disingenuousness," and noting that "[r]eporters from the Jamaica Information Service appeared before and after the meeting with photo and video equipment, and as Phillips clearly intended, the meeting received prominent coverage in the weekend news."[7] Kingston Mayor Desmond McKenzie tells the press that the issue has "jerked this country" at the highest levels.[8]

What were the Jamaican officials so keen to discuss, and to be *seen* doing so, with the Americans?

Now fast forward once again, this time to June 2008. A dispute between Oman and the US is making headlines in diplomatic cables from Muscat, which describes Oman as "indignant." Sayyid Badr al-Busaidi, the Secretary General of the Ministry of Foreign Affairs, goes to the US embassy on June 9 and, visibly agitated, warns the ambassador that Oman might be "forced to reassess all aspects of its relationship with the US," due to an incident that he calls "a 'knife in the back' of a friend" and describes as a personal insult. The shaken US ambassador writes Washington noting that he has never before known a senior Omani official to question the long-standing US–Omani relationship, which the Omanis usually view as "strategic." He is shocked that the Omani Secretary General has suggested that the Free Trade Agreement, which is a personal initiative of the Sultan, could even be in jeopardy. The ambassador notes that as an indication of just how seriously Oman views the matter, Sayyid Badr al-Busaidi has canceled an upcoming meeting with a US delegation coming to Oman to discuss civil nuclear cooperation.[9] Reporting that the Sultan feels "dishonored" and that Oman's "national honor has been impugned," the embassy laments to Washington: "We therefore are caught in a dispute in which there is little common ground, and with a partner that has indicated its willingness to wager the relationship on the outcome of the matter."[10]

---

[6] 05KINGSTON1531.
[7] 05KINGSTON1611.
[8] 05KINGSTON1531.
[9] 08MUSCAT425.
[10] 08MUSCAT431_a.

Why were the Omanis so upset?

SCORECARD DIPLOMACY AND THE POWER OF REPUTATIONAL CONCERNS

The answers to all three of these questions revolve around states' concern for their reputation, a central theme of this book. Understanding power and influence among states is one of the most enduring issues in international relations.[11] It is central to global governance, order, and peace. Coercive uses of power like interventions or sanctions get considerable attention, partly because they are high profile and have traditionally monopolized the concept of power. Subtler uses of power, such as institution building or appeals to shared norms, are often overlooked because they are difficult to trace and their effects less blatant.

This book focuses on one such subtle type of power, namely the power to shape the reputations of states. Nowadays, when information is more easily disseminated and protest more easily coordinated, the reputation of states in the eyes of their citizens and the world at large matters more than ever.[12] The word reputation here is used in its broad, conventional linguistic sense: States want social recognition and their governments care about how they are viewed by their own citizens and the global community.[13] Because states value their reputation, the ability to influence it is a form of power.[14] This book shows how eliciting states' concern for their reputation, broadly defined, can influence their behavior – a crucial insight for how we govern our increasingly interdependent world.[15]

To explain what the situations above in Israel, Jamaica and Oman above have to do with the power to shape reputations, some background is needed: In 2000, the US Congress adopted the "Victims of Trafficking and Violence Protection Act" (TVPA) to fight human trafficking, also called trafficking in persons (TIP). Human trafficking is the trade in human beings usually for sexual or labor exploitation. In recent decades, such trade has flourished to create a multi-billion dollar industry that exploits millions of human beings in unfathomably degrading ways.[16]

---

[11] Dahl 1957, Baldwin 2016.

[12] Nye 1990, 100, Grant and Keohane 2005.

[13] Wendt 1999, Ch. 5.

[14] Barnett and Duvall 2005, 42.

[15] Throughout this book I sometimes refer to "states" or "countries" as unitary actors. This is not an evisceration of individual agency, which this book affirms. These terms are used to refer to the aggregate elites that drive decision-making within a state.

[16] For more discussion of the nature and extent of the problem, see Chapter 3.

Sadly, while crime gangs are the primary perpetrators, government officials are involved in human trafficking in nearly one-third of countries
worldwide.[17] This makes the problem thorny to tackle both logistically
and politically. The international community has become concerned and,
also in 2000, adopted the Palermo Protocol to Prevent, Suppress and
Punish Trafficking in Persons, especially Women and Children to supplement the Convention against Transnational Organized Crime (the
Palermo Protocol).

The US had been one of the leaders on the Palermo Protocol, and
the new US policy signaled US intent to become a global leader on this
issue.[18] The nature of the problem and the fact that officials are so often
involved in this crime led the US to a government-centered approach. The
TVPA created the Office to Monitor and Combat Trafficking in Persons
(US TIP Office) within the Department of State (DOS) to issue an annual
report describing the efforts of other governments to combat human trafficking.[19] These were to be tied to some aid allocations, although the
president could easily waive any repercussions.

The act and the report might have gone unnoticed in the sea of government information were it not for the fact that the US TIP Office had
an additional mandate: to *grade* countries on their anti-TIP efforts. This
monitoring and grading exercise, which I call *scorecard diplomacy*, was
intentionally public. The drafters believed that "countries would only get
serious about their failure to address human trafficking if their deficiencies were publicly identified."[20] Although the World Bank and others had
produced global indices and rankings on various topics, *countries* had
never graded *all* other countries in the manner proposed by the TVPA.
Other US reports had been less comprehensive. The Special 301 Report
on intellectual property laws, for example, published since 1989, focuses
only on problem countries, leaving others alone. Not so with the TIP
Report: Since 2001, the report has come out with fanfare every summer
and assessed governments' efforts on prevention, protection, and prosecution of human trafficking.[21] In addition to criticizing countries and recommending various policy actions, it has also rated countries on "tiers,"

---

[17] Police and government officials have been identified as sources of trafficking in no
    less than 68 countries. Their participation is topped only by organized criminal gangs.
    Protection Project 2014, 41.
[18] DeStefano 2007.
[19] This office was originally named the G/TIP office and later renamed the J/TIP office.
    Often I refer simply to the US TIP Office.
[20] US Congress 2002, 8.
[21] Later a fourth "P," for partnerships, was added.

with Tier 1 being the best and Tier 3 the worst – and clearly failing – grade. Importantly, the tiers reflect government *efforts*, not outcomes.[22]

Scorecard Diplomacy and the Broader Grading Phenomenon

The TIP Report is not an isolated phenomenon. Grading countries' performance is becoming an increasingly common way to try to exert influence. The US itself uses this strategy in areas ranging from aid to religion. The US Millennium Challenge Corporation (MCC) developed scorecards to determine eligibility criteria for foreign aid. The afore-mentioned Special 301 Report reviews the global state of International Property Rights protection and enforcement and places US trading part-ners on a Watch List or a Priority Watch List. Similarly, the US Bureau of International Narcotics and Law Enforcement Affairs publishes the annual International Narcotics Control Strategy Report, which identi-fies countries with failing counternarcotics strategies. More recently the US Department of Labor has begun to place countries into performance categories in the annual Findings on Worst Forms of Child Labor, and the DOS has begun to flag the most restrictive countries in the International Religious Freedom Report. Notably, the model of the TIP Report is gain-ing favor. In July 2015, new legislation was introduced in the Senate to apply a "tier" grading system for countries' anti-corruption efforts explicitly modeled after the Anti-TIP Report.[23]

The US is not alone in its use of ratings, rankings, and blacklists. Going back as far as sovereign risk ratings, and gaining in popularity with the introduction of reports such as the Freedom in the World, by Freedom House, a range of actors has started to use global performance indicators as a tool of governance.[24] Today, non-governmental and inter-governmental organizations (IGOs) and even private actors rate and rank countries in different issue areas – for example, the World Bank uses the "Ease of Doing Business Index" to motivate governments to improve their business environments.[25] Ratings and rankings are also used at the subnational levels and may assess cities, firms, non-governmental orga-nizations (NGOs) and other entities.[26] Illustrating this boom in indices,

---

[22] For a comprehensive discussion of this policy, see Chapter 3.
[23] United States Senate Committee on Foreign Relations 2016.
[24] Davis et al. 2012b, Broome and Quirk 2015, Kelley and Simmons 2015.
[25] Chapter 2, note 24 lists some of the scholarship that has evolved around this emerging phenomenon.
[26] One example is firm level audits on labor standards as discussed in Locke 2013.

recent studies have uncovered over 150 efforts to rate, rank, or bench-mark countries on various dimensions.[27] While many focus on economic issues, these run the gamut from the environment, to health, gender issues, development, peace and security, and so forth.

As students and teachers know, grades can be powerful motivators, especially if they are public and recurring. Highly comparative and easy to understand numbers or categories stigmatize low performers because they provide an easy basis for others to point a finger.[28] Grades also facilitate competition. Global rating and ranking is clearly something that has caught on, but research on whether it works is nascent; nobody really knows. This makes the US efforts on human trafficking particularly interesting.

Back to the Cases

So what had the Omani, Jamaican, and Israeli officials so upset? They were all angry about the "grades" their countries had received in the recent reports. They called the meetings to discuss their grades with the US, to express their disappointment, and to show their citizens and the world that they were taking the criticism seriously.

But why did they react so strongly? Why would they care about a US report on a narrow human rights issue? Some countries like Oman rou-tinely sign human rights treaties and violate them, so why worry about this? The US had criticized countries for human trafficking issues in the larger DOS human rights report for years without provoking such reac-tions,[29] so why were the officials reacting so strongly to US criticism now?

Perhaps their reactions were just showmanship. Surely these officials might puff themselves up to impress the US officials, but what does that matter? Is there anything to show for all this huffing and puffing? This book will argue that it *does* matter, that many countries *do* change their policies, and that this reveals something interesting about the nature of influence in the international system.

Let's revisit the cases above just briefly. First, Israel: Here the US becomes a steadfast participant at the TIP policy table. The Israelis engage on the highest levels through meetings between officials such as Attorney General Alberto Gonzales and Prime Minister Ehud Olmert.[30]

---

[27] Bandura 2008, Kelley and Simmons 2014, Broome and Quirk 2015.
[28] Kelley and Simmons 2015.
[29] For an elaboration of the comparison between reactions to the human rights report and the trafficking report, see Chapter 5.
[30] 06TELAVIV2620.

The momentum and focus on trafficking changes drastically with the TIP Report. Political insiders call it a "shakeup" and a "complete turnabout."[31] Israel eventually passes anti-trafficking legislation that aligns with US preferences on both sex and labor trafficking and the annual reports receive ample coverage in the media, which often notes the US impetus behind government action.

Next, Jamaica: In the meeting described above, Phillips demands to know "definitively what further steps would be required for Jamaica to receive a 'passing grade.' " The Kingston mayor publicly credits the 2005 TIP Report with "focusing attention on the issue."[32] Between June and September, when the Tier 3 designation would be reassessed, the government undertakes several reforms.[33] By 2007 attitudes and behaviors have changed. Whereas in 2005 no Jamaican official even acknowledged the problem, two years later officials discuss it routinely, the police are investigating cases, and the Ministry of Justice is cracking down on employment ads used to lure women into prostitution.[34] When Jamaica eventually earns an upgrade in the TIP Report in 2007, the government proudly issues a press release touting "[T]he improved Tier 2 status [as] a welcome recognition by the international community in general and the United States Government in particular, of the intense efforts being undertaken by the government to tackle this growing problem."[35]

Finally, Oman: The US meets frequently with Omani policymakers and helps focus attention on human trafficking in Oman. Embassy officials confront Omani officials and society with the nature of the problem, particularly the practices of using small, trafficked boys for camel racing. Omani officials literally take notes in meetings with US officials about what they needed to do to get a better grade.[36] Eventually, the US directly advises on the text of new anti-trafficking legislation, which passes.[37] The debate around human trafficking significantly changes how the problem is perceived and defined and, although trafficking problems persist, the camel racing issue eventually is actually eliminated through new technologies.

[31] Efrat 2012, 204.
[32] 05KINGSTON1531.
[33] Ribando 2005, 19.
[34] 07KINGSTON927.
[35] Jamaican Information Service 2007.
[36] 08MUSCAT409.
[37] 08MUSCAT830_a.

This pattern has repeated itself in several countries around the world. The US has influenced policies in Argentina, the Dominican Republic, Japan, Malaysia, the Philippines, Indonesia, Armenia, Cambodia, Madagascar, United Arab Emirates, Jordan, Mozambique, Nigeria, and Ecuador, among others. Figure 1.1 maps one of the changes that the US has helped bring about, the domestic criminalization of human trafficking. Criminalization matters because countries need domestic statutes that allow them to arrest and prosecute offenders. The modern nature of the crime is such that by the end of the 1990s, most countries relied on a hodgepodge of unrelated statutes to piece together prosecutions and sometimes they lacked ways to charge offenders despite what was so obviously heinous and wrongful behavior. Thus, criminalization is not as a cure-all, but a *sin qua non* of anti-trafficking efforts. Furthermore, as later chapters will show, often criminalization has been connected to subsequent government efforts. The top map shows that few countries had adopted anti-trafficking legislation when US scorecard diplomacy began in 2001, while the bottom map shows the progress just 13 years later. The US has not been alone in pushing for these policies,[38] but this book will argue that its use of scorecard diplomacy has influenced the definition and norms and motivated and shaped many policy responses.

The term "influence" does not imply that scorecard diplomacy has reduced human trafficking, which is currently unknowable because of the poor data, or that its approach has been unproblematic. What US scorecard diplomacy *has* done is shape how many governments tackle this issue, including legislation, treatment of victims and other policies. Thus "influence" is the ability to change how a country behaves: to get it to pay attention and to adopt – and hopefully also implement – the recommended policies.[39] The approach doesn't work everywhere, and the influence is subtler than the blunt Cold War arm-twisting, but it is pervasive and consequential, and, given the relatively low cost, rather efficient. Sometimes scorecard diplomacy has allowed the US to influence which laws countries pass, train domestic security officials, comment on domestic administrative personnel decisions, and force issues on the domestic agenda. Indeed, the human trafficking issue illustrates

---

[38] Foot et al. 2015.

[39] This accords with the definition of social power. Baldwin 2016, 24. Influence does not require that actors are made to act *against* their own interest. Rather, it can include empowerment, facilitation, and encouragement to get others to progress toward behaviors that are in their interests. If a policy encourages adoption of a behavior faster than would otherwise occur or in a different form, the policy is influential.

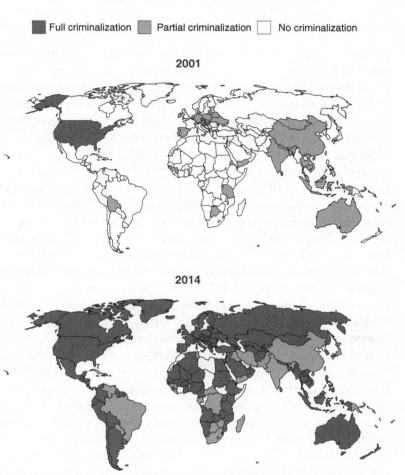

FIGURE 1.1. The spread of domestic laws criminalizing human trafficking.
Source: Author's data.

that the US is far more intrusive and influential in the domestic politics of many countries than is commonly understood. While the TIP Report is public, the engagement it elicits goes largely under the radar, but it has been strong.

So to return to the larger question about power and reputation: Why has the US had such influence and how has it wielded it? Why did the officials above react as they did? How did the US policy bring about changes? And, most importantly, what can this teach us about international relations, state behavior, and the power of reputational concerns?

THE ARGUMENT IN BRIEF

This book argues that the power to elicit states' concern about their reputation can be used to influence states. It contends that states care about their reputation in terms of how others perceive their performance relative to a broad set of norms and standards, and that, consequently, external actors can influence states by eliciting these concerns about their reputations – and indeed have found new ways to do so.

Specifically, the US has exercised such influence through what I call *scorecard diplomacy*. Scorecard diplomacy is the embedding of recurring monitoring and comparative grading of countries in traditional diplomacy. This contrasts in several ways with conventional "naming and shaming" or criticism of state misconduct. First, whereas shaming singles out individual countries, scorecard diplomacy gains validity by explicitly focusing on *all* countries, not just offenders. This reinforces the sense that the norms and standards are global and that everyone is being held accountable, which boosts the legitimacy of the monitoring and grading. In contrast with shaming, this inclusive approach facilitates *comparisons*, which can be powerful in the context of reputations. Second, scorecard diplomacy works not just by pointing out negative behaviors, but also by identifying desirable behaviors and plans of action. Moreover, whereas shaming is *ad hoc*, scorecard diplomacy is *recurrent*, which facilitates long-term engagement and subsequent anticipatory pressures, or what I call "status maintenance" effects. Scorecard diplomacy is thus much more than shaming. Countries are literally assigned periodic, and highly comparable, performance scores. These scores, derived by simplifying complex information, take on symbolic value and can be employed by others as well as the creators.[40] This allows NGOs, IGOs, and the media to augment the effect of the scores. Thus grades have outsized ability to shape states' reputations.

The US use of scorecard diplomacy is part of a larger phenomenon of using rating and rankings to influence states as a broader exercise of authority in global governance. The use of grades, rating or rankings is a particularly potent way to elicit reputational concerns. Grades are powerful symbols that shape perceptions about the performance of the graded.

---

[40] In *Economic Statecraft*, Baldwin references Harold Lasswell's work *Politics: Who Gets What When?* which referred to four different types of influence techniques, one of which was "words" or information, or symbolic means, also sometimes called propaganda. Lasswell 1958. Based on this Baldwin defines propaganda as "influence attempts relying primarily on the deliberate manipulation of symbols." Baldwin 1985, 13. For a discussion of the politics of numbers as symbols, see also Broome and Quirk 2015.

Grades are far from neutral, however. They reduce a complex reality to a preferred interpretation and in so doing select what to call attention to and designate that as meaningful.[41] Symbols such as grades are thus a political exercise to label and therefore shape perceptions of reality.[42]

A scorecard report or a rating or ranking may capture and issue space by propagating its definitions and norms until they dominate discourse on the issue. The annual reporting and related meetings open conversations with policymakers about how to define and frame the problem. In this sense, it can define discourses, through what some have called "productive power."[43] Successful scorecard diplomacy allows creators to become opinion leaders in the international system, which can change how policymakers in other countries define their interests and preferences.[44] A good example of this is the World Bank's Doing Business Report, which has framed the discourse on regulation. The issuance of grades becomes a form of standard-setting activity that constructs "scripts for action" and defines "legitimate social practice."[45]

States may become concerned about their reputation on the graded issue for instrumental or normative reasons. They may worry about their image or legitimacy for its own sake, or they may worry about practical implications of a poor reputation.[46] Practical concerns could be about material consequences, but they could also be about states' need to be able to justify their actions to be seen as legitimate for electoral or other purposes. Thus, the use of reputation as a tool of influence is neither limited to the idea of soft power nor does it deny hard power.[47] Rather, it acknowledges that power is multidimensional and can work "in and through social relations."[48]

The argument, however, is not a simple narrative about reputation as the lone driver of change. Rather, concern about reputation is *catalytic*; it facilitates other engagement. In the case of human trafficking, scorecard

---

[41] Bourdieu 1989, 20.

[42] Bourdieu 1989, 22. Eagleston-Pierce draws on Bourdieu's notion of symbolic power to explain how relatively weaker actors can frame a situation to enhance their position in bargaining with the WTO. Eagleton-Pierce 2013.

[43] "Productive power concerns discourse, the social processes and systems of knowledge through which meaning is produced, fixed, lived, experienced, and transformed." Barnett and Duvall 2005, 55. Merry et al. have a related concept called "knowledge effects." Merry et al. 2015.

[44] Barnett and Finnemore 2004.

[45] Hansen 2011, Büthe 2012, Davis et al. 2012a.

[46] Erickson 2015.

[47] Nye 2004.

[48] Barnett and Duvall 2005, 42.

diplomacy combines the symbolic use of grades with traditional diplomacy and assistance that can influence state behaviors. These include things like building productive coalitions with other stakeholders to pressure for change or information exchanges that can shape understandings and habits. Once states worry about their reputation, they become more receptive to these other efforts and interactions. Combined, the scorecard and the diplomacy aid institution building and learning, which generates further reputational concerns, which motivate countries to improve in anticipation of the next cycle. The iteration is crucial; it reinforces the norms and motivates action.

Whether scorecard diplomacy works depends on three factors: the degree and credibility of the exposure of the gap between its performance and the ideal; its sensitivity to this performance gap, which will depend on the instrumental and normative salience of this gap; and, finally, its ability to prioritize the issue sufficiently to respond.

Scorecard diplomacy is interesting not just as a story about US influence in human trafficking, or even about the wider use of rankings or ratings, but for what it reveals about state behavior more generally. The officials above reacted to the ratings because they cared about their personal reputations and the reputations of their countries. As this book will show, officials shun stigmatization and find public criticism embarrassing, upsetting, and sometimes infuriating; often they seek advice on how to improve their countries' ratings. The ratings are powerful because they invoke global norms and facilitate comparisons with other countries. Officials worry about their country's relative standing in the international community; they dislike being grouped with states they perceive as worse offenders, and they don't want to lag behind their neighbors or peers. They boast when they are praised. In today's interconnected and dense information environment, policymakers react to criticism or denouncement of their country.

Thus, the particular exercise of scorecard diplomacy elaborated in this book may be unique, but it demonstrates the importance of reputation to states and its potential as a tool of influence more generally. This validates yet another facet of power, which many scholars have come to understand as not simply an artifact of capabilities or direct force, but also as a multifaceted product of institutions, structures, and discourse.[49] It also demonstrates the oft-invoked – but seldom systematically examined – claim that states worry about their standing and image in

---

[49] Barnett and Duvall 2005, 44.

the international community of states, a claim that is fundamental to so many other arguments about how the world works.

This book will show that US scorecard diplomacy has influenced state policies by making states concerned about their reputation in the area of human trafficking. The primary tools have been the recurrent monitoring, comparative grading, and engagement. The use of sanctions has been marginal, although the possibility has been present. The US has not been alone in the anti-trafficking fight nor has the US accomplished everything it wants. Human trafficking is an ugly and deep-seated problem. Driven by entrenched poverty, increased trans-border mobility, and unscrupulous demand, trafficking will not cease; at best it can only be managed.[50] Most governments still have a long way to go in addressing it adequately, including the US. Yet, this book shows that the US policy has been a major factor in this fight. It has defined the international and national discourses, engaged and empowered NGOs and IGOs, and motivated and shaped policy responses around the world. That the US has accomplished this primarily by making states worried about their reputations underscores that more subtle methods of interstate diplomacy can influence states.

One might object that this is just another story about the predominance of US power.[51] Clearly, its strong position is surely an advantage, and may even be a prerequisite, although examples of weak actors wielding scorecards effectively also exist, as discussed in the conclusion. However, attributing everything this book reveals to US strength alone would overlook important insights about how scorecard diplomacy works.[52] Indeed, the US is not quite the master of ceremonies that it used to be; alternative narratives of more diverse worldviews are emerging everywhere, from India to Turkey and China to Russia.[53] Furthermore, even if the US still commands considerable conventional power, such power does not obtain results by itself; it must be wielded effectively. The status and strength of the US have facilitated scorecard diplomacy, but the story is not purely a function of power asymmetry. It is about the *way* that a particular strategy has been used to exert influence. Dictating national policies is not easy, even for the powerful. Scorecard diplomacy *harnesses reputational*

---

[50] Kapstein 2006.
[51] On network position as an important condition for exercising influences through assessments, see Kelley and Simmons 2016.
[52] Or, in the words of Ikenberry and Kupchan, "Power is not reducible to coercive capacities." Ikenberry and Kupchan 1990, 289.
[53] I thank Peter Katzenstein for making this point.

concerns and enables the user to wield power more effectively. It uses reputation like a sculptor might use a chisel: to target and deliver her power more effectively than the use of her hammer alone.[54]

HOW DOES IT WORK? SCORECARD DIPLOMACY
IN FIVE STEPS

Scorecard diplomacy combines traditional diplomacy with recurring monitoring and public, comparative grading of the performance of countries around the world. This approach is gaining prevalence; both the US and other actors increasingly use related approaches to rate and rank countries.

Importantly, however, scorecard diplomacy amplifies simple ratings and rankings in several ways. First, it embeds them in a web of regularized diplomacy and pushes the issue to the highest domestic players. Second, it can link the issue to other issues in the diplomatic relationship, including aid or trade. Third, localized diplomacy makes it easier to request information directly from states and local actors and to exchange ideas about possible solutions. Finally, funding to local and international actors can reinforce the central message. Thus, scorecard diplomacy creates an environment of continual policy engagement that exceeds the practices of most global performance indicators.

Figure 1.2 lays out the basic dynamics of what I call the *cycle of scorecard diplomacy*. The entire cycle is embedded within an existing normative environment. The public monitoring and comparative grading combines with ongoing diplomacy and assistance and is augmented by the indirect pressure created by media and other organizations. The grading and pressure generate concern about both present and future grades, which opens further engagement between policymakers and US diplomats. This concern and interaction increase countries' efforts to improve their ratings, thus they become more receptive to outside advice and practical assistance and keen to communicate actions taken so they can be considered for the next report. The most important feature of scorecard diplomacy, however, is its *cyclical* nature. While the steps might overlap,

---

[54] As Harold Lasswell notes, there are many tools or instruments of influence. Lasswell 1958. Cited in Baldwin. Baldwin 1985, 13. Sometimes these add up to more than the sum of their parts. As even Morgenthau noted, "[A] competent diplomacy can increase the power of a nation beyond what one would expect it to be in the view of all the other factors combined." Morgenthau 1950, 105.

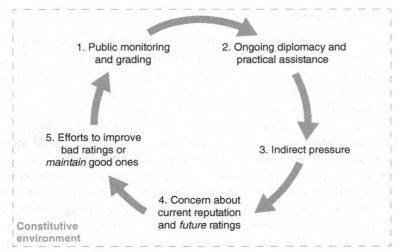

FIGURE 1.2. The cycle of scorecard diplomacy.

it is their recurrence that makes them powerful. The next section explains the components briefly.

The Constitutive Environment

Scorecard diplomacy is rooted in and depends on prevailing standards and expectations.[55] Users of scorecard diplomacy may either tap into the existing norms, be part of a prior effort to establish such norms, or, through the use of scorecard diplomacy and appeals to reputation, be part of redefining and shaping these norms.[56] Actors who publicly assess the performance of others are actively engaged in a debate around the definition of the basic norms, and sometimes one goal of the scorecard diplomacy may be not only to shape state behaviors directly but also to shape this evolving environment. Indeed, as part of a larger conversation, the many indices that gained visibility during the 2000s and contained the word "sustainable" have likely contributed to the framing of the "Sustainable" Development Goals finalized by the United Nations in 2015. In Figure 1.2 a surrounding box represents this environment. Although for ease it is omitted in later uses of the figure, it is an essential component.

---

[55] For a broader discussion of the role of a constitutive environment, see Wendt 1999.
[56] See Chapter 2, note 24.

Step 1: Public Monitoring and Grading

The heart of scorecard diplomacy is the regular publication of public reports that includes ratings or rankings of countries. These grades are often accompanied by recommendations for policy solutions. Recurrence is important for generating concerns about future grades.

Grades reduce complex reality to simple symbols that resonate easily with audiences and that other actors can employ easily to assess performance relative to a global set of norms and standards. These ratings reward or punish the non-conformant novice, and either mark or devalue their status.[57] Ratings and rankings mean that countries can be compared easily and movement relative to previous periods is obvious, a point elaborated by the recent body of research on global governance indicators.[58] This makes the information easy to process and magnifies the comparative element of status and reputation, especially when the reporting and monitoring are accompanied by concerted efforts to publicize the reporting. The monitoring furthermore has the potential to induce reflectivity, the concept that individuals change their behavior when they are aware of being observed, an idea also identified with the famous "Hawthorne effect"[59] and underscored in many recent experiments that show how people act more responsibly when they think someone is watching. Finally, the reporting may include narratives that help spread ideas and practices across countries.

Step 2: Ongoing Diplomacy and Practical Assistance

Engagement is a crucial step in scorecard diplomacy and separates it from the use of rating or rankings alone. Public criticism may be sufficient to get the attention of national officials, but not enough to produce policy reforms, which may have to compete with other priorities or engender opposition. That is why scorecard diplomacy is as much about diplomacy as it is about scoring. Importantly, the two are connected: the ratings and

---

[57] Johnston defines "social influence" as "a microprocess whereby a novice's behavior is judged by the in-group and rewarded with backpatting or status markers or punished by opprobrium and status evaluations." Johnston 2008, 24. For the power of symbols, Bourdieu 1989, 20. On status, see Dafoe et al. 2014.

[58] For a discussion of the literature on ratings and rankings, see Kelley and Simmons 2015. For general references, see Hansen 2011, Büthe 2012, Davis et al. 2012a, 2012b, Merry et al. 2015.

[59] Adair 1984.

rankings provide what some scholars have called "external inducement" for policymakers to engage in dialogue.[60]

The engagement that goes along with scorecard diplomacy takes many forms. The diplomacy is often intentionally less visible than the report. The diplomacy may consist of meetings with national officials in various agencies, where diplomats can call attention to the problem, persuade policymakers of the nature of the problem, flesh out recommendations, and work with domestic officials to formulate solutions. Meetings may also bring together stakeholders to help form coalitions for reform.

Scorecard diplomacy may also link aid or other practical consequences to the ratings. When such direct or indirect issue linkage is salient, scorecard diplomacy approximates more traditional forms of conditionality. The extent to which this occurs likely depends on the issue area, but also on the actor practicing scorecard diplomacy. More powerful actors are better positioned to link issues.

If scorecard diplomacy is linked to funding, training or know-how, this can build important capacity when states possess the will but not the means to change.[61] Such programs can also increase coordination and collaboration among NGOs, IGOs, and the government and contribute to domestic institution building.[62] Diplomacy and assistance thus boost attention to the issue and provide opportunities for interaction, institution building, and information transfers.[63]

Step 3: Indirect Pressure by Third Parties

The creators of scorecard diplomacy do not operate in a vacuum; other actors join in. Because governments worry about their reputations with multiple audiences, the greater environment and broader scope of actors are important to scorecard diplomacy. When other actors use the grades and reports, they increase the pressure on the target state.

Media is particularly keen to cover information packaged as rating or rankings rather than mere narrative reports. News stories often lead with the ratings. Sometimes they simply reprint the entire content of the

---

[60] Ikenberry and Kupchan discuss external inducement as one venue for socialization and learning. Ikenberry and Kupchan 1990, 290. In their scenario, coercive measures are used to induce elites into adopting new policies that they later internalize. In this case, the ratings and rankings may produce a non-coercive form of inducement.

[61] It is a long-standing argument that many countries want to comply with various international standards, but lack the capacity. Chayes and Chayes 1993, 1995.

[62] Finkel et al. 2006.

[63] Risse and Sikkink 1999, Johnston 2001, Checkel 2005.

reports more or less unedited. Other times the media itself may blame the government for underperforming. Of course, strong governments may prevent media criticism, but often both government and opposition figures comment on the accounts.

IGOs and NGOs can also boost scorecard diplomacy. If they get funding to implement related projects or use or promulgate the information in the reports, they legitimize and augment the central message. They can seize on poor ratings to pressure on their governments to reform and use information to inform their demands. Similarly to how NGOs mobilize around international legal commitments, they can use scorecard diplomacy to hold officials accountable.[64] Finally, NGOs also gain influence by becoming information *sources* for the reporting. This type of "information politics"[65] increases the influence of NGOs: When governments realize that NGOs have some input into the rating, they are likely to take NGOs more seriously.

Depending on the issue, other actors might also exert pressure on the government because of the ratings. This could include lenders, investors, or other market mechanisms. In such ways, third parties play a crucial role in the promulgation of scorecard diplomacy. Indeed, the public nature of scorecard diplomacy combined with the in-country engagement and resource provision is designed to empower such actors.

Step 4: Concern About Current Reputation and *Future* Ratings

The central step in the cycle of scorecard diplomacy is the generation of concern about the reputation generated by the tier ratings. Without this, the motivation to respond is absent. As the next chapter discusses, scorecard diplomacy can give rise to reputational concerns at both the level of the state or government, and at the level of the individual policy maker or bureaucrat responsible for a given policy area.

On a national level, governments may worry about practical consequences such as sanctions or loss of aid, trade, or other benefits. They may also worry that criticisms can damage their international or domestic legitimacy and harm their standing in the international community. A government's concern about its reputation on a given issue may increase because the scorecard diplomacy or the associated assistance increases attention to the issue or even changes the national position.

[64] Simmons 2009.
[65] Keck and Sikkink 1998.

If they worry they will be held personally accountable or fear for job security, individual elites may also be concerned about practical consequences of poor performance.[66] They may also be concerned morally if they identify with the normative issues but know that their conduct, or that of their state, is contradictory. On a personal level, they may become concerned about the issues as they interact with and learn from the creators of the scorecard. Whatever the source or reason, the ratings can ignite concern that incentivizes state actors.

Step 5: Efforts to Improve Bad Ratings or *Maintain* Good Ones

The goal of all this activity, of course, is to encourage policy reform, the last step in the cycle of scorecard diplomacy. Scorecard diplomacy usually offers many recommendations for policy actions and may stipulate what is required to improve a given grade. It thus also brings resources and know-how to the issue. As attention to the issue increases and domestic institutions begin to engage with the issue, capacity grows and becomes more institutionalized. The issue has an easier time making it onto policy agendas, and the creation of concrete capacity and programs may find more support.

This is not to say that the process ends here with perfect outcomes. Reforms are possible but not certain. If there is funding for programming, this may lead to *some* implementation, but a country's framework may need to evolve further or implementation may remain a challenge. Some countries may not respond, or perhaps a satisfactory solution for a problem does not exist. Further, countries may backslide, especially if the problem is unwieldy. Progress may occur in one cycle, regression in another. This is why scorecard diplomacy is a cycle, and why its recurrent nature is so important. Iterative practices help stabilize meaning and action,[67] and game theorists argue that iteration helps establish the "rules of the game" and create norms through expectations.[68]

WHY STUDY SCORECARD DIPLOMACY?

Scorecard diplomacy brings a fresh perspective to the age-old, but challenging quest to study influence. Because diplomacy usually is distinctive

---

[66] Not surprisingly, survey experiments show that those most responsible for a policy are held most responsible. Renshon et al. Forthcoming.
[67] Pouliot and Cornut 2015, 306.
[68] Schelling 1980, 107, 168–169.

to each country or even each situation, most research consists of valuable – but idiosyncratic – case studies. Scholars are rarely able to examine diplomatic efforts across countries on a single topic and observe the relative merits of the various tools or differences in state responses to any given tool. This is why, although scholars have long argued that states care about their standing and image in the international community, studies have not shown this systematically. Studies that engage these ideas typically invoke them as explanations for correlations in cross-national studies but struggle to document the causal mechanisms across multiple cases. We lack rigorous investigations of how government officials respond to public criticism, whether those reactions translate into behavioral changes, and what factors facilitate or hinder such changes.

The US promotion of anti-trafficking policies offers an opportunity to overcome some of these challenges to the study of influence because of its cross-national scope, which makes it possible to compare responses to the pressure on the same issue across many countries. This is facilitated by an unprecedented availability of primary documents that makes it possible to study the causal mechanisms and derive insights about how evoking concern for reputation can work as a tool of influence.[69]

A good understanding of power and influence is central to the study of international relations. This book is by no means the first to argue that power is not primarily about force and coercion, but that it is also normative and symbolic: power can flow from shaping and invoking conceptions of what is normal.[70] However, this book brings novel evidence to bear on this argument and provides unprecedented micro-level evidence of how elites react to monitoring and to criticisms and how this connects to outcomes.

While not its main focus, the book also addresses the ever-debated role of the US in the system of global governance. Claims of the decline of US influence have become common,[71] but these miss subtle channels of US influence. This book shows that much consequential diplomacy happens in the background: the provision of grants that empower local actors, meetings proffering detailed advice that often gets followed, legislative council, funding for international organizations to carry out programs

---

[69] A case for testing of mechanisms in the context of randomized controlled trials is made by Mullaninathan et al., and the general insight applies. Mullainathan et al. 2011.

[70] Note that Manners defines normative power as "ability to shape conceptions of 'normal.'" Manners 2002, 240. Scorecard diplomacy holds countries to standards of behavior and shapes their reputation in terms of conceptions of these.

[71] See Layne 2012, 203. For a discussion of this debate, see Nye 2010.

aligned with US preferences, etc. These are all ways that the US continues to exert influence, albeit in subtler ways.

Although the book focuses on US scorecard diplomacy on human trafficking, the systematic use of reputation as a tool of power is also worth studying because the use of ratings and rankings, benchmarking, and the like is gaining popularity. The US uses it in many different issue areas, and many other actors, including IGOs and NGOs, use related approaches such as rating and ranking countries' performance across a range of different topics, some which trigger clear material payoffs and others less so. The findings may therefore provide insights into a broader range of global efforts to exert influence.

In addition to exploring the nature of influence, the book also brings useful attention to US anti-trafficking policy. IGOs and NGOs all over the world are engaged in fighting TIP,[72] but the US program has been one of the leaders. Opinions of the program vary greatly.[73] Both the US Government Accountability Office and the US Inspector General's Office have pointed out flaws in the program. Other countries have berated it as inconsistent or arrogant. Some commentators have criticized its relationship to international law[74] or questioned its accuracy or effectiveness.[75] Others accuse the policy (as well as the international Palermo Protocol itself) for harming victims, while some credit the policy with reinforcing the core provisions of the Palermo Protocol.[76] Yet Mark Lagon, a former US Ambassador at large to Monitor and Combat Trafficking in Person, has testified before Congress that: "[I]n case after case, we have seen how the report and rankings have worked, even among allies unused to prodding from the United States ... When some say this 'tough love' has not worked, it is flatly untrue. The US TIP Office and the report focus the mind of other governments on the problem."[77] This book doesn't provide definitive evidence one way or the other, but it casts more light on the subject and offers insights on the US efforts.

In sum, US scorecard diplomacy on human trafficking offers a unique opportunity to learn about the central question of influence in international relations while assessing a contested diplomatic effort on an important topic.

[72] Foot et al. 2015.
[73] DeStefano 2007.
[74] Chuang 2013.
[75] Chacon 2005–2006, Chuang 2005, Nathan 2005, Wooditch 2011, Horning et al. 2014.
[76] Gallagher 2015.
[77] Lagon 2010, 5.

OUTCOMES, SOURCES, AND RESEARCH METHODS

This book uses the example of human trafficking to explore how score-card diplomacy can generate reputational concerns that can bring about change. But change in what? What is the outcome of interest?

Importantly, the empirical focus of this book is neither the moral uprightness nor the efficacy of national trafficking policies, but the exercise of influence. It is not about whether the US has promoted the "best" policies, which is a matter of opinion, or whether those policies have reduced trafficking, which poor data renders elusive to assess.[78] Rather, this book focuses on diplomatic efficacy: has US scorecard policy been able to get governments to change their behavior – in terms of both policy and practice – by accepting the problem and undertaking reforms the US was promoting? The goal is to understand the nature of influence, what drives state behaviors, and bring us closer to that holy grail of international relations research: to understand the ability of one nation to influence another, which is the foundation of global order.[79]

To this end, the book studies multiple types of outcomes at various levels. As the Methods section describes further, given the complexity of the outcomes, they are explored in depth for some cases and in other cases measured cross-nationally over time. The outcomes examined are as follows:

State criminalization of human trafficking: Have countries criminalized human trafficking? One of the major foci of the Palermo Protocol was for countries to criminalize human trafficking in domestic laws. The measure and the appropriateness of its use and the extent to which it is meaningful are discussed more fully in Chapter 6, but essentially this captures whether states have sufficient legal measures criminalizing all forms of human trafficking with appropriately stringent penalties.

Policy implementation: To what extent do countries take practical measures to implement anti-TIP policies? This includes consideration of how the criminalization measure is implemented, for example, whether countries arrest and prosecute traffickers. It also includes attention to

---

[78] Tyldum and Brunovskis 2005. Much scholarship calls for greater attention to whether anti-trafficking policies effectively address root causes to reduce trafficking levels. This research is both important and much more voluminous than can be covered here, but Chuang is a good starting point for learning about much of this interesting and relevant work. Chuang 2006.

[79] An important reason for understanding power is, as John Harsanyi has pointed out, to understand policy options for influence. Harsanyi 1971, 80.

protection of victims as well as prevention efforts and other implementation efforts.

Institutionalization: Does scorecard diplomacy influence domestic designations of agency operations, change how agencies operate, or build new institutions and practices such as training academies or regularized data gathering?

Adoption of new definitions of trafficking: Do the norms and practices around the problem change? Does the government become more open and accepting of the problem of human trafficking, do officials change the way they discuss the problem, do laws adopt new definitions, and do attitudes and practices towards victims change?

The reactions of officials to US grading and diplomacy: How do officials react to the grading and issuance of reports on their government's performance on human trafficking? What responses do they have and what types of questions or concerns do they raise? Do officials compare their countries with others?

The extent of media coverage: Does media coverage respond to the issuance of the report and does it magnify the criticisms in the report or do officials use it to defend themselves against those criticisms?

The behavior and views of NGOs and IGOs in the field: Are NGOs and IGOs engaged by scorecard diplomacy? Do they discuss and use the report? Do they collaborate with the embassy, and what are their views about US efforts?

The research relies on extensive original data collection and combines multiple methods in an eclectic approach that includes the following techniques:[80]

Document analysis: The project analyzes thousands of media accounts and hundreds of other primary documents from intergovernmental organizations, the US Department of State, and other sources. The research is enhanced by the new and unprecedented availability of the quarter-million diplomatic documents from the 2012 Wikileaks release, about 8,500 of which refer to human trafficking from 2001 to early 2010.[81] These are US diplomatic exchanges between Washington and embassies around the world. Many of these documents reveal interactions between

---

[80] Barnett and Duvall 2005, 67–68, Sil and Katzenstein 2010, 10.

[81] Note that my use of these cables was revealed in my initial application to the NSF for funding and that the NSF passed the proposal through a review to ensure that it was in the national interest (as required at the time by law following an amendment to the budget from Senator Coburn (Rep-OK)). After this review, the NSF decided to sponsor this research, full knowing the use of the Wikileaks cables.

embassy staff with national officials on trafficking and report discussions in detail, as experienced by the local US diplomats. The discussions are interesting because they were not intended for publication and thus contain some frank observations and cannot easily be dismissed as public posturing.[82] This unconventional evidence is therefore unusually rich and promising. While the record is much fuller for some countries than others, even this incomplete archive reveals information that – combined with other evidence – is extraordinarily useful. Based on the embassy cables and media reports, I coded all official reactions to the release of the TIP Report.

Interviews: The book draws on interviews with 90 people from governments, NGOs and IGOs in 19 countries from all continents, conducted between 2012 and 2016. The majority were phone or Skype interviews, with about 20 one-on-one in-person interviews, three group interviews with a combined 18 people, and a few email correspondences. The interviews generally varied in length from 20 to 90 minutes. Questions were tailored to the knowledge and experience of each interviewee so that the interviews were partly structured, but open to follow-up on new information. Several were anonymous, although all but a few people agreed to be listed as sources in the Appendix.

Interviewees were selected based on research about who had played key roles in the development of US trafficking policy and inquiries with IGOs about suitable interviewees. NGO interviewees were often people who had been invited to participate in the NGO survey and preferred a personal conversation. In addition, systematic interviews were done in a few countries where research assistants connected with the project were traveling. The list of interviewees was expanded using snowball techniques, which entails asking interviewees for other recommendations of whom to interview, a technique that was also useful for confirming the appropriateness of those interviewed. While it proved difficult to get the International Organization on Migration (IOM) to agree to interviews, perhaps because it receives extensive funding for anti-TIP efforts, and while some interviewees requested anonymity, those asked to participate were generally willing and forthcoming.

A global NGO survey: Between 2012 and 2014 I assembled a database of over a thousand NGOs working on TIP issues around the world. During the summer and fall of 2014, 480 NGOs working in 133 countries

---

[82] Gill and Spirling 2014, 2.

responded to a survey designed to understand their engagement with the US and the TIP Report, as well as their assessments of the role of the US in their countries and their own governments' performance. Because some NGOs working in several countries filled in the survey for each country they worked in, this provided 561 separate country-level responses.

The NGO survey garnered an unusually high response rate of 43.5 percent, and those NGOs that participated were similar in terms of whether their primary focus was on human trafficking or a broader set of issues. The survey took care to minimize signaling about its purpose and any overt focus on the US, thus reducing the likelihood that any opinions of the US and its efforts influenced NGO decisions to participate in the survey. There were only slight geographic differences in participation rates, and nearly 90 percent of respondents were based outside the US, so the US organizations did not drive the findings. Furthermore, most organizations reported being very knowledgeable about TIP policy in their country.

Case studies: Drawing on interviews, the NGO survey, and the document analysis, 15 case studies were used to examine the evidence for the steps in the scorecard diplomacy cycle to identify outcomes and analyze the likelihood of causality between US efforts and the observed outcomes. Each case study includes construction of a chronology to facilitate analysis of sequencing of events, examination of the congruence between recommendations and outcomes, comprehensive overviews of factors driving change, and observers' own inferences. In addition to the 15 cases, other relevant examples are drawn from other countries.

Statistical analysis: Original data created for this project included a measure of NGO presence, US TIP grants, a dataset of public and private reactions to TIP Reports, updated data on media coverage of human trafficking, original data on sanctions waivers by the US president, data on embassy interaction with NGOs and IGOs, and data on criminalization updated from a prior project with Beth Simmons. Other pre-existing data was also merged with the above.

The Methods Appendix explains these methodologies further, describes the relevant data and lists the interviewees. It also discusses the survey methodology and participation rates, coding of data, methods for identifying and coding relevant media documents and State Department cables, as well as the case study selection and methodology. Many related materials are available on the book's resources site (www.cambridge.org/ScorecardDiplomacy).

The analysis explores many observable implications of the argument with a variation of data. Such "triangulation" of evidence cross-validates findings in multiple ways that are not all subject to the same sets of assumptions or weaknesses.[83] Analysis of mechanisms at the micro level improves causal inference both by checking for evidence of the proposed mechanism and by allowing discovery of alternative explanations.[84] The main focus is on demonstrating the overall effects, but the methods also permit some inferences about the relative strength of the causal mechanisms.

THE PLAN OF THIS BOOK

The next chapter lays out the argument about reputation and scorecard diplomacy in three parts. It elaborates on the broad *definition* of reputation and discusses the notion that states hold multiple reputations in the eyes of multiple audiences and why states value a good overall reputation. It then considers the factors that *condition* whether states worry about their reputation on a given issue. It ends by exploring how the *features* of scorecard diplomacy stimulate concerns about reputation.

The chapters that follow unfold along the steps of the cycle of scorecard diplomacy. Chapters 3 and 4 focus on how scorecard diplomacy around human trafficking is produced. Chapter 3 presents the background of human trafficking to provide context for the normative environment in which scorecard diplomacy operates. It then discusses Steps 1 and 2 in the scorecard diplomacy cycle. Using the NGO survey, data about US TIP-related aid, and interviews, it describes how the US conducts scorecard diplomacy and presents data on the volume and nature of diplomatic interactions and the nature, volume, and distribution of financial assistance. The chapter also examines whether the US scorecard diplomacy treats countries differently, which is important for exploring its effectiveness.

Chapter 4 examines Step 3 in the cycle of scorecard diplomacy: indirect pressure, or how scorecard diplomacy engages other actors. Drawing on interviews and the NGO survey, the chapter highlights interactions between states, NGOs, and IGOs and illustrates how scorecard diplomacy facilitates indirect pressure from these actors. It also overviews the

---

[83] Greene and McClintock 1985.
[84] George and McKeown 1985, Legro 1997, 45–58.

use of funding to NGOs and IGOs and provides examples of indirect pressure in different countries.

While Part I of the book focuses on how scorecard diplomacy is produced and delivered, Part II focuses on how countries react and respond. Chapter 5 examines the evidence for Step 4 in the cycle: concern about ratings. The premise of scorecard diplomacy is that elites care about the report, take it seriously, worry about their grades etc. Is this what happens? This chapter analyzes elite reactions to tier ratings. The analysis draws on the cables from US embassies chronicling discussions with officials about their countries' tier ratings. It codes the reactions and uses case studies and statistical analysis to demonstrate the volume of reactions to the rating and the nature of concern they reveal. Finally, the chapter shows how elites react differently in private and in public, which underscores their concern with reputation.

Chapters 6 through 8 focus on how scorecard diplomacy influences state behavior, Step 5 in the cycle. Chapter 6 looks at several outcomes. It first analyzes the domestic criminalization of human trafficking, a top policy priority of US pressure. It shows that countries ramp up efforts closer to the US reporting deadline. It also shows that inclusion in the report, tier ratings, and drops in tier ratings correlate with criminalization. Importantly, it shows that countries that have documented reactions also are more likely to criminalize, indicating that reputational concern is a plausible mechanism for the established relationships. The chapter also synthesizes the case study evidence about broader outcomes such as influences on domestic institutions and implementation issues. To get at broader perceptions of the policy's effectiveness, the chapter also shares insights from the NGO survey and interviews with IGOs.

Because the effectiveness of scorecard diplomacy varies, it's important to understand why. Chapter 7 draws on the ideas developed in Chapter 2 about sensitivity, exposure, and prioritization, and uses statistical analysis and case studies to discuss the factors that have impeded or facilitated scorecard diplomacy.

The penultimate chapter uses the cases of Israel, Japan, Armenia, and Zimbabwe to illustrate how variation in the elicitation and presence of reputational concern influences how states respond to the policy demands. The cases provide a glimpse into the intensity of the diplomacy, the reactions on the ground, and some of the conditioning factors as well. Hopefully, they might entice the reader to visit the book's resources site (www.cambridge.org/ScorecardDiplomacy) for more case study examples.

The book concludes by synthesizing the evidence and asking larger questions. What do the findings tell us about the influence of reputational concerns in today's world? What does scorecard diplomacy reveal about the nature of power and influence more broadly? What might be objections to these claims? What are the insights for US policy on human trafficking and how might these transfer to similar efforts to use ratings and rankings?

2

Scorecard Diplomacy and Reputation

It was really a reputational issue. Kazakhstan wanted very much to be seen as a modern country, or it has aspirations for that. It wanted to be accepted.
– *Larry Napper, Ambassador to Kazakhstan*[1]

Trafficking in persons was not a big priority for Kazakhstan's government in the late 1990s. In 1999 the government's National Commission on Women's and Family Issues even declined to include trafficking in its list of priorities. However, after the 2001 TIP Report labeled Kazakhstan as Tier 3, interactions with the embassy spiked as high-level officials became concerned about this bad rating.

The use of public grades is a core element of scorecard diplomacy. This book argues that these grades are central in making countries receptive to broader diplomatic engagement. In a world more accustomed to "muscle diplomacy" this is odd. Why should meager grades make a difference, especially on issues that are not high profile? Why should countries care about a grade, especially if it is good enough to avoid consequences such as aid loss? And perhaps most puzzling: why should countries care what grades *other* countries get?

The answers to these questions lie in the concept of reputation. This chapter delineates the role of reputation in states' behavior and explains how the features of scorecard diplomacy raise states' concerns about their reputations. It argues that states care about their reputation not simply in terms of the credibility of their promises and threats, but more broadly in terms of how others perceive their performance. States want social recognition and governments care about their reputation vis-à-vis

---

[1] Napper interview.

their citizens and the global community because this directly affects their standing and legitimacy to govern.[2]

This desire means that others can seek to influence states by influencing their reputation. As others have noted, power "is a social process of constituting what actors are as social beings, that is, their social identities and capacities" to determine their fate.[3] While this has always been true, the digital age has made it cheaper to generate and disseminate criticism and accountability systems have become more transparent.[4] Thus, the ability to influence the reputation of states is an increasingly valuable tool.

Reputational concerns are only one of many factors that influence states. Sometimes it carries more weight than others. Reputational concerns won't compel North Korea's Kim Jong-un to resign or stop human rights repression in China, but it curbed the ability of the US to use torture and has tempered countries' trade in weapons.[5] Furthermore, even if reputational concerns may not *constrain* China's ability to repress human rights, it still imposes inconvenient *costs* that China must factor into its interstate relations.

This chapter has three parts. It first provides a broad definition of reputation and argues why it is valuable to states. It then creates a simple model to explain when states are more likely to worry about their reputation and act accordingly. Finally, it explains how scorecard diplomacy stimulates countries concern with their reputation.

***

THE CONCEPT OF REPUTATION
IN INTERNATIONAL RELATIONS

Some scholars argue that reputation matters "most in trade and security and least in environmental regulation and human rights"[6] because misbehaving governments know that while important allies or trade partners prefer to tolerate violations on soft issues like human rights rather than let misconduct spill over into higher priority areas like trade and security.[7]

---

[2] Wendt 1999, Ch. 5.
[3] Barnett and Duvall 2005, 42.
[4] Nye 1990, 100, Grant and Keohane 2005.
[5] Erickson 2015.
[6] Downs and Jones 2002, S112.
[7] Downs and Jones 2002, S97. Simmons discusses, but does not endorse, these views. Simmons 2009, 122.

However, this pessimistic view rests on too narrow a use of the word reputation that equates reputation with "credibility of commitments," or a reputation for resolve not to back down in the face of opposition.[8] Following this hard "reputation-as-credibility" logic, a reliable reputation enables states to gain from repeated cooperation with other states.[9] Reputation thus defined is about the predictability of a state's actions and it signals a state's military resolve or reliability as a partner on trade issues and so forth.[10] Indeed, reputation has become so synonymous with credibility of commitment that many use the terms almost interchangeably.[11] Even if reputation is defined more broadly as general beliefs about an actors' behavior, its consistently applied narrowly to topics such as threats, retaliation, reliability as an ally, or treaty compliance, perhaps because the study of reputation came of age during the Cold War and the study of deterrence.[12] Some even call this the "rational dimension of reputation that is chiefly of interest to economists and most political scientists," as if other dimensions of reputation are irrational or of less interest.[13] It is unfortunate that the concept of reputation has become shorthand for this narrower meaning.[14] As a result, much of the empirical research on "reputation" has focused on issues that involve iterated cooperation, such as security and economic issues.[15]

---

[8] Kreps and Wilson 1982, Alt et al. 1988, Jervis 1989, Sharman 2007. On resolve, see Dafoe et al., 375.

[9] Keohane 1984, 94, Schelling 1980.

[10] See in particular Mercer 1996, 6. Also Mercer 1996, Sartori 2002, Crescenzi 2007, Crescenzi et al. 2007, Walter 2009, Levy and Thompson 2011, Hugh-Jones 2013. Keohane notes that "[t]o a government that values its ability to make future agreements, reputation is a crucial resource; and the most important aspect of an actor's reputation in world politics is the belief of others that it will keep its future commitments." Keohane 1984, 116. For a treatment on sanctions see Peterson 2013. For reputation and sovereign debt, see Tomz 2007b. This conceptualization figures in some work on legalization and international law. See Abbott and Snidal 2000, Simmons 2000, 2010. On "Reputational capital," see Guzman 2002.

[11] Tomz 2007b. Even domestic audience costs have been conceptualized as a reputational cost of breaking commitments or being caught bluffing. Fearon 1994, Sartori 2002, Tomz 2007a. Joseph Nye also uses "reputation" to refer to credibility. Nye 2008, 100.

[12] See for example Dafoe et al. 2014.

[13] Downs and Jones 2002, S96, fn 2.

[14] Dafoe et al. 2014, 375. Even scholars those who disagree with these schools of thought use of the word reputation to refer to credibility. See Johnston 2008, 7.

[15] Mercer 1996. I myself have used a narrow definition of reputation as synonymous with concerns about the benefits of future exchange, a view I now consider too narrow. Kelley 2004b, 428.

A Broader Definition of Reputation

In the spirit of Malthus who advocated that scholars use words according to their common understanding, this book uses the word reputation broadly and more consistently with everyday usage.[16] Rather than being foremost or only about credibility of threats or promises, reputation here refers to the basic Merriam-Webster dictionary definition as the "the common opinion that people have about someone or something," or "the overall quality or character as seen or judged by people in general."[17] That is, a state's reputation reflects how others view it or – where responsibility can easily be allocated – its officials.[18] Reputations are usually based on past behaviors and can be updated with new information that indicates changes in the track record.[19] Reputation in this broad sense is not just about keeping promises; it's about perceptions of performance, both in terms of processes and outcomes across a range of issues. Thus, reputation is about character more broadly. Such a conceptualization that includes a notion of reputation as image or status has long existed. It is akin to what some now call "social reputation," or "diffuse reputation or image," which is the "the package of favorable perceptions and impressions that one believes one creates through status consistent behavior."[20]

Reputation is not a fixed property but is in the eye of the beholder. States can have reputations in relation to multiple actors: citizens, national elites, other governments, and the global community. These audiences

[16] Thomas Malthus, writing in 1827, thought it incumbent upon social scientists seeking to use common words to denote concepts to use those words in ways that accord with common usage. Those who narrowly equate reputation with credibility of commitments, etc., violate this basic advice. Thanks to Baldwin 2016, 44–45, for highlighting these insights of Malthus.

[17] See also Sharman 2007, Erickson 2015. Erickson (Ch. 2) has an outstanding discussion of reputation as "image and social status," or "credible cooperation," or "credible threat." See in particular her Table 2.1. For a similar broad definition, although their application is more narrowly to conflict, see also Dafoe et al. 2014.

[18] Indeed, much theory on reputation and image moves easily back and forth between analysis of individual and state level. A large debate exists about whether reputations are attached to states or leaders, but this most likely depends on whether the issue and related decisions are diffuse or can easily be identified with individuals who can be held accountable. For a longer discussion and a survey experiment backing this intuition in the context of war, see Renshon et al. Forthcoming.

[19] Tomz 2007b, 17–20.

[20] For use of the term "social reputation," see Risse and Ropp 2013, Erickson 2015. For the notion of "diffuse reputation or image," see Johnston 2001, 500, 2008. See also related discussions of status as communal proficiency assessments. For a discussion of the relationship between image and reputation, see Erickson 2015, 25–26.

may assess a state's reputation differently depending on which standards they each use, what they know, or how they weigh the evidence.[21]

Reputation, Behavior, and the Existing Normative Environment

Widely accepted rules or practices that prescribe appropriate or desirable behavior are central to how states and governments assess each other, and how citizens assess their governments.[22] One can think of reputation in an idealized form. In Figure 2.1, point "I" represents the internationally defined ideal behavior along some spectrum. For example, this could be the degree of freedom of speech, policies to promote gender equality, or per capita carbon emissions. The ideal point could be embedded in an international agreement or in common practices. It could be about policy behavior, but it could also be about behavioral traits, such as generally abiding by the rule of law, or keeping international commitments. The more the global community agrees on and adheres to the ideal standards, the greater their weight and the more these standards act as prerequisites for international legitimacy.[23]

Based on Figure 2.1, a country's international reputation is the way the international community at large assesses the gap between ideal point "I" and the state's actual behavior, "B." The smaller the gap, the better the reputation. Countries have a "good" reputation when they approximate "I." In reality of course, "I" might be more or less well established, and the understanding of "B" may vary with the level and quality of information, but the idea is that the international reputation is the assessment of the gap by international audiences, and this assessment is more favorable the smaller the gap.

Importantly, however, this reputation may or may not be the same as the one the government has at home. If the state subscribes to different ideals than the international community, domestic audiences may assess

---

[21] Tallberg and Zürn 2015.

[22] For a broader discussion of the role of a constitutive environment, see Wendt 1999. Baldwin links the constructivist notions about a socially constructed reality to earlier ideas by Harold Lasswell and Abraham Kaplan about power being "situational." Baldwin 2016, 153–154.

[23] Complete consensus around norms need not exist for states to gain reputations in a given issue area. Different ideologies or competing norms may dictate different behaviors and different groups may judge states differently depending on which ideologies they subscribe to. For example, some states may have a reputation as abiding by the principles of the free market, while others may have a reputation for managing their economies more closely. In this case reputations are not necessarily measured against a universal right or wrong, but are labels for different – sometimes competing – ideologies.

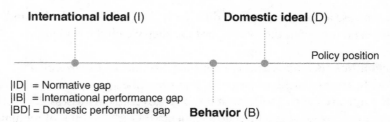

FIGURE 2.1. Performance gaps and the relationship between ideals and practice.

the state's behavior differently. For example, in some countries a widespread acceptance of female circumcision differs from the more widely held international taboos. In Figure 2.1, "D" represents the domestic ideal point. If the international norms conflict with more locally held norms, then "I" and "D" will be far apart and the state may have a different reputation at home than abroad because of the assessment of the gap between the domestic ideal point and behavior differs.

This can place a government in a conundrum. Internationally it is concerned about the gap between its behavior and the international idea, |IB|, while domestically it is concerned about |BD|, the domestic performance gap. Naturally, "D" could also lie between "I" and "B," in which case the direction of the gap is the same, representing less of a dilemma, but still leading to differential pressure domestically and internationally. Or "D" and "I" could coincide, in which case international criticisms ring true at home. In either case, reputations form relative to existing ideal points and behavior. Because there can only be one behavior, differing ideal points may pull government policies in opposite directions.

Importantly, ideal points need not be fixed. The very act of invoking certain ideals can be an exercise not only in rule enforcement but also in standard setting. That is, those assessing performance are simultaneously shaping the interpretation of what is acceptable performance. In this way, invoking norms is also an act of influencing the very definition of these standards and norms.[24] Invoking the norms and calling for their implementation can help institutionalize the norms and standards.[25] Indeed, information is powerful because it promotes accountability, but

---

[24] This is akin to the argument that contestation over norms shapes their form. Finnemore 1996. Much of the literature on governance indicators engages this argument. See for example Löwenheim 2008, Merry 2011, Büthe 2012, Davis et al. 2012a, Kelley and Simmons 2015, 2014, Merry et al. 2015.
[25] Finnemore and Sikkink 1998.

also because the producers of the information and assessments influence the definition and salience of ideas.[26]

Multiple Reputations Across Issues

In accordance with this broader definition, countries not only have multiple reputations across different audiences, but also across different issues or traits.[27] For example, countries that stimulate positive economic growth, lead humanitarian rescue efforts, or advance international peace talks may earn a good reputation in the view of those who favor such policies. Conversely, countries that monopolize domestic markets, confiscate private property, or slash and burn its virgin forests might earn a poor reputation in view of those opposed to such practices. Generally, huge environmental disasters tarnish a government's reputation as a competent and responsible caretaker. The selling of arms to human rights abusers brands a government as opportunistic in the eyes of most. Conduct in trade and war will brand a government's reputation for credibility and resolve.

While states have multiple reputations, they also accumulate a general reputation based on their performance across many issues ranging from the provision of services and the stewardship of resources to various international matters. As others have noted, "to say that a state has a particular reputation implies that most observers hold the relevant belief about the state."[28] In this sense, states may "acquire reputations as law-abiding global citizens."[29]

Importantly for whether countries are concerned about their reputation in a given issue area, many issues cannot be compartmentalized. If countries repeatedly disregard negative externalities they impose on their neighbors in different areas, for example, other states may worry that poor consideration for neighbors is a general quality.[30] In an age when states are considering much broader approaches to "human security," this is increasingly true. Thus, the potential for spillovers remains for most issue areas. This means that a state's overall reputation can be damaged by a poor performance in any issue area that reveals a fundamental

[26] Keohane and Nye Jr 1998, 86, Kelley and Simmons 2014.
[27] For a discussion stressing this, see Dafoe et al. 2014, 374.
[28] Dafoe et al. 2014, 374.
[29] Lebovic and Voeten 2006, 885.
[30] Crescinzi argues for an experiential model of reputation in which states learn from how other states behave more broadly in the international community, not just from dyadic interactions. Importantly, the way that states assess information depends on the similarity of context. Crescenzi 2007.

disregard for qualities of broader universal values.[31] This can be true even if the issue area itself is rather narrow. For example, in 2005 when Mugabe razed local slums in "Operation Murambatsvina," his reputation suffered generally, not only on the issue of local housing, or even human rights more generally, but also on his governance more broadly. He was widely seen as ruthless and power-obsessed and his state as edging ever closer to pariah status, as noted by a condemning report from the United Nations.[32] Just like bad news tends to dominate the media, so government failures that attract considerable attention tend to dominate their reputations. States therefore have reason to be concerned about their reputation in any given issue area that threatens to attract public attention.

Furthermore, as opposed to a purely credibility-based conceptualization of reputation, a broader performance and image-based conceptualization sees human rights as central, because it involves moral responsibility and justice, which are the fundamental building blocks of state "character." Maintaining legitimacy requires states to conform to the international community's minimal justice requirement.[33] Because of the substantive international support for human rights norms, countries that violate human rights struggle to maintain legitimacy.[34] Thus, states may value having a compliant reputation in areas such as human rights that undergird their overall character.

Why Care? The Value of a Good Reputation

A narrow definition of reputation stresses that states value their reputation because they want to gain from cooperation or be able to make credible threats in wartime. In the context of the latter one might allow that some leaders actually value a reputation for unpredictability, ruthlessness,

---

[31] See Erickson's excellent discussion of scandal and domestic politics. Erickson 2015, 31–34.

[32] Tibaijuka 2005.

[33] Barkin and Cronin 1994, 113, Buchanan 2003, 282. States are considered responsible when they observe human rights including broad social and economic rights. Franck 1990, Wendt 1999, Lebovic and Voeten 2006. Thus, countries that violate human rights struggle to maintain legitimacy.

[34] Hawkins 2002, 31. States cannot maintain their own image as upright if they ignore blatant human rights violations in their own or other countries. Thomas 2001, 51. Indeed, theories of shaming assume that states do care about their human rights reputation and that elites worry about others' assessment of their performance or their character. Lebovic and Voeten 2006, Franklin 2008, Efrat 2009.

and so forth. That is, some leaders might prefer a bad reputation – they actually wish for their behavior to be assessed as far from the international ideal point.

That said, a broader definition also stresses that governments and citizens value their reputation as part of their state's identity or image, similar to how a citizen may desire to be viewed as law-abiding.[35] If states have a good reputation – if others assess their behavior as aligned with international ideals – this gives states and their governments a sense of belonging, facilitates cooperation with other states, and allows them to consider themselves as upright members of the international community.[36] A positive reputation can be a policy goal in itself, not merely a means to an end.[37] Indeed, at times states may value their reputation so highly that they are willing to forego other immediate or more concrete gains.[38]

That states and elites care about their reputation in terms of image and broader legitimacy does not imply that states are not instrumental or strategic. States may adopt certain norms and behaviors to reap social benefits and avoid social costs; in this sense, they respond rationally to social incentives.[39] A good reputation can confer respect and influence, which enables states to accomplish other goals.[40] Thus, for states, concern

---

[35] Lutz and Sikkink have argued that "as members of an international or regional society of states [leaders of authoritarian governments have] been 'socialized' into caring about what other states think of them." Lutz and Sikkink 2000, 659. See also Finnemore 1996, Risse et al. 1999, Erickson 2015. In prior work I have argued that citizens may expect their governments to respect international law as part of their state's identity. Kelley 2007.

[36] Thus, Franck argues that states seek to become members of a club of states, and others argue that shaming is meaningful because it places states in an out-group, and causes some states to "feel deeply offended, because they want to belong to the 'civilized community' of states." Franck 1990, 38. In international relations, identity or image is often related to "social identity theory" and used to denote the idea of belonging to certain groups, and to the concept of "othering," as part of a state's own identity construction. Risse and Sikkink 1999, 15.

[37] Erickson 2015, 24. Johnston proposes that "actors in world politics value image and status as ends in and of themselves." Johnston 2008, 75.

[38] Johnston notes that often status markers are uncorrelated with material gains, and desires to maximize status need not even be about topping others. Johnston 2008, 83. Others note that "reputation is often crucial for status. The loss or acquisition of certain reputations can lose or gain an actor a particular status." Dafoe et al. 2014, 375.

[39] For a discussion of social incentives, see Erickson 2015, 17–24. Both Hurd and Johnston note that states act rationally within a social context. Hurd 2008, Johnston 2008. Kelman refers to this behavior simply as compliance. Kelman 1958.

[40] Gilpin 1981, 30–31.

about their image "is always in the national interest."[41] In other words, a good reputation is just plain useful.

Favorable reputations boost states' legitimacy, both internationally and domestically. "International legitimacy" is coveted because it is foundational to the state and international society and underscores the right to govern.[42] Even strong states and their leaders seek international recognition and may assign value to upholding norms that are widely accepted in the international community – a point that some have argued explains why many states joined in sanctions against South African apartheid.[43] The US, for example, has worried about anti-Americanism worldwide and has sought to manage its international reputation.[44]

A favorable overall reputation is also useful domestically.[45] Citizens assess their states both for their procedural legitimacy and for the outcomes they produce. It is procedural reasons that have compelled states to invite international monitors to verify the legitimacy of electoral processes.[46] If citizens perceive their government as corrupt or irresponsible, they may lower their support for the government.[47] States and their elites may fear economic repercussions or worry about their own political survival.[48] Although most violations of international norms won't topple the government, cumulative misconduct can erode its reputation over time. For example, the revelation of human rights violations by the US military in the Abu Ghraib prison in Iraq brought protests at home and undercut

---

[41] Baldwin 2016, 171. For the value of national image, see also Jervis 1989. Public criticism can harm a state's ability to cooperate with other states and can damage its domestic authority to govern. Gilley 2013.

[42] On the role of legitimacy in international society, see Bull 1977, Hurd 1999, Clark 2005. International legitimacy, too, is a social concept – in the eyes of the beholders – and denotes the extent to which others accept the *authority* of a regime and view it as having the right to govern. Reus-Smit discusses legitimacy as a social concept and argues that it cannot be separated from the concept of power, but is a source of power. Reus-Smit 2007.

[43] Klotz 1995.

[44] Johnston 2008. On anti-Americanism, see Katzenstein and Keohane 2007. On US standing, see American Political Science Association 2009.

[45] See Lutz and Sikkink 2000, Newton and Norris 2000, Reus-Smit 2007, Hurd 2008, 29–30, Kelley 2012, Risse and Ropp 2013. Wendt notes that legitimacy derives from possessing "identity criteria which define only certain *forms* of state as legitimate." Wendt 1999, 292. Erickson has a particularly extensive discussion of the importance of national reputation. Erickson 2015, Ch. 2.

[46] A survey of eight African countries shows that individuals who perceive election conduct as proper are more likely to consider the regime legitimate. Elklit and Reynolds 2002. See also Kelley 2012, Ch. 2.

[47] For a discussion of procedural and performance legitimacy as it pertains to international organizations, see Tallberg and Zürn 2015.

[48] Batson 1987.

support for the president. Thus, governments need good reputations to maintain domestic support.

Although some dictators may seek to inspire fear by deviating from international norms, support is important for all regime types. Even authoritarian governments experience pressures to perform and are vulnerable to external criticisms, which is one reason so many of them hold "elections" and invite international election monitors to gain some sheen of legitimacy.[49] Indeed, because authoritarian states compromise on procedural legitimacy, some governments, such as Singapore and China, rely on a reputation of being able to deliver certain policy outputs to sustain their legitimacy.[50] For example, Singapore prides itself on its top placement in the Heritage Foundation's Economic Freedom Index as a form of validation, which is why the government has worked so hard to maintain the top spot for decades and brags about it.[51] Indeed, some research has found that authoritarian states are more susceptible to public exposure of human rights violations than are democracies.[52] Naturally, authoritarian regimes may compare themselves with different "reference" states, but the principle remains if for some issues they wish to be viewed favorably by a peer group or by domestic constituents.

In addition to the benefits of domestic and international legitimacy, a good reputation also boosts status and standing in the international community. A state's status refers to its position relative to a comparison group,[53] and denotes a more hierarchical structure of state relations. Higher social status and prestige are valuable as means to boost recognition and influence in international society or to attract investment or other benefits.[54]

Although the discussion here has mostly focused on states and their governments, individual leaders and elites also have reasons to worry about their *personal* reputation. Most want to be respected by their citizens and leaders of other states with which they identify.[55] They want their country to compare well with other countries and they shun "the

---

[49] Hawkins 2002, 30, Johnston 2008. On election monitoring, see Hyde 2011, Kelley 2012.
[50] Zhu 2011.
[51] Interview with staff, by Judith Kelley, August 12, 2014, Washington, DC.
[52] Hendrix and Wong 2013.
[53] Dafoe et al. 2014.
[54] Gilpin 1981, 30–31, Erickson 2015, 27.
[55] Hawkins 2004. Leaders seek to maximize their personal "esteem." Finnemore and Sikkink 1998, 898. Research on status from economics, sociology, and psychology shows that people are motivated by status. Harsanyi 1966, Blader and Chen 2012, Ridgeway 2013. For a discussion see Kelley and Simmons 2016.

stigma of backwardness."[56] Not withstanding those who actually desire a negative reputation for unpredictability or toughness, if leaders are sensitive to the international status markers of their state or to domestic legitimacy concerns, these might activate psychological desires for a positive self-image and for social approval.[57] Enhanced status has psychological benefits and elites may value these as part of their identity and fear being ostracized.[58] Johnston argues, "The most important microprocess of social influence ... is the desire to maximize status, honor, prestige – diffuse reputation or image – and the desire to avoid a loss of status, shaming, or humiliation and other social sanctions."[59]

Thus, states and their elites may value their broader reputation for instrumental reasons and "strategically [adopt] popular policies out of social concern for their international reputations rather than out of any existing practice or norm internalization."[60] This also means that governments or officials do not need to be persuaded or have internalized the norms and standards; all that matters is that they believe that others will view them as failing with respect to these norms, that *others* ascribe validity to these.[61] Political elites may become "trapped" by the prevailing rhetoric, unable to "craft a socially sustainable rebuttal," and therefore "compelled to endorse a stance they would otherwise reject."[62]

In sum, states and their elites may care about their reputation for both normative and instrumental reasons. Such motivations are often both

[56] Weyland 2009, 33. For example, sociological intuitionalists see policymakers as striving to enhance their international status by borrowing policy solutions from abroad to demonstrate their modernity. Meyer and Rowan 1977, DiMaggio and Powell 1983.

[57] See discussion by Johnston of the appropriate level of analysis when considering efforts of social influences. Johnston 2008, 95–99. See also Lumsdaine 1993, Shannon 2000, Efrat 2009. Even scholars who question the role of reputation for states stress that individual leaders worry about "their own reputations and status." Dafoe et al. 2014, 381. Young argues that like private individuals, policymakers "are sensitive to the social opprobrium that accompanies violations of widely accepted behavioral prescriptions." Young 1992, 176–177. If they believe in the norms but find their own behavior at odds with them, they may also dislike experiencing "cognitive dissonance." Festinger 1962.

[58] Franck 1990, 32, 58, Lutz and Sikkink 2000, Johnston 2008, 76, 84.

[59] Johnston 2001, 500.

[60] Erickson's discussion of arms transfer policies provides an example. Erickson 2015, 25.

[61] The sociologist Max Weber acknowledged as much. Jackson 2002, 449. For a discussion of "social reputation," that makes similar points, see Erickson 2015. Elites need not be persuaded; they may simply strive for public conformity to protect their reputation. Johnston discusses social influence versus mimicry versus persuasion in his book, *Social States*, in which he quotes from Leon Festinger that it is possible to have "[p]ublic conformity without private acceptance." See Johnston 2008, 24–26. See also Kelman 1958.

[62] Schimmelfennig 2001, Krebs and Jackson 2007, 36.

compatible and indistinguishable, depending on how one defines costs and benefits.[63] They likely operate in concert, either because individual policymakers respond to a combination of these, or because different policymakers in the same country respond differently. In either case, the values states place on their reputations are likely heterogeneous.[64] Indeed, the sources of concern may not fit as neatly into theoretical boxes as one might suppose. For example, do elites worry about possible consequences like sanctions because they fear losing the funding, or because sanctions are shameful? Some research suggests that sanctions can be used symbolically to influence states, and Arab states have done so at times.[65] Minor sanctions might be financially bearable; yet the stigma might be unacceptable. Similarly, cognitive dissonance may not just be about emotional stability; individuals may be concerned that others will spot and punish their hypocrisy.

For some reason, however, even scholars who acknowledge that intrinsic and instrumental logics are intertwined default to the instrumental logic and argue "what is at issue is the extent to which these mechanisms lead behavior to deviate from the ideal instrumental policy."[66] The burden is always to show that something is not instrumental. From a policy perspective, however, what is at stake is when behavior deviates from norms.

Although these sources of concern can't all be disentangled, this book will argue and document that reputational concerns are not limited to immediate credibility-based, material repercussions; they are also social and image-based in the sense that states care about being seen as in conformance with the norms in the society of states. This is important for scorecard diplomacy because it means that reputation can be elicited as a tool of influence with or without material leverage, and that it can be elicited across a broad range of issues, not only – as argued by others – "most in security and trade."[67]

---

[63] Dafoe et al. 2014. For a thoughtful discussion of "social reputation," that makes similar points, see Erickson 2015. For a similar discussion around the concept of status and war, see Renshon 2016.

[64] Ragin 2000.

[65] For a discussion of how "symbolic sanctions" worked in the Arab context during the 1950s, see Barnett 1998. Barnett argues that these worked because states wanted to maintain their dignity, honor, and face.

[66] Dafoe et al. 2014, 383.

[67] Downs and Jones 2002, S112.

WHEN DO REPUTATIONAL CONCERNS OPERATE?
A SIMPLE MODEL

When do broad reputational concerns arise and translate into policy? The answer to this question may vary with the nature of the issue. Conflict-focused research argues that reputational concerns vary with cultural values such as honor and standing and with the number and type of separatist movements or other challengers.[68] But reputations on war and resolve can often be identified with singular decisions that are likely attached to individual leaders and entail direct interstate interaction, as is also the case in international lending and repayment, for example.[69] This contrasts with issues such as human rights or environmental performance, which are more diffuse and focus on broader policies, performance, and implementation over time that often involves many actors. Here I present a simple model of three factors that the arguments above suggest will interact to generate reputational concerns on such broader issues and whether these then produce behavioral changes. These factors are *sensitivity* and *exposure*, which together drive the level of concern, and *prioritization*, which drives the translation of concern into policies, as discussed below.

Sensitivity

Reputational concerns depend on how sensitive a government is to any reputational pressures. Sensitivity depends on the salience of the possible practical stakes of low performance, both for states and political elites, as well how much the government sees itself as being in conflict with existing norms and expectations.

One source of sensitivity is what one might call *instrumental salience*: to the extent that reputational concerns are connected to the desire to obtain certain goals, their activation will depend partly on the salience of such goals. These are usually some form of international benefit such as aid, trade, tourism, and office holding in international institutions, or membership in international institutions. For example, when countries want cooperation from the international community, they seek external legitimacy more, as evident when Mexico was negotiating for the North American Free Trade Agreement and President Carlos Salinas was campaigning for the World Trade Organization presidency.[70] Thus,

---

[68] For a discussion of this literature, see Dafoe et al. 2014.
[69] For a theory on reputation and international debt see Tomz 2007b.
[70] Kelley 2012, Ch. 2.

when such benefits are more salient, states will be more sensitive to the reputational damage that can block access to these benefits.[71]

The extent to which individual elites face consequences may also vary. The more likely officials are to be held directly responsible for poor performance, they more likely they will be to worry about their personal careers. Policymakers may also worry that they or their party might be blamed for underperforming. Bureaucrats may worry about being singled out for inaction or mishandling.[72] Officials may worry about such practical consequences, even if citizens are not protesting. Rather, they may worry simply if they anticipate criticism.[73] If they fear that bad publicity can produce protest or lower their public approval ratings or job evaluation, they will be more sensitive.[74]

Complementing instrumental salience, states will also be more sensitive to reputation if the underlying norms are salient. The *normative salience* depends foremost on how well established the international norms are. Norms encoded in legally binding treaties that most states have signed will be most compelling, whereas the least compelling will be those where considerable contestation remains. Some "norms" are not so much moral in character as ideological. For example, the international community is less likely to have consensus on business regulations than on torture. Even if a norm or expectation is well established, the normative salience of a given state also depends on whether the state and governmental elites identify with these. Certain countries may be comfortable deviating from some norms, even if they are well accepted internationally. For example, some countries may have different views on women's rights that the state justifies based on religious grounds. Finally, the normative salience will depend on the extent to which actual behavior diverges from expectations. To return to Figure 2.1, the salience of norms depends on the gap between the domestic and international ideal points, and greater discrepancy between these and actual behavior stokes reputational concerns.

Public international commitments can be important in this context. If a state has committed to an international treaty that embodies a set of norms, its declared ideal point is close international norms that outside actors might invoke.[75] This makes the discrepancy between performance and the standards more damaging. On the other hand, if domestic norms

---

[71] Keck and Sikkink 1998, 208, Risse et al. 1999, 13–14, Risse and Ropp 2013, 20–21.
[72] Batson 1987.
[73] Cook et al. 1983, Mutz 1998.
[74] Hendrix and Wong 2013.
[75] On the importance of public commitment, see Lutz and Sikkink 2000, 657.

differ markedly from international ones, the state will not be as harmed, at least domestically, for failing to live up to standards to which it does not subscribe. This decreases the sensitivity to reputational concerns.

This may lead one to conclude that democratic states are more likely to worry about their reputations because their domestic ideal is likely closer to the international ideal, or because citizens can protest more easily. However, this may vary across issue areas. Domestic ideal points can align well with international ideal points, even in autocracies. This may be especially true if the issue concerns state competencies to deliver services and protect its citizens, to which citizens of autocracies may feel as entitled or with which autocracies may mollify its citizens, a point that aligns well with Huntington's notion of "negative legitimacy." Pollution, for example, has become a huge domestic liability issue for China, around which domestic protests have festered. On the other hand, even democracies may veer from international norms. For example, while Australia has been criticized by the international community for its policy to turn back refugees at sea, the mood at home is one of agreement: many people do not want the large influx of refugees and the government has successfully stoked this sentiment to avoid domestic reputational damage for its non-compliance with international norms.[76]

Normative salience also depends on the relationships between the target and the source of the norms. Because reputation is about legitimacy and identity, criticisms from a desired in-group carry more weight.[77] If states see themselves as having a certain identity, then they are sensitive to status markers from others who share this identity.[78] Thus, reputational concerns are likely greater when affinity to the actors eliciting the concerns is greater. Relatedly, because reputational concerns arise when information discredits performance, the authority of the source is important. Those advancing norms must be credible and trustworthy and must exemplify the norms they promote, which imbues them with what some call "normative power" to shape conceptions of norms.[79] The same might be true if the country has strained political relations with the source, in which case it's easier to dismiss the criticisms as politically motivated. That noted, active efforts to discredit the source signal concern about

[76] Maguire 2016.

[77] See Johnston 2001, 2008. Social psychology research finds that people may adopt behaviors if they are associated with the desired in-group. Kelman 1958.

[78] For a discussion of identity and how it relates to cooperative behavior, see Johnston 2008, 74–75 and Ch. 3 generally.

[79] On trust as a filter for processing information, see Rieh 2002, Espeland and Sauder 2007. On the value of exemplary behavior, see Sikkink 1993, Monks and Ehrenberg 1999. On normative power, see Manners 2002.

reputational damage, underscoring the presence and weight of such concerns.

Finally, it may matter how good a country's overall reputation is. For example, Norway is able to deviate from the international consensus on whaling without too much damage, because it has a lot of "reputational capital" to draw on. It is well regarded and can afford a light dent in its reputation on this issue. Still, reputations, particularly on issues like debt repayment or peacefulness, can easily be squandered, especially if they are accompanied by leadership changes so that others might infer that a structural change has occurred.[80]

Exposure

Reputational concerns depend not only on how sensitive states are on the issue, but also on the availability and clarity of information and on the exposure that the relevant information brings about. The public element is crucial – reputation depends critically on "the extent to which a behavior is publicly observed."[81] States may be missing the mark but suffer no reputational consequences if nobody knows about it. Clear information is essential for domestic and international actors to evaluate performance and pressure governments.[82] Exposure is the degree to which a country's behavior, "B," is actively brought into question. Exposure depends on the abundance and clarity of the information as well as on the attention by third parties and the media and focal events.

Active third parties such as NGOs or IGOs can bring attention to the issue in the media and in public discussion.[83] A large literature stresses the role of civil society in holding domestic governments accountable. Domestic interest groups may care about the international norms referenced and pressure governments to comply.[84] Societies with active civil societies may therefore be more susceptive to reputational concerns.[85]

Similarly, large events in a country that focus attention on an issue might also increase the exposure of government officials to the criticisms and heighten the costs of inaction. Media play a particularly critical role.

[80] For a discussion in the context of debt repayments, see Tomz 2007b.
[81] Dafoe et al. 2014, 376.
[82] Keohane 1998, Erickson 2015, 30, Guzman 2002.
[83] For a discussion of the role of civil society in exposing reputational gaps in state behaviors on arms transfers, see Erickson 2015, Ch. 3.
[84] Young 1979, Schachter 1991, Sikkink 1993, Jacobson and Weiss 1997.
[85] Simmons 2009, Erickson 2015, 19.

Even the threat of bad publicity may worry officials.[86] Underperformance or scandals can attract outsized attention.

Finally, if the source is unreliable or inconsistent, exposure will be diminished, and governments can dismiss criticism more easily and therefore lessen any reputational damage.[87]

Prioritization

When states are sensitive and their performance exposed, they are likely to worry about their reputations. But whether these concerns translate into action depends on their prioritization. Even if a government is concerned about its reputation on a given issue, it may not be able to pay attention or change its behavior. Like others, government officials have limited capacity for attention and action. Agenda-setting theory suggests that when the agenda is crowded with high priority items – for example, all-consuming crime or drug problems as in Honduras – it's harder to generate attention for other issues.[88]

Furthermore, the individual agency of elites may influence prioritization. Elites may incur personal costs to change. Local issue champions who can act as "sympathetic interlocutors" can help rally domestic reformers and channel the exchange of information and ideas, but if they are absent or irregular, this can stifle progress.[89] If reforms could interfere with practices from which officials benefit, such as official corruption, opposition will be high, so even if reputational concerns are present, they may be squashed by such corruption. On the other hand, reform-minded elites – be they bureaucrats, government officials, or opposition politicians – can boost attention to the issue and any international criticisms to highlight the reputational concerns within the country. The more such bureaucrats worry and are in a position to make things happen in government, the more their concern matters, as has been pointed out by the literature on the importance of reform-minded teams within countries.[90]

A country's ability to address an issue will also be affected by its stability: distraction by internal or international wars or uprisings, or political turmoil, can undermine the attention of any government to address

---

[86] Mutz 1998.
[87] Guzman 2002, 1863.
[88] Kingdon and Thurber 1984.
[89] Corrales 2006, Chwieroth 2009, Parks 2014. Note that Alter similarly speaks of "compliance partners." Alter 2014.
[90] Haas et al. 1993, Jacobson and Weiss 1997, Corrales 2006, Chwieroth 2009, Parks 2014.

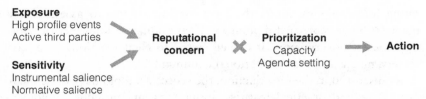

FIGURE 2.2. Factors that influence reputational concern and its translation into action.

less pressing issues. Political instability may also undermine the personal stakes of elites who face uncertain futures and thus may be less motivated to advance their course. When time horizons shrink, investments in reputations are likely to be less valued.

Capacity is also crucial. Even if reputational concerns bring an issue on the agenda, lack of capacity to design or implement change can end good intentions. Such capacity-deficits are known to hamper international reform efforts as well as compliance with international human rights and environmental treaties.[91]

Figure 2.2 illustrates how sensitivity and exposure influence reputational concerns, and how prioritization mediates whether these concerns translate into action.

HOW DOES SCORECARD DIPLOMACY ELICIT REPUTATIONAL CONCERNS?

Scorecard diplomacy shares some traits with international institutions, which embody norms and expectations and often provide mechanisms for information sharing.[92] Through these interactions, institutions can stoke reputational concerns.[93] Scorecard diplomacy operates as a type of quasi-institution that promotes information sharing and accountability, and facilitates comparisons of state performance. Like international institutions, scorecard diplomacy can set norms and expectations and provide transparency between citizens and their governments, as well as relative status markers between states. New information, such as indicators or

---

[91] Haas et al. 1993, Weiss and Jacobson 2000, Kelley 2012, Risse and Sikkink 2013.

[92] In international relations, information has long been thought to influence the cooperation among states and so international organizations have often gathered and disseminated information about state performance as a tool of influence. Keohane 1984.

[93] For the importance of institutions as social environments see Johnston 2001, 2008, Hurd 2008, Erickson 2015.

rating and rankings, alters the base that actors use to assess performance.[94] Since scorecard diplomacy often evaluates states' performance
or criticizes governments, it is well suited to elicit reactions from civil
society, media and the international community.

As discussed in the introduction, the scorecard diplomacy cycle incor-
porates several practical features: monitoring and grading, diplomacy
and practical assistance, and third party pressures. The next section discusses how these tap into and elicit concerns about reputation.

The Role of Monitoring and Grading

Scorecard diplomacy engages reputations by using public monitoring and
assessment. Importantly, it strategically packages and distributes information in a way that invokes relevant norms, and invites comparisons
and judgment. It holds states to some behavior that is simultaneously
promoted as ideal.

The grades are crucial. Scorecard diplomacy literally assigns periodic,
and highly comparable, performance scores. The scores seek to boil down
the distance between the international ideal point, "I," and the state
behavior, "B," down to a grade. They thus become a direct representation
of the reputational gab. Numbers, as often used for scorecard diplomacy,
are frequently treated as authoritative and lodge themselves in people's
minds.[95] Because grades are easily understood representations of government performance and the gap with international standards, politicians
may worry that a bad rating can lower their citizens' confidence in their
government's legitimacy and thus its ability or right to rule.[96] Conversely,
if a government suffers from poor legitimacy at home, positive international rankings can be a sign of "good housekeeping, which will add
luster to the moral and political credentials" of the government's reform
efforts, as the chief of staff of the Philippine president said in 2009 about
the MCC eligibility criteria.[97]

Grades, ratings, and rankings are potent symbols that shape perceptions about performance. By reducing complexity they designate a preferred interpretation as meaningful. Symbols such as grades are powerful,

---

[94] Merry 2011, Davis et al. 2012a, 2012b, 2015.
[95] Yalch and Elmore-Yalch 1984, Baesler and Burgoon 1994. For more on the power of
numbers, see Robson 1992, Andreas and Greenhill 2010, Hansen and Mühlen-Schulte
2012, Kelley and Simmons 2016, 457.
[96] Finnemore and Sikkink 1998, 903, Hawkins 2002, 32.
[97] Ermita 2009. Reported in Parks. Parks 2014.

because, as sociologist Beaulieu argued, humans are engaged in "symbolic struggles over the perception of the social world" and they exercise power by trying "to transform categories of perception and appreciation of the social world, the cognitive and evaluative structures through which it is constructed."[98] Thus, the use of symbols such as grades to name and label is a political effort to shape perceptions of reality and powerful actors can use such symbols to impose their perspectives.[99] By categorizing, grades thus socially construct reference points for normative standards of appropriate conduct and encourage others to gauge state behavior against the reference norms. In this way, grades can stimulate the reputational concerns of states and shape perceptions of interest.[100]

In addition to their symbolism, their comparative nature makes grades particularly well suited to elicit reputational concerns. Comparisons can shape and reinforce social identities.[101] States want to belong to a community, but they also seek to place as high as possible in a social hierarchy, which is why rankings are particularly status-oriented.[102] Thus, states are not only concerned with how they are viewed by other states, but also how they compare to other states. Grades can introduce a competitive element. When states are grouped they can compare themselves with others – a fundamental status exercise. Citizens may not understand the issue, but they understand that their country has been grouped with pariah countries, or has been put on a blacklist of sorts, or is performing worse than similar countries. Thus, by putting the "scores" front and center, scorecard diplomacy engages exactly the kind of out-group feeling that is foundational to theories of shaming.[103] Grades thus allow governments to reference their state's standing within a certain category of

---

[98] Bourdieu 1989, 20.

[99] Bourdieu 1989, 22. Eagleston-Pierce draws on Bourdieu's notion of symbolic power to explain how relatively weaker actors can frame a situation to enhance their position in bargaining with the WTO. Eagleton-Pierce 2013. In *Economic Statecraft*, Baldwin references Harold Lasswell's work *Politics: Who Gets What When?* which referred to four different types of influence techniques, one of which was "words" or information, or symbolic means, also sometimes called propaganda. Lasswell 1958. Based on this Baldwin defines propaganda as "influence attempts relying primarily on the deliberate manipulation of symbols." Baldwin 1985, 13. For a discussion of the politics of numbers as symbols, see also Broome and Quirk 2015.

[100] For a discussion of normative approaches to compliance, see Simmons 1998.

[101] The sociological concept of "commensuration" captures how actors make sense of the world by grouping and judging objects or entities. For further discussion see Espeland and Stevens 1998, Espeland and Sauder 2007.

[102] For a discussion of this, see Erickson 2015, 27.

[103] Risse and Sikkink 1999, 15.

states.[104] States might worry about their peer group for various reasons. For example, investors or other actors may use a country's perceived peer groups to make decisions about investment.[105] Grades therefore allow comparisons that stimulate reputational concerns.

Furthermore, the recurrent nature of scorecard diplomacy – assessments are usually issued annually – reveals whether countries are on the right trajectory or whether performance is deteriorating. This iteration engages the country's reputation both relative to others and to itself over time. Crucially, iteration activates anticipation. A country never actually has to be rated poorly to experience concerns about reputation; countries respond to the anticipation of another round of rating or ranking. Thus, similar to a straight "A" student concerned not to get a "B," scorecard diplomacy can stimulate *status maintenance* behavior: once a country achieves a good rating, it wants to maintain it.[106] For example, when she was told in February 2005 that failure to pass an anti-TIP law could affect Ghana's Tier 1 status, Ghana's Minister of Women and Children Affairs exclaimed, "[W]e must keep Tier 1."[107] Reiterative and public monitoring and grading is thus a form of systematic "deployment of normative information," which creates an environment of continuous accountability.[108]

Finally, the monitoring aspect is important. Monitoring signals social importance.[109] The philosopher Michel Foucault famously characterized monitoring as a form of control and thus power.[110] Research has also identified the famous "Hawthorne effect," when individuals change their behavior in response to being aware of being observed, akin to what sociologists call reflectivity.[111] Election monitoring, for example, can improve the conduct of elections without any formal sanctions.[112]

In sum, monitoring and grading have unique abilities to elicit reputational concerns.

---

[104] Checkel 1998, 902, Finnemore and Sikkink 1998.
[105] Gray 2013, Brooks et al. 2015.
[106] Kelley and Simmons 2015, 65.
[107] 05ACCRA364_a.
[108] Kelley and Simmons 2015, 56.
[109] Larson and Callahan 1990.
[110] Foucault 1995, 201–202.
[111] Adair 1984. Kelley and Simmons note, "Sociologists use the concept of *reflectivity* – the tendency for people to change their behavior in response to being evaluated – to explain the effect, for example, of US News and World Report rankings on university priorities." Kelley and Simmons 2014. See also Espeland and Sauder 2007.
[112] Kelley 2012.

The Role of Diplomacy

While ratings and rankings schemes differ in their degree of interaction with the targets, a fundamental feature of scorecard diplomacy is its engagement on the ground. Scorecard diplomacy takes advantage of the fact that the initial grading increases concerns, which makes policymakers more receptive to other efforts. The second step in the scorecard diplomacy cycle is therefore the ongoing diplomacy and practical assistance. Diplomacy can increase reputational concerns, because it gives international actors a chance to share information, to educate local elites, and to underscore the importance of the international norms. The reporting and meetings launch conversations with policymakers about how to define and frame the problem.

Individual level interaction is important. Even Morgenthau recognized the value of interacting with responsible officials who can be identified and held accountable.[113] As discussed earlier, drivers of reputational concerns such as the desire to belong to the in-group or fear of opprobrium operate foremost at the individual level. More recently political scientists have emphasized the interpersonal elements of social influence and socialization.[114] Borrowing from the neuropsychology, a study of face-to-face diplomacy suggests it may stimulate unique neurocognitive processes, because "[d]uring face-to-face interaction we move from private to shared experiences."[115] This also aligns with literature in social psychology and sociology, which argues that shame, in particular, is felt in face-to-face encounters, leading people to *avoid* potentially embarrassing encounters.[116]

New information shared in meetings and reports can influence policymakers' causal beliefs about the roots of the problem or their understanding of its scope or possible solutions.[117] This can lessen the gap between the international and the domestic ideal point and thus increase the normative salience of outside criticisms.[118] The provision of new data and

---

[113] Morgenthau 1950, 189.

[114] Johnston 2001, Checkel 2005. Erickson also notes this point. Erickson 2015, 25.

[115] Holmes 2013, 839.

[116] Scheff and Retzinger 2000, Rutten 2006, 355.

[117] This can happen even if policymakers do not change their overall objectives or if they are only self-interested. Goldstein and Keohane 1993, 13. Deutsch 1963, 92 defines simple learning as learning that does not change the goals of actors, but educates them about the state of the world, so that they may choose different ways of accomplishing their goals. This resembles Levy's notion of causal learning (Levy 1994) and learning in epistemic communities (Haas 1992). Grobe 2010 calls this functional learning.

[118] Colonizers, for example, came to see empires as inconsistent with their values of democracy and equality. Jackson 1993.

statistics can motivate states to act when they learn the scope of a problem, something that occurred in connection with the campaign against landmines.[119] Scorecard diplomacy may also shape views by requesting information from the domestic government. Research has found that engaging individuals directly in active data collection, processing, and dissemination can shape their cognitive framework,[120] in effect priming the international norms in local minds and thus increasing attention to performance on those norms. If elites change their beliefs and internalize new ones, that can be considered a form of socialization.[121] That said, beliefs are difficult to observe, and in any case not necessary for the dynamic to operate. Policymakers may simply realize that others view the issue as important and seek to behave more appropriately. This essentially moves the domestic ideal point "D" closer to the international ideal point "I," which may increase reputational concerns as the gap between "I" and behavior "B" then grows.

Policymakers are particularly likely to seek information about policy alternatives because these often require detailed knowledge.[122] Policymakers surveyed about their attention to performance assessments mention such information as far more influential than financial incentives.[123] The availability heuristic also suggests that policymakers are more likely to adopt solutions that are placed on their radar.[124] This is perhaps why studies of diffusion have shown that countries often look to similar countries when designing and advocating for new policies at home.[125] Thus, diplomatic interaction that highlights policy solutions can increase attention to the problem and make policymakers more receptive to proposed solutions.

---

[119] Price 1998, 322. A study on pension reforms in Latin America found that the World Bank influenced reforms more through the provision of information than through conditionality. The Bank provided information that had escaped the attention of policymakers, who, unable to process all relevant information fully, allowed the Bank to influence policy choices, or perhaps was able to use the Bank's suggestions to push for change. Thus the Bank had more influence through knowledge provision than through conditionality. Weyland 2009, 126–127.

[120] Von Bogdandy and Goldmann 2008, 242.

[121] Checkel 2001, Johnston 2001, Checkel 2005. This resembles what some call argumentative learning (Risse 2000, Deitelhoff 2009) and Grobe calls sincere learning (2010). This requires "value-based rationale," more so than scientific-based evidence. Adler 1992, 3.

[122] Kingdon and Thurber 1984.

[123] Parks et al. 2015, 73.

[124] Weyland 2009.

[125] Linos 2013.

Diplomatic interaction and repeated requests for information may also stimulate new bureaucratic structures or habits that institutionalize attention to the issue area and facilitate ongoing learning about the problem and possible solutions. New administrative structures, in turn, can transform the capabilities of the states and foster bureaucratic expertise.[126] This matters, because new institutions can routinize behaviors and change domestic norms. Max Weber argued that habituation was an important mechanism for shaping behavior.[127] More common behaviors can become routinized because bureaucrats and politicians are "habit-driven actors."[128]

In sum, the individual diplomacy calls attention to the issue and shapes local views and ideal points. The more this occurs, the more concerned elites become with the issue and their related reputation.

The Role of Practical Assistance

Not all ratings and rankings are connected to extensive assistance, but those that are will be more likely to work. By funding the government or NGOs or IGOs, scorecard diplomacy can contribute to structures that might shape local norms and practices and thereby increase reputational pressures to live up to those standards. Funding for capacity building or training may introduce new solutions to problems and normalize certain behaviors. Even if the assistance itself may not be effective, it can empower recipients and broaden the set of voices that participate in the national discussion.[129] Diplomacy and assistance extend attention to the issue far beyond the peak attention it might receive surrounding the release of the report itself and provide ongoing opportunities for interaction, institution building and information transfers.[130] Thus, while structures are often thought to prevent change,[131] new exogenously introduced structures can explain change in local norms and practices.[132]

Practical assistance or aid can also increase the *instrumental salience* of the grades. If ratings or rankings are linked to aid or other economic

---

[126] Pierson 1993, 58, Skocpol 1995.
[127] Weber 1968 [1925], Hopf 2010.
[128] Rosenau 1986, 861–870.
[129] While the extensive literature on building and technical assistance is mixed with respect to results, research suggests that targeted assistance like this is more likely work than general foreign assistance. Collins 2009, 371–381, Scott and Steele 2011, 53.
[130] Risse and Sikkink 1999, Johnston 2001, Checkel 2005.
[131] See discussion in Hopf 2010 and references to Bourdieu 1989.
[132] Neumann 2007, Hopf 2010.

advantages, this resembles standard uses of conditionality or sanctions. Because a strong country like the US can obstruct the flow of economic benefits to other countries, elites may fear economic fallout for their country. The linkage of the Special 301 Report and US trade, for example, generated concerns about costs to trade with the US.[133] That said, scholars have long questioned the efficacy of direct economic leverage in achieving policy changes[134] and criticized them as impracticable and harmful.[135] Some successes nonetheless exist: Sanctions were widely credited with reforms in South Africa, some research has found that economic pressure can destabilize leaders, the European Union (EU) was able to incentivize reforms in candidate states by linking them to membership, and the US inclusion of human rights clauses in preferential trade agreements has been effective.[136] More recent work finds that *ex post* performance-based incentives such as the Millennium Challenge Corporation's (MCC) use of performance indicators to award aid can induce reforms, although this so-called MCC effect may wear off over time if the conditionality is implemented inconsistently – a lesson that might well also apply to scorecard diplomacy more generally.[137] Thus, targeted economic pressure that credibly links policies with economic consequences should matter.[138]

Because the assessments are repeated they may also produce anticipatory effects similar to the "hidden hand" of sanctions: the very threat of punishment may lead to efforts to avoid them.[139] If the rating is linked to punishments or rewards then the recurrent assessments represent an ever-present possibility of economic consequences. Even well performing countries fear the potential consequences of downgrades, a dynamic that has been played out in the Special 301 reports with their more concrete trade implication.[140]

---

[133] Newby 1995.

[134] Collier 1997, Killick 1997.

[135] Hufbauer et al. 1990.

[136] On South Africa, see Klotz 1995. On destabilizing leaders, Marinov 2005. For discussion of EU incentives for reform, see Schimmelfennig et al. 2003, Jacoby 2004, Kelley 2004b, Vachudova 2005. Finally, for the use of human rights conditions in trade, see Hafner-Burton 2005.

[137] On the inducement of reforms, see Parks and Rice 2013. On the fading of the MCC effect see Öhler et al. 2012.

[138] On the importance of credibility see Kelley 2004a, 51, 190–191.

[139] Drezner 2003. This also relates to anticipatory compliance effects of trade negotiations, which suggest that states change their behaviors before agreements enter into effect. Kim 2012, Dür et al. 2014.

[140] Newby 1995, 36.

Even if the scorecard linkages to aid or trade are not explicit, elites may still worry about economic consequences of a poor reputation in a given area.[141] This may be true even in the human rights area, where shaming by international NGOs has been linked to lost investment for targeted states.[142] In Thailand, for example, the business community was concerned that the 2014 Tier 3 rating would harm trade, especially the fishing industry. This continued even after President Obama waived the sanctions threat.[143]

The Role of Third Parties

Scorecards are designed to engage third parties and increase *exposure*. Because reputation is relative to existing norms and multiple audiences, the attitudes of other parties are important. Third parties can amplify reputational concerns because they reinforce the larger global set of norms and standards. Once scores are public, other actors such as NGOs, IGOs, and the media augment the visibility of the scores and thus increase exposure and subsequent reputational pressure. This can also trigger market pressures of various kinds. Third parties are not necessary to the success of scorecard diplomacy, but they boost the odds.

The media disseminates ratings or tiers easily, which increases the exposure that activates reputational concerns. For example, the media coverage following the US Special 301 reports about intellectual property rights has been described as media hysteria. Ratings are much simpler than narratives,[144] and thus easier to use as "psychological rules of thumb"[145] and to present in media stories. Importantly, media coverage can worry policymakers even if citizens don't take to the streets. Even the anticipation of publicity and negative domestic reactions can pressure government officials.[146] Research has shown that elites in general pay much more attention to media than the general public, because they believe that the media does, in fact, affect public opinion.[147] Thus, negative media coverage can create pressure if it creates the *expectation* of

---

[141] Lebovic and Voeten 2009.
[142] Barry et al. 2012. Research also suggests that investors care more about appearances (as in having ratified treaties) than actual human rights performance, which suggests that global ratings and rankings should matter. Garriga 2016.
[143] Charoensuthipan 2014a, 2014b.
[144] Espeland and Stevens 1998, 316, Löwenheim 2008, 257–258.
[145] Sinclair 2005, 52.
[146] Cook et al. 1983.
[147] Mutz 1998.

protest or of lowering public approval.[148] Of course, domestic officials can also use the media to try to save face by rebutting or rejecting the content of the public scorecard. Indeed, it's noteworthy if domestic elites feel pressured to do so in the first place. Governments are also not always successful at controlling the flow of information, and cannot control the international press, much of which now reaches citizens through the Internet. Thus, media, both international and domestic, can increase the reputational concerns of domestic elites.

IGOs and NGOs can also increase the exposure to scorecard diplomacy. Funding these actors allows them to carry out programs, and boosts their standing within society.[149] Their programs, in turn, increase attention to the issue and therefore the exposure of the state to any criticisms of its performance. This is the *inverse* of a tactic scholars have called the "boomerang" effect, in which domestic NGOs unable to pressure their own governments directly can harness the power of outsiders who then pressure the government of those NGOs.[150] In the case of scorecard diplomacy, NGOs are not necessarily unable to pressure their own governments, that is, it is not limited to unreceptive authoritarian settings. Furthermore, the pressure is initiated internationally in an ongoing – rather than ad hoc – fashion. Still, a similar dynamic can ensue: NGOs can use poor ratings to augment their pressure on their governments.

The reports may also provide NGOs with more specific substance with which to pressure the government. One global survey found that over half of civil society actors agreed they were empowered to advocate for reforms because the Millennium Challenge Corporation tied aid eligibility to measures of policy performance.[151] NGOs can also use scorecard diplomacy the way they mobilize around international legal commitments by using the commitments to hold officials accountable.[152] A study of the Extractive Industries Transparency Initiative (EITI), which declares countries to be in or out of compliance, has found that the EITI "improves the capacity of civil society to hold governments to account, whether governments like it or not."[153] Thus NGOs can use scorecard

---

[148] Hendrix and Wong 2013.
[149] Collins 2009, 371–381, Scott and Steele 2011, 53.
[150] Keck and Sikkink 1998.
[151] Parks 2014, 229.
[152] Simmons 2009.
[153] David-Barrett and Okamura 2013, 3.

diplomacy reports for information, but also directly for advocacy and to engage in conversations about problems and needs, all of which increases the governments' exposure to the reputational concerns.

IGOs can also boost scorecard diplomacy. They have long been argued to play important roles in transnational advocacy.[154] Their work on the ground encourages information exchanges with the creators of scorecard diplomacy: IGOs may become sources for information into the regularized reporting, but they may also become primary consumers – and thus legitimizers – of that information, which increases the weight of the grades in the minds of policymakers. For example, organizations such as the United Nations (UN) and the IOM use the TIP Report as a source of information.[155]

Other actors can also increase the consequences of scorecard diplomacy by incorporating scorecards or performance assessments into their own criteria for actions, as the Millennium Challenge Corporation has done for awarding aid. At other times, the link is more direct, for example, if the creators of scorecards fund other actors to engage in efforts that align with the basic goals. In this way, concerns about funding may increase, thus increasing the instrumental salience and, therefore, concerns about reputation.

EMPIRICAL EXPECTATIONS

About the Production of Scorecard Diplomacy

The arguments in this chapter suggest a multitude of hypotheses and observable implications. On any given issue the actual set of these will vary with the available evidence and the context. In general, however, if scorecard diplomacy operates as proposed, then, in an information-rich environment, we should observe evidence of the conduct of diplomacy and the engagement of third parties. We should see active reporting and monitoring connected with diplomacy at meaningful administrative levels, and we should see media coverage of the reports, and involvement of NGOs and IGOs. NGOs, in particular, should use the report to pressure their governments.

Chapters 3 and 4 examine these behaviors in the context of human trafficking.

---

[154] Keck and Sikkink 1998.
[155] This is evident in their reports. See for example UNODC 2009.

About the Verbal Reactions to Scorecard Diplomacy

Furthermore, if scorecard diplomacy generates concern about ratings as argued, then to the extent that it is possible to observe how countries react, we ought to see that those who fare the worst react more often, and in many instances react negatively. In an effort to minimize the normative salience of the criticism, attempts to discredit the creators of the scores might occur. There may also be contestation over the norms if international and domestic ideal points differ. Countries that get more exposure through media coverage, for example, might also react more.

This chapter has also stressed that countries' reputational concerns are broad, that is, they are both instrumental and normative, and they include concerns about image and standing in the international community. While it may not always be possible to observe, countries might explicitly express such concern about their image or standing, even if they don't face any aid or trade threats as a result of the score, or they may underscore such concerns by explicitly comparing their scores with those of other countries, especially those they consider peers. If the reference to international norms is important for states, we might also see that those that have publicly committed to the international norms underlying the scores might react more often. On the other hand, if countries worry about ratings because of aid or trade, we might see discussions in reaction to poor grades in particular, and countries whose aid is threatened might react more.

Chapter 5 examines these behaviors in the context of human trafficking.

About the Policy Responses to Scorecard Diplomacy

The goal of scorecard diplomacy, of course, is not just to get states riled up, but to get them to change their behavior, whether that be policies, regulations, programs, or whatever the relevant outcomes are. If states care about monitoring and grading, then we should observe that they respond when they are included in the monitoring scheme, when they get harsher grades, and when they are downgraded in their rating or ranking.

How would one know that these patterns are really due to the scorecard diplomacy? Here one can derive further observable implications. For example, since the ratings are supposed to affect change through concerns about reputation, then it might be possible to observe not only that scores relate to the level and nature of verbal reactions, but also that countries that react are more likely to change their behavior. Furthermore, if states are motivated by the prospect of a rise in their rating, if one has good information, then one might also be able to observe extra efforts by states to accomplish certain goals as the deadline for the next scorecard cycle approaches. Indeed, with very good access to information, one might even be able to observe that officials explicitly state that they are undertaking reforms with the hope of improving their scores.

Chapter 6 explores these behaviors in the context of human trafficking.

About the Factors Modifying the Policy Reactions to Scorecard Diplomacy

Finally, this chapter has presented a simple model for understanding when scorecard diplomacy is more likely to matter. Specifically, policy responses should depend on states' sensitivity, exposure, and prioritization. Therefore, policy responses should be more likely when states are more sensitive, that is, if the country wants to boost its international image, if its norms align with the international norms, or if it faces economic repercussions of a low score. This sensitivity will be heightened the more credible the scorecard creator is. Policy responses should also be more likely when states are more exposed. That is, when third parties are actively attracting attention to the issue, or when local events bring attention to issues, and when scorecard diplomacy is credibly implemented in a country, giving it greater weight. Finally, states are more likely to change their behavior in response to scorecard diplomacy, the more they are able to prioritize the issue, such as when local officials take the issue on, when the government is stable and crisis free, or when domestic actors do not have large stakes in preventing change.

Chapter 7 examines these behaviors in the context of human trafficking.

SUMMARY

This chapter has defined reputation as used in this book, explained its nature, and discussed why states and their governments value a good reputation. It has offered a simple model to explain the factors that modify whether states become concerned about their reputation on a given issue and whether they actually do something about it. Finally, it has considered how the features of scorecard diplomacy stimulate states' concern for their reputation.

The argument takes its starting point in the claim that states are not merely concerned about their reputation in terms of the credibility of their threats and promises in keeping commitments or their resolve in war; rather, states care about their reputation about their broader performance across many issues as assessed by multiple audiences. A good reputation is important for states' image and identity. Governments know that others – citizens, civil society, and other international and domestic actors – assess their performance relative to a set of standards and norms across a number of issues and that this assessment undergirds their legitimacy and status, both of which bolster their ability to govern and interact with other states.

States sustain a good overall reputation when they adhere to norms more broadly and adopt productive policies, yet, in a world of increasing publicity and accountability, their reputation can suffer even when they falter in a narrow area that attracts attention. Governments therefore worry about their reputations across multiple areas and generally prefer to satisfy the norms and ideals promulgated domestically and internationally. A few exceptions notwithstanding, even authoritarian governments have reasons to worry about their performance. Since the procedural foundation for their authority is weak, to suppress revolt they depend even more on successful performance in other areas.

Performance gaps arise when a state veers from established norms and expectations. How concerned a state becomes about this gap depends on several factors that influence its *sensitivity* and *exposure* to criticism. Sensitivity describes the weight that governments assign to the performance gap. Such gaps are more salient to a state if those promulgating the standards belong to a group with which it identifies and if the norms or ideals are well established. Nonetheless, if the domestic standards differ markedly, the international gap will be less salient and the state will be less concerned. Likewise, a state is more sensitive to performance gaps that might affect other objectives, for example, if the state is seeking some benefit that's tied to the specific issue area. Exposure describes how much credible attention the performance gap gets. This depends both on the authority of the sources of criticisms, as well as the volume and quality of information about the government's performance. Third parties can magnify the exposure.

States' concern about their reputations gives the international community an opportunity to influence them. The use of scorecard diplomacy and similar efforts can garner attention and highlight the performance of a state over time and relative to peers. The repeated nature of this exercise makes countries concerned about current and future ratings. Its public nature lets other actors reinforce the norms, which increases the government's reputational concerns. The use of monitoring and grading therefore can raise governments' concern about their reputations, especially if the efforts are further supplemented by diplomatic engagement.

Whether concern translates into action depends on the priority the government can give it. States have crowded agendas, experience instability, and may lack capacity. Some states may assign a lower relative value to its reputation on a given issue when the domestic agenda is very crowded. Surely, when leaders gas their people, as has Syria's president Bashar al-Assad, the reputational cost to them is considered tolerable in light of their other objectives. Getting from concern to action thus remains a context-dependent challenge. Nonetheless, without other surefire tactics to influence recalcitrant governments, it makes sense to attend to the question of reputation and how to stimulate concerns about performance. In the absence of military or strong coercion, reputational concern is a prerequisite for action, so it's important to understand how it arises and can be stimulated. This book therefore moves on to examine what we can learn about reputation and scorecard diplomacy from the case of human trafficking.

3

The Case of Human Trafficking

We were incredibly involved. We were the prime mover in all of the TIP
activities.

    – John Ordway, former Ambassador to Armenia and Kazakhstan[1]

To study the influence of reputation among nations this book focuses
on the case of US diplomacy on human trafficking. This case is useful
because the policy has been similar all around the world, has emphasized
reputation through ratings, and is rich in information. The questions at
hand are: Has the strategy elicited reputational concerns? Have governments undertaken the reforms the US wanted? Why do governments
respond and why do their responses differ? And what do the answers to
these questions teach us about the nature and influence of reputation?

    Addressing these questions is a considerable task. Therefore, this book
does not engage the larger debates about global anti-trafficking norms,[2]
nor address whether policies have reduced the incidence of human trafficking. The data is too poor to know.[3] Rather, given the vastness of the
topic of human trafficking, this chapter focuses on a few questions that
bear directly on scorecard diplomacy such as: What is human trafficking?

---

[1] Ordway interview.

[2] NGOs, IGOs, and governments working to fight trafficking disagree about the optimal
approaches. Some external organizations may lack cultural understanding. Some argue
that some anti-trafficking policies harm the victims more than they help. Raids of brothels
followed by possible prosecutions and criminal proceedings may accuse victims of crimes
and deport them to places where they may face more suffering. Global Alliance Against
Traffic in Women 2007.

[3] Prosecutions and convictions have increased, but this could be because the problem is
growing, because we have more information, or we are cracking down on it more.

How did it arrive on the international agenda? Does a global prohibition exist? How has interstate cooperation developed? The chapter then explains how the US conducts scorecard diplomacy in the case of human trafficking. It walks through Step 1 of scorecard diplomacy, monitoring and grading, and Step 2, active diplomacy. It also discusses US choices about which states to initially include in the report as well as any biases in the tier system, because these choices and biases are essential to understand to be able to assess the policy's effectiveness.

*** *

THE PROBLEM OF HUMAN TRAFFICKING

What Is Human Trafficking?

Human trafficking is the sale and exploitation of human beings. It differs from smuggling, which illegally moves people across borders at their request.[4] Article 3, paragraph (a) of the 2000 Palermo Protocol (discussed more below) defines Trafficking in Persons as:

[T]he recruitment, transportation, transfer, harbouring or receipt of persons, by means of the threat or use of force or other forms of coercion, of abduction, of fraud, of deception, of the abuse of power or of a position of vulnerability or of the giving or receiving of payments or benefits to achieve the consent of a person having control over another person, for the purpose of exploitation. Exploitation shall include, at a minimum, the exploitation of the prostitution of others or other forms of sexual exploitation, forced labour or services, slavery or practices similar to slavery, servitude or the removal of organs.

In some ways the problem is old, linked to traditional forms of slavery going back thousands of years to a time when such exploitation was normal and even legal. The terms "human trafficking" or "trafficking in persons" apply to the modern and more varied and hidden forms of severe exploitation of human beings.

The scope of the modern problem is difficult to assess but clearly large. The Palermo Protocol notes that trafficking can be for sexual exploitation or forced labor or organ removal. It is commonly understood to involve forced labor, bonded labor, child marriage, forced marriage, or the use of children in begging, warfare, prostitution, and much more. The UN Office on Drugs and Crime (UNODC) notes that of all the detected cases, nearly 40 percent are labor-related. Labor trafficking affects workers in

---

[4] International Labour Organization 2012.

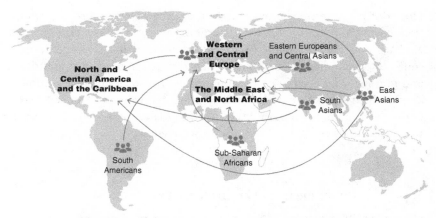

FIGURE 3.1. Human trafficking patterns of major origin and destination regions,
2010–2012.
The arrows show the flows that represent 5 percent or above of the total victims
detected in the sub-regions.
Source: UN Office on Drugs and Crime (UNODC).

sectors such as agriculture, domestic service, hospitality, construction,
and garment and shoe production. Some trafficking, like Uzbekistan's
forcible cotton production, is government-sponsored. About half of all
victims are thought to be women, one-fifth girls, and 12 percent boys,
while about 72 percent of traffickers are male.[5]

Actual numbers of victims are unreliable.[6] In 2002, the US State
Department estimated there were between 700,000 and 4 million. A
2012 ILO estimate of forced labor came in at 20.9 million.[7] By 2014, the
US State Department noted that 44,000 actual victims had been identified in the past year, but that the real number of victims could be as high
as 20 million. In 2014, a UNODC report covering the years 2010–2012
reported having detected 510 actual trafficking flows of citizens from 152
different countries, but noted that these observed events are but the tip
of the iceberg.[8] It's big business: A 2014 ILO Report estimated the illicit
profits from forced labor and human trafficking at $150 billion.[9]

The pattern of movements varies across countries. Some countries
are mostly sources of trafficking victims who are transported or travel

[5] UNODC 2014.
[6] Kessler 2015. The number in the Global Slavery Index are deeply flawed. Gallagher 2014a.
[7] International Labour Organization 2012.
[8] UNODC 2014.
[9] International Labour Organization 2014.

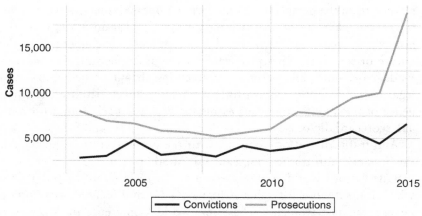

FIGURE 3.2. Human trafficking prosecutions and convictions worldwide, 2003–2014.
Source: 2007 and 2016 TIP Reports, section on "Global Law Enforcement Data."

to destination countries where they are victimized. Countries can also be transit countries, meaning that the victims travel or are transported through the country but neither originate nor remain there. Many countries can be classified as all three types. Given that trafficking can also take on many guises, countries face mixed challenges. Figure 3.1 displays the major movement patterns. Despite an increase in prosecutions and convictions, compared to the number of victims estimated above, human trafficking goes largely unpunished (see Figure 3.2).

The Backdrop for Reputations: The Emergence of a Global Prohibition Norm

Scorecard diplomacy is a symbolic exercise that only works if it is grounded in a global normative or regulatory milieu such that violations or poor performance are widely considered undesirable. Global norms provide the mirror and the standards against which actors assess reputation.

In the area of human trafficking, such a global norm is now widely shared by multiple actors, including an array of intergovernmental organizations. However, for many years the world lacked an internationally accepted definition of trade and trafficking in human beings. Smuggling and illegal migration were lumped together with trafficking – a confusion still perpetuated by the media. Although trafficking has clear links to slavery, from the perspective of modern national criminal justice, human trafficking was a new crime lacking a proper legal framework. Over the last two decades, an international legal consensus has emerged on the nature of the "trafficking problem."[10] Even as implementation remains inadequate, states are increasingly accepting that it is their moral and legal responsibility to punish traffickers and protect victims. The emergence of this global consensus forms the essential background for anti-TIP scorecard diplomacy.

Anti-trafficking efforts date back to the anti-slavery movement, but the modern anti-trafficking regime is more recent.[11] The precursors include various world conferences on women in the 1980s and 1990s, which framed women's rights as human rights and focused attention on violence against women.[12] The 1995 World Conference on Women in Beijing called for action against trafficking in women and children. For many years the issue of human trafficking had been framed around sexual exploitation, but in Beijing, forced labor and forced marriages were also included.[13]

Meanwhile rising concerns about transnational crime led the UN General Assembly to ask the Commission on Crime Prevention and Criminal Justice to analyze the incidence of various transnational organized criminal activities.[14] The Assembly established an ad hoc committee to draft a multilateral protocol against transnational organized crime in 1998. Prompted largely by NGOs and faced with a rising incidence of human trafficking, poor domestic legislation and an inadequate international legal system, the issue of human trafficking was also making its way into the convention.

The topic of human trafficking also heated up in the US during the 1990s, propelled by an unusual coalition of feminists and religious conservatives. Efforts to fight the "moral scourge" of human trafficking found cross-party appeal and received broad support.[15] After first being introduced by Representative Chris Smith (R-NJ) in 1998, on October 18, 2000 the Trafficking Victims Protection Act (TVPA) became the

---

[10] Gallagher and Holmes 2008, 318–319.
[11] Oldfield 1998.
[12] This section draws on Bertone 2008, 21ff.
[13] A thorough treatment of the rise of anti-trafficking policy both internationally and in the US including various ideological debates can be found in Bertone 2008 and in Efrat 2012.
[14] United Nations 2000, 610.
[15] Miller and Horowitz interviews. Also DeStefano 2007.

backbone of the US anti-trafficking policy abroad.[16] While the US domestic efforts to pass the TVPA gained momentum, the efforts to extend these efforts globally also got underway. The US quickly dominated the global policy arena and took a leading role in negotiations over the protocol and in the development of the norms embedded in the protocol.[17] On Women's Day, March 1998, US President Clinton referenced the "3Ps" that eventually made it into the protocol: to prevent trafficking, protect victims of trafficking, and prosecute traffickers.[18] Later that year during the development of the proposed convention, the US introduced a resolution calling for a protocol on trafficking in women and children.[19] After the resolution was adopted, the US and Argentina introduced the draft protocol.[20] In November 2000 the Assembly adopted the Palermo Protocol to Prevent, Suppress, and Punish Trafficking in Persons (Palermo Protocol) to the Convention against Transnational Organized Crime and opened it to signature from December 12 to December 15.[21] The protocol entered into force on September 29, 2003.

The drafters of the Palermo Protocol overcame many disagreements to reach the definition above. The NGO community was present in remarkable force and developed among themselves "a clear and savage rift."[22] The text was a compromise and some things were left unclear to accommodate differing views. In particular, "sexual" or "exploitation" was not defined clearly, reflecting a deep disagreement about whether prostitution can ever be voluntary. Some abolitionist groups in the US wanted the protocol to include voluntary prostitution. The coercion–consent debate necessitated some compromises that allowed both sides to claim victory.[23]

---

[16] Others have described the history and spirit of this act. See for example DeStefano 2007, Efrat 2012, Ch. 5.

[17] Bertone 2008, 24, Chuang 2015, 610.

[18] Clinton 1998.

[19] Hyland 2001, 1. Argentina had already suggested drafting a convention against trafficking in minors and Greece had followed up by suggesting this be broadened to all trafficking. Ollus 2008, 16, 20.

[20] Ad Hoc Committee on the Elaboration of a Convention against Transnational Organized Crime 1999. See the procedural history at the Convention website United Nations 2000.

[21] Hyland 2001, Fredette 2009. Hyland attributes the new protocol to five factors: NGO lobbying of governments on behalf of trafficking victims, an increase in victims with more data becoming available to document the trend, a turn to view trafficking as a crime issue with increasing negative externalities, the difficulties of prosecuting trafficking offenders in the absence of national laws, and the inadequacy of international legislation to address the modern aspects of the problem, including the recognition of a broader range of victims and acts that qualified as trafficking.

[22] Gallagher 2001, 1002.

[23] Doezema 2002.

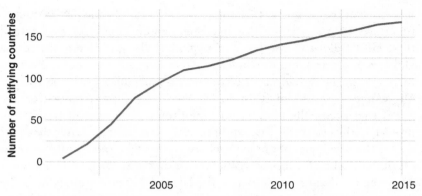

FIGURE 3.3. Number of state parties to the Palermo Protocol to Prevent, Suppress and Punish Trafficking in Persons (Palermo Protocol) to the Convention against Transnational Organized Crime.
Source: UNODC.

Ultimately the protocol made consent irrelevant in an effort to prevent offenders from using it as a defense,[24] but it did not equate prostitution with trafficking.

Since the passage of the protocol, the legal and political landscape around human trafficking has been "radically transformed,"[25] and contributed to the global culture against human trafficking that forms the foundation of reputational concerns. Ratifications grew steadily after the protocol was created (see Figure 3.3). By 2015, 169 states were parties to the protocol, and several regional legal and policy instruments had emerged. In 2002 the UN developed the Recommended Principles and Guidelines on Human Rights and Human Trafficking and in 2005 the Council of Europe adopted the Convention on Action against Trafficking. These measures were supplemented by global efforts of several regional and international government organizations, as well as countries' own expenditures on law enforcement, victim protection and assistance, awareness-raising programs, and so forth.[26]

IGOs focused on human trafficking include the United Nations Office on Drugs and Crime (UNODC), which started the Global Programme against Trafficking in Human Beings in 1999, the International Labour Organization (ILO), the International Criminal Police Organization, and the International Organization for Migration. In 2007 UNODC launched

[24] Gallagher 2001, 985.
[25] Gallagher and Holmes 2008, 318.
[26] Sychov 2009.

UN.GIFT (United Nations Global Initiative to Fight Human Trafficking) with a large gathering in Vienna, Austria. In 2002 the Organization for Security and Co-operation in Europe (OSCE) adopted the Declaration on Trafficking in Human Beings that created so-called national referring mechanisms to facilitate coordination. The Council of Europe and the European Union have also been active, though the focus has largely been limited to member and neighbor states. The US has been at the forefront of leaning on governments around the world to live up to international standards.

The US definition of human trafficking used in the TIP Report has stimulated discussion about legal norms, the relationship between prostitution and trafficking,[27] and the Western imposition of ideas. Some saw early US anti-TIP efforts as the president's campaign to "promote restrictive policies on reproductive rights and sexuality throughout the world."[28] The issue of a person's "consent" to transactional sex has loomed large in the US efforts to shape the Palermo Protocol and has, at times, created tensions that intersect with the US efforts on the ground. These debates are left outside the scope of this book, but are treated in depth elsewhere.[29]

Broadly speaking, however, a global prohibition against human trafficking clearly exists and has been growing over the last two decades. This has given the US a foil against which to reflect the performance of countries. The protocol provides standards that are widely accepted by major actors, lending moral force to efforts of US scorecard diplomacy to elicit reputational concerns by invoking these norms.

Doesn't Everyone Want to Fight Human Trafficking?

One might argue that human trafficking stands apart in its ability to generate moral outrage. Certainly, it's easier to generate opprobrium against human trafficking than against less morally abject issues such as banking

---

[27] Lerum et al. 2012. The creators behind the TVPA wanted to eliminate prostitution and sought bans on funding to anything related to prostitution or to organizations that did not renounce prostitution. This became part of the Bush administration's global anti-prostitution policies, which prohibited anti-TIP funding to some organizations. These policies were eventually eliminated in a 2013 Supreme Court ruling.

[28] Foester 2009, 153.

[29] Butcher 2003, Weitzer 2005, Masenior and Beyrer 2007. A critical discussion of the way the US has defined trafficking norms compared with the UN protocol can be found in much of the work of Chuang and is also discussed in various Congressional research reports. Wyler et al. 2009, Wyler 2013, Chuang 2005, 2012, 2013, 2015.

regulations. Countries should therefore naturally want to address it, so little outside pressure should be necessary. Furthermore, one might argue that addressing human trafficking should not threaten domestic power holders in the way that curbing political repression or other human rights abuses might. This would suggest that there should be less resistance to curbing TIP than to increasing freedom of speech, for example.

However, other factors push *against* governments' prioritizing this issue and lower the government's sensitivity to problem, and, as discussed in Chapter 2, prioritization and sensitivity are crucial to success.

Few Direct Material Linkages

While countries might fear that a poor rating could affect trade, investment decisions, or tourism, and while such fear has been warranted in some cases such as Thailand,[30] generally such fears are less common than for issues that bear directly on a state's investment climate, such as its respect for intellectual property or its rule of law. TIP is mostly a soft issue that, as shown later, even the US has failed to tie to any real economic repercussions. Poor ratings do not predict less foreign direct investment (FDI), aid, or trade, for example, so countries may be less concerned about spillover effects on these. This decreases the instrumental salience discussed in Chapter 2.

Domestic Barriers to Addressing TIP

Addressing TIP poses several challenges, many of which lower its prioritization, and its normative and instrumental salience as discussed in Chapter 2.

First, *human trafficking victims are often not constituents.* Whether governments want to address a difficult domestic problem, such as illicit trade, depends on the domestic political economy of the issue. The illicit nature of trafficking rarely promotes a set of prominent and vocal actors. The victims are often from overseas or lack political empowerment, so, posing no threat at the ballot box, they are marginalized. Israel, for example, initially saw trafficked women as foreign prostitutes who could be ignored.[31]

Furthermore, *cracking down on trafficking is costly and difficult.* Addressing the problem may in itself attract attention to it, thus initially bring more costs than benefit for the government. Because it is driven by

---

[30] For more on Thailand, see Chapter 5.
[31] Richards 2004, Efrat 2012.

crime and poverty, it is also a difficult problem to address.[32] It involves border issues, labor regulations, investigations and increased law enforcement, training, shelters, and inter-agency cooperation, which can create friction. This makes it hard for TIP to compete with other government priorities.

In addition, *elites often benefit from trafficking*. Where corruption thrives, the government may lack the will to combat illicit trade.[33] Authoritarian governments often depend on loyalty among security forces and police, and if these forces benefit from trafficking in their districts – as is often the case – then cracking down on TIP can sow discontent and erode loyalty that is so often important for non-democratic power holders. Indeed, government complicity is rampant. Corrupt officials may take bribes for altering documents, or allowing border crossings. In 2014 police and government officials were sources of trafficking in 68 countries, topped only by organized criminal gangs.[34] In Argentina, for example, the IOM Country Representative "identified official complicity at provincial and local levels and poor interagency coordination at all levels as impediments to effectively combating the problem." He recounted a conversation he'd had with the interior minister who had told him that, "if the anti-TIP law applied to adult victims as well, the [government] would have to go after half of all provincial governors" and that this was why although "high-level officials may not be directly involved in trafficking activities, they are likely aware of the problem and are currently doing little to stop it."[35] Some governments outright exploit workers themselves, some of the most egregious examples of this being Uzbekistan's cotton production program, Japan's Industrial Trainee and Technical Internship Program, and the many forms of state-sponsored labor exploitation in Belarus.[36]

Another challenge is that, while international law bans human trafficking, *different cultural or domestic traditions are more accepting*. Different domestic norms lower the normative salience of the issue, as discussed in Chapter 2. Some Middle Eastern countries have long traditions of using domestic servants. They do not see it as a form of trafficking that workers have their passports taken away and are only allowed to

---

[32] Mertus and Bertone 2007.

[33] Efrat 2012, 278.

[34] Protection Project 2014, 41.

[35] 07BUENOSAIRES1353.

[36] US Congress 2014. See also the 2015 US TIP Report narrative on Belarus. US Department of State 2015.

be in the country if they work for one given employer, to whom they are entirely beholden. Also in the Middle East, children used to be trafficked to serve as jockeys for camel racing, a practice widely condoned by inner circles of the regimes. Some countries view child marriage as culturally acceptable. In other countries such as Ghana, families send their children to work for the fishing industry, which is difficult to escape, or simply give children to extended family.[37] In Chad, children are used for herding, and the cultural environment regards youth employment as normal.[38] The president of the State Human Rights Commission has said that most TIP occurrences were instances of "indigenous citizens ... participating in 'cultural practices' such as selling young daughters."[39] Cracking down on such traditions is challenging.

Conservative religious views may dismiss concern for victims. In some countries the views toward trafficking can be not only dismissive, but also outright condemning. In Iraq, for example, the US embassy reported:

Member of parliamentarian, [Nada] Ibrahim related that some officials could not overcome their personal and religious beliefs about trafficking to view TIP as a political issue. She recounted a conversation with Women's Committee Chairwoman Sameera Al-Mousawi, who walked off the stage in the middle of a televised interview with Yanar Mohammed, an NGO activist, regarding female victims of sexual exploitation and trafficking. Ibrahim remembered that when she confronted Mousawi after the incident and asked her why she did not acknowledge the situation of female victims of trafficking as a political issue, Mousawi had responded by declaring that these women were "prostitutes who must die." Ibrahim lamented that some [Iraqi] officials who might otherwise help Iraq make progress on TIP harbored strong personal beliefs that precluded their objective consideration of human trafficking as a political issue.[40]

Sometimes religious groups are outright complicit. For example, in Guinea-Bissau religious teachers lure boys by offering them education, but instead force them to beg in neighboring countries. In the 2014 TIP Report, religious groups are mentioned as sources of trafficking in 16 countries, so one cannot assume that the preferences of religious leaders align with the US in fighting trafficking.

Denial is often easier. While governments may not see human trafficking as an immediate threat to their own power, denial is often easier than admitting to such an ugly problem. One IOM staffer noted how

---

[37] Mahamoud interview.
[38] 09NDJAMENA230.
[39] 09MEXICO3173.
[40] 10BAGHDAD480.

governments often refuse to acknowledge the problem: "The Bahamas really changed their song about this issue over time. First, they would say: 'I don't know what this country in that the report is about, but it's not mine.' Two years later they admitted they were wrong. Now we are working, talking about the TIP Report as well."[41] Such denial is common. In many countries, such as Algeria, US embassies have reported similar attitudes. Some governments consider human trafficking simply "an illegal immigration issue," for example. Libya's government lacked "even a rudimentary understanding of the phenomenon" and how to respond.[42] In Tajikistan, the US embassy noted that government officials had "very little comprehension of our concerns about TIP ... some prefer denial to engagement on difficult issues which require reform and self-criticism."[43] Such refusal to recognize the problem is a common obstacle to progress.

In sum, it's probably easier to generate moral outrage about human trafficking than on many other issues. However, even if it is easier than, say, banking regulations or freedom of speech, this does not make it an *easy* case per se. It still requires political will, education, capacity, and resources. Just like murder and other heinous crimes, it is not about to be eradicated. Furthermore, even if governments care about their reputation on the issue, many lack the capacity and know-how to deal with the issue.[44]

As the previous chapter noted, the way a country views an issue and the extent to which it prioritizes it will modify its concern. Chapter 7 will examine how some of these factors discussed above modify the influence of scorecard diplomacy. For now, having discussed the global regime against human trafficking and the nature of human trafficking as a policy problem and subject for influence by international actors, this chapter turns to explain how the US has implemented the first two steps of the scorecard diplomacy cycle.

STEP 1: PUBLIC MONITORING AND GRADING

The US Victims of Trafficking and Violence Protection Act

The US was, as noted, an early adopter of national anti-trafficking legislation. The 2000 TVPA was one of the first dedicated national anti-trafficking laws, and its international dimension was striking. The Act

---

[41] Interview #3.
[42] 06TRIPOLI671.
[43] 09DUSHANBE1319.
[44] Efrat 2012, 222.

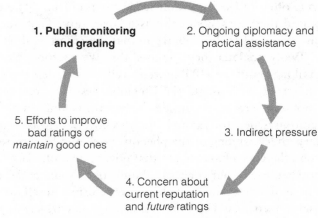

FIGURE 3.4. The cycle of scorecard diplomacy.

created the Office to Monitor and Combat Trafficking in Persons within the State Department (TIP Office) to evaluate countries' progress in the areas of "trafficking prevention, protection, and assistance to victims of trafficking, and prosecution and enforcement against traffickers, including the role of public corruption in facilitating trafficking." Countries were to be placed into tiers, *not according to the scope of the problem, but according to their efforts.* The Act set "minimum standards"[45] for the elimination of trafficking: Tier 1 was for countries that meet the minimal standards, Tier 2 for countries who do not meet them but are making significant efforts to do so, and Tier 3 was for countries failing to meet the minimal standards. The Watch List, first used in 2004, was for countries at risk of falling to Tier 3.

The use of public ratings was by design. As Rep. Chris Smith noted, the US TIP Report was deliberately designed to expose countries:

[W]hen the [Trafficking Victims Protection Act] was enacted, there were many people that didn't want to publicly name offending countries. The experience of the first two "TIP Reports," however, supports the argument that I and others made, that some countries would only get serious about their failure to address this travesty of human rights if their deficiencies were *publicly* identified [emphasis added].[46]

Interviews reveal that the people who created the TVPA wanted a "tool." The ratings were intended to shame countries, even if their ostensible

---

[45] Section 108 US Congress 2000.
[46] US Congress 2002, 8.

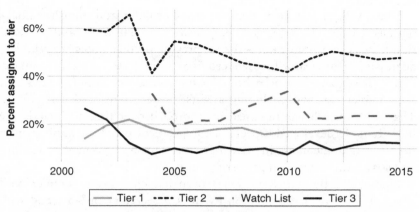

FIGURE 3.5. US Department of State tier ratings of countries on human traffick-ing, 2001–2015.
N = 79 countries in 2001; 186 countries in 2015.
Source: US TIP Report.

purpose is merely to assess whether a country meets US TVPA criteria for aid – an assessment that would not require tiers. The link between action and future ratings is often used in diplomacy, with US embassy staff warning that a country risks a downgrade, or will only be able to achieve an upgrade if certain steps are taken. That the rating is less about the scope of the problem than the government efforts is clear from cases like Oman where, between 2005 and 2007, the US government lost patience and worsened Oman's ratings until it responded. Figure 3.5 shows the distribution of tier ratings over time, keeping in mind that the number of countries included in the report also has expanded.

The Act also authorized monetary assistance to help countries meet the criteria and prohibited US "nonhumanitarian, nontrade-related for-eign assistance" to countries making insufficient efforts. The US may also "work to deny" such countries funding from international finan-cial institutions, although the president can waive any punitive measures. Importantly, however, the Act necessitated an additional interim assess-ment in the wake of a Tier 3 rating, so in this follow-up period the focus on the problem often increases. Congress reauthorized the Act in 2003, 2005, 2008, and 2013, and along the way also classified failure to pro-vide the US with data as evidence of lack of a sufficient anti-TIP effort (2003) and asked the TIP Office to "intensify the focus of the Office on forced labor" (2005).[47]

[47] Section 105 (2) US Congress 2005.

The TVPA requirement that countries prohibit and punish trafficking has led the TIP Reports to emphasize criminalization and prosecution. One commentator notes the US pressured other states "to establish aggressive, perpetrator-focused criminal justice responses to trafficking."[48] This focus has been both on the passage of anti-TIP laws and their implementation, including arrests, prosecutions, and convictions. That said, the US has modified its approach over time to include the initially underdeveloped aspects of the protocol that have subsequently been clarified, including increased attention to the treatment of victims, and structural issues such as corruption.[49]

Since 2001 the TIP Report has been launched every summer with a big press event in Washington by the US Secretary of State and with accompanying events around the world. The report covers the "Three Ps" – protection, prosecution, and prevention. Today the report captures a wide array of behaviors often referred to as "modern day slavery," an expansive label that some criticize as "exploitation creep" to broaden the US sphere of influence.[50] The US considers prostitution of minors,[51] forced marriages, and all forms of forced labor as forms of trafficking. It does not require the person to be transported across state borders or even domestically to be trafficked. Those born into exploitative conditions are also considered victims of trafficking. Over the years the US definition has evolved somewhat, which has led some countries to criticize the US for "moving the goal posts," particularly with the greater emphasis on labor trafficking after the 2005 reauthorization act.[52]

The report uses data gathered from multiple sources. First and foremost, US embassies around the world request information on a wealth of policies, practices, and statistics directly from governments and communicate with local NGOs to obtain their perspectives. The office in Washington also draws on information from IGOs around the world, including UNODC, IOM, ILO, and others.

---

[48] Chuang 2015, 610.

[49] Gallagher 2015, no page numbers.

[50] Chuang 2015, 611. Gallagher offers an excellent analysis of the TIP Reports. Gallagher 2011.

[51] Thus the US publicly criticized Switzerland when it discovered a loophole in Swiss law that failed to criminalize prostitution of 16 year olds. The Swiss were originally appalled by the US criticism, which was accompanied by a fall to Tier 2. Subsequently, it did not take long for Switzerland to amend the relevant laws.

[52] The Act mandated "[a]dditional activities to monitor and combat forced labor and child labor." US Congress 2005, §7112.

Importantly, the report does not rate countries according to the *scale* of the problem, but according to government *efforts* to fight trafficking. Some countries with large trafficking problems can be rated Tier 1 if their governments are working hard to address the problem, while those with fewer problems can be rated Tier 3 if their governments are completely apathetic. Furthermore, a change in tiers does not necessarily reflect a change in underlying conditions. On the contrary: Since the tiers assess government efforts, a country might receive a certain tier for a while under the understanding that it is in the process of addressing the problem. If time passes and nothing happens, the report is likely to lower the rating to exert pressure. The ratings usually appear in an overview section of the TIP Report and can be easily accessed online. The body of the report assesses government actions, often critically. It also recommends policies, such as urging a country to pass or implement anti-trafficking legislation, to open a shelter, or to increase awareness of the problem. Such recommendations can penetrate domestic discourse.[53]

The Inclusion and Scoring of Countries

Initially, the US did not include all countries in the TIP Report, and it took many years before all countries were included. To understand whether inclusion of countries in the report matters, it is necessary to understand the pattern of inclusion. Specifically, if the US simply engages with countries that are already seeking to combat human trafficking, one might misattribute improvements to the US efforts. That's not what's happened, however. The 2001 report included only 80 countries, supposedly based on whether information existed about at least 100 identified victims. As data improved, more countries were included and the 100-victim threshold was eliminated in 2009. By 2011 most countries were included, as Figure 3.6 shows.

The first 80 countries were not chosen because they were the most receptive to US influence – Iran, Cuba, China, and Russia are hardly bastions of US influence. Rather, countries were selected according to criteria listed in the TIP Report methodology. Additionally, Beth Simmons and I analyzed what other factors may have driven inclusion in the report. We found that the perceived prevalence of the problem (as measured by a UN

---

[53] For example, in 2008 Australia's parliament referenced the report's criticism of Australia's failure to link victim assistance to viable prosecutions. Phillips 2008, 5.

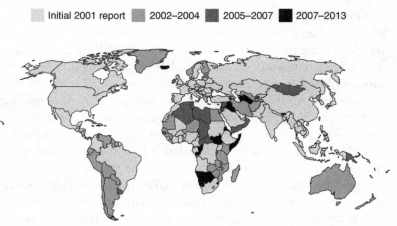

FIGURE 3.6. The timing of inclusion of countries in the US State Department TIP Report.

count of reports about the problem in a given country) as well as the quality of information in a country (as measured by an average availability of data on a number of basic national statistics) best predict when the US included countries in the report. Countries did not appear to be included because they seemed likely candidates for good performance on TIP.[54] Indeed, countries with *worse civil liberties* were more likely to be included, although those might be less susceptible to US pressure or less motivated to fight TIP. In sum, the report's explanation that inclusion was driven by available information about trafficking appears accurate, and it does not seem that the TIP Office was gaming the system by excluding harder cases.

Although inclusion in the report appears neutral, the ratings are not.[55] Critics have characterized the tier assignments as political maneuvering.[56] The US government has acknowledged the weaknesses. A 2006 Government Accountability Office (GAO) report criticized the reports as subjective and too incomplete to guide policy, noting that the rankings sometimes resulted from political "horse trading."[57] Likewise, the

[54] Kelley and Simmons 2015. The models are in Table A3.1 in the Results Appendix. We found no correlation with other factors that might influence the tendency to give in to US pressure such as aid, trade, or a country's wealth, or whether a country had joined the Palermo Protocol. Inclusion in the report also does not correlate with a country's *bureaucratic quality*, *rule of law*, *corruption*, or the *share of women holding seats in parliament*.

[55] Wooditch 2010.

[56] Garcia 2006, Rosenberg and Cochrane 2015.

[57] GAO 2006, i, 33.

Inspector General's Office has identified inconsistencies and revealed that regional bureaus, embassies, and the TIP Office in Washington wrangle over the ratings.[58] A blatant case was Malaysia's 2015 upgrade to the Watch List to facilitate the Transpacific Partnership after Congress had prohibited the inclusion of Tier 3 countries in the deal.[59] Nonetheless, many countries, including US allies, do end up in the worst categories. Countries with Tier 3 rankings have included Israel, Greece, and Turkey, while the Watch List has included Egypt, Estonia, and Japan. That said, to address the reluctance to place countries in the Tier 3 category, in 2008 Congress mandated that starting with the 2009 report, countries could no longer be on the Watch List for more than two years, forcing the first set of "automatic" downgrades in 2011 to countries such as Thailand, China, and Russia.

Despite criticism, the report is still credited as "the most influential and the most trusted indicator of states' performance vis-à-vis human trafficking."[60] Many interviewees from IGOs and NGOs staff said that they consider the report a good source of information and rely extensively on it.

What does all this mean for how one assesses the influence of the ratings on state behavior? Although biases in the ratings threaten their credibility and cause political tension, this only matters for the purpose of evaluating their influence if the biases lead to a false impression that the tier system is influential. If the TIP Office consistently assigned harsher ratings to countries already on the verge of improving, this would mislead the analysis. Note that this would require harsher ratings, not the lenient ones that critics have identified. Furthermore, the evidence does not suggest such gaming. Rather, a mix of factors predict tier ratings, including some that correlate with a propensity to fight trafficking and others with the opposite propensity.[61]

---

[58] Office of the US Inspector General 2012, 13.

[59] Rosenberg and Cochrane 2015.

[60] Zaloznaya and Hagan 2012, 18.

[61] Transit countries tend to have better tiers. Beth Simmons and I used a statistical model designed to predict the probability of shaming, defined as either Watch List or Tier 3 status in a given year. Kelley and Simmons 2015. States were more likely to be shamed the more US aid they get, the smaller they are, the more NGOs interact with the US on trafficking in the country, and if they have ratified the 2000 Palermo Protocol. On the other hand, countries were also more likely to be shamed the *less* democratic they are, the *more* corrupt they are and the *lower* their rule of law. These are exactly the countries one would expect would be harder for the US to influence and that would be less inclined to address their trafficking problem. Overall, while the ratings are far from unbiased, we found "no systematic evidence that the US merely criticizes countries that would have criminalized anyway." Kelley and Simmons 2015, 64. See Table A3.2 in the Results Appendix.

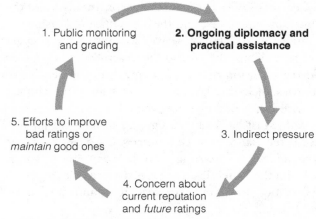

1. Public monitoring and grading

2. Ongoing diplomacy and practical assistance

5. Efforts to improve bad ratings or *maintain* good ones

3. Indirect pressure

4. Concern about current reputation and *future* ratings

FIGURE 3.7. The cycle of scorecard diplomacy.

STEP 2: ONGOING DIPLOMACY AND PRACTICAL ASSISTANCE

Scorecard diplomacy is much more than the report. The TIP Office operates more independently than most in the State Department. Although it consults with embassies and regional bureaus, and superiors can veto the ratings, the office has extraordinary leeway in determining the ratings. The staff has grown from just a few in 2001 to over 50 people in 2015 and is headed by an ambassador-at-large. The office also works with the Department of Justice (DOJ), the Department of Labor (DOL), and the US Agency for International Development (USAID). The DOJ provides legal assistance in drafting of laws. The Criminal Division's Overseas Prosecutorial Development, Assistance, and Training (OPDAT) sends resident legal advisors to countries and also conducts various anti-TIP programs. In 2011 the DOJ undertook 42 such activities.[62] USAID carries out awareness programs, and supports cross-border referral mechanisms. Between 2001 and 2010 USAID spent $163.3 million on counter-TIP activities in 68 countries and Regional Missions. Officials in embassies and regional offices do much of the groundwork. Indeed, some regional bureaus have complained that they spend "as many resources on TIP issues as on all other global issues combined."[63] The TIP Office also

---

[62] The United States Department of Justice 2012. I tried repeatedly to get data for other years, but the DOJ was unresponsive.
[63] Office of the Inspector General 2012, 7.

consults with NGOs and issues a public call for information in connection with each report.[64]

Scorecard diplomacy has enabled the US to capture the issue space of human trafficking. NGOs attest to the intense activity of the US diplomacy. The NGO survey (on which more information can be found in the Methods Appendix) asked respondents to name which embassies were active in anti-TIP work in their countries, and which of those governments were most active. This was a free-response question before the survey broached questions about the US, so there was no priming or prompting. NGOs mentioned the US embassy far more often than any other embassy. NGOs identified 64 different foreign or regional governments as active, but 78 percent of respondents included the US embassy or government in their list (see Figure 3.8) – six-fold higher than the next most common country, the United Kingdom. Furthermore, 71 percent of those respondents named the US as the *most active* embassy, which is 14-fold more often than the European Union, the runner-up. When later asked directly about US activities, only 39 NGOs (7.3 percent) said that the US had *not* been active in any of the countries they work in.

Policy Interaction to Increase Attention and Concern

Government officials are more likely to become concerned about their reputation on a problem they know and care about. Scorecard diplomacy can increase their understanding of the problem or prompt new institutional approaches that bring attention to the problem.

The Power of Information Gathering and Exchange
The information gathering process engages government officials and local law enforcement officials, who are asked to provide certain information every year. The Trafficking Victims Protection Reauthorization Act (TVPRA) of 2003 made data provision a requirement for Tier 1 status. That incentivized local officials to institutionalize data gathering capacity, an activity that in and of itself can be agenda setting because it brings the issue to the forefront. Of course, the US Congress has no authority to mandate foreign governments to share this information, but the repercussion of not doing so is public criticism in the report. Many officials therefore deliver the data by the requested deadlines.[65] This repeated

---

[64] US Department of State 2012–2013.
[65] 09BRUSSELS1605.

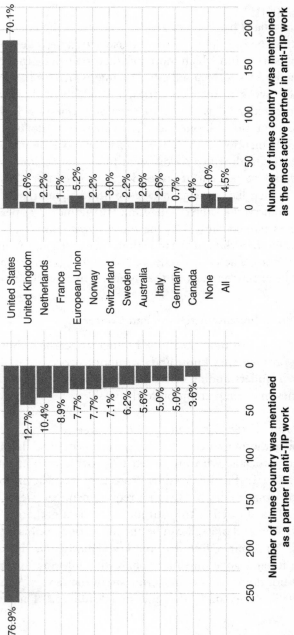

FIGURE 3.8. Embassies or foreign governments that NGOs reported as active partners in the fight against human trafficking. N: 657 responses mentioned 64 unique countries as partners; 325 responses mentioned 40 unique countries as most active partner. Total responses varied because this was an optional write-in question. Source: Author's NGO survey.

information gathering sometimes spurs new institutional structures or practices. For example:[66]

- Singapore now issues its own TIP statistics just a few days before the US embassy deadline for reporting to the Washington TIP Office.
- Concerns about a drop in tier ratings led the acting justice secretary in the Philippines to order "all government prosecutors nationwide to submit immediately the status of cases involving anti-trafficking in persons, including those undecided by the courts."[67]
- The Bahamas appointed an inter-ministerial committee to review the 2011 TIP Report and mandated it to consult with NGOs.[68]
- In Armenia, the US TIP Report was "one of the principal driving forces for the activities of the Government Anti-TIP Commission."[69]
- Israel appointed new administrative structures to discuss the report.

Relatedly, scorecard diplomacy can also facilitate cooperation and information exchange that can translate into new domestic institutions. For example, the US embassy in Chile organized a working group of 20 entities from the government, the UN, NGOs, and foreign embassies to strategize about how to implement Chile's anti-trafficking legislation and raise awareness among journalists and the general public. The group was institutionalized through a seven-organization steering committee to ensure long-term sustainability.[70]

The report's recommendations also place policy solutions before policymakers, which research suggests may make them more likely to adopt those solutions.[71] Sar Kheng, who has been both the Deputy Prime Minister and Minister of Interior in Cambodia, and led its anti-TIP efforts, told the US embassy that Cambodia had gained "experience and ideas" from interacting with the US embassy.[72] Maybe he was just being nice, but given how much information the embassy has shared and that subsequent policy choices reflected this information, he may well have been telling the truth.

---

[66] Cooley 2015.
[67] No to Trafficking 2009.
[68] BBC Monitoring Latin America 2011.
[69] 06YEREVAN214.
[70] US Department of State and the Broadcasting Board of Governors 2012–2013, 27–28.
[71] Weyland 2009.
[72] 08PHNOMPENH463.

Face-to-Face Diplomacy

The report and the ratings provide impetus for engagement. Officials are often keen to discuss the ratings. One might think of these less visible efforts as *backstage diplomacy*. After the report comes out, embassy staff, often the ambassador, usually meets with national officials to discuss the report and recommendations. Throughout the year the local embassy also discusses the issue with domestic officials, NGOs, and other stakeholders. Notably, in many of these meetings the US and local officials discuss the TIP Report and the tier ratings, and US officials repeatedly emphasize actions required to maintain or improve a given tier rating. As the US embassy in Armenia noted: "We pushed hard on the areas in which there has been insufficient progress, using the TIP Tier rankings as both carrot and stick, in hopes of spurring the [government] to action."[73] It is normal for such meetings to go over detailed recommendations, for US embassy officials to push local officials to advocate for certain outcomes, for officials to engage in discussions about the definition of trafficking, or for the US to share model language for proposed legislation. Interactions may also consist of embassy officials sitting in on official meetings related to TIP, visiting with NGOs in the field, or organizing stakeholder meetings.

One good example comes from Kazakhstan, where throughout the process, the US – along with the US-funded IOM and OSCE – attended the inter-agency TIP working group and were involved in the discussion of the language of the draft amendments.[74] Then-Ambassador Larry Napper reported:

We would go up to Astana and meet with the Minister of Justice and meet with his team. First order of business was to get the [TIP] legislation right. ... We went up and discussed it in conceptual terms, walked through the kind of legislation we wanted to see; we went into it in very fine detail. They undertook to take it to the parliament. We monitored it very closely. I'd go and talk with parliamentary deputies about it ... At the time that they were actually doing the legislation I would go up two or three times within the month or so. We worked on it together.[75]

The frequency of diplomatic interactions varies across countries. In Oman, for example, the State Department cables document about six meetings annually where there is some discussion of trafficking issues. This is a low estimate, of course, as it only accounts for those meetings that happen to be revealed in the available cables. The local embassy also

[73] 06YEREVAN1548.
[74] 05ALMATY406.
[75] Napper interview.

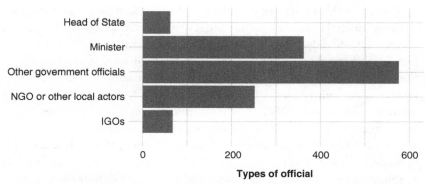

FIGURE 3.9. Distribution of types of officials meeting with US officials, 2001–2009. N = 1,320.
Note that if two ministers meet at the same time, this is coded as one instance. The same is true for multiple NGOs, IGOs or "other government officials."
Source: Author's coding of US embassy diplomatic cables from Wikileaks.

may arrange workshops or training for government officials. The TIP Office also sends emissaries. The ambassador usually makes several trips a year to multiple countries to reiterate the recommendations.

Figure 3.9 shows the observed number and type of individuals meeting with US officials from 2001 to 2009 (the information is based on the embassy cables; see the Methods Appendix). These are meetings where trafficking was discussed, although other issues could also have been covered. The total of 1,320 individuals is an underestimate, because sometimes multiple actors of the same kind might be present.[76] Still, the measure provides some sense of the overall breakdown of the types of officials the US would meet with. Furthermore, it also suggests something about the frequency of interactions, which, given that the cables cover only between 5 and 10 percent, can be estimated to be between 8 and 16 occasions a year per country.[77]

[76] For example, there may be several different NGOs, but the coding of that encounter would just be "NGOs." It's also difficult to infer from this how many meetings this represents as sometimes a US official might meet with a minister and another government official in the same meeting, or a description in the cables of a US official meeting with several government officials might represent several meetings but not be specified.
[77] If 1,320 meetings represent 10 percent only, then the total number is 13,200. This divided by 9 years and roughly 180 countries brings the number to about 8 meetings a year. If instead the meetings represent only 5 percent of the total, then the estimate doubles. Because the available cables likely constitute considerably less than 10 percent of the total (perhaps less than 5 percent), the 1,320 documented meetings is an underestimate of the number of individuals involved or the number of meetings; a conservative estimate of the true total is closer to 23,250, an average of discussions with 8 individuals per year

The figure shows that most of the discussions occur at the level of government officials such as police, judges, parliamentarians, bureaucrats, and agency officials. Usually even these meetings are at a fairly high level. Over a fifth of the individuals are at ministerial level, which could be the minister, or a deputy, an attorney general, or someone of that rank. Finally, 4 percent of the individuals are heads of state, so that about a quarter of the individuals are *either* a minister or a head of state. Based on estimated figures, this could mean that from 2001 to 2009, about 3,500 ministers or heads of state discussed human trafficking with US officials, or nearly 400 per year. That's a lot of high-level discussions that enable embassy staff to engage with officials who often are not experts on the issue and to bring the issue to their attention.

On the US side, the discussions also occur at high levels. Of the 1,055 documented cases of US officials discussing TIP with domestic officials, 406 encounters (38 percent) were with US ambassadors, 38 of which were with the TIP ambassador from Washington. Add to these 46 cases of "other high-level US officials," including the secretary of state in two cases, or sometimes the US attorney general. That means that nearly 43 percent of US personnel involved were senior US officials. Political officers accounted for about a quarter of cases. US visiting politicians or other visits from the US TIP Office contributed about 7 percent. In sum, the issue is commonly handled at high levels.

The meetings are important, not only for the exchange of information, but also because traditional diplomatic interactions build trust and personal connections.[78] For example, former anti-TIP Ambassador John Miller spoke about the importance of "cajoling," and recalled how he would talk about what the US, too, needed to do and what other countries needed to do and that he would try to create a sense of shared identity and responsibility to do better:

We are all in this together, the US has a problem – we are working on it, we are in this together to create a worldwide movement against slavery, we are all against slavery. ... I didn't berate them. I was diplomatic, but I laid out what was wrong and what could be done better. ... That's part of the cajoling. Maybe more than shaming. You can't just shame if you haven't cajoled them.[79]

per country, if we assume the US embassies are active in about 180 countries between 2001 and 2009. If we extrapolate directly from the percentage of cables we believe are missing, then the high end of the estimate could be closer to 16 meetings per year per country. For a discussion of the missing cables, see the Methods Appendix.

[78] Pouliot and Cornut 2015, 307.
[79] Miller interview.

Practical Assistance

US scorecard diplomacy also uses economic tools. First, the US offers practical assistance to IGOs and NGOs, and, although the program is small, it is one of the biggest sources of anti-trafficking funding in the world. Various US entities, including the grants program within the TIP Office and the DOJ OPDAT, deliver assistance, for example in the form of legal advisors or training sessions for police or prosecutors. The greatest influence of such assistance is probably through its delivery of logistical capacity and knowledge than economic incentives, since the funds remain small. The effectiveness of these programs is unknown, but clearly the US engages with the various stakeholders through these programs. This aid could be given even if the TIP Report and ratings did not exist, but they facilitate one another by connecting reputation and practical engagement. For example, the Argentinian embassy facilitated partnerships between NGOs and the Argentine Federation of Trucking Companies to introduce an anti-TIP training component into the mandatory annual training required for teamsters to retain their licenses, a program that reaches 20,000 teamsters a month.[80]

Sometimes the funding is used to establish new institutions within governments. For example, to help Egypt's government build capacity, the US gave a million dollars to start an anti-trafficking unit in the National Council on Childhood and Motherhood, which, among other things, became involved in drafting the anti-TIP law as well as data collection and a national action plan. The head of the unit came directly to the US to ask for help in drafting the plan.[81] In this way, US funding led to a new government unit that in turn connected closely with US embassy staff and was receptive to their advice. Similarly, the US funds training of government officials. For example, in Jordan, a USAID-funded ILO "Better Work Program" trained inspectors on forced labor issues.[82]

Between 2001 and 2014 the US disbursed $532 million for 3,349 anti-TIP projects. The projects span prevention, protection, and prosecution purposes. Figure 3.10 shows that most grants, which also represent the biggest chunk of the money, go toward prevention purposes. Contrary

---

[80] US Department of State and the Broadcasting Board of Governors 2012–2013, 29.
[81] 08CAIRO2525.
[82] 08AMMAN2822.

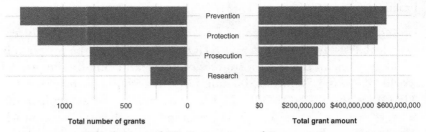

FIGURE 3.10. Distribution of US Department of State grants across purposes, 2001–2014.

Note: A grant can have more than one purpose, so some double counting occurs. Does not include separate funding through other US agencies or some direct funding of IGOs.

Source: US Department of State.

FIGURE 3.11. Distribution of US TIP Department of State funding across countries, 2001–2014.

Note: Does not include separate funding through other US agencies or some direct funding of IGOs.

Source: US Department of State.

to criticism that the US is overly focused on prosecution issues, this area receives the least funding of the "3Ps."

Figure 3.11 shows that funding has gone mostly to countries with large trafficking problems. Some top source countries for trafficking victims into the US are Mexico and the Philippines, both of which have received considerable funding, as have populous countries such as India, Indonesia, and Brazil.

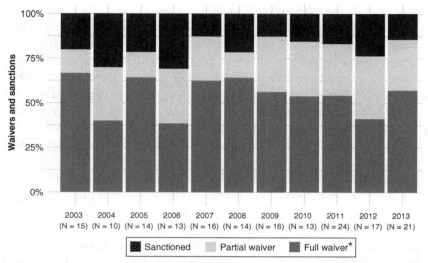

FIGURE 3.12. Distribution of waivers and sanctions across Tier 3 countries, 2003–2013.

Number in parentheses is the total number of Tier 3 countries facing the possibility of sanctions that year.

*Full waivers under sections 110(d)(4) or as recognition of ameliorating actions or promises under 110(d)(3) of the TVPA.

Source: Presidential Determinations With Respect to Foreign Governments' Efforts Regarding Trafficking in Persons, 2001–2013.

Sanctions

One of the ways that scorecard diplomacy generates concern for ratings is fear of material repercussions. Officials might worry that a poor reputation could harm national economies or fear punishments linked to a low rating. In the case of trafficking in persons, the potential certainly exists. As the deputy director of the TIP Office has noted: "We have had a foreign minister ask the TIP Office how [his country] can move up a tier, because it was hurting their credit rating."[83] While the link from TIP to credit ratings is a long causal path, policymakers might fear that a bad reputation can spill over into other issues areas.

Although the TVPA ties sanctions with Tier 3 ratings, the US rarely enacts these.[84] Figure 3.12 shows what happened to sanctions-eligible

[83] Friedman 2013.
[84] Presidential Determination Nos. 2003–35, 2004–46, 2005–37, 2006–25, 2008–4, 2009–5, 2009–29, 2011–15, 2011–18, 2012–16 and Presidential Determinations 2013, 2014, 2015.

countries (those who get rated Tier 3) between 2003, the first time the tiers were tied to sanctions, and 2013. The probability of full sanctions has remained around 10–20 percent, occasionally 30 percent. In reality, however, usually only two to four countries a year are sanctioned, and those were mostly countries *already* under sanctions, like North Korea, Cuba, and Myanmar, and sometimes Syria or a few others. Thus, the probability of *new* sanctions is low. A few countries have experienced partial sanctions, but that means little when aid is fungible. Indeed, statistically tier ratings do not predict subsequent aid; even countries such as Venezuela and Zimbabwe tend to get partial waivers. A 2012 *Washington Times* editorial called out both the Bush and Obama administrations' failure to enforce sanctions, labeling it "appalling," and noting that they have used every loophole to avoid punishing countries.[85]

US efforts to bar funding from international financial institutions are also rare,[86] although Venezuela found itself in trouble under these provisions. Bad rankings can also affect eligibility for the Millennium Challenge Account (MCA) funds, but this too is rare. It did occur in Moldova in 2008 when, as part of an interim review, the Millennium Challenge Corporation (MCC), which administers the MCA, put projects on hold to pressure Moldova.[87] In a few other cases the MCC has worked with countries such as Lesotho and Senegal on TIP issues,[88] but overall, according to interviews, the MCC has rarely been part of the conversation about TIP.

In sum, states might fear various economic repercussions from poor ratings, but the precedent of implemented sanctions is very low. While the mere possibility of sanctions can contribute to the instrumental salience of the gap between ideal points and behaviors, as discussed in Chapter 2, in reality the sanctions threat doesn't appear to loom large.

SUMMARY

The previous chapter discussed the nature of states' reputational concerns and how scorecard diplomacy can elicit such concerns. This chapter has begun to apply these ideas to the area of human trafficking. It has provided the necessary background and described Steps 1 and 2 in the

---

[85] Neubauer 2012.

[86] This point had been contentious between Democrats and Republicans, with the latter pushing for the sanctions option. Bertone 2008, 186.

[87] Millennium Challenge Corporation 2008, Office of Inspector General 2010.

[88] After the 2010 TIP Report, the MCC wrote Senegal's finance minister to emphasize the importance of addressing TIP issues. Office of Inspector General 2011.

cycle of US scorecard diplomacy and documented how the US has combined the public grades in the TIP Report with traditional diplomacy, expanded publicity, and practical assistance.

Importantly, a global prohibition on trafficking has provided a powerful backdrop for eliciting reputational concerns. As trafficking in persons gained increasing attention since the 1990s, the US led in defining the content of a global protocol and anti-trafficking activities. Human trafficking was codified in the Protocol to Prevent, Suppress and Punish Trafficking in Persons, especially Women and Children. This forms a necessary constitutive normative environment for scorecard diplomacy.

Nonetheless, it's hard to motivate countries to combat human trafficking. Laws are difficult to pass and the issue competes with other priorities. Countries have norms and practices that diverge from the Palermo Protocol and many governments shirk their responsibility to address human trafficking or may disagree with US-preferred strategies. In about one-third of countries, government officials are even involved with human trafficking. Corruption and endemic crime make it a tough issue for governments to tackle and some are unwilling or unable to prioritize it.

To elicit reputational concerns about human trafficking, the US adopted a global strategy, spearheaded by an annual report that grades countries on their efforts to fight trafficking. The TIP Report has become widely recognized and used despite its acknowledged flaws. The report was deliberately designed to engage countries' reputations. Interviews and primary documents show that the designers of the policy believed that it was crucial that the report be public and use grades.

Consistent with the argument about scorecard diplomacy, this chapter has illustrated how the recurrent reporting has become the foundation for activities that involve the US embassies around the world and how the US has aimed to empower other actors such as the media, NGOs, and IGOs, sometimes by funding their activities. The reporting process has spurred domestic institutional responses, such as the creation of committees to review the report and gather information for the embassy. Funding sometimes also goes to build new institutions within governments. A breakdown of US TIP funding shows that despite the strong emphasis on prosecution, more grants have gone to prevention and protection.

Importantly for later analysis of what triggers reputational concerns, the data shows that the US has rarely used sanctions. While a poor rating in the report could technically trigger sanctions according to the law, in reality these have rarely been meaningfully implemented. The president has waived most threats, such that only countries under other pre-existing sanctions would be listed as sanctioned. Statistical analysis cannot detect any relationship between tiers and aid flows.

Further important for later analysis, although the report is far from unbiased, there is no statistical evidence that the US has cherry-picked countries to initially include nor graded them in ways that would make the report look more influential. Although the report initially did not cover all countries, inclusion in the report appears to reflect the stated criteria of reliable information about a certain level of trafficking victims. Similarly, although some tier ratings have been biased, nothing suggests that these biases were designed to make the US policy look more effective. If anything, the inconsistencies have harmed rather than helped US influence. Thus, any correlation between US efforts and policy outcomes is unlikely to be because the US gamed the system to appear powerful.

With this in mind, the remaining chapters examine whether US scorecard diplomacy has indeed worked: Has it generated the dynamics that could meaningfully prompt change in states' behaviors? Has the policy been able to build a coalition with third party actors such as NGOs and IGOs? Have countries been concerned about their reputations? Have they interacted extensively with the US on the issue? Have these concerns prompted institutional changes or new policies on human trafficking? How do such behaviors compare with the policy recommendations of the US? And what do the answers to all these questions teach us about influence and state behavior more generally? The next chapter moves on to Step 3 in the scorecard diplomacy cycle by examining how scorecard diplomacy interacts with IGOs, NGOs, and the media to increase the indirect pressure.

4

How Third Parties Boost Reputational Concerns

The American campaign was used by some local activists to grow a movement.

– Cecilia Varela, researcher with the Argentinian National Scientific and Technical Research Council (CONIZET), 2015[1]

The TIP Report is an incredibly useful tool for anyone working in the anti-slavery sector ... As an advocacy tool you don't get much better than that. ... If you have strong evidence then the TIP Report is probably the most effective way of getting governments to actually take notice of what you're presenting. ... Feed in your work, build those relationships with the embassy and you're also opening up channels to the highest levels of policymaking on trafficking in the world.

– Steve Trent, Chief Executive, Environmental Justice Foundation, 2013[2]

This local NGO, which specialized in helping the victims of trafficking, is itself supported by IOM, which is funded in part by the United States.[3]

– Comment by the US embassy about an NGO in Indonesia, 2007

Chapter 2 discussed how scorecard diplomacy stimulates states' reputational concerns, but also stresses that their concern depends on the degree to which their performance is *exposed*. More attention to the issue amplifies the weight of any criticisms, makes shortcomings more salient and increases pressures to ensure a good grade in the future. This means that states are more likely to worry about their reputations when more actors pay attention to the scorecard information and join in stressing the issues.

[1] Varela interview.
[2] Kelly 2013.
[3] 07SURABAYA3489.

Scorecard diplomacy can increase the coalition of actors engaged in pressuring the state in several ways. For example, funded by the US, IGOs may implement projects congruent with its central norms and objectives. This reinforces the norms of the monitoring and grading scheme and augments the social pressure. In particular, IGOs can boost the message of scorecard diplomacy when it might otherwise run up against a wall. Some governments may be more inclined to appear to be cooperating with IGOs, which are perceived as more neutral, than to be seen as weak by responding to pressure from powerful states. Cooperation between IGOs, NGOs, and other actors boosts the importance of the issue by signaling that the views of multiple reputational audiences are aligned.

In addition to bolstering norms, civil society, IGOs, or the media also increase attention to the issue and the government's performance. Internationally backed information can bolster NGOs watchdog capability by providing data that strengthen their claims.[4] This is akin to what scholars have called the boomerang effect[5] and similar to how NGOs can mobilize around international legal commitments to hold officials accountable.[6] This chapter will show that many NGOs use the report for information and to engage in conversations about particular problems and needs. The report and the rating become rhetorical tools for shaping discourse and action.[7] NGOs can also help shape perceptions of reality by for government elites by becoming information sources for reporting. This type of "information politics"[8] increases the influence of NGOs: When governments realize that NGOs have some input into the rating, they are likely to take NGOs more seriously. In addition, some NGOs receive funding from the US to conduct various forms of advocacy or provide services, all of which raises their visibility and that of the issue domestically. Thus funding increases the direct pressure from the scorecard diplomacy.

The media also plays an important role in boosting exposure and therefore reputational concerns. As creators of ratings and rankings know, media coverage can increase attention to the public monitoring and grading. Simple ratings are easy to communicate and dramatize,[9] which makes them appealing for the media. Sometimes news stories may

---

[4] Parks 2014, 229.
[5] Keck and Sikkink 1998.
[6] Simmons 2009, David-Barrett and Okamura 2013.
[7] Schimmelfennig 2001, Krebs and Jackson 2007.
[8] Keck and Sikkink 1998.
[9] Espeland and Stevens 1998, 316, Löwenheim 2008, 257–258.

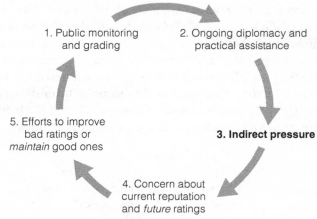

FIGURE 4.1. The cycle of scorecard diplomacy.

simply recount the ratings; other times the media may criticize the government for underperforming. Authoritarian governments worry about such public criticism,[10] but may be unable to control the flow of information from international sources. Reporting can also inform and empower opposition figures or NGOs to pressure the government. Indeed, sometimes even the *anticipation* of negative publicity can make policymakers receptive to pressure because they fear a public backlash.[11]

In sum, other actors can boost attention to the issue, reinforce a shared alignment behind norms, and gain visibility and standing through funding or information sharing. In these and other ways, they become part of the broader social pressure on the government.

This chapter explores the evidence for these mechanisms. If scorecard diplomacy engages these actors and facilitates their work, it should be possible to observe some of this activity. Certainly, NGOs should be aware of US efforts, and interact with them. They should use the ratings and reports themselves to engage with policymakers. IGOs, too, should work with the US on the human trafficking issue, and perhaps note that the ratings affect their work. The media should write not just about the trafficking problem more generally but about the ratings specifically.

The chapter uses several methods to investigate these observable implications. First, it follows the money, that is, it analyses US funding to NGOs and IGOs to explore the strength of these interactions. This is

[10] Hawkins 2002, 30.
[11] Cook et al. 1983, Mutz 1998, Hendrix and Wong 2013.

supplemented with interviews with staff of NGOs and IGOs as well as the survey of NGOs around the world, described in the introduction as well as the Methods Appendix. Throughout, excerpts from the case studies illustrate the presence and interaction of third parties with anti-TIP issues and US efforts. Together, the survey, the interviews, the analysis of document and funding streams, and the examples form the case studies demonstrate how the indirect pressure from NGOs and IGOs fuels reputational concerns and the effectiveness of scorecard diplomacy.

***

HOW THE US FUNDS OTHER ACTORS: "IT WAS *ALL* ABOUT THE US [EFFORTS]"

The US anti-TIP funding program began in 2001, and by 2014 it had disbursed over half a billion dollars to a total of 3,349 anti-TIP projects. Figure 3.10 in the previous chapter showed that the grants varied across prosecution, prevention, and protection purposes, while Figure 3.11 showed the distribution across countries. These grants are substantial in a field where funding is sparse; indeed, the US is probably the biggest source of anti-TIP grants and funds a wide array of organizations. Because many governments do not like to be perceived as merely responding to US pressure sometimes grantees can accomplish goals in ways that are better received by recipient states than if the US implemented the programs itself. Engaging these other actors enables the US to remain a driving force behind the efforts.

Mohamed Mattar, the Executive Director of the Protection Project at Johns Hopkins University, has advised over 45 governments on drafting and implementing anti-trafficking legislation. Most his efforts, as well as those of IGOs or NGOs he has worked with, were driven by US funding, and he stresses that, ultimately, it's really about the US efforts:

I traveled five times to Syria, working with the IOM while providing technical assistance on how you draft the law. ... *The IOM program was financed by the US, so it's all about the US efforts. The US has really great influence*; I witnessed it directly. I went to Mexico, testified before Senate, Russia Duma, and the one who invited me was the US. I did it in Egypt too. *It was all about the US. I was there at the time and I know it. It was because of US pressure.* In Morocco, I worked for the UNODC but it was the UNODC funded by the US [emphasis added].[12]

---

[12] Mattar interview.

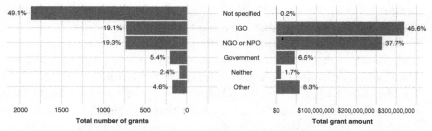

FIGURE 4.2. Distribution of US Department of State TIP funding across sectors, 2001–2014.
Does not include separate funding through other US agencies or some direct funding of IGOs.
Source: US Department of State.

Indeed, the US funding for TIP goes mostly to NGOs and IGOs, not to governments directly. The right side of Figure 4.2 shows that nearly half of all US funding goes to IGOs and that NGOs receive 37 percent.[13] The distribution differs if one considers the number of grants, because many tiny grants go to other types of recipients, but what clearly matters most is the magnitude of the transfers. The next two sections examine the role of IGOs and NGOs.

HOW IGOS HELP INCREASE THE ISSUE SALIENCE AND BUILD CAPACITY

Funding of IGO programs often underscores the urgency and importance of the issue. *It's evident that third parties serve as vital amplifiers of the scorecard diplomacy message, and that this has sometimes been a deliberate strategy.* As one IOM staff interviewee noted, IGOs can extend the work of the US when the US itself cannot be effective.[14] For example, in Zimbabwe, the US embassy has sought to operate in the background by cooperating with and funding the NGOs and IGOs, and helping to organize meetings between stakeholders.[15] The embassy frequently acknowledged that its own relationship with the government was not conducive to exerting much direct influence. Instead, the government partnered with NGOs and the IOM, which had a much better working relationship with

---

[13] IGOs were eligible for the general competition for grants up until 2011, and after that have been funded through a separate mechanism.
[14] Interview #3.
[15] 06HARARE1490.

the government. For example, the US gave the IOM half a million dollars to help Zimbabwe enact domestic anti-trafficking legislation.[16]

Similarly, in Indonesia in 2007, the US hosted a meeting with donors and NGOs to discuss collaboration and how to lobby the government. Over 40 people attended, including staff from the United Nations Children's Fund (UNICEF), the IOM, as well as the US-based NGO Save the Children. The US embassy reported that the collaboration helped "take the [US government] out of the position of being the only strong voice calling for stronger political action," and that the effort was meant as a way to amplify US pressure: "We hope to leverage this new grouping into our effort to further improve Indonesia's Tier Two standing after it was removed from the Watch List earlier this year."[17] The wish to stay in the background while supporting NGOs was evident in later cables as well.[18]

As Figure 4.3 shows, the most frequent IGO grant recipient is the International Organization for Migration (IOM), which received 459 grants accounting for 62 percent of all IGO grants and 36 percent of total value of IGO funding. The International Labour Organization (ILO) received only 72 grants, however those grants accounted for nearly 47 percent of all IGO funding going to the ILO. Other notable recipients include the UN Office on Drugs and Crime and UNICEF, as well as the Organization of American States, the Organization for Security and Cooperation in Europe, and the UN Development Programme.

One ILO staffer highlighted a massive multi-year, multi-million dollar project for the International Programme on the Elimination of Child Labour (IPEC), and noted that this directly enhanced ILO work, which otherwise would be limited to a small international budget. The US has also supported global projects such as IOM's data collection capacities. Similarly, a UN High Commission for Refugees (UNHCR) legal officer noted that "the US is an important donor, so we have regular briefings with the US and highlight issues we have been confronted with." Such a symbiotic relationship exists in many countries.

Funding of projects is the core type of cooperation with IGOs. Importantly, the US does not give lump sum grants to IGOs for general budget support. All TIP grants have designated purposes, which allows the US to shape IGO programs. In some countries, like Afghanistan, the

---

[16] US Department of State Office to Monitor and Combat Trafficking in Persons 2010.
[17] 07JAKARTA3238.
[18] 08JAKARTA269.

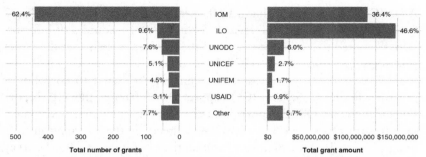

FIGURE 4.3. Distribution of US TIP funding across IGOs and other agencies. Does not include separate funding through other US agencies or some direct funding of IGOs.
Source: US Department of State.

IOM has received extensive support from the US government. One IOM staff person stressed the importance of the US funding:

It would look very different if you took the US out of the picture. The US puts money where their mouth is. ... We have a lot of open J/TIP projects all over the word. People, missions look to J/TIP to decide what to fund. I would say that the US is making a big mark in terms of dictating the agenda or the type of programming that should be in a country.[19]

Funding is not the only important factor for IGOs. The IOM was the most common collaborator mentioned in the US diplomatic cables and by interviewees.[20] Sometimes the embassy even intercedes to facilitate the work of the IGOs. In the United Arab Emirates (UAE), the embassy facilitated an official visit from the head of IOM in Kuwait,[21] pressured the government to allow the IOM to open an office,[22] and urged the government to sign a formal agreement with the IOM to aid in the resettlement of trafficked child camel jockeys.[23] Getting the government to acknowledge these problems is one way to increase the issue salience.

Scorecard diplomacy helps IGOs become more informed and thus more empowered to attract attention to the issues. Staff from several IGOs interviewed said they relied on the US TIP Report as a source of information, with one calling it "the most detailed report available."[24]

[19] Interview #3.
[20] Ordway interview.
[21] 04ABUDHABI814.
[22] 04ABUDHABI2034.
[23] 05ABUDHABI1167.
[24] Haddin interview.

A UNICEF official noted that his office follows the TIP Report, calling it "a big event" that UNICEF regards as one of many sources of information. He noted that in some countries the TIP Report helps set the policy priorities.[25] Similarly, a UNHCR legal officer noted the UNHCR uses the TIP Report "to get an understanding of the issues to corroborate our own findings." Several IGO reports also reference the TIP Report. For example, an OSCE report discusses Serbia's tier rating over time.[26] Finally, sometimes the US involves IGOs directly in the information gathering process. In Armenia, for example, the US funded an IOM survey. US embassies also exchange information with IGO representatives in the field. In Bangladesh, for example, IOM and the embassy would meet to discuss labor trafficking and migrant labor violations.[27] Similarly, in Kuwait, the ILO and the embassy would update each other on the nature of trafficking legislation.[28]

Sometimes the work aligns so well the US TIP Office and the IGOs more or less become partners. This presents a more united front on the issue to the local government, bolstering the appearance of strong international norms. An IOM staffer explained how IOM works with the US TIP Office both in setting priorities and around information gathering issues:

We work really closely with J/TIP. We get most of our [TIP] funding from J/TIP. We do also meet with them on strategy. ... We have really good personal relationships. We collaborate on working out strategies for different countries. I am emailing with someone from J/TIP almost daily. I speak with at least one of them weekly. I join them on monitoring trips when they go to inspect an IOM project that the US funded. Sometimes I serve as interpreter to people in the different offices when "J/TIP speak" doesn't translate with everyone.[29]

IGO staff says that the TIP Report empowers their work and that the TIP rankings sometimes give them more leverage. One official noted, "The IOM does sometimes tell countries that if they do certain things, this might improve their rating in the TIP Report, so that it is a tool."[30] An ILO official stressed that while the ILO has to maintain independence, "sometimes if you are trying to do a program in some countries with a lower TIP ranking, they may be sensitive to what the US says. ...

[25] Neil interview.
[26] OSCE 2008, UNODC 2014, 23.
[27] 07DHAKA275.
[28] 09KUWAIT1134.
[29] Interview #3.
[30] Anonymous interview.

I've had it brought up by countries: 'Would this help our TIP ranking?' "
Similarly, an interviewee from the Organization of American States
(OAS) noted that "we would not have been able to develop or implement certain activities, either related to raising awareness or protection
or prosecution, if country A, B, or C would not have been on the Tier 2
watch-list," suggesting that the IGOs are able to capitalize on the motivation that scorecard diplomacy generates. Finally, a staff member with the
Australia-Asia Program to Combat Trafficking in Persons also noted that
while the report has its problems, "I could not have done what I do in my
work without the report. It would be so much harder. The report really
helps facilitate contact with the policymakers that I deal with. And when
the tier drops, that does make those countries vulnerable, like Thailand,
and then they do listen more to us."[31]

*IGOs boost attention to human trafficking and thus the normative
salience of the issue, which makes it more likely that countries will care about
their reputation on human trafficking.* Examples abound. In Argentina, the
US funded IOM training and program implementation, including handling
of individual cases, training of judges, and regional coordination workshops.[32] In 2007 the IOM Country Representative said this had helped the
IOM put the problem on the public agenda in Argentina and the region.[33]
In Armenia, where many IGOs were involved in fighting TIP, the US funded
the OSCE to organize an exhibition in Yerevan to raise awareness about
TIP,[34] and the IOM to conduct a survey on TIP. In Indonesia, where the
IOM, the ILO, and UNICEF were all active,[35] the US helped the ILO conduct workshops to educate government officials about human trafficking –
a way to make the issue more normatively salient for the government.[36]

*A specific way to increase the normative salience is to engage IGOs
in pushing for legislation.* In Armenia, the US funded the OSCE efforts
to spearhead legislative changes in June 2006.[37] In Mozambique, the US
supported IOM's involvement in the drafting of the anti-TIP legislation,[38]
and funded IOM research and a capacity building program to strengthen
civil society efforts to combat TIP and identify trafficking patterns.[39] Such

[31] Gallagher interview.
[32] 06BUENOSAIRES309.
[33] 07BUENOSAIRES1353.
[34] US State Department 2002.
[35] 08JAKARTA1345, 07JAKARTA1560.
[36] 08JAKARTA191.
[37] 06YEREVAN960.
[38] 04MAPUTO513_a. IOM was funded in 2005.
[39] 05MAPUTO114.

efforts not only bring attention to the issue, but also help prioritize it for the government and provide the tools to move from concern to action.

Finally, the TIP Report influences the interaction within the IGOs themselves. One interviewee noted that:

> [It's] not just the TIP Report itself. It also generates discussion of trafficking and knowledge of trafficking. So a great example is the main ASEAN body that we work with at the policy level is the Senior Officials meeting of transnational crime. ... They have 8 issues they deal with and one of them is trafficking. There are only two permanent committees set up under that, and one of them is trafficking. So this is something people are talking about. And the TIP Report has a lot to do with that. I think without that they wouldn't get a basis for the conversation, but it kind of evens things out, every country has a dog in this fight to a greater degree.[40]

In sum, the US interacts with and funds IGOs in ways that enhance the roles of IGOs and amplify the scorecard diplomacy message. While they draw on varied sources and have many independent contributions, sometimes IGOs rely extensively on US funding, work with countries to achieve goals related to the TIP Report, and in general work closely with the US. IGOs and the US exchange information in connection with the TIP Report and any shared or funded work on the ground. By funding IGOs the US is able to influence IGO engagement in different countries to align with US scorecard diplomacy. IGOs gain leverage from the fact that the TIP Report motivates governments to reform, and the US efforts at times can facilitate cooperation between IGOs and other actors. All this increases the attention to the issue and boosts its normative salience. IGOs thus help reinforce the normative expectations and feed the government's reputational concerns.

HOW CIVIL SOCIETY CAN USE SCORECARD DIPLOMACY TO HOLD THE GOVERNMENT ACCOUNTABLE

The trafficking case also illustrates how NGOs can use scorecard diplomacy as an advocacy tool and how they can play the role of sources and partners. NGOs are aware of the report and many use it as a focal point for engaging with their government. Local media coverage can also increase the salience of the tier ratings and criticism in the report, or NGOs can use the media to voice their report-based criticisms of the

---

[40] Gallagher interview.

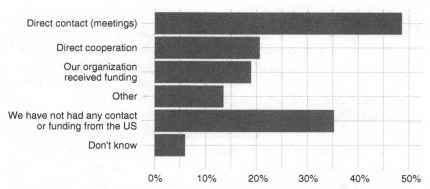

FIGURE 4.4. NGO responses to the question: "Over the last 10–15 years, has your organization worked directly with or had direct contact with the US embassy or government on human trafficking issues?"
N = 533 responses.
Source: Author's NGO survey.

governments. Finally, as with IGOs, funding to NGOs can align their activities with US priorities. Although the US funding is modest, from 2001 to 2014, the US funded 737 NGO projects on TIP in 120 countries.[41] In the survey of NGOs worldwide, 90 organizations reported having received some funding from the US. Funding to NGOs allows them to provide services, foremost, but also to engage with their governments.

The global survey also found that many NGOs interact extensively with the US embassy or government. In the global NGO survey, nearly 40 percent of NGOs knew of workshops or conferences organized by the US. Nearly two-thirds said they had engaged in some way with the US government over the last 10–15 years. Figure 4.4 shows that about half said they had had direct contact with US officials in the country they worked in, and about a fifth reported some form of direct cooperation, similar to the number that received funding. Note that the different categories do not correlate highly, so, for example, while there is some overlap, it is not the same set of NGOs that get funding that also cooperate directly.

Examples from the case studies showcase how NGOs help implement programs inspired and funded by the US, which increases attention to the issue. In Mozambique, funding to NGOs amplified US efforts, both to help victims and to implement the criminalization law. The US also

---

[41] The biggest recipient countries of NGO grants have been Indonesia, Cambodia, the Philippines, Nepal, and India.

funded the start-up of a reception center for women and children. The Mozambican co-director of the project had visited the US in 2004 as an International Visitor Program grantee and toured several "safe houses," which served as inspiration for the new center.[42] The US also funded an NGO, Rede CAME, to help disseminate the new law, train police, border guards, and judicial officials; and build synergy between civil society and the government.[43]

Many NGOs survey respondents credited the US for being especially good at bringing government and civil society together and providing space to "express their opinions [and] share their experiences" with policymakers.[44] Some viewed workshops to link NGO and government policy efforts as especially effective,[45] although others noted that such efforts alone are insufficient.[46]

Several examples illustrate how NGOs amplify US scorecard diplomacy by using the TIP Report as an advocacy tool. In Honduras, the US supports NGO efforts to lobby the government for policy change. The president of the Honduran Commission Against Trafficking in Persons, Nora Suyapa Urbina Pineda, whom the US declared a local TIP Hero, stressed the importance of the funding for NGOs and noted that the Commission holds a public forum on the US TIP Report every year and passes the recommendations on to the authorities.[47] NGOs in Argentina reported that they had a good relationship with the US. One staff member reported that the embassy works with her organization all the time, although they don't receive funds.[48] To the frustration of some politicians, these NGOs used the TIP Reports to persist in making demands.[49] One interviewee recounted that,

NGOs took the [TIP] report as a tool to pressure the government ... you can look in newspapers, each time the TIP Report came the organizations took it to say "see, the government is doing nothing" – it was a very useful tool. ... *The American campaign was used by some local activists to grow a movement* [emphasis added].[50]

[42] The embassy later introduced the NGO Save the Children Norway and the Peace Corps to the project. See 07MAPUTO1475.
[43] 07MAPUTO464, 08MAPUTO651.
[44] Response 1104.
[45] Response 1351.
[46] Responses 1254, 1457, 1227, 1457, 1372, 1378, and 1254.
[47] Pineda interview.
[48] Interviews with Majdalani, Altschul, and Caminos.
[49] Varela 2012, 49.
[50] Varela interview.

Malaysian NGOs also used the report to push for reforms and hold officials accountable. When Malaysia was moved to Tier 3 in 2006, Aegile Fernandez with Tenaganita, a prominent rights group, told the media that the report was a "warning" that she hoped would spur the government to improve conditions, rectify shortcomings, and get out of the "denial syndrome."[51] In Thailand, NGO efforts have long bolstered the scorecard diplomacy. In her dissertation detailing anti-trafficking efforts in Thailand, Bertone notes, "Thai non-state actors have leveraged the hegemonic response of the US government to improve the Thai government response to the issue of trafficking, as well as acquire additional resources for themselves from other donors," and quotes a Thai NGO consultant as saying that "pressure was coming from the US government and the Thai media," and that "the Thai NGOs love that the US government is pressuring the Thai government."[52]

Third parties also boost scorecard diplomacy through conferences and networking that increase attention to the issue and pressure officials directly. In 2006, the US helped to organize the "Vital Voices Conference" in Thailand to promote anti-TIP collaboration among NGOs, government agencies, as well as representatives from the UN Office on Drugs and Crime. The conference provided a regional forum for "NGOs to express their view directly with representatives of their own governments," sometimes for the very first time.[53] In Kazakhstan, the embassy and the IOM conducted a roundtable with NGO representatives and mid-level government officials to analyze the impact of the March 2006 anti-TIP law and recommended practical actions. Two conferences followed to launch future cooperation.[54] Finally, in Mozambique in 2005 the ambassador hosted NGOs along with government officials from key ministries to discuss anti-trafficking legislation.[55] These officials became instrumental in the push for new legislation, which passed in 2008.

The information provided in the TIP Report also helps NGOs mobilize transnational pressure.[56] For example, ECPAT International ran a three-year campaign with the retailer The Body Shop to push for government action against child sex trafficking. Like the US TIP Report itself, ECPAT published its own scorecards on over 40 countries, grading them

---

[51] Kuppusamy 2007.
[52] Bertone 2008, 36 and 222.
[53] 06BANGKOK3955.
[54] 06ASTANA368, 07ASTANA1061, 07ASTANA1147.
[55] 05MAPUTO378.
[56] Kelly 2013.

according to government performance across a range of issues. To do so, they drew both inspiration and information from the TIP Report, thus strongly reinforcing the anti-child sex trafficking message of the TIP Reports. An ECPAT employee recounted that: "For me [the TIP Report] was a useful tool, I reviewed all the countries one by one."[57] Still, not everyone finds the report an asset. One NGO called it unhelpful and superficial;[58] others said that it does not reflect the reality of trafficking issues.[59]

In addition to NGOs using the TIP Report as an advocacy tool, some embassies have involved NGOs in the efforts to promote anti-TIP legislation, thus increasing the normative salience of the issue. Larry Napper, ambassador to Kazakhstan in 2003, said that whenever he traveled he met with NGOs to discuss the legislation.[60] In Indonesia, NGOs provided information for the report and partnered in many efforts.[61] The embassy noted that: "The [comprehensive anti-TIP] bill's passage represents the culmination of over two years worth of intense anti-trafficking collaboration between Post, its NGO partners, and the [government of Indonesia]."[62] Also, in Chad where progress has been slow, the US funded a technical workshop on the TIP legislation in 2015. The workshop, lead by the UNODC, brought together "legal practitioners, academics, sociologists, members of civil society, government departments involved in the topic, as well as representatives from international organizations."[63]

The global NGO survey showed that these examples are normal experiences in many countries. The survey asked NGOs who had said they were aware of the TIP Report whether they had used it to discuss trafficking issues with others. Generally, the NGO respondents reported that they and many different stakeholders in their countries consider the State Department's annual TIP Report a useful tool and common reference point when discussing trafficking issues.

Figure 4.5 shows that in the global survey, over half of NGOs said they'd used the report to discuss TIP with their governments. Sometimes NGOs also use the report to talk with foreign governments, and more

---

[57] Altamura interview.
[58] Response 1157.
[59] Responses 1076 and 1079. See also responses 1254 and 1060. One NGO said that using the TIP Report posed a political risk due to anti-American sentiment in their country. For more discussion of NGO reactions, see Heiss and Kelley 2016.
[60] Napper interview.
[61] 06JAKARTA2849, 09SURABAYA99, 07JAKARTA2167.
[62] 07JAKARTA778. See also Green 2007b.
[63] UNODC 2015.

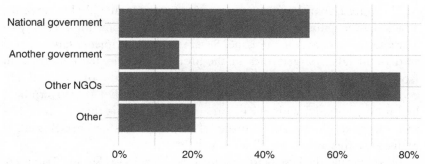

FIGURE 4.5. Stakeholders with whom NGOs report discussing the US Department of State TIP Report.
N = 402 responses.
Source: Author's NGO survey.

than three-quarters of NGOs use it to talk with other NGOs, showing that the report contributes to the general dialogue around the topic and that NGOs are helping to disseminate the report. The survey allowed respondents to write in some comments, and they cited the information in the report, especially the recommendations, as subjects of discussion, noting that they talk with individual members of parliament, courts, national and local police forces, and community leaders.[64]

Embassies also rely on NGOs for information gathering, which may increase the NGOs' position vis-à-vis the government. In Argentina, NGOs say that the embassy regularly asks them for information: "Yes, the embassy of the US has been holding meetings in the last year or so with the NGOs and the [government] office working with TIP, and to share information. And also every year they ask us to inform on the TIP Report."[65] In Armenia, the embassy interacted frequently with the NGO community, which has been aggressive in fighting TIP and skeptical of the government efforts. The US has used NGOs as a source of information on TIP and funded NGOs to do research.[66] Knowing this, the government has sought to sometimes pressure and at other times work with the NGOs, who have had to walk a fine line between exercising influence and yielding to pressure. As the government became more accepting of the TIP problem, the collaboration with NGOs became more constructive.[67]

[64] Survey responses 1077, 1165, 1280, 1296, 1343, 1349, and 1473.
[65] Altschul interview.
[66] 04YEREVAN1344.
[67] 06YEREVAN1161, 07YEREVAN351.

The State Department also bestows several annual TIP Hero awards, which, by recognizing the efforts of individuals, become another way to increase the salience of the issue. Several award recipients have gained status and taken larger roles in the anti-TIP fight in the countries. In Israel, the award helped Rachel Gershuni become the official anti-TIP coordinator.[68] An NGO worker told the embassy that the government had not cooperated with her before and that "This is the first time I've seen [the government] visibly proud of her," and Gershuni herself said, "I plan to use this award for all it's worth."[69]

In Argentina, the US awarded a local NGO activist, Susana Trimarco, as "International Woman of Courage." NGOs recognized this as a key moment that boosted attention to the issue.[70] While Trimarco provided the US with information, the embassy pressured officials to meet with her. For example, in a May 4, 2007 meeting, the ambassador and Trimarco agreed that the latest draft of the anti-TIP bill was flawed, and discussed activism strategies. The ambassador then met with Interior Minister Anibal Fernandez and encouraged him to meet with Trimarco, which he did on May 15, after which Trimarco followed up with the embassy.[71] This was possible because Fernandez cared about the tier rating and knew the embassy cared about Trimarco. Another Argentinian, Marcelo Colombo, Head of the Prosecutor's Office for the Combatting of Trafficking and Exploitation of Persons, also received a TIP Hero award, which he said "made the work of the prosecutor's office in my charge known in other parts of the world."[72]

Unfortunately the limelight of scorecard diplomacy may also have ill effects on NGOs. Repressive governments may crack down on NGOs, as experienced by the Cotton Campaign in Uzbekistan. The US TIP Report has criticized Uzbekistan for its labor exploitation and abuses in the forced cotton harvest that occurs during Uzbekistan's cotton harvest. In response, Uzbekistan has sought to appear to be improving, while simultaneously cracking down on NGOs to silence their alternative narrative.[73] NGOs report similar crackdowns in Belarus, where lots of people are jailed for trafficking as a means of ordinary repression, while the government casts itself as a hero in anti-trafficking efforts.[74] In this way,

[68] 06TELAVIV1391.
[69] Both quotes are from 06TELAVIV1652.
[70] Varela interview.
[71] 07BUENOSAIRES965.
[72] Colombo interview.
[73] Skrivánková interview.
[74] Ferghana Information Agency 2015, Kelly 2015.

authoritarian governments may silence NGOs precisely because they fear that they would otherwise augment the reputational pressure.

THE MEDIA'S ROLE IN ELICITING REPUTATIONAL CONCERNS

Attention to an issue and to any criticisms of the government's performance is essential to elicit reputational concern. The grades and comparisons in the report lend themselves to media coverage, which then attracts more attention to the issue. The TIP Report clearly correlates with more coverage of human trafficking in the news, whether those stories mention the report specifically, or address trafficking more generally. Statistical analysis predicting the volume of news articles about human trafficking shows more coverage for countries in the report than those not in the report. The increase for the first year in the report for a given country is small, but in general it is true that countries in the report get more coverage.[75]

Coverage also often spikes when the TIP Report is released. For example, Figure 4.6 shows coverage by months for Oman in the years when a TIP Report came out. June – when the TIP Report comes out – shows a drastic increase. In sum, the media acts as a megaphone for the report, thus enhancing scorecard diplomacy and augmenting the potential reputational concerns that come with poorer ratings.

As in Thailand where the media magnified the criticisms of the Environmental Justice Foundation's report and also brought attention to the TIP Report itself, the media can magnify the pressure of the report or of NGOs who use the report to criticize their governments. For example:

- In Turkey, in 2009 a researcher name Mine Yokel, who was the "'go-to' person on TIP for NGOs, journalists and the diplomatic community," met with Minister of Interior to discuss the TIP Report, and used the report to raise awareness on a radio talk-show and push for enactment of anti-TIP legislation immediately following a meeting with the embassy.[76]

---

[75] Countries also get more media coverage of human trafficking the larger they are and the more civil liberties exist. See Table A4.1 in the Results Appendix. On average, being in the report is associated with 50 percent more media coverage (or an average increase of about 15 to 23 stories per year in a given country), and this holds when controlling for the initial media coverage when a country is first added to the TIP Report. If one controls for the perceived incidence of human trafficking, the effect decreases to 34 percent but remains significant.

[76] 09Nicosia432.

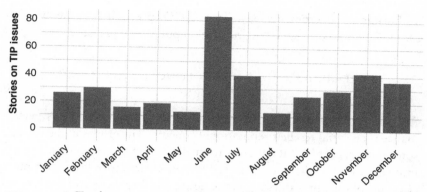

FIGURE 4.6. Total news coverage of human trafficking issues in Oman, by publication month, 2005–2014.
Source: Lexis Nexis.

- In Nepal in 2008, the largest-selling newspaper published the entire Nepal report as an op-ed.[77]
- In Argentina, NGO staff said they would use the media to highlight the report.[78] After the 2006 TIP Report came out, the leading newspaper *Clarin* argued that in view of the Watch List placement, "the Government should promote the enactment of the draft bill against TIP, which is now in Congress ... as well as take the struggle against the TIP seriously."[79] After the 2007 report, the media noted which countries the Watch List was grouping Argentina with, and criticized Congress for delaying the anti-TIP legislation.[80]
- In Israel, the media has covered the report extensively,[81] with the embassy holding digital videoconferences and working to keep the issue in the media.[82]
- In Mozambique, the media, with embassy encouragement, also took a lead role in exposing TIP.[83] For example, during a visit from an Africa Reports Officer from the Washington TIP Office, the embassy arranged a lunch with a dozen local journalists who then filed stories on the

---

[77] 08KATMANDU659.
[78] Varela interview.
[79] 06BUENOSAIRES1340.
[80] 07BUENOSAIRES1162.
[81] 05TELAVIV669, 06TELAVIV2072, 06TELAVIV2157, 06TELAVIV2239, 07TELAVIV1727, 07TELAVIV3314, 08TELAVIV1185, 09TELAVIV1564.
[82] 07TELAVIV930.
[83] 08MAPUTO651.

interview for their newspapers, outlining the problem in Mozambique and emphasizing the US efforts to help fight TIP.[84]

- In Malaysia, few Members of Parliament knew of the downgrade in the 2009 TIP Report until the media covered it extensively.[85] *The Star* even published an entire interview with the US Ambassador on TIP,[86] and in 2014 the international media covered another downgrade widely. Thus both the domestic and international media strengthened US efforts in Malaysia.

SUMMARY

This chapter has examined Step 3 in the cycle of scorecard diplomacy – indirect pressure – and documented how NGOs, IGOs, and the media increase attention to the government performance on the issue and thereby bolster *exposure* and reputational concerns.

Scorecard diplomacy creates indirect pressure in several ways. Funding is a primary mechanism: The US anti-TIP funding program began in 2001 and by 2014 had disbursed over half a billion dollars to 3,349 anti-TIP projects. Nearly half the funding has gone to IGOs and over a third to NGOs. The case studies provide several examples of how the US funds programs that reinforce the message of scorecard diplomacy. Some IGOs exchange information with the US and collaborate with the US TIP Office in developing strategies. The IOM has been a particularly strong partner.

Funding IGOs and NGOs can be particularly helpful when the US itself has less favorable relations with a government. Scorecard diplomacy relies on a strong relationship with the government, but sometimes this works poorly. When this happens, the presence of other actors is crucial. Sometimes the US can fund IGOs or NGOs to do work in countries that would not otherwise accept the US influence.

Embassies also rely on NGOs for information gathering, which can increase NGOs' position vis-à-vis the government. Bestowing the TIP Hero honor similarly empowers actors. Some recipients have gained in status and taken on larger roles in the anti-TIP fight in their countries. These are examples of the types of activities enabled by scorecard diplomacy. As one interviewee said, "[I]t's not just the TIP Report but *the things that go on around* the TIP Report."[87]

---

[84] 05MAPUTO1030, 08MAPUTO651, 06MAPUTO564, 07MAPUTO886.
[85] 09KUALALUMPUR491.
[86] 09KUALALUMPUR632.
[87] Gallagher interview.

Third parties can also amplify the message of the TIP Report by using the it to pressure or criticize the government. In a global survey, over half of NGOs said they use the TIP Report to discuss TIP issues with their national governments. Several case studies illustrate that scorecard diplomacy can facilitate wider cooperation regarding trafficking issues between governments, donors, NGOs, IGOs, and other actors.

The media also amplifies the message of scorecard diplomacy. The TIP Report gets coverage, either because NGOs use the media to point to the report, or because the US embassy works with media to publicize the report. Statistical analysis shows that countries in the report get more coverage of human trafficking.

All told, scorecard diplomacy is not conducted in isolation; third party actors – IGOs, NGOs, and the media – interact with scorecard diplomacy in important ways. This underscores that the US is by no means a lone champion on human trafficking and that much of the credit for any accomplishments are shared among actors. However, the chapter has illustrated how scorecard diplomacy fosters and harnesses these collaborative activities and uses them to bolster the effectiveness of the ratings, because they augment the global normative environment that scorecard diplomacy invokes. The other actors help magnify the message and also facilitate action through practical assistance.

Documenting these mechanisms demonstrates how scorecard diplomacy has the potential to influence government behavior. This makes it less likely that any observed relationship is merely incidental. Still, these mechanisms might be present, but governments might not care or respond. Therefore this book now moves on to examine the next steps in the cycle of scorecard diplomacy, namely whether governments care about the monitoring and grading and therefore change their behavior.

PART II

EFFECTS

5

Micro-Level Evidence of Reputational Concerns

[His] face went pale when told.
– *US embassy description of the reaction of Albania's foreign minister
to the news that Albania would drop to the Watch List, 2008*[1]

If scorecard diplomacy works, it does so because the recurrent public ratings increase officials' concern with reputation. This generates a desire to improve a rating in the following year or to maintain a good rating once achieved – what I term "status maintenance" – as well as an increased receptivity to policy suggestions by those who created the ratings. For example, Australia has never fallen below Tier 1 in the TIP Report, but an Australian legal expert assesses that the report has nevertheless spurred it to follow several US recommendations such as increasing the focus on labor issues and improving its treatment of victims.[2] This concern about public exposure is an essential link in the argument about how scorecard diplomacy elicits reputational concerns – without concern there would be no action, and no cycle.

But why might a rating engender reputational concern? Chapter 2 offered some explanations: First, in line with the argument that states care about their reputation because of its *instrumental salience*, states and their elites may be concerned that a poor tier rating may have immediate practical or material consequences. Officials may react because they fear that if they are held accountable for their country's poor performance they might lose their influence or position in the government

---

[1] 08TIRANA469_a.
[2] Anne Gallagher, a legal expert on human trafficking and an Australian, makes this assessment in Gallagher 2011.

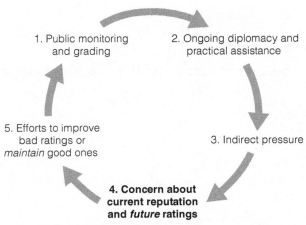

FIGURE 5.1. The cycle of scorecard diplomacy.

hierarchy or their professional status. At the same time, governments might worry that poor ratings could damage the economy by leading to sanctions, impacting trade or decreasing foreign investment, or that poor ratings might damage other practical aspects of their cooperation with other states.

Second, governments may focus on the *normative salience* of the issue. This concern may derive from a basis of principles. Officials who are directly accountable for a policy area targeted by scorecard diplomacy may fear the social opprobrium that can come when international actors single out their policies for criticism. If officials believe the criticism is warranted because they subscribe to the same set of internationally shared values, they may want to reduce the cognitive dissonance between their actions and beliefs. That is, they, and government officials more generally, may feel compelled to do something because they believe it's right. Such logic is not necessary, however, for governments to become concerned about their reputations. Even if the government does not agree with the criticisms, they might worry that a poor tier rating may harm the national image because it shows the country is performing poorly with respect to international norms. As Chapter 2 argued, states value their image and reputation so a state might especially dislike having its national image tarnished if it is seeking to improve the country's standing or legitimacy in the broader international community, just as it would if domestic audiences become critical. This is a concern about reputation-as-image about how a country is perceived to perform across a number of issue areas.

But in reality, in the deluge of information, do policymakers care at all about a mere report? How would we know? And what can we learn about why they might care? This chapter explores the presence and nature of reputational concern by examining the trafficking case further. The chapter has two goals: First, to study whether and how often officials express concern about the ratings. Documented concerns make it more plausible that behavior that correlates with the goals of scorecard diplomacy is actually motivated by it. Second, to understand what policymakers say drives the concerns: What types of reactions are more common and do the patterns and the content suggest that policymakers mostly worry about hard economic fallout, about their image, or something else?

The chapter explores these questions in several ways. It begins with an illustration from when Thailand was dropped to Tier 3, which is an interesting case because the drop was highly anticipated and only imposed by the US DOS reluctantly. Thus the reaction is purely in response to the drop, and not other underlying conditions, making it a good case for understanding the vital role of the assignment of grades.

Next, it analyzes reactions across countries systematically. Normally we lack access to such information, so scholars usually have to infer what policymakers think based on how they behave. This is difficult, because many factors might explain their behavior. In this case, however, the US State Department cables allows us to peek behind the scenes at how officials react in private conversations with the US embassy officials, who are first in line to hear any reactions when they deliver the news of the tier rankings.

Before analyzing these documents, the chapter discusses the source documents and methods for classifying them for the analysis. The chapter then overviews the types of reactions government officials might have and provides examples. This categorization makes it possible to analyze the overall and relative prevalence of the different types of reactions to see which are most common.

To understand the nature of the reactions, the chapter explores statistical patterns that cast light on why officials react. For example, if they are concerned about their country's image, they should worry about harsher tiers, and they should be more likely to react if they've committed to relevant international standards. On the other hand, if they react because they worry about losing aid, then countries receiving greater aid should be more likely to react. The chapter also explores evidence from the case studies to supplement this analysis.

Finally, the chapter uses two other techniques to probe the nature of state reactions. To isolate the role of grades, the chapter compares reactions to the graded TIP Report with reactions to another *un-graded*, but otherwise similar US government report, namely the State Department's annual human rights report, which contains a section on human trafficking. This comparison helps identify whether officials merely react to the substantive criticism of trafficking in their countries, or to the use of public grades, which I've argued is more likely to stimulate reputational concerns.

Similarly, to understand the extent to which officials are particularly concerned with maintaining domestic legitimacy, the chapter compares reactions expressed by government officials in private to those they express in the media to see if they differ, and whether officials are more likely to object to the report in public or otherwise attempt to save face.

***

THE TALE OF THAILAND'S 2014 DROP TO TIER 3

Reactions to ratings in the TIP Report are particularly stark when countries are dropped to Tier 3. Thailand is a great example when, forced by the 2008 legislation forbidding that a country remain on the Watch List for more than two years, in the summer of 2014, the US TIP Office finally dropped Thailand to Tier 3. This drop was not the result of domestic Thai politics or an opportunistic strategy by the TIP Office, nor of changes to the underlying trafficking conditions. It happened merely because the law said it had to.

Because of the law, the possible drop was anticipated. An upgrade to Tier 2, the only other option for the TIP Office, was indefensible with media attention to the horrific and ongoing abuses in the fishing industry.[3] In a demonstration of how much the downgrade meant to Thailand, the government spent US$400,000 to hire a US lobbying firm as the report was being drafted.[4] Attention to the concern about a drop was so strong that Thailand's *The Nation* even entitled a story "Anxious wait for TIP Report,"[5] including a graphic with bold red headings that depicted people with "price tags" as well as the TIP tier scale, using a red arrow to indicate Thailand's possible downgrade. It also showed as a "price tag" a list of countries currently on Tier 3 whose company Thailand would join, as

[3] Lagon 2014.
[4] Lawrence and Hodal 2014, McCauley 2014.
[5] Tumnukasetchai and Pratruangkrai 2014.

well as a bullet list of "impacts of being on Tier 3," which included export barriers and a note that "the image of Thai products will be tarnished." This last point was very salient because Thailand feared that the EU, its third largest trading partner, would impose sanctions over the human trafficking issue. The message to the reader was clear: this is bad – even alarming – news for Thailand's image and economy. A week before the report was due out the government tried to counter the blow of the anticipated downgrade by issuing a press release entitled "Thailand's anti-trafficking progress exceeds US State Department criteria for upgrade."[6] The press release showcased increased trafficking arrests, prosecutions, and convictions and, in a notably comparative spirit, stressed that "Thailand's progress" is "greater than progress made by other countries previously upgraded in the US TIP Report." The government knew that the report had been finalized, so the press release was a purely pre-emptive face-saving effort; its primary goal was to counter any reputational damage.

Once the US dropped Thailand to Tier 3, the news spread immediately and even made a headline in *The Economist*.[7] The negative publicity spurred the new military government to action. At first there was clearly concern about sanctions, but even after President Obama waived the sanctions as expected, concerns about the ratings continued, especially from the fishing industry. Thailand took several steps to mitigate the effects of the rating: A formal delegation visited Washington to meet with the TIP Office and the business community.[8] Thailand's ambassador published a letter to the editor in the *New York Times*.[9] In addition, Thailand sought to impress the US by increasing arrests, opening a call center, and by making some high-level appointments to spearhead policy changes. General Prayut Chan-o-cha, the leader of the coup and the new post-coup prime minister, charged a committee explicitly "to work towards upgrading Thailand's status from a 'Tier 3' country in the United States' report on human trafficking by next year."[10] In March 2015, just in time for the reporting deadline for the TIP Report, the parliament followed the General's orders and overwhelmingly voted to amend the trafficking law to increase punishments for human traffickers, including life imprisonment and the death penalty if victims had died.[11]

[6] Ministry of Foreign Affairs of the Kingdom of Thailand 2014.
[7] *The Economist* 2014.
[8] Gallagher interview.
[9] Isarabhakdi 2014.
[10] Fernquest 2014, Jikkham 2014.
[11] Reuters 2015.

The reason for these moves is clear. One news headline read "The true motivation: Seeking to impress Washington."[12] The labor ministry even announced the report "on Thailand's efforts to improve its Trafficking in Persons (TIP) ranking" would be translated into English.[13] The General also spoke to the Government House promising to get tough on TIP and laid out several measures – this, likewise, just as the US embassy was filing its 2015 report with the DOS.[14] Furthermore, the government sent a 159-page report detailing actions taken in response to each TIP Report recommendation to the US embassy by the filing deadline.[15]

It's clear that efforts to solve the problem were secondary to efforts to fix the reputation. As the general-turned-prime minister exhorted: "[R]eporters should not elaborate on this problem. You need to consider the damage it does to the nation."[16] While it is sad that a passion to address the problem itself was not more in the forefront – an issue this chapter returns to at the end – the fact that it *wasn't* highlights the strong power of reputation tied to the tier rating itself. Indeed, when the 2015 TIP Report kept Thailand on Tier 3, *The Nation* again reported the news as one of relative standing, noting Thailand was "on the bottom," and that "none of other Asean nations is in the bottom list [*sic*]."[17]

HOW TO STUDY REPUTATIONAL CONCERN?

The Thai narrative is based entirely on behaviors that were observable due to the high profile of the case. In most cases, however, it is difficult to study whether countries really care about their reputations or what the source of their concern is. This is a problem for most research about shaming, for example, which assumes that someone feels ashamed, but cannot document this aside from showing that behavior change follows

---

[12] Charoensuthipan 2014b.

[13] Charoensuthipan 2014a.

[14] Jikkham 2015a, Jitcharoenkul et al. 2015, Thai Anti-Human Trafficking Action n.d.

[15] Thai Anti-Human Trafficking Action 2014.

[16] Jikkham 2015b.

[17] *The Nation* 2015. Thailand's responsiveness to the 2015 TIP Report is consistent with the findings of other research of Thailand's past responsiveness to the US. In Thailand many NGOs have been active in fighting trafficking and in pushing for the creation of the Palermo Protocol. Throughout the years, the pronouncement of the TIP Report has therefore weighed heavily on Thailand. One scholar who devoted an entire dissertation to Thailand's anti-trafficking fight and interviewed nearly 60 individuals concluded, "[A]lthough Thai NGOs and the community of various international organizations were also pressuring the Thai government to improve its policies ... the weight of US government pressure was heavier than the other two." Bertone 2008, 221.

the act of shaming.[18] Furthermore, public behavior often has multiple audiences and meanings.[19] Who is an official addressing when he or she makes a statement? Is it an effort to impress the public? Is it a criticism of a fellow policymaker? Is it a signal to international actors? Is it a strategic lie?

One way to minimize this ambiguity is to examine how officials react *privately* when the target audience is known and the array of motives can be narrowed. What actors say is as revealing as what they do. Two states may respond differently to scorecard diplomacy, but their words might reveal that they are both concerned about their reputations. As scholars have noted about international law, "communicative dynamics may tell us far more about how robust a regime is than overt behavior alone."[20]

Most of the time scholars lack access to private statements, but this is where the case of human trafficking shines. In connection with the report's release, US embassy staff usually notify government officials in person. The meetings are often high level. In addition, throughout the year, national and embassy officials may discuss the country's tier ranking. These discussions, which are sometimes recounted in diplomatic cables to Washington, make it possible to study how public policymakers in different countries react to the TIP Report and to US efforts on trafficking in persons. If officials do not react much at all, this suggests they are not worried about any reputational fallout. If they do react, however, we can learn about the intensity and nature of their concern.

A Note on the Data

Normally it's not possible to access State Department cables, but this study uses a rare database of a quarter-million cables leaked in September 2011. As discussed in the Methods Appendix, the availability varies, ranging from under 1 percent in 2001, the first year of the report, to over 20 percent in 2009. This produces gaps in how well any country is covered at any given time. That said, of the nearly 9,000 cables about TIP, almost 500 documents recounted explicit reactions by government officials to the annual Trafficking in Persons reports. After accounting for repetitious responses, it was possible to identify 481 types of reactions to 217 reports on 99 different countries. During this period, the US issued 1,142 tier rankings, so that means that overall a documented reaction

[18] Friman 2015, 210.
[19] Hurd 1999, 390–391.
[20] Kratochwil and Ruggie 1986, 768.

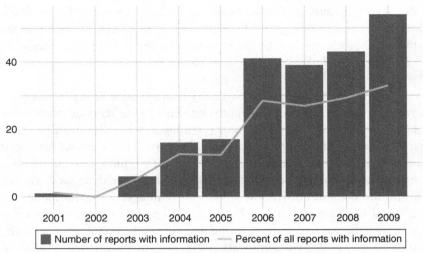

FIGURE 5.2. Percentage of US Department of State TIP Reports with a documented reaction by the rated state.
Source: US Department of State diplomatic cables, Wikileaks.

exists for 19 percent of the reports. Figure 5.2 shows the variation over years, indicating that in some years we have a documented reaction in over 30 percent of cases. This is plotted against the percent of all reports with some information on TIP, which in 2009 surpasses 50 percent.

Statistical Analysis of the Pattern of Cable Availability

The "missing" reactions represent a mix of cases: (a) for which there truly was no reaction to the TIP Report; that is, no country official reacted, (b) for which there was a reaction, but the embassy never recorded it, and (c) for which a reaction was recorded but we lack the record. Importantly, with regards to (c), as the Methods Appendix shows, the documents appear to track the overall availability of cables. Statistical analysis of the cable availability also suggests that while it was not random, it was not correlated with factors related to TIP. This analysis was done by first using the numbering system of the cables to calculate the total number of cables likely issued for each embassy or consulate for each year.[21] For each year the actual number of available cables was then tallied for each

---

[21] Diplomats verified the validity of using the numbering system in this way. For each country-year, the last available cable ID number was used to calculate the rate of cables in that year to that date and then extrapolate the total for the year.

country.[22] This was then used to derive the percentage of cables available for a given year for each country. Several factors were then used to try to predict this percentage with a standard regression model.

The results show that, although the cable availability is not random, the pattern is not statistically correlated with TIP factors. While the cable availability is predicted by per capita Gross Domestic Product (GDP), overseas aid, and level of democracy, neither the tier level, nor whether a country has ratified the international Palermo Protocol, nor whether it has criminalized human trafficking predicts the availability of the cables. Neither do the basic, albeit crude, measures of the level and type of human trafficking problem in a country. (The analysis can be found in the Methods Appendix, Table A1.1). This suggests that TIP related documents are missing as if at random, which means that although the absence of a particular reaction cannot be interpreted as the absence of a response, analyzing the available reactions *is essentially like analyzing a random sample* of cables. This makes it possible to draw inferences about the overall pattern or likelihood of reactions.

Given so few available cables, documented reactions to nearly one-fifth of all reports seems high and suggests that for some embassies multiple cables likely discussed the TIP Report, which increased the likelihood that the sample contained at least one reaction for any given report. Accordingly, whether a country has a documented reaction may well be an approximate measure of the *intensity* of the reaction in that country. Indeed, discussions with staff in the DOS TIP Office suggests that most countries react in some form nearly every year.[23] In this case, whether the archives contain a recorded reaction therefore captures the intensity of reported reactions, given that the more cables that discuss reactions, the more likely it is that a random release of cables would contain a cable documenting a reaction for a given year. Furthermore, it is probably also the case that embassies are more likely to report reactions in cables when these reactions are noteworthy.

HOW DO OFFICIALS REACT?

Each documented reaction was sorted into categories and sub-categories shown in Figure 5.3. The main categories represent the inferences it is possible to make from them. The category "material concern" is reserved

---

[22] We counted the total number of cables available by country in Wikileaks, after collapsing embassies and consulates by country.

[23] Miller interview.

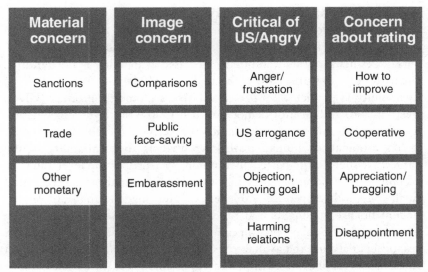

FIGURE 5.3. Reaction coding categories.
For more details, please see the Methods Appendix.

for reactions that entail discussions of practical consequences of the rating. "Image concerns" are those where the reaction can be interpreted as expressing concern with image or reputation. The other two types of reactions, "Critical of the US" and "Positive" are reactions for which the motive is less apparent. Officials might ask how they can improve their ranking, but while that shows that they are concerned about the ranking, it does not tell us why. Similarly, they might be angry about the US practice, but such anger could have many sources. The Methods Appendix describes the coding methodology and the content of each of the subcategories. The categories are not mutually exclusive. A country may have multiple types of reactions in one year – indeed many do. The section below illustrates each type of reaction.

Reactions Concerned With Material Factors

Officials sometimes express concerns about sanctions, trade, or other types of material concerns. In 2004, for example, the first year of possible sanctions, a Venezuelan official "asked exactly what programs would be affected by the sanctions, and for clarification on whether the United

States government] would oppose international loans."[24] Sometimes the embassy brings up the issue, at other times government officials inquire about the possible sanctions, so the incidence of such concern might be overstated since the fact that the US brings it up does not necessarily mean it was on the minds of the national officials.

Smaller countries sometimes fear the loss of US aid, suggesting that they might be more vulnerable to scorecard diplomacy. In 2005, Jamaican officials asked what they needed to do to avoid the sanctions and the National Security Minister "also expressed concern that a downgrade of Jamaica to Tier 3 could endanger [US government] security assistance badly needed by the Jamaica Defense Force and the Jamaica Constabulary Force." Senior officials, all the way up to the prime minister, vowed to take actions to avoid sanctions. Similarly, in 2006, Belize officials were concerned about freezing International Military Education and Training and Foreign Military Financing even though those were not the funds potentially affected by TIP. In 2008, a Moldovan official expressed concern that the TIP ranking might derail Millennium Challenge Account (MCA) programs, and that clearly motivated the government. However, this might be more the exception that proves the rule, since cases of such MCA concern were rare.

Do concerns about repercussions spill over into trade? In a few cases officials worry that bad ratings might affect trade. In 2008, the United Arab Emirates labor minister, who was involved with negotiations on a Free Trade Agreement, noted that "a fall to Tier 3 would mean [the UAE] could 'kiss [a free trade agreement] goodbye.' " In another example, in 2008 the embassy recounted concern by Omani officials that the "latest Trafficking in Persons (TIP) report would adversely impact the country's ability to promote trade and investment." On the other hand, some countries show contempt for the sanctions. Thus, in 2009 Burma was already under various US sanctions and it blamed these for making workers lose their jobs and becoming more vulnerable to trafficking. In 2007, Malay officials commented that they simply did not care about US non-humanitarian, non-trade related aid, or about military training assistance and scholarships and the like. Similarly, the Algerian justice minister reacted to the US Ambassador's references to the financial implications

---

[24] This chapter provides examples of how officials react to the TIP Report. All quotes in this section are from embassy cables and can be found in the author's coding document entitled "Reactions" posted on the book's resources site (www.cambridge.org/ScorecardDiplomacy).

of Tier 3 status by saying that US–Algeria relations were not constrained by money.

Reactions Concerned With Image and Standing

Comparisons and Relative Standing

It's remarkable how candidly officials think in comparative terms, which underscores a strong focus on reputation. Officials often reference countries with better ratings and argue that their country should be rated likewise. This might be thought of as a general objection, but because it is based on comparison with peers it suggests a concern with relative standing and image. Argentina has done this repeatedly. In 2007 the foreign minister asked the US ambassador, "[H]ow can anyone think that the TIP problem is worse in Argentina than in surrounding countries?" The next year he again protested to the US ambassador that Argentina surely was not performing any worse than countries not on the Watch List such as Mexico or the Dominican Republic. In 2009 he complained that the better placement of Bolivia, Paraguay, Brazil, and other Central American countries was "unbelievable" and "objectively false." Similarly, in 2003 a Turkish Ministry of Foreign Affairs official told the embassy that she had researched all the countries with better rankings, and that none had done as much to fight TIP as Turkey. Sometimes officials make comparisons to figure out how to improve. For example, in 2007 when preparing a new action plan in response to the TIP Report, Armenia's Americas Director described how he and his staff had analyzed the reports for reports Azerbaijan, Turkey, and Georgia, to understand why they were getting better grades.[25]

Illustrating that countries do not simply make comparisons to argue for a better rating, officials are often concerned with their standing *within peer* groups like immediate neighbors. In 2009 a Bahraini official told the embassy that he was concerned about how "Bahrain stacked up against its GCC [Gulf Cooperation Council] neighbors." A Belarusian official from the Ministry of Foreign Affairs also complained in 2007 asking, "What other eastern European country has done as much as Belarus in this field?" Or on the flipside, countries might balk if a rating puts them in what they consider a decidedly *non-peer* group.

Not only countries with bad ratings worry about their ratings. *Even Tier 1 countries think about the ratings in comparative terms.* The

[25] 07YEREVAN888.

TABLE 5.1. *Countries that given countries compare themselves with in discussions with US embassies, as documented in the Department of State Cables, 2001–2010*

Country referencing	Countries referenced
Algeria	Morocco and Tunisia, Saudi Arabia
Argentina	Suriname, and Venezuela, Dominican Republic, Mexico, Western Hemisphere (WHA), Bolivia, Paraguay, Brazil, and Central American countries, Italy
Armenia	Azerbaijan, Turkey, and Georgia
Bahrain	Gulf Cooperation Council members
Belarus	Eastern European countries
Belize	Venezuela and Cuba
Croatia	Bosnia and Serbia and Montenegro
Egypt	Thailand
France	United Kingdom, Germany, the Netherlands, Nigeria
Israel	Holland and Germany
Japan	Other Tier 1 countries, other G8 countries
Kuwait	Qatar, United Arab Emirates, neighboring countries, the rest of the Gulf, Gulf Cooperation Council members
Lesotho	Other African states
Malawi	Botswana
Malaysia	ASEAN member-states, neighboring countries
Oman	United Arab Emirates
Turkey	"Neighboring countries"
Uzbekistan	Commonwealth of Independent States, Georgia
Venezuela	Colombia, Mexico and Guatemala, Cuba

director of France's anti-TIP Office responded to criticisms in the report by arguing that France was much more proactive than Germany or the United Kingdom. Sometimes countries make generic references to "other countries," but Table 5.1 shows the references and reveals a clear geographical pattern.

Not everyone references geographic neighbors; some reference other peer groups, or they *contrast* themselves with countries that are decidedly *not* part of their envisioned peer group, as an Egyptian official noting, "After all, Egypt is not Thailand."[26] Israeli officials compare Israel

[26] 07CAIRO1776.

with European countries, and similarly, when Japanese officials protested Japan's Tier 2 ranking in 2007 they compared Japan to "other G8" countries. In some cases officials worry that a low grade can stigmatize their country by grouping it with other low-performing countries. Thus, in 2007 Venezuelan officials expressed anger about being in the same category as Cuba, with one Ministry of Foreign Affairs official saying, "[W]e are not as bad as Cuba on this issue." Similarly, in 2010 an Algerian official exclaimed, "You can't put us in with countries like Saudi Arabia." In 2005, after Kuwait was ranked Tier 3, the Prime Minister's Economic Advisor "objected to Kuwait being 'lumped in with other states' and ... asserted that Kuwait was 'not like the rest of the Gulf.'" The Foreign Minister similarly argued that "Kuwait was very different from its neighboring countries," indeed, "superior" to its neighbors. Even France was concerned about with whom it might be grouped. One cable noted an "incredulous" official asking: "You're telling me that France could easily be in Tier Two, with Nigeria?" That officials compare their countries with other countries shows the emphasis on image, and also reveals whom they consider their peers. It is also interesting to see how states compare themselves with the countries in a group that place them in a more favorable light. For example, when the TIP Report elevated Sri Lanka to Tier 2, the government issued a news release that noted that Sri Lanka was now in the company of Iceland, Japan, and Switzerland, arguably the three most democratic and well-functioning states in that category.[27]

This evidence of reference to peer groups is empirically groundbreaking. I know of no other systematic analysis of this, a deficit to which scholars have pointed given the many claims that states care about their relative status.[28]

Public Face-Saving

Another indication that reactions are foremost about image is that governments frequently try to save face publicly. The cables sometimes describe such reactions. Most extreme, in 2008 Sudan simply censored the report by removing it from an English-language publication before it went to print. More common was the behavior of Belize's prime minister in 2006 when he went on the evening news to defend his governments' record on trafficking after the TIP Report ranked Belize a Tier 3.

---

[27] Sri Lanka Ministry of Defence 2011.
[28] See for example Renshon 2016, 529.

Public objections could reflect a government's true position rather than attempts at face-saving. However, it seems like face-saving when governments cooperate with the US in private, but criticize the report in public. The cables sometimes reveal this. As discussed more in Chapter 8, the Armenian embassy noted in 2006 that "[t]he deputy minister's lack of complaint behind closed doors illustrates a larger phenomenon whereby the government has criticized the TIP Report's methodology in public, but indicated in private that it takes the rating seriously."[29] Jamaica's reaction in 2005 was similarly two-faced. The embassy noted that "senior [government] officials publicly defended Jamaica's record and demanded 'tangible evidence' of a trafficking problem in Jamaica, while the [government] simultaneously professed concern for trafficking victims and cited actions that have and will be taken to combat the problem locally." In 2008 the Oman government went to extreme lengths to criticize the report and defend government practices in the press. The embassy notes that top officials were even "feigning surprise," and commented that:

This is astonishing to Post given the dialogue, sometimes intense, that Post has had with the [Ministry of Foreign Affairs] and other ministries on the trafficking issue. The journalists who interviewed the Ambassador were surprised to hear that US and Omani officials have been discussing TIP, including the need for Oman to move on multiple fronts, for the past two years.

The embassy noted that this face-saving effort occurred in the midst of Oman's government taking serious steps to address the criticism in the report.

Embarrassment

The diplomatic exchanges sometimes convey scenes of embarrassment or recount officials' direct references to national image or reputation. In 2003, for example, the UAE deputy prime minister and minister of foreign affairs said to the US ambassador that trafficking in women was "detrimental to our society and reputation."[30] In 2005 a Jamaican official commented that the report "reflected badly on Jamaica," and expressed "concern over damage to Jamaica's public image caused by the Tier 3 designation."[31] In 2008, Algeria was concerned that the TIP Report was so "public," and Albanian officials told the embassy that they wanted to avoid the "black mark" of being on the Watch List.[32]

[29] 06YEREVAN836_a.
[30] 04ABUDHABI496.
[31] 05KINGSTON1784_a.
[32] 08TIRANA469_a.

The same year the embassy in Kuwait reported that "Kuwaitis across the board express shame at seeing their country in the spotlight over labor exploitation and related TIP issues"[33] and Malaysia's foreign minister told the US ambassador in 2007 that the report "affects our country's reputation and dignity."[34] Oman reacted particularly strongly to criticism in 2008, with officials arguing in a private meeting with the embassy that the "Sultan has been dishonored and its national honor has been impugned." A UAE Sheikh said that the camel jockey issue had become "frankly embarrassing for the country."[35] An official told the embassy that, "although the Sultan was very upset about the report, Qaboos was more concerned about the international image of his country."[36] The CEO of the Oman Petroleum Services Association (OPAL), who also advised the Minister of Manpower on labor affairs, told the embassy "that it was unfortunate that the [US government] published its report while the Sultan is outside of Oman on his European trip and therefore more exposed to international scrutiny and criticism. 'You likely caught him by surprise,' Balushi surmised, forcing the Sultan to defend his country before Western leaders and explain why Oman is not like the other countries on Tier 3."[37]

Officials sometimes stress the recognition of the international community as important, suggesting a concern with international standing. For example, when Jamaica was upgraded to Tier 2 in 2007, it issued a long press statement noting, "The Government of Jamaica considers the improved Tier 2 status to be a welcome recognition by the international community in general and the United States Government in particular."[38] Or on the flipside, Venezuelan legislators made connections to international reputation when they accused the US in 2007 "of trying to smear the [country's] international image"[39] with the Tier 3 rating. In Algeria in 2007, the embassy noted that the government was interested in the negative perception associated with Tier 3 status and assessed that "the

[33] 08KUWAIT913.
[34] 07KUALALUMPUR1375_a.
[35] 05ABUDHABI1274.
[36] 08MUSCAT634.
[37] 08MUSCAT464.
[38] Jamaican Information Service 2007. Interestingly, five years later the Jamaican TIP office found it compelling to stress publicly in a press release that "We have been doing a lot because we recognize the negative impact of human trafficking on our people and all persons within our shores. We are not motivated *just* to improve our tier rating [emphasis added]." Jamaican Ministry of National Security 2012.
[39] 07CARACAS1218_a.

[government] has interpreted its Tier 3 listing as an attack on Algeria's bona fides as a champion of social justice issues in the region."⁴⁰

Angry or Critical Reactions

Several reactions are negative but cannot easily be characterized as grounded in concerns about image. Officials may for example express disappointment or surprise, anger or frustration, criticize the US for "moving the goal posts" by which they are assessed, or outright accuse the US of arrogance for rating other countries.

Anger or Frustration

Government officials often express frustration over poor ratings. For example, in a seminar in 2006, Burmese "participants expressed frustration that, despite their anti-trafficking efforts, Burma would retain its Tier 3 ranking." Similarly, in 2008, the embassy reported that Dominican officials were "clearly frustrated." A Turkish official in 2009 told the embassy that, "While the [US government] report allows TIP to remain at the forefront of government objectives, it is frustrating to implement many anti-TIP steps only to be told later they are not sufficient."⁴¹ In 2009, the Egyptian Deputy Assistant Foreign Minister for Human Rights told the embassy "the [government] was 'frustrated' with the 2009 TIP Report. He said that Egypt felt like it had done enough in the past year to be moved off the Watch List, and the report 'left a bitter taste,' especially in light of overall increased US-Egyptian dialogue and cooperation." Emotions were so high that "some officials wanted to stop cooperating with the [US government] on TIP, but he stated that everyone agreed to revisit the issue at a later date to give some time for feelings to subside."⁴²

Some officials are more angry than frustrated. As the above quote by 2007 Venezuelan officials suggested, they "reacted angrily to the ... designation of Venezuela as a Tier 3 country," a pattern consistent with 2004 when numerous government officials reacted with "indignation and condemnation." This could be attributed to the poor relationship between the US and Venezuela, but other countries have reacted similarly. Uzbekistan's government was "angry" about the 2007 Tier 3 ranking; so angry in fact that local NGOs officials warned embassy staff. Some embassies even

⁴⁰ 07ALGIERS1099.
⁴¹ 03ANKARA4066_a.
⁴² 09CAIRO1222_a.

refer to "rancor," as in Algeria's 2007 reaction. Most striking was Oman's anger in 2006 when "[t]he normally imperturbable [Ministry of Foreign Affairs Under Secretary] reacted harshly to the report, calling its assessment of Oman 'unfair, arrogant, discourteous and unfriendly,' and charging that it ignored Oman's serious, constructive engagement on TIP over the past year as well as the Sultanate's mature, positive relations with the US. He said his ministry is 'extremely frustrated' that their efforts have been ignored."[43]

Moving Goal Posts

Officials sometimes get angry because they think that the US is changing the standards over time, which the US has indeed done.[44] The fact that officials rebel against changing goals indicates that they have been striving to meet the goals and are at least partly motivated by a desire to improve their rating. For example, in 2008 the UAE complained in the national media that the standards were changing. Others did so privately with the embassy. Hong Kong officials asked the embassy directly in 2009 if the US "was 'moving the goal posts' on TIP," and Jamaica complained of "moving goal posts" in 2007. In 2007 Japan complained, "the United States needs to offer further explanation concerning the inclusion of apparently new criteria into this year's report." In 2007, Thailand asked for more time to "adjust to new benchmarks," given the report's recent focus on labor trafficking. In 2008 the Qatari embassy reported, "[O]fficials often tell us that they don't know where our end game lies." In 2009, a UAE official told the embassy that it "'changed the goal posts' by emphasizing labor issues while the [government] was focused largely on fighting sexual exploitation."[45] Such comments about moving goal posts reveal that efforts are often focused on what might improve tier ratings, not simply on fighting TIP regardless; that is, countries are focused on getting better ratings.

Harming Relations With the US

Sometimes officials get so angry they threaten to withdraw or actually withdraw cooperation on TIP issues. Japan did so in 2007, frustrated at what it saw as inconsistencies in the report, criticizing the report as unsubstantiated. For example, it noted that

---

[43] 06MUSCAT907_a.
[44] See Chapter 3 for how the standards and content of the report has varied over time.
[45] 09ABUDHABI1096_a.

Following last year's TIP Report, it refers to the 2005 penal code and repeats that "Application of these statues, however, has been hindered by the difficulty of establishing a level of documentary evidence required for providing a trafficking crime." Last year we mentioned that this is not true and asked for clarification of such statement. We need to know on what basis such statement in the report relies.

It provided a long list of specifics of the report that it disagreed with and set out a list of conditions for further cooperation on TIP, noting "if the United States cannot clearly explain its Tier ranking criteria and give Japan assurances that meeting those criteria will result in a Tier-1 ranking, [the Ministry of Foreign Affairs] will no longer cooperate with the US Embassy in compiling data for the report." Likewise, in 2008, Indian officials reacted to the Watch List status with "indignation" and subsequently refused to discuss TIP with US officials.

The reaction to the report can also spill over into other aspects of the relationship with the US. In 2006, officials there said that the Watch List ranking could interfere with ongoing process of ratifying the free trade agreement (which eventually went into effect only on January 1, 2009), in 2007 they threatened that the Ministry of Foreign Affairs undersecretary would avoid meetings with key officials during an upcoming trip to Washington, and in 2008, Oman officials said they "felt 'stabbed in the back' by the US report" and said they would cut off US access to criminal statistics or other law enforcement data, and threatened "to re-appraise 'all aspects' of [the] bilateral relationship" unless the US retracted the Tier 3 designation. Several serious counteractions were implemented even affecting a discussion of nuclear issues. As the embassy summed up in 2009: "Oman's placement on 'Tier 3' ... greatly angered the Omani government and threatened to damage bilateral cooperation on a variety of fronts." Such a reaction is clearly not aimed at improving diplomatic relations with the US or ensuring that the US continues to pour favors on the country. It signals clear concern with the rating.

Objections to the Report Content or Accuracy
While many reactions can be labeled as some form of objection, sometimes governments object to the report itself or to specific elements of the report. They call the report unfair, unjust or unfounded, biased, prejudicial, politically motivated, unsubstantiated, inaccurate, erroneous, or untrue. As a Kuwaiti official stated in 2005 in protest of the Tier 3 rating: "Your report says it, but I am not convinced. ... You have no

numbers, just like us." Governments often object if they think the report does not take into account changes they have undertaken. Turkey argued that the 2003 report "was clearly 'not made on its merits.'" Similarly, in 2008, an Egyptian official said the report "does not match the legal and factual realities in Egypt." In 2004 Malawi wrote to the US embassy calling the report "exaggerated and not professionally done. The Report is debatable and not substantiated by a list of identifiable interviewees, credible sources or reliable statistics. ... The Ministry would, accordingly, appreciate a review of its case based on the real situation as exists on the ground so that a genuine classification is given." Japan has been particularly upset by its repeated Tier 2 ranking, and in 2008 said that "[t]he report's language about Japanese law not criminalizing labor recruiting through fraud is 'completely false.'"

Accusations of US Arrogance

Some governments criticize the very fact that the US is issuing the report in the first place. This is a common defense strategy for countries seeking to evade international criticism.[46] The more a country can discredit the source of criticisms, the more they can undermine the reputational damage. In 2007, for example, Argentinian officials referred to it as "paternalistic." Officials call the reports "arrogant," and criticize the US for passing judgment on others or dictating values to other countries. A few call it "interference," or, as Qatar in 2008, view it as an infringement on their sovereignty. In 2007 Venezuela criticized the report as "unilateral" and urged that the monitoring be left to multilateral organizations, a view seconded by other Latin American countries, such as Guatemala and the Dominican Republic, and understandable in the context of the history of US dominance in the region. There is also some sense that the US is supercilious in issuing the report, considering its own huge trafficking problem. In 2006 Belize's prime minister made this point on the evening news: "But those who seek to judge us should perhaps examine their own decadent societies before they come and pass judgment on us." A Kuwaiti parliament speaker grabbed headlines by calling the report "laughable" and invoked the old adage that "those who live in glass houses should not throw stones."[47]

---

[46] For example, countries criticized for poor implementation of anti-money laundering measures in turn criticize the process. Nance 2015.

[47] 05KUWAIT3221.

Concern About the Rating

Many reactions are focused specifically on the rating itself, either by seeking specific advice on how to improve, by bragging about the rating, or by being disappointed or surprised about the number itself.

Specific Advice on How to Improve

Indicative of the concern with the damage done by the rating itself, not simply the country's performance, many countries seek specific information from the US about what they can do to earn a better tier rating. In 2009, for example, officials from Albania, Chad, Ghana, and Malaysia all posed this question to the embassy. In Malaysia's case, officials requested a meeting to figure out how to improve its rating. In 2004 Croatia, likewise, "wanted to know our intentions, as well as what Croatia must do to demonstrate that it is vigorously working to eliminate all forms of TIP," and in 2009 a Philippine official asked the ambassador how to restore the Tier 2 ranking. Similarly, in 2005 a Jamaican official wanted "to know definitively what further steps would be required for Jamaica to receive a 'passing grade.' " Two years later, Jamaican officials asked the embassy "to explain G/TIP criteria for deciding how many arrests/ prosecutions/ convictions move a nation into Tier 1 status." At other times, officials may ask the US if a particular action will prompt criticism, as when the UAE in 2004 asked whether "the US would criticize the UAE for putting long-term bans on deported prostitutes." This shows clear concern with the rating itself and with the *criticism* it implies. Other times it is clear that the reason for making improvements is to earn a better tier rating. Thus, in 2005, UAE officials reportedly "wanted assurances that the [US government] would raise the UAE from Tier 3 to the Tier 2 Watch List if the UAE accomplished all six steps suggested in the action plan."

Embassy officials sometimes report that country officials have studied the report closely, highlighted needed changes, and take notes avidly during meetings. They may ask for assistance from the US directly, as in 2008 when Albania worked with the embassy to draft a short-term action plan to identify trafficking victims. Sometimes officials contact embassy staff to find out what the deadline is for making changes before the next report comes out, clearly indicating that any actions would be driven by a desire for a better rating.

It's interesting that officials often do not want to be seen as bowing to the pressure of scorecard diplomacy. Even here they are concerned about their image. Thus, actions may be taken specifically with the intent to qualify for a tier improvement, even if officials do not like to admit it. For example, although a Bahraini official opened up the conversation with the US political officer by stressing that Bahrain was not acting due to US pressure but because it was the right thing to do, he nonetheless made sure to note later in the conversation that "once both of these pieces of legislation are enacted and begin being enforced, Bahrain should have in place all the minimum standards to qualify for Tier 1."

Appreciation and Bragging

The weight that many countries place on the rankings is revealed not only in their embarrassment or anger or disappointment when they get low rankings, but also the enthusiastic responses they often give when their rankings improve. Officials may say they see it as "recognition" of their efforts or express "relief." Sometimes officials even brag when the rating improves. In 2009, the US embassy reported that the Albanian government had "touted its improved ranking" in both the media and in a press conference at the ministerial level. After its 2007 upgrade, the government of Jamaica issued a press release showcasing "the improved Tier 2 status [as] a welcome recognition by the international community in general and the United States Government in particular, of the intense efforts being undertaken by the government to tackle this growing problem."

Disappointment or Surprise

That officials are concerned about their rating is also evident from their pure emotional reactions to it. Officials often anxiously await the news of their country's ranking in the report and are disappointed or surprised when they discover the rating. When US staff delivered the report to a Taiwanese vice minister, he greeted them with "I hope you are bringing good news." Often, however, the news is not good and this creates disappointment. For example, in 2008, when the US ambassador to Albania briefed top officials on Albania's drop to the Watch List, the ambassador reported that "[the foreign minister's] face went pale when told." This is a very striking reaction. This minister was clearly and genuinely concerned about this news, and it was the rating itself that mattered. Similarly, in 2008 Costa Rica's main official dealing with TIP was "visibly unhappy" when told of Costa Rica's placement on the Watch List. It's hard to fake such reactions. Their private and explicit nature shows just how disappointed some official are when their country's tier rating drops. Other descriptions that the embassies commonly use to describe reactions include dismay, disappointment, shock, and regret. Often the disappointment is connected to statements that the officials think their country deserves better.

Cooperative

A common reaction is to strike a cooperative stance, welcoming advice and engaging in constructive dialog. Officials may explain what actions the country has taken, or stress that officials have met to consider the report. Embassy reports often note that officials were "receptive" to the suggestions in the report, or "agreed to continue to work with the US." Countries may invite the US embassy staff to participate in the TIP-related policy process. In Armenia in 2006, for example, the US embassy reported that the head of the inter-agency Anti-TIP Commission said:

[T]he Anti-TIP Commission would take our concerns into consideration as they work on Armenia's new National Action Plan. He said that, given the [US government]'s concern about victim-blaming, the Commission would emphasize victim protection during the formulation of the new plan. [He] also agreed with the [Deputy Chief of Mission] that the participation of Post's new resident legal advisor in the discussion was a good idea.

When Bahrain was moved down to the Watch List in 2006, officials were cooperative: "Sheikh Abdul Aziz said he was not surprised that Bahrain moved down to the Tier 2 Watch List. He pledged to transmit the TIP Report to the inter-ministerial TIP taskforce and include a cover letter recommending that the [government] move quickly on implementing anti-TIP measures."

RELATIVE PREVALENCE OF REACTIONS

The volume of reactions reveals how concerned officials are with the TIP Report rating. Reactions to the reports are fairly common, suggesting that countries are concerned about their reputational consequences. The reactions often seem genuine: Many are not ingratiating toward the US (they might be angry or criticize the US for arrogance), and thus cannot be dismissed simply as sweet talk. If countries didn't care about their reputations we wouldn't expect these types of reactions. The reactions thus show that countries do care about public criticism of their human trafficking records.

But how common are the different types of reactions relative to one another? Many reports solicited an array of reactions from government officials. It is striking, though not surprising given the desire of many

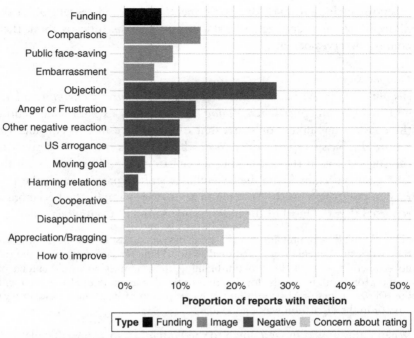

FIGURE 5.4. Distribution of reactions documented in Wikileaks US embassy cables.
N = 491 reactions.

countries to maintain good relations with the US and the rather low cost of being friendly, that nearly three-quarters of all reports received some positive reaction, with over half signaling that they wanted to cooperate. Yet, despite this trend, countries also reacted more candidly, expressing anger, or protesting the rating, both of which suggest that they take the rating seriously. One way to look at the data is to group the reactions by the expressed nature of the concern, which have been grey-scale coded in Figure 5.4. If one asks how many reports had at least one reaction from each of these categories, then for nearly a quarter of all reports, officials reacted in a way that can be classified as concerned with image, with the most common type being that officials made comparisons to other countries. It's noteworthy that there were so few mentions of funding concerns, especially given that any discussion of funding, trade, or aid was coded as a concern, even if the US official initiated the discussion. Indeed, the reactions about image dwarf those about material concerns by a factor of about 3.5.

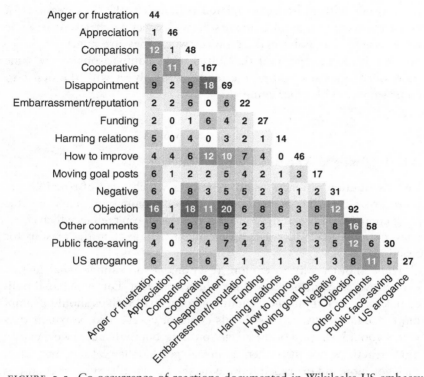

FIGURE 5.5. Co-occurrence of reactions documented in Wikileaks US embassy cables.
N = 738 reactions.

Co-occurrence of Reactions

What does the co-occurrence of different reactions tell us about the nature of any one given reaction? The matrix above analyzes each individual reaction, so that if two different officials had the same reaction in a given year, these both count. This makes it possible to analyze which types of reactions are likely to occur to the same report. For example, when officials ask how they can improve their country's ranking, what other reaction are they likely to have alongside this question? In the co-occurrence (or correlation) matrix in Figure 5.5, darker shades indicate greater co-occurrence. The numbers are the actual counts of co-occurrence. For example, it shows that policymakers are most likely to ask how they can improve when they are disappointed with their ranking and want to be cooperative. However, this sentiment also tends to co-occur with more image-related reactions such as expressions of embarrassment or making comparisons with other countries. Also, while it's expected that policymakers object when they are angry or disappointed, it's interesting that they often make comparisons at the same time, once again associating the tendency to object with the desire to compare well with other countries.

WHO REACTS AND WHY?

Who Is Silent and Who Reacts to Tier Ratings?

The distribution of reactions above tells us which *types* of reactions are more prevalent. This helps describe the dominant sentiments and the most common nature of the concerns. But this doesn't tell us which *countries* are most likely to react, which might help explain the reasons for reactions.

Thus, another way to explore reactions is to examine what factors explain which countries react and which are silent. For example, if policymakers worry about their country's image, bad ratings should prompt more documented reactions.[48] This could of course also be true if they worry about losing aid or trade relationships, but in that case we'd expect more reactions not just when countries got harsher ratings, but when they got more aid or traded more with the US. Furthermore, if countries have ratified international treaties, they are more likely to worry about their image if they are violating them.[49] Therefore countries singled out with harsher ratings should be more likely to react if they have ratified the Palermo Protocol. Finally, if officials are concerned with image, we might also expect them to worry about public perceptions. Officials may worry that a bad rating will lead to public criticism of the government, which could undermine its legitimacy to rule. Research has shown that media and press coverage of human rights issues correlated with greater respect for human rights.[50] We might therefore observe that officials are more concerned about ratings when the issue of trafficking gets more domestic media attention.

In sum, if policymakers are concerned about their country's image or criticism of their behavior, then *documented reactions should be*

---

[48] Given that the documented reactions resemble a random draw of all the available cables. See the Methods Appendix.

[49] Kelley 2007.

[50] Sen 1999, Apodaca 2007.

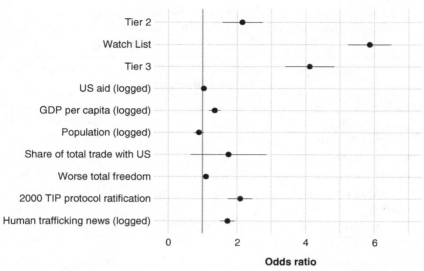

FIGURE 5.6. Odds ratios of Model 5.1.3.
Logit model of probability of a documented reaction. N = 1118.
Source: Author's data.

associated with (1) *harsher tier ratings,* (2) *ratification of the Palermo Protocol,* and (3) *more domestic media coverage.* On the other hand, if policymakers are concerned about material consequences of their ratings, then countries should be (4) *more likely to have documented reactions the more aid they get* and this should be more true (5) *when they get harsh grades.* In addition, the relationship might also hold for trade if countries fear that harsh grades might harm (6) *trade with the US.*

To examine these propositions, I use multiple regression models to estimate the probability that a country has a documented reaction to the TIP Report in a given year. Since they by definition cannot react, countries not in the report are excluded. The Methods Appendix describes the method and data and the complete models are in Table A5.1 in the Results Appendix. Figure 5.6 shows the coefficients from one of the models. The coefficient is indicated by the black dot and the confidence interval by the line through it. Dots and lines not touching the vertical line are statistically different from an odds ratio of 1, meaning dots to the right indicate an increased likelihood of the outcome, in this case a country having a documented reaction.

The model supports some of these propositions. Consistent with image concerns, harsher ratings or ratification of the Palermo Protocol

TABLE 5.2. *Summary of results of regression analysis of factors correlating with the presence of a documented reaction to the TIP Report in the US Department of State cables, 2001–2010*

	Correlation with documented reactions?	Inference
Harsher tier ratings	Yes	Analysis supports claim that image is important.
Ratification of the Palermo Protocol	Yes	
Domestic media coverage	Yes	
US aid level	Not significant	Analysis about material consequences is inconclusive.
US aid level × harsher tier ratings	Not significant	
US trade level	Not significant	

both correlate with greater likelihood of a country having a documented reaction. Greater media coverage of TIP also correlates with reactions. However, there is no evidence that aid recipients are more likely to react to the TIP Report, nor that they are more likely to react if they get harsher tiers that might threaten that aid. This does not prove that aid or trade does not matter, but it is consistent with the fact that we observe rather few conversations in the cables about the fear of losing aid.

The analysis also shows that richer countries are more likely to have documented reactions, but this is likely because more cables are available for richer countries as prior analysis showed (see Table A1.1 in the Methods Appendix). Finally, less democratic countries are also slightly more likely to react. This is consistent with an argument that others have made that governments with less freedom of information suffer greater reputational costs when critical information becomes available.[51] Other explanations are possible, however, or democracy could correlate with other unobserved but important factors. Table 5.2 summarizes the results of Models 5.1.1–5.1.3.

WOULD OFFICIALS STILL REACT IF THERE WERE NO TIERS?

Are the reactions to the TIP Report driven by the rankings or simply by the narrative reporting? If the harshness of the ranking correlates with

[51] Hendrix and Wong 2013.

TABLE 5.3. *Comparison of TIP-related reaction frequencies in the TIP Report and HR Report*

Report	Total reports (2001–2009)	Total documented reactions in cables	Scope and government effort discussed in report	Ranking	Percent of reports with documented reaction about TIP
US TIP Report	1,142	217	Yes	Yes	19.00%
US HR Report	1,755	13	Yes	No	0.74%

the harshness of the narrative, it would be hard to know. Ideally we could compare reactions to the TIP Report with reactions to a report that covered the same issues without assigning grades. Fortunately the annual Country Reports on Human Rights Practices (HR Report), which the State Department has issued since 1977, has, since 1999, included a section on human trafficking under a dedicated heading. The discussion in the HR Report is as extensive as the one in the TIP Report. For example, in 2009 the Nigeria HR Report section on TIP was 1,428 words and the dedicated Nigeria TIP Report was 1,340 words. Similarly, in 2006 the Afghanistan HR Report section on TIP was 572 words and the dedicated Afghanistan TIP Report was 608 words. Their structure differs, but both reports describe the scope of the problem and the governments' efforts. The main difference is that the annual human rights report does not grade each country's performance.

The difference in the number of documented reactions to the TIP treatment in the two different reports is striking. Relying on all the embassy documents that contain any discussion of human trafficking, Table 5.3 shows that reactions to the TIP discussion in the HR Report were rare. While there might well be reactions to other parts of the report in other cables – and indeed countries do sometimes protest the HR Report – the trafficking portion of the report receives little notice. However, countries react 25 times more often to the rated TIP Report than to the non-rated HR Report, although the latter has been around more much longer.[52]

Governments may pay less attention to the TIP criticisms in the HR report, because it is not dedicated exclusively to TIP issues or because it

---

[52] Assuming that discussions of human rights reports and TIP Reports are missing at similar rates, which seems plausible.

lacks grades. Given how focused reactions to the TIP Report are on the grades, the latter makes a lot of sense. The difference in these reports lies in how the information is packaged and targeted. The TIP Report delivers a clear message by being solely about TIP and by containing the rating as an easy assessment. That countries react more to crisply delivered grades than to the message alone again suggests concern about reputation.

FACE-SAVING EFFORTS: PUBLIC VERSUS PRIVATE

The discussion of face-saving above signals concern about image. To examine this further, the analysis below compares how the private reactions in the cables differ from officials' public reactions in the media. If, as much of the analysis suggests, countries are concerned about their rating in the TIP Report and if this concern stems not just from fear of material repercussions, but from concerns with image or standing, then officials should object to the facts in the US report more often in public than in private. In private, the objection serves only to protest the rating or the content of the report. In public, however, an objection is a face-saving mechanism to repair one's image.

Officials do in fact object more often in public than in private. Using English language news in LexisNexis, one can apply the same rules as were used in the cables to code how public officials react to the report in the media. This may miss some local media reactions, although LexisNexis includes some translations. That said, in stories that mentioned the TIP Report, it was possible to locate 480 instances that could be coded as 306 distinct types of reactions by public officials to 176 different reports.[53] Figure 5.7 compares the full range of private and public reactions. The most notable difference is that objections occur nearly twice as often in public. Also, over half of all reports receive some cooperative reaction from a government official in private, which is much higher than in public. Cooperation when the report is critical may appear as an admission of failure that officials concerned about image do not want to make publicly.

Importantly, the data in Figure 5.7 simply compares the cases in the cables with other cases documented in the media. These cases are not the same set, although they overlap. This might matter if the media covers a unique set of cases – perhaps those that are more controversial. Therefore, it is interesting to look at cases where we have *both* a public

---

[53] The search was conducted in September 2012.

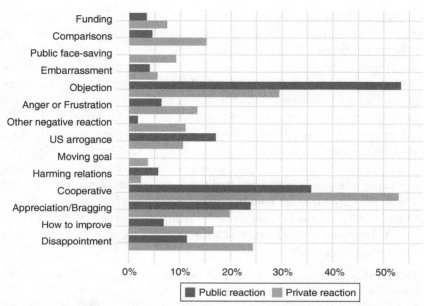

FIGURE 5.7. Distribution of public versus private reactions, as percentage of all reports with a reported reaction.

N = 306 reports.

Public reactions are those published in the media. Private reactions are those documented in US Department of State embassy cables from Wikileaks.

Note: Public face-saving reactions were only relevant in private, as embassies could not report in the media that officials were making efforts to save face.

and a private reaction recorded to the very same report, that is the overlapping cases from the two sets. The overlap covers only 50 cases, but the pattern confirms the overall tendency for officials to object more in public to save face: Half of the countries that had no objection in private nonetheless stated one in public. The reaction of Singapore was extreme: it started issuing its own TIP statistics that come out just a few days before the US reporting deadline along with reports that rebut US criticisms point by point.

SUMMARY

Ratings are at the heart of scorecard diplomacy; for scorecard diplomacy to work, officials must care about their countries' ratings. This is the fourth and crucial step in the scorecard diplomacy cycle and the focus of this chapter.

Starting with the example of Thailand's reaction to its 2014 drop to Tier 3 this chapter has shown that government officials care about their country's rating in the report. The evidence also shows that reactions are common, which we would expect if countries care. The diplomatic cables suggest that nearly a fifth of all reports have at least one documented case of officials reacting to the tier rating in a meeting with the local US embassy. Given that we likely have less than one-fifth of all US cables over the time period, this suggests that countries frequently react to their tier ratings. Indeed, interviews suggest that nearly *all* countries react in some form. That the grades themselves – rather than the substantive criticisms – matter is supported the fact that reactions to the graded TIP Report are far more common than to a similar, but non-graded, section about TIP in the US human rights report also issued by the DOS.

An Armenian official expressed the importance of ratings well in a 2004 BBC news story:

The fact that according to the US State Department, Armenia is among the countries of the second group is satisfactory. It is also good for Armenia that the report said if Armenia continues its fight against trafficking in the same way and with the same consistency … the country may be included in the first group in the future. … In the report drawn up four years ago, our country was in the third group. This assessment of Armenia was *like a cold shower*, as their approach was very strict and unexpected. In any case, we were not disappointed ending up in such a situation, but were given an incentive and concentrated all our efforts on making the fight against trafficking more organized [emphasis added].[54]

The quote illustrates how concern for the rating can drive scorecard diplomacy: First, the report can be a wake-up call; a bad rating attracts the attention of officials. Second, the ongoing ratings provide a continued incentive to strive for a higher rating. Furthermore, the report allows for credit taking. In this case it was the Head of Armenia's Migration and Refugees Department who boasted.

This chapter has also shown that officials worry about their country's image and standing. In nearly a quarter of documented cases, officials act embarrassed, try to save face, or compare themselves with others. Also consistent with image concerns, countries are more likely to have a documented reaction when they receive harsher ratings, have more media coverage of TIP, or have ratified the Palermo Protocol.

That countries tend to compare themselves with a geographic or other identity-based peer group suggests concern with status and standing

---

[54] BBC Summary of World Broadcasts 2004.

within groups that countries identify with. Indeed, the data on references to peer groups is ground-breaking. While many scholars claim that states care about their relative status and consider themselves as belonging to peer groups, few studies have shown this systematically and identified peer groups.[55]

It is also revealing that officials not only react strongly in private, but that their public reactions often differ. A comparison of reactions in meetings with embassies and statements in the national media show that officials object nearly twice as often in public than in private, while they tend to be less cooperative in public. Officials are keen to salvage their image, protect their government's reputation, and demonstrate to citizens and foreign audiences that they are doing a good job. Indeed, some countries have even hired public relations firms when their ratings dropped.[56]

If concern about the report were mostly about international aid or the possibility of US sanctions, comparisons or face-saving efforts would be futile. However, explicit references to status or image were 3.5 times as common as conversations about aid, trade or sanctions. Countries with greater aid or trade relationships with the US were also not more likely to react, nor did they react more when they received harsher grades that might threaten their aid or trade. Aid and trade likely matter some, but this once again suggests that material concerns cannot be the whole story of why officials respond to scorecard diplomacy. Interviewees for this project also reflected this view. One IOM staffer noted that: "Some of the countries that care more are the ones that get attention and funding from the US government. But it's not so black and white, it's *not* just about money."[57]

Finally, the analysis in this chapter also highlights some of the perils of scorecard diplomacy. Countries react because they care, but that also means they may get upset if they perceive the report as unfair or unjustified. Some displays of anger or criticism of the report may be evasive tactics, but much of it may also be genuine. Rating other countries invites criticisms, especially if the rating and reporting is not perfectly objective or consistent. Countries have criticized the US for "moving the goal posts" when they thought that the criteria were changing over time. This criticism is not just cosmetic. If countries think the goals are changeable,

[55] See for example Renshon 2016, 529.
[56] Notably Thailand and Malaysia. See 09KUALALUMPUR652 and Lawrence and Hodal 2014, McCauley 2014.
[57] Interview #3.

they may become discouraged. Some countries also push back on the rating scheme as arrogant. The book's conclusion revisits some of these points.

Because of their concern about the ratings, officials also become discouraged if their efforts fail to earn an upgrade, which creates a dilemma similar to the use of conditionality or other assessments. My earlier work on conditionality for EU enlargement found that a common dilemma for the EU was how much to praise a country when it was making great progress in one area but not in another.[58] Similarly, my work on international election monitors showed that in response to partial progress some monitors were torn between calling the glass half full or half empty.[59] The situation is the same here: A country may have passed a law to criminalize trafficking, yet the implementation of that law may be completely absent. Do you upgrade the country or keep it the same? This is a question the TIP Office faces annually for many countries. The cables often reveal embassy officials pleading with the TIP Office to reward the momentum.

Furthermore, scorecard diplomacy invites scorn. Some countries call the US unilateral, even arrogant. They criticize the report as biased or of low quality. When such emotions run high, this can damage the relationship. Countries may withdraw cooperation on TIP or, as with Oman, cancel other meetings. Grading others comes at a cost.

In sum, this chapter has revealed the mechanisms of scorecard diplomacy by uncovering and analyzing private and public reactions to the US efforts. These examples of concern make it more plausible that any correlations between a country's report status and its behavior are causal, because we can observe how countries react, that they care, and that they do think of how their status is affected by how their rating compares with others. They also highlight that concerns with image and standing are prevalent.

But, are *reactions* also connected to *actions*? Thailand, despite its overtures, changed little in the next year and did not earn an upgrade. But the scorecard diplomacy argument is that the reports creates concern which in turn changes behavior. Do some countries that react verbally actually behave differently? Are reactions fleeting, or do countries follow up by taking action? Chapter 6 takes up this question by examining some outcomes that scorecard diplomacy seeks to accomplish.

[58] Kelley 2004a.
[59] Kelley 2012.

6

From Reputational Concerns to Effects on Laws, Practices, and Norms

> If it were not for the US, [the Counter-TIP Act] would probably not have come.
>
> *– Kenyan NGO worker*[1]

> There was always the risk that this new, high-level anti-TIP council we had urged upon the [government of Armenia] might prove in its execution to be an empty formality – a formulaic sop to international pressure.
>
> *– US embassy Yerevan, 2008*[2]

Countries might be concerned about their reputation but never do anything about it. Have states translated their reputational concerns into action? If you want to know if something works, there is a lot to be said for asking the people close to the action. Chapter 4 showed just how involved IGOs and NGOs are with anti-human trafficking efforts and that many of them interact with the US on the ground. As first-hand observers of the policy in their countries, what do IGOs and NGOs think of US efforts? The global NGO survey found that in most countries NGOs view the US as by far the most active embassy in their countries. Indeed, they were 14 times as likely to rate the US as active than other embassies. That's a lot! Furthermore, 44 percent of those who knew of the TIP Report said that they had heard government officials refer to the report, showing that the report enters local TIP discussions.

But what do they actually think of the role of US scorecard diplomacy? Do they believe the TIP Report and accompanying efforts have been

---

[1] Adhoch interview.
[2] 08YEREVAN555_a.

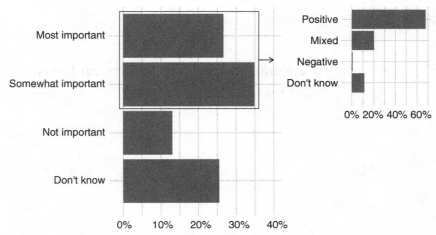

FIGURE 6.1. NGO assessments of US anti-TIP efforts in their countries.
Responses related to importance: 522. Responses related to positivity: 316.
The N exceeds the total number of respondents because some NGOs work in
more than one country and answered the question for each country.
Source: NGO survey by author.

important? The answer is a surprisingly resounding "yes." As Figure 6.1
shows, nearly two-thirds of the NGOs said that the US had played the
most important or a somewhat important role in their country. The share
of countries in which at least one NGO attributed a most important or a
somewhat important role was even higher, at 83 percent.

Still, NGOs might see US scorecard diplomacy as important, but in
a negative light. The survey, therefore, asked those who said that the
US had played an important role whether that role had been positive
or negative or mixed. The rarity of negative replies was astounding. Of
the 316 NGOs who said the US had been important, over three-quarters
were positive (214) and about one-fifth were mixed (64). Only two said
the US had played a negative role. This is less than 1 percent! In the light
of pervasive anti-American sentiment and academic criticism of US anti-
TIP policy,[3] this appreciation suggests that scorecard diplomacy is having
some effect – at least in the eyes of those close to the problems.

Interviews with NGOs reflect these views as well. Jessica Van Meir,
who assisted with research for this book, interviewed five Kenyan NGOs
about their views of US efforts there. One NGO staffer reported that

---

[3] On anti-Americanism, see Katzenstein and Keohane 2007. On academic criticisms of US
TIP policy, see Chuang 2015, 2005.

someone from the Kenyan intelligence service had asked her organization for assistance because the TIP Report was making Kenya look bad, and said that the TIP Report "shows where we are," and that it's important to have a "transparent report," that high-level officials read.[4] Another NGO staffer said the report is "like a mirror" of the situation, and that even donors "are taking the report very seriously. ... Other NGOs look at the TIP Report like the Bible."[5] Yet another NGO worker said that US efforts were crucial in the passage of the anti-TIP law and contributed to the wording of the law,[6] while another described the TIP Report as "one of the main instruments that describes the situation of trafficking," though sometimes it can be inaccurate.[7] Finally, an NGO staffer said the report was "a good accountability document" that led to more traffickers being convicted and noted that the Kenyan government has needed to be "pushed" by the American government on every step regarding TIP.[8] These NGO views suggest that scorecard diplomacy indeed makes officials concerned about their country's reputation and that officials, NGOs and donors take the report very seriously.

While some IGO staff question the breadth of the US definition of human trafficking, they generally appreciate the TIP Report. An ILO staff person noted the report improves the application of the ILO conventions when the US asks mentions it in the report: "That sort of pressure is much, much stronger than the ILO telling off the governments. Some countries ratify, etc., but never did anything until one day the US sort of, not even imposing trade barriers, just consider it."[9] Another ILO official said: "The US has been a major player. The US did help propel a lot of legislative changes in many countries, so definitely it has had an impact." A staff member of the Office of the High Commissioner for Human Rights said that that the US has advanced victim protection, and increased awareness of the issue:

Many countries did not know about it or they would deny it, and the report is very important in putting TIP high on international agenda. If you go to the Gulf countries, they really pay a lot of attention to what is being said about them in the TIP Report. They really care about what has been written in the TIP Report. In the absence of a comprehensive UN report the TIP is very valuable and the best there is.[10]

[4] Gachanja interview.
[5] Otieno interview.
[6] Minayo interview.
[7] Malinowski interview.
[8] Adhoch interview.
[9] Noguchi interview.
[10] Haddin interview.

IOM officials, though generally reticent to offer interviews, perhaps because the organization receives generous US funding, made similar comments. As discussed more in Chapter 8, one official argued that before the TIP Report IOM efforts had fallen flat as the Armenian government denied the problem, but that the report changed the government's actions.[11] Similarly, the IOM has noted that progress on trafficking legislation in Guyana was "spurred on by its inclusion in Tier Three of the US State Department Trafficking in Persons Report in 2004" and attributed the text of the law to "the United States model legislation issued by the US State Department's Office to Monitor and Combat Trafficking in Persons, which provides legal building blocks for countries attempting to reform their criminal law."[12]

In sum, NGOs and IGOs view scorecard diplomacy efforts surprisingly favorably. And as Chapter 5 showed, domestic policymakers in many countries pay attention to the TIP Report, take it seriously and, by and large, want to improve their rating. This suggests that scorecard diplomacy has traction with the players who can make a difference on the ground. Alas, alone none of this shows that scorecard diplomacy actually changes government policy, which is what is most important. That is what this and the next two chapters therefore set out to assess.

OUTCOMES UNDER STUDY

It is important to be clear about how to think about outcomes. One way is to consider whether the problem of human trafficking has been mitigated. If this were a study about how to reduce human trafficking, that would be the way to go, although that approach surely would face insurmountable data challenges. Because this book is about the efficacy of scorecard diplomacy, it instead considers the efforts of countries to fight trafficking and more specifically their responses to US recommendations for how to do so. In other words: are countries following US advice? Importantly, implementation matters.

Regardless of how one defines the outcome, in most countries results have been mixed. Human trafficking persists even in countries that fight it hard. It's a stubborn problem. Like murders, government efforts can reduce their frequency, but not eliminate them. The problem is unlikely

---

[11] Hrach Kajhoyan, coordinator of the International Organization for Migration (IOM) programs. Cited in Kalantarian 2006.
[12] International Organization for Migration 2010, 16.

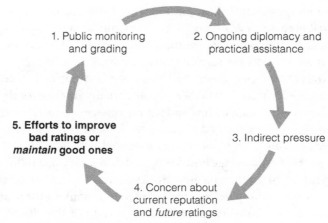

FIGURE 6.2. The cycle of scorecard diplomacy.

to be mitigated without eradicating deep-seated poverty and societal criminal elements. Most government efforts to fight trafficking cannot be measured at any given time as being accomplished or not. The challenges and the corresponding efforts may ebb and flow. Indeed, the fluctuating nature of government efforts is a central motivation for the TIP Report's ongoing nature and a key advantage for scorecard diplomacy as a policy tool. Performance and reputations are never permanent. Government efforts must be sustained to maintain good tiers.

The cases studies, a few of which are discussed two chapters hence, examine the fate of policies the US was pushing. Because of the changing nature of government efforts, the outcomes focus not just on cases overall, but also on discrete diplomatic successes or failures. The cases identify incidents or periods when scorecard diplomacy had traction and moved things forward and other times of stagnation or backsliding. Progress may occur when a policy advances, a new agency is created, a shelter is built, or a new action plan is drawn up. That does not mean that the country has solved the problem, or that the efforts have been maintained at high standards. It simply illustrates instances where some progress was made, or, conversely, where it failed.

Specifically, this chapter examines three policy outputs and outcomes. The first is the criminalization of human trafficking into domestic law, one of the foremost requirements of the Palermo Protocol and a primary goal of scorecard diplomacy. The chapter examines not only whether the scorecard diplomacy influenced the passage of such laws, but also whether it influenced their content and implementation. The chapter also examines institutionalization, that is, whether scorecard diplomacy has contributed to new practices, the creation of new commissions or agencies, new data gathering routines and so forth. The final focus is on change at an even deeper level, namely in norms around the problem of human trafficking. One might call this socialization, but since it's not really possible to observe whether people actually internalize the norms, this book makes no such claims and simply observes how these issues are discussed and operationalized in policies. Changes at this level are meaningful because this is how policies are executed.

The chapter first assesses how scorecard diplomacy has influenced the criminalization of trafficking into domestic law. As an introduction to this assessment, it discusses the importance of criminalization of human trafficking and explains its suitability for a study of the effectiveness of US scorecard diplomacy. Next, the focus turns to different outcomes that might be observed if scorecard diplomacy influences criminalization. This starts with examining the timing of the passage of laws to see whether countries appear to pass these with an eye to the internal State Department reporting deadlines for the US report. After this, the chapter draws on previous work with Beth Simmons and examines the effects of the TIP Report on criminalization behavior. If grading in and of itself matters, then countries included in the report (and therefore graded) should respond to the pressure, regardless of their tier rating. Similarly, countries should respond to the rating itself by being even more likely to criminalize trafficking when they receive lower ratings and when their ratings first drop to low tiers.

After exploring these relationships, the analysis asks a crucial question: Are the established correlations between tier ratings and criminalization plausibly connected with the diplomacy itself? That is, are countries with documented reactions more likely to criminalize? This would suggest that reputational concerns help explain the relationship between tier ratings and criminalization.

Next, the chapter explores the US influence on the content and implementation of laws, on institutionalization related to human trafficking, and on norms and practices. It addresses these outcomes by synthesizing findings from the 15 case studies completed for this book, which examined the development of legislation in each country as well definitions of trafficking, implementation issues, and the building of domestic institutions to address trafficking.

***

CRIMINALIZATION

Criminalization of trafficking is the enactment of domestic laws to prohibit trafficking in person and prescribe punishment for the crime of human trafficking. In this analysis, a country is considered to have "criminalized" if it prohibits all forms of human trafficking with sufficient penalties. This can be through a dedicated anti-trafficking law, or by adopting provisions in other laws, usually the penal code. For the statistical analysis, this is recorded for the period after the report comes out and before the next report. The measurement of criminalization is explained in the Methods Appendix. Figure 6.3 shows the number of countries included in the report and the number of countries that have criminalized trafficking.

While criminalization of illicit activities won't end trafficking,[13] it is a meaningful outcome for a number of reasons. First, the policy feedback literature shows that policies are consequential structures.[14] Criminalization, therefore, has been a major priority of both the UN Palermo Protocol and the US anti-TIP efforts. It is a *sine qua non* to further progress. Indeed, when the early TIP Reports sometimes awarded Tier 1 status to countries that had not criminalized trafficking, Human Rights Watch protested: "While legislation is just the beginning of providing a legal structure to address trafficking, and laws alone do not guarantee state action, passing legislation is vital to the effective prosecution of traffickers and to ensure that the victims' rights are respected."[15] A UNODC report similarly cited the "non-existent national legislation against trafficking in human beings"[16] as a major obstacle to addressing trafficking in West Africa. Indeed, real-world examples demonstrate the problems when legislation is missing: in 2008, "Chadian authorities detained some suspected offenders, but could not legally arrest them because there was no law in place."[17] Thus legal authorities agree that criminalization is "the central element of the required legal framework fight."[18]

Second, anti-TIP legislation can shape debates around the definition of the issue and serve an important socializing function. In Kazakhstan, the embassy noted that "[t]he process of drafting this set of amendments built

---

[13] Efrat 2012.
[14] Pierson 1993, 624.
[15] Human Rights Watch 2003.
[16] UNODC 2006, 11.
[17] 08NDJAMENA528.
[18] Gallagher and Holmes 2008, 322.

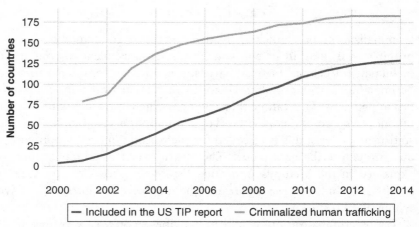

FIGURE 6.3. Number of countries with domestic criminalization of human trafficking and number of countries included in the US Department of State TIP Report, 2000–2014.

a cadre of TIP experts spread across the [government], the NGO community, and international organizations."[19] In Chad, for example, part of the efforts to push through legislation was about changing long-standing acceptance of practices such as using children for herding, which political interests opposed including under trafficking legislation.[20] In Indonesia, bonded labor was a widespread practice that the US succeeded in including in the TIP legislation. In Argentina, the initial version of anti-TIP law required adult victims to prove that they had not consented, which ran against the Palermo Protocol, but was nevertheless supported in Argentina. The issue was contentious. The US and some NGOs pushed hard for the legislation to make consent irrelevant. A later amendment finally did so.

In addition to contributing to such conceptual debates, passing anti-TIP legislation can spur efforts to create national action plans and designate responsibility to new or existing government agencies. All this helps to establish TIP partners for the US within the government, which increases attention to the issue and raises the stakes of performance. Or anti-TIP legislation may change criminal behaviors. For example, in Indonesia, NGOs reported that the new anti-trafficking law had made local officials much more hesitant to issue false documentation, making it harder for traffickers to function. As required by the law, Indonesia also began to set up special interview rooms for trafficking victims, "complete with video cameras to record testimony for victims who do not

[19] 05ALMATY406.
[20] 07NDJAMENA89.

want to appear in court and special materials to help with interviewing children."[21] Therefore, TIP legislation, while far from a silver bullet, is essential to progress on the issue, contributes to the debate around the concept and helps institutionalize national-level approaches to the problem. These are important tangible policy responses.

This notwithstanding, some observers criticize the promotion of anti-TIP legislation. One IOM interviewee stressed that the US influence on laws around the world can be a mixed blessing:

I have seen countries that have literally copied and pasted from the US law. They put them in because they think that's what makes a strong law. A lot of countries have pushed to get a law in place because of the TIP report, so sometimes that produces good results, other times it's too hasty. In some countries, prosecution increases as the TIP reporting deadline draws closer. So instead of going towards bigger things it becomes: How quickly can we count numbers?[22]

Indeed, some in the anti-TIP movement have been disappointed with the overall lack of impact legislation has on the basic conditions of victims. Some even wonder if the Palermo Protocol itself has simply attracted more attention to superficial actions.[23]

Although it's common to criticize legislation as cheap talk, in the case of trafficking, criminalization is important and has often been difficult. Chapter 3 already discussed the opposition and obstacles in many countries. Furthermore, trafficking experts have argued that of the three possible areas of compliance with the Palermo Protocol (prevention, protection, and prosecution), prevention, not prosecution, is the preferred choice for "strategic compliance" to please major powers, because they are the least costly, whereas

[P]rosecution policy requires lengthy and expensive judicial processes to implement. To comply with the obligations for prosecution prescribed by the Protocol, countries need to enact anti-trafficking law that reflects the newly adopted definition of human trafficking in national legislation, i.e., the criminalization of human trafficking with specific and strict penal codes, as well as the delegation of anti-trafficking enforcement personnel including police and prosecutors (article 5 of the Protocol). The criminalization of human trafficking calls for amendments to general immigration law and careful interpretation in the court proceedings of related cases. This may have the potential to cause political disputes and administrative burdens, especially in countries with lower institutional capabilities – i.e., most developing countries.[24]

---

[21] Both quotes from 08JAKARTA415.
[22] Anonymous IOM source.
[23] Skrivánkova interview. Hathaway 2008.
[24] Cho and Vadlamannati 2012, 252.

Thus, criminalization is by no means the easiest test for scorecard diplomacy. Thus, the focus on trafficking legislation provides a methodologically sound, as well as substantively important, way to examine US influence on a government's TIP policy choices.

Finally, studying criminalization has methodological advantages. While data on other trafficking-related outcomes such as the number of victims are notoriously flawed, legislation can be tracked and compared. Furthermore, one can isolate countries that have not yet criminalized and study what factors affect whether they do. Other trafficking policies are harder to compare across countries and that increases the difficulty of disentangling the effect of the tier rating from the fact that the rating itself might reflect different underlying realities. Maybe those rated the lowest simply have more improvements to make, and do so, not because they get a low rating, but because they have lots of room to improve. When comparing countries that *all* do not have trafficking legislation, however, we can study how differences in the rating or monitoring itself, rather than the policy starting point, matters.

Is Criminalization Meaningful or Just Cheap Talk?

Whether criminalization of TIP is meaningful depends on whether countries behave differently after they criminalize. If passing a law is a cheap signal – a way to get the US off your back and take some credit while otherwise halting any further efforts at improvement – then we should observe stagnation or even backsliding. However, at least on average, this appears not to be the case. Indeed, while the records are clearly mixed, many countries that criminalize continue to boost their efforts. In Indonesia, for example, after the law passed the embassy reported that:

Law enforcement action to rescue children from prostitution and other trafficking was vigorous. Police carried out significant action to shut down manpower placement companies, which were complicit in trafficking, including the arrest and prosecution of two owners. Important progress was made in fighting trafficking-related corruption, including the arrest and prosecution of several immigration officials.

Additionally, NGOs noted that enforcement of such legislation had "a severe chilling effect" on government complicity, "thus greatly inhibiting the ability of traffickers to obtain false documents."[25]

---

[25] Both quotes from 08JAKARTA415.

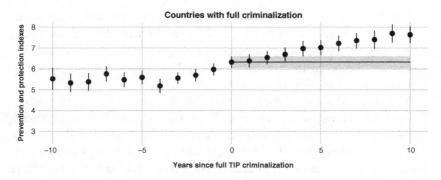

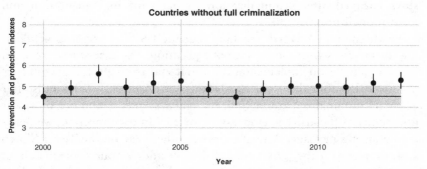

FIGURE 6.4. Performance of countries on prevention and protection measures, 2000–2014, by criminalization status.

Highest possible score is ten.

Countries with full criminalization: ten years before (N = 45); year of criminalization (N = 124); ten years after (N = 33). Countries without full criminalization: 62. Source: Author's data and Cho 2015.

Figure 6.4 uses data from the "3P Anti-trafficking Policy Index,"[26] which codes countries' policies on prevention, protection, and prosecution. It is based on the TIP Report and UN sources, but differs from the tier ratings by coding policies in place, and not government efforts overall. For example, in the face of no change the Department of State may drop a tier rating to prompt more attention to the issue, whereas the Index would remain steady. Figure 6.4 displays only the combined prevention and protection scores to avoid counting the act of criminalization itself. Thus, the maximum score is 10.

The top figure displays the average scores in the years before and after criminalization for all the countries that criminalized trafficking at some point. It's clear that government efforts do not wane after

[26] Cho 2015.

criminalization – if anything they continue the positive trend of government efforts to combat trafficking. This contrasts with the bottom figure, which displays countries that have *not* criminalized. Here the average scores are displayed from 2000 to 2013, demonstrating little change in government effort over this period.

The comparison of the two groups thus suggests that criminalizing human trafficking, while no cure-all, is also not simply empty rhetoric. After they criminalize, countries outperform those that don't on a number of dimensions related to trafficking policy efforts. Furthermore, the case studies, summarized later, also demonstrate that the US effort stays engaged after criminalization to push for implementation and institutionalization.

Furthermore, it's worth recalling that the US does not stop advocating for progress with the passage of legislation. The case studies reveal a continued focus on implementation, and it's far from given that countries are upgraded after they pass legislation. For example, four months after Armenia criminalized trafficking, the embassy met a number of senior government officials. The embassy reported, "In each meeting, we delivered a strong message: Armenia risks another year on the Tier 2 Watch List, or worse, if the [government] doesn't address our concerns about investigatorial [*sic*] misconduct, the unfunded and behind-schedule draft National Action Plan, and the low working level of the interagency Anti-Trafficking Commission."[27] The embassy pushed so hard they called their efforts the "anti-TIP blitz."[28]

Underscoring this persistent focus of the US efforts is the breakdown of US TIP funding in 3, which showed that despite the strong emphasis on prosecution, more US grants have actually gone to prevention and protection. Thus, criminalization is neither merely an empty gesture nor a naive end goal of the US; many countries continue to improve after criminalization.

Has Scorecard Diplomacy Promoted Anti-TIP Legislation?

Given that criminalization is associated with other positive outcomes, whether scorecard diplomacy has contributed to criminalization meaningfully measures not only whether countries have responded to the policy recommendations by the US, but also whether they've taken on the fight

[27] 06YEREVAN1548.
[28] 07YEREVAN106.

against human trafficking. The chapter uses four different ways to examine whether scorecard diplomacy has promoted legislative changes on TIP policy around the world. The first is to examine the timing of criminalization. The second is to look at the connection between reactions and criminalization: Are countries that react to their tier rating more likely to criminalize? The third method is to use statistical analysis of the relationship between countries presence and rating in the TIP Report and how long they take to criminalize trafficking. The last method is to explore the influence of legislation through the case studies.

Inferences From Timing

Estonia had been rated Tier 2 since 2005. In 2011 the US dropped Estonia to the Watch List and recommended that Estonia "draft a trafficking-specific criminal statute." Estonia adopted comprehensive TIP legislation in March 2012. The US embassy usually reports to the Washington TIP Office around March, so this was right in time for the US TIP Report deadline. The timing suggests both that the drop to the Watch List expedited the passage and that Estonia made an effort to pass the legislation in time for the next report. This suggests an interesting observable implication: *Countries that are motivated to pass legislation to gain recognition in the TIP Report should try to get it passed in time to make the report.* Anecdotally, NGOs note that they do see governments working harder up to the reporting period. Linda Alkalash, who works with a Jordanian NGO, noted in an interview that: "[t]he Government tries to work on trafficking to avoid the TIP Report bad tiers. That is a big motivating factor. You find that all the development in this issue happens in the period of reporting usually in January and February."[29]

This is a "hard test" because legislative timing is difficult to control. Even if countries want to pass legislation, they may not be able to do so in the time they would like. In most countries, passing laws is complicated and time-consuming. Efforts to pass TIP laws often drag on for years. This makes it a hard test, because even if the political will is there, it may not manifest itself in the data. That said, if a country is motivated by scorecard diplomacy, then we might expect efforts to pass these laws in time for inclusion in the TIP Report, and indeed staff in the Washington TIP Office experience increased efforts around this time.

Is there any evidence of this? Figure 6.5 shows the raw distribution of the months when countries passed, or, if different, enacted TIP legislation.

[29] Alkalash interview.

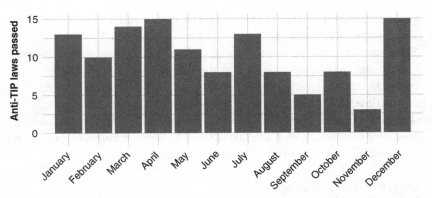

FIGURE 6.5. Number of laws passed to criminalize human trafficking, by month, 2001–2014.

These are not estimates, but actual numbers. We might expect that activity to be highest in the months leading up to the internal US reporting deadline for the report. The figure therefore starts with December, four months before the US embassies report back to the State Department for the next year's report. It turns out that 53 percent of the laws were adopted between December and April, which is 12 percent higher than would be expected if they were evenly distributed across months. April is usually the last month the US can make an adjustment to the June report and sometimes April events do make it into the report. Burundi's passage of legislation in April 2009, for example, featured in the report that year. Not too much can be inferred from the timing alone since legislative schedules vary in different countries, but it's worth noting that the passage of laws peaks before the reporting period in April. This suggests the laws are directed toward satisfying US pressure and getting credit for it as soon as possible, a point that the case study research supports when politicians make this timing point explicit. For example, in the United Arab Emirates, after the ambassador had discussed with key leaders how the US TIP Reporting system worked, on March 14, 2005, the government revised the effective date of the new camel jockey law to March 31, *explicitly stating that they did so to coincide with the last day of the TIP reporting year.*[30] It's possible the July peak reflects an attempt at an immediate reaction after the release of the report if legislation was pending. December might be a push to pass legislation before the reporting deadline in the face of uncertain productivity in the beginning of coming

[30] 05ABUDHABI1167.

year. Thus, while the data is noisy and the pattern is only suggestive – it is not statistically significant – it is nevertheless interesting and supportive of the trend.

Criminalization and Status in the TIP Report

If countries indeed do push for new laws because they care about their tier ratings and the monitoring of the report, what other evidence might exist? Beth Simmons and I explored this in earlier work, which I elaborate here.[31]

The scorecard diplomacy argument is that the recurrent monitoring – in and of itself – triggers concerns in countries about their behavior and causes them to engage with US diplomacy. The basic idea is that if countries care about their reputation, and if scorecard diplomacy derives part of its influence from recurrent monitoring, then countries featured in the report should be more likely to take actions consistent with behaviors that the report promotes, and countries with harsher tier ratings should be even more likely to do so. Again, if we consider criminalization as the outcome of interest, we should expect inclusion in the report and harsher tiers to promote criminalization. The best way to test this is by measuring the time it takes a country to criminalize, since criminalization is something that can only happen once. This leads to the following testable proposition, namely that *countries included in the report should criminalize faster.*

Furthermore, the theory of scorecard diplomacy also argues that countries worry about and respond to lower tier ratings either because their scores embarrass them or because the possibility of economic repercussions through sanctions or reputational damage to trade seems imminent. Thus, *countries with harsher tiers should criminalize faster.*

Finally, as was seen in Thailand in the summer of 2014, a drop in the tier rating can solicit a strong reaction from the government. Demotion may be especially worrisome for countries because it signals that the country is doing worse than could be expected and is not living up to expectations. Although it may simply reflect the US assessment that the country is not doing enough and has been lagging in its efforts for some time, a drop in the rating is likely to be perceived as a sign the country is worsening; that it is performing more poorly than expected. If this matters to countries, then, if they've not already done so, *we should expect demoted countries to criminalize trafficking faster.* The expectation that

[31] Kelley and Simmons 2015.

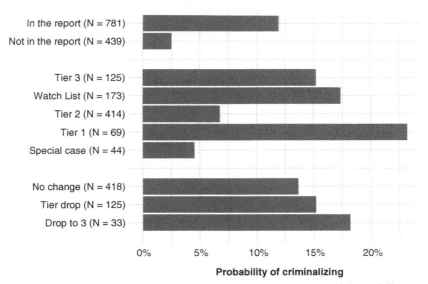

FIGURE 6.6. Probability of a country criminalizing human trafficking fully in a given year if it had not already done so, by tier status in the US Department of State TIP Report, 2001–2010.

countries should react to demotions and harsh tiers by criminalizing is a hard test for scorecard diplomacy, because those harsh grades were given precisely because these countries were not making an effort.

These three expectations, that countries should criminalize faster if they are (1) in the report, (2) get harsh tiers, or (3) are demoted, reflect the expectations developed at the end of Chapter 2.

It is useful to examine the data before showing the results of testing these propositions. Figure 6.6 shows the basic incidence with which countries criminalize trafficking in the next year, given that they had not already done so in the current. The unit of observation here simply is the country-year, so each year a country appears in the report is a separate observation. A country can change from being not in the report to being in the report over the time, or can change its tier over time. The outcome of interest in each country-year is what happens in the following year in terms of criminalization. Once a country criminalizes it is no longer part of the data reported in Figure 6.6. The top bars compare country-years in the report to those not in the report, the middle bars breaks down the country-years in the report by their tier status and the bottom bars compare country-years where the tier rating remained steady to those that experienced a drop (of any kind) and those that dropped to Tier 3. It is clear that countries in the report criminalize at a much higher rate, 4.6 times as often, and that countries rarely criminalize the next year if they were not in the report in the current year. Countries rated Tier 1 have the highest rate of criminalization in the following year, showing that the difference in criminalization associated with being in the report is not simply that those ranked harshly drive the action. The data does suggest, however, that those rated most harshly are more likely to criminalize than those rated Tier 2 and, given the distribution of cases, most of the progress is made by the countries on the Watch List and Tier 3. Finally, countries that get dropped to Tier 3 have a higher rate of criminalization in the next year than countries whose rating remains steady.

How do these trends hold up when using multiple regression analysis that can account for other concurrent influences? When Beth Simmons and I examined these propositions in our earlier work, we found support for all three. Because we were considering how long it takes a country to criminalize, we used so-called duration models that make it possible to model time to a certain event. We controlled for the factors that that predict inclusion in the report, as well as those that predict harsher tier ratings and trafficking more generally as discussed in Chapter 3. All three of the propositions found support. Full specifications of the models can be found in the appendix Tables A6.1–2. Meanwhile, Figure 6.7 shows the coefficients for the main models of being in the report (Model 6.1.2), of specific tiers compared to not being in the report (Model 6.2.2), and of being downgraded (Model 6.2.3). A coefficient is indicated by the symbol (dot or triangle) and the confidence interval by the line through it. Symbols and lines not touching the vertical line are statistically different from an odds ratio of 1, meaning dots to the right indicate an increased likelihood of the outcome.

First, as Figure 6.7 shows, countries do indeed criminalize faster when they are in the report.[32] Furthermore, as suggested by the descriptive data above, this is not just driven by the lower tier ratings; Even Tier 1 countries criminalize faster than those not in the report.[33] Furthermore, countries with harsher tiers criminalized fastest. Finally, we examined the effect of demotions, allowing variables for demotions one, two, or three years ago. We found a positive relationship between demotion and criminalization, with demotion two and three years before having the strongest relationships, perhaps because reform takes a bit of time.[34]

[32] See Models A6.1.1–A6.1.3 in the Results Appendix.
[33] See Table A6.2 Models A6.2.1 and A6.2.2.
[34] See Model A6.2.3 in Table A6.2.

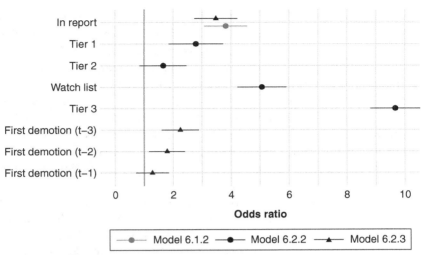

FIGURE 6.7. Odds ratios of the variables representing scorecard diplomacy. Duration models of time to criminalization. N = 1,307 (Models 6.1.2 and 6.2.5) and 1,392 (Model 6.2.3).
Source: Author's data. For full results, see the Results Appendix.

Examining Alternative Explanations

Is the relationship between the reporting and the tiers real or is it simply picking up on other factors that drive the outcome? Chapter 3 already examined whether the TIP Report has strategically included or shamed countries in ways that might make it appear to be effective. It found no evidence for this.[35] While political biases in the grading have long been obvious, these do not favor a portrayal of the strategy as more effective. That is, the biases are not highly aligned with factors that are likely to drive progress on anti-TIP policy. Still, it's important to consider whether the relationships in the analysis above are robust to the inclusion of other factors that are likely to drive trafficking policy.

One such factor is democracy. Countries with greater civil liberties allow greater accountability of officials.[36] Civil liberties also often correlate with greater levels of democracy and democracies are more likely to make and comply with human rights commitments. Indeed, the analysis finds that civil liberties are associated with a greater propensity of countries to criminalize trafficking.

---

[35] See Table A3.1.
[36] See Table A6.1.2.

Along the same line of reasoning, countries with more women in parliament also criminalize trafficking faster, which is understandable because human trafficking often is seen as a gendered issue and the more women that are present in the legislature, the more support the issue is likely to have.

Regional patterns also exist: countries are more likely to criminalize when their neighboring countries have done so, which again underscores that this is an issue where countries compare themselves with other countries, as evidenced in Chapter 5 where officials made so many comparisons with neighboring states. And indeed, the US TIP report could act as a vehicle for spreading information about the behavior of one's neighbors, because the narratives in the report often expand on country policies and because US embassy officials direct the attention of local officials to such examples from other countries.

Another possibility to consider is that rather than scorecard diplomacy, international legal obligations to the Palermo Protocol drive criminalization. To test for this, the analysis included a variable to capture whether a country had ratified the protocol. Results showed that countries that have signed the Palermo Protocol do criminalize faster, which makes sense because these countries have already sent a signal that they are interested in doing something about trafficking and indeed have agreed in that protocol to criminalize trafficking.

Finally, perhaps it's not ratings, but US aid that matters. However, this does not seem to be the case: no models show that more US aid or trade is associated with a greater propensity to criminalize. As a matter of fact, it may even be the case that countries that get more US aid are less likely to criminalize, perhaps because they are poor and have fewer resources and political attention span to devote to an issue such as human trafficking.

Importantly for the initial question of whether these are valid alternative explanations, it turns out that the association between the scorecard ratings and criminalization is robust to the inclusion of all these factors. In addition, controlling for other things such as GDP per capita, proxies for information capacity, proxies for the scope of the problem or the density of NGOs working on human trafficking are not significant in predicting criminalization, but, more importantly, also does not change the results. Scorecard diplomacy is not merely picking up on effects of the commitments countries made by signing on to the Palermo Protocol, on US aid flows, or on other domestic drivers of criminalization; it contributes directly to changes in policies. All these results can be found in Tables A6.1–2 in the Results Appendix.

Actions and *Reactions*: Do Countries That React Also Criminalize?

The analysis above suggests that tier ratings are related to outcomes – in this case criminalization. We know from Chapter 5, furthermore, that ratings are related to the likelihood of reactions. Since the argument is that this correlation is driven by concern about ratings, if further evidence can uncover a substantial link between concern and outcomes, then it is more likely that this relationship between ratings and outcomes is not merely coincidental, because we then have evidence of the full chain: Ratings → Concern → Outcomes, where the arrows indicate correlation. Indeed, the analysis of the second arrow is the missing link in research on shaming which tends to only show that Shaming → Outcomes; largely it has never been done.[37]

This project offers a rare opportunity to establish evidence for this link, however. Such evidence might be found by looking back to Chapter 5, which showed that countries are more likely to have a documented reaction if they get a lower tier rating or have ratified the Palermo Protocol. These patterns make sense if countries care about their domestic and international reputations. This supports the argument that scorecard diplomacy engenders reputational concerns. But does this concern translate into action? If reactions are meaningful expressions of intent, then *countries with a documented reaction in a given year should be more likely to criminalize trafficking in the following year.* Furthermore, if countries that care more also react more, then *countries with more types of documented reactions should be more likely to criminalize trafficking in the following year.*

By examining countries in years when they have not yet criminalized but are included in the TIP Report, one can compare rates of criminalization in the following year for countries that did and did not have a documented reaction or not to their tier rating.[38] If the countries with documented reactions are more likely to criminalize, this suggests that reactions are connected to actions.

---

[37] As far as I know, nobody has gathered cross-national data both on shaming and its outcomes, as well as the intervening reaction of policymakers to examine if these are all connected. Friman acknowledges how difficult and rare this is. Friman 2015, 210.

[38] As noted earlier, the cables containing a reaction may be missing, which would likely underestimate the effect of documented reactions by removing the measurable differences between countries with and without a documented reaction. Again, examining criminalization in the following year is also a stringent test since such processes often take longer.

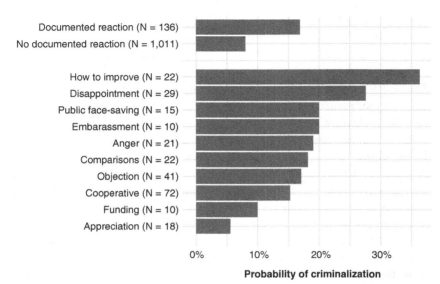

FIGURE 6.8. Probability of a country criminalizing human trafficking fully in a given year if it had not already done so, by prior year's reaction (as documented in the US embassy cables) to the US Department of State TIP Report, 2001–2010. Note that the total N for the sub-types adds to more than the N for the documented reactions. This is because the sub-types are not mutually exclusive. Source: Author's data.

Figure 6.8 describes the basic data. It shows the distribution of criminalization for countries with and without a documented reaction as well as the types of reaction shown. The data ends in early 2010 when no more embassy cables were released and we therefore no longer have data on reactions. Of the 825 country-years where the country has not yet criminalized and when a report was issued in the previous year, 130 country-years have a recorded reaction and 695 country-years do not. It is important to recall here that, as discussed in Chapter 5, these are only *recorded* reactions, so it is not possible to infer that therefore countries only reacted in 130/695 or 19 percent of country-years.[39] Indeed staff in the TIP Office has noted that following the release of the annual report nearly every country in the world routinely contacts it. The cables we do have, however, probably sample from the countries where the reactions were more pronounced, as the embassies exposed to these reactions are

---

[39] It is clear that many more countries must have reacted to the TIP Report. For a discussion of the pattern and rate of missing cables, see the Methods Appendix.

more likely to have reported them. Whether a reaction is documented is thus likely to be a measure of the intensity of the reaction.

The data shows that countries with documented reactions to the TIP Report are more likely to follow up with action. The two top bars in Figure 6.8 compare the behavior of the countries in the country-years with and without recorded reactions. They clearly differ. In country-years *with* recorded reactions countries are 50 percent more likely to criminalize the following year, a statistically significant difference. The remaining bars below compare the criminalization rate for different types of reactions. Because some countries react in multiple ways, some double counting occurs in these bars. Furthermore, conclusions should be tempered by the fact that sometimes the total number is low, which is why this analysis does not push the sub-type data further. For example, only ten countries that have not yet criminalized have a funding reaction, so a 10 percent criminalization rate only means that one country criminalized. Nonetheless, the only group that criminalizes less often than those with a funding-reaction is the "appreciative" group – likely countries that improved their tier rating and that may therefore be less motivated to take further action (a point the book's conclusion returns to). All the other groups are *more* likely to criminalize the next year than the group with no recorded reaction. Furthermore, countries where officials explicitly asked how they could improve were most likely to criminalize, suggesting that this is a more earnest group than might be expected. Note that those where funding is discussed differs only slightly from the group with no information.

A simple descriptive analysis of the data also suggests that governments that were initially rated poorly but then criminalized within a few years often discussed the report with the embassy. For example, 17 countries that were placed on the Watch List or Tier 3 for the first time ended up criminalizing trafficking within the next year. Of these 17, eight have a documented reaction. This is a lot, given the high volume of missing cables, and knowing that overall we only have documented reactions to 19 percent of the report. For example, Israel is dropped to the Watch List in 2006. The report engenders a media backlash against the government, officials share their disappointment with the rating to the US embassy, and the government then proceeds to criminalize trafficking fully, incorporating labor trafficking as the US had stressed.[40]

---

[40] Of the 14 countries that criminalize within two years of first receiving a Tier 3 or Watch List rating, a documented reaction occurred in five. Finally, of the 14 countries that criminalize within three years of first receiving a Tier 3 or Watch List rating, a documented reaction occurred in seven of the cases.

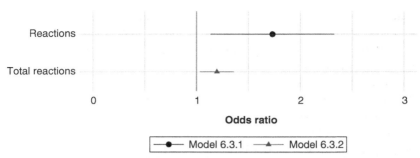

FIGURE 6.9. Odds ratios of the variables representing scorecard diplomacy. Logit models of probability of criminalization in the next year. N = 758. Source: Author's data. For full results, see the Results Appendix.

Finally, it is also useful to examine reactions and criminalization with multivariate analysis that can account for other factors that may influence whether a country criminalizes. I have done so using a simple logit analysis of whether countries criminalize in a given year if they had not already criminalized the year before. Such a model analyses the binary likelihood of some event occurring in a given year. This full models are in the Results Appendix in Table A6.3. Figure 6.9 shows the odds ratios for the two models that examine the relationship between two different measures of reactions. The first is a binary measure of whether a country reacted to the TIP Report, while the second is a count of the number of reactions a country had in a given year. Both measures correlate positively with the probability of criminalization in the following year after the reaction. Thus, the analysis confirms the descriptive data above. Countries with a recorded reaction are statistically more likely to criminalize faster. There is also an intensity effect: The more types of documented reactions countries have in a given year, the more likely countries are to criminalize faster.

In sum, both descriptive and regression analysis show that countries where officials react more are more likely to change their behavior. The display of emotion is not just a show of ruffled feathers; for many countries it is a sign of intention to act. *Reactions* also mean *actions*.

US TIP Funding: Varied Engagement by the US Embassy

Public monitoring and grading is but the first step of the delivery of scorecard diplomacy; variation in the ongoing diplomacy and practical assistance also matter. Some embassies engage more than others, sometimes due to the domestic factors discussed above, but other times simply because the individuals in the embassy differ in their commitment to the issue. For example, in Armenia, the embassy made the issue a top mission priority.[41] Why does one ambassador or diplomat prioritize the issue more than others? The reasons for such choices are unclear. But, as even Morgenthau recognized, and as more recent scholarship on the practice of diplomacy is highlighting, the particulars of diplomacy matters.[42] As we'll discover in Chapter 8, TIP Ambassador John Miller's meeting with the wife of the Japanese ambassador clearly influenced the latter's stance. Miller also recounted his contact with a prime minister's aide, Yukio Okamoto, whom he persuaded to ask the prime minister to set up a special task force, which he did.[43] John Ordway, the ambassador to Kazakhstan, also notes how engaged the embassy was and that the Ministry of Justice "had a serious group of people, but we brought a lot of ideas to the table," and that, "it's the combination of the people and the circumstances that makes history."[44] Larry Napper, US ambassador to Kazakhstan before Ordway, noted a similarly close involvement: "At the time that they were actually doing the legislation I would go up two or three times within the month or so. We worked on it together."[45]

It is difficult to capture this type of activity systematically. Far from all activities are logged and we know many cables where such information is recorded are missing. To understand how variation in US efforts influences outcomes, I examined whether the *engagement* of US diplomatic efforts as measured by TIP grants from the US to a country in a given year mattered in the analysis of criminalization. This captures the level of practical assistance to the country for addressing trafficking problems and the assistance often entails more on the ground collaboration.

TIP grants are positively associated with criminalization, meaning the more funding or embassy engagement a country gets, the more likely it is to criminalize (see Table A6.4). The relationship is small, but so are the grants, so that's not surprising, but it suggests practical engagement is a meaningful component of scorecard diplomacy. Indeed, in the global NGO survey, NGOs that work in countries that get more funding were also more likely to believe that the US is an important actor. This was not simply a co-optation effect: Only about 20 percent of the NGOs

---

[41] 08YEREVAN244.
[42] Morgenthau 1950, 105.
[43] Miller interview.
[44] Ordway interview.
[45] Napper interview.

respondents get funded, and those that do were not more likely to view the US efforts as positive.

EFFECTS ON IMPLEMENTATION, INSTITUTIONS, NORMS, AND PRACTICES

It is important to examine a fuller spectrum of outcomes beyond legislation. To do this, this project's most intensive research has been the case studies, which can be accessed on the book's resources site (www.cambridge.org/ ScorecardDiplomacy). The Methods Appendix explains the choice of cases and the methods used to analyze the interaction between the US Department of State, the local embassy, and the many stakeholders in each country. In addition to the 15 formal cases, I gained knowledge about several others over the six years this project lasted. For example, when a research assistant traveled to Kenya, we took the opportunity to conduct several interviews there, as noted above. Also, some cases, such as Thailand, have been prominent in the media, or have been studied by others.

To systematize the knowledge from country studies, 15 cases were chosen to be geographically representative, but also to provide an array of experiences. Because they were chosen partly due to the availability of information, they likely oversample cases where the US has had extensive interaction, which, if the scorecard argument is right, correlate with greater effects. Thus, the level of success in the case studies should not be extrapolated to the world as a whole. That said, as Figure A1.4 in the Methods Appendix shows, they represent the general trend. Basic data suggests that both cases and non-cases have improved over time. It's also important to remember that the cables, which provided the richest source of information for the case studies, ended in February 2010, so the narratives are richest before 2010 and peak in 2007–2009.

Because the goal of this section is to understand any causal relationship between the scorecard diplomacy efforts and each country's human trafficking policies, the case studies have paid close attention to three things: sequencing, congruence, and testimony. Sequencing refers to the fact that cause must precede effects. The cases therefore trace timing of meetings, advice, and actions to see if causation is plausible. Congruence refers to whether the advice given about a specific topic, for example on legislative language, resembled that adopted. Finally, testimony refers to direct statements by stakeholders about their opinions of cause and effect. The case studies also examined the connection between scorecard diplomacy and a set of policy-related outcomes. The outcomes are behaviors that constitute successes from a diplomatic perspective, meaning they are outcomes that demonstrate an influence on the policy behavior of the target government. They are not complete accounts of the outcomes in these areas, but they are evidence of outcomes that involved scorecard diplomacy. I consider five types:

Effects on the passage of legislation are outcomes where the case reveals though the sequencing of interactions that the US played a role in pushing for legislation. The US pressure may come through the TIP Report itself, but usually the US embassy staff amplifies this pressure through frequent meetings with local interlocutors, often ministers or other high-level officials. The US may bring up the need to pass a law and stress the necessity of doing so to achieve a better tier rating. Sometimes the US has worked simultaneously with multiple domestic actors in an effort to smooth the way for legislation to be placed on the legislative agenda. Table A6.5 in the Appendix summarizes the key points about each case with respect to the influence of US scorecard diplomacy on the passage of legislation. For each country, the US influence on the outcome is scored, with "3" indicating the greatest influence and "0" indicating no influence. This coding is used on Tables A6.5–A6.9; for fuller explanations, the case studies summaries (available on the book's resources site, www.cambridge.org/ScorecardDiplomacy) can be referenced. Table 5.1 summarizes the influence across all categories and cases. The passage of legislation was the area where the US had most traceable impact. As Table 5.1 shows, strong influence is apparent in over half the cases, and a medium influence in another four. There is no country where scorecard diplomacy did not somehow address the issue of legislation. It's clear this focus was a priority for scorecard diplomacy.

Effects on the substance of legislation are outcomes where the case reveals that the US had significant input into the wording or content of the legislation. This may occur when the US provides model legislation to the local officials, or when the US embassy staff or US-paid legal advisors participate in governmental meetings about the drafting of the law or are provided opportunities to comment on the text.

Table A6.6 in the Appendix summarizes and scores the key points about each case with respect to the influence of US scorecard diplomacy on the substance of legislation. As Table 5.1 shows, this is another area where scorecard diplomacy has been influential. Indeed, the US has an extensive program of legislative assistance coming out of the Department of Justice and many embassies provide legislative council. Trafficking laws have been on the agenda of many of these staffs. The US has also worked through the American Bar Association, and as noted earlier,

Mohamed Mattar, the Executive Director of the Protection Project at Johns Hopkins University, has advised on legislation in over 45 countries, usually funded by the US government. In addition, the US has funded the OSCE and other actors as well to work on legislation. The effort has been considerable and appears to have paid off.

Effects on the implementation of legislation occur when the US succeeds in encouraging implementation of the law. The US may fund efforts to implement the law or push the government to do so. The key issue is whether it gets done. It may highlight specific cases for arrest and prosecution or encourage the government to increase its identification of victims. The US may also fund training of police and judges so they can implement the law more effectively.

Table A6.7 in the Appendix summarizes and scores the key points about each case with respect to the influence of US scorecard diplomacy on the implementation of legislation, an admittedly difficult area to influence. Nonetheless, as Figure 5.3 shows, the law is associated with meaningful change. The question here is how much the US efforts contribute to implementation efforts. As Table 5.1 shows, the results have been mixed, but not absent. This puts significant focus on implementation and is sometimes successful in encouraging meaningful change.

Effects on policy institutions occur when the US efforts can be tied to the formation of new government bodies such as governmental committees, new agencies or task forces, the appointment of specific people to such bodies, or new data gathering capacities or service institutions like shelters or hotlines for victims. Also included might be the creation of new reporting routines.

Table A6.8 in the Appendix summarizes and scores the key points about each case with respect to the influence of US scorecard diplomacy on the creation of institutions. As Table 5.1 shows, the US has had some success in this area, with some meaningful changes in about half the cases.

Effects on understanding around trafficking norms and practices occur when US efforts contribute to new understandings of trafficking or new practices in anti-TIP efforts. This could include new definitions of trafficking, a broader acceptance of its scope, greater willingness to take ownership of the problem, or training about better ways to treat victims, and so forth. Sometimes deeper belief changes are difficult to identify, so the case may not capture all such outcomes.

Table A6.9 in the Appendix summarizes and scores the key points about each case with respect to the influence of US scorecard diplomacy on norms and practices. As Table 6.1 shows, it's therefore understandably an area where scorecard diplomacy only has resonated in some countries.

Overview of Case Study Outcomes

Table 6.1 summarizes the insights from the case studies on these outcomes by aggregating the scores from Tables A6.5–A6.9 referenced above. The darkest shading indicates the greatest influence on a given outcome. The table has then been sorted to show the countries and outcomes with the greatest assessed US influence.

As the table shows, congruent with the statistical analysis in this chapter, US scorecard diplomacy has influenced the passage of legislation in half the country case studies. In the process of pushing for legislation, scorecard diplomacy has also shaped the content of legislation. To the extent that laws set important norms and principles and define issues, this approaches an exercise of norm-setting influence. In many countries, we also observe influences on domestic institutions. US scorecard diplomacy has been able to suggest new governmental committees or has influenced who sits on such committees. This is an influence on norms and practices.

It's also important to note that the US has often kept a focus on implementation of the law. It's not generally the case that as soon as a country criminalized trafficking, the US lets up the pressure and gives better tier ratings. Some countries have found themselves kept at lower tiers because they lacked implementation. The US has often funded efforts to improve implementation aimed at the root of addressing the trafficking problem. Not surprisingly, success in this category is hard to achieve and even when it happens, backsliding can and does occur. Given the complete lack of efforts not long ago, this certainly qualifies as progress.

Finally, the hardest outcome to track is influence on norms, such as how countries define and approach human trafficking. Whether people's minds are truly changed and whether this was due to US scorecard diplomacy efforts is nearly impossible to ascertain. That said, the US has engaged several countries in discussing the concept of trafficking. Around the world, embassies have sought to explain the difference between smuggling and trafficking or wrestled with deeply-rooted domestic practices such as the use of child jockeys for camel racing in the Middle East; the use of children in the fishing industry in Ghana; or even the normalization of the sexual exploitation of women in countries where the line between prostitution and trafficking might blur because of the normalcy of the former.

TABLE 6.1. *Summary of case-study evidence of US influence in given areas (tally of details in Tables A6.5–9)*

	US influence on passage of legislation	US influence on substance of legislation	US influence on institutions	US influence on implementation of legislation	US influence on norms and practices	Total
Armenia	3	3	3	3	1	13
Indonesia	3	3	3	3	1	13
Ecuador	2	3	3	2	2	12
Kazakhstan	3	3	2	1	2	11
Argentina	2	3	2	2	1	10
Israel	3	3	2	1	1	10
United Arab Emirates	3	3	1	1	2	10
Mozambique	3	3	1	1	1	9
Malaysia	2	1	2	1	2	8
Nigeria	1	0	3	2	1	7
Oman	3	3	0	0	1	7
Honduras	2	2	2	0	0	6
Japan	3	1	0	0	0	4
Chad	1	1	1	0	0	3
Zimbabwe	1	1	0	0	0	2
Total	35	33	25	17	15	125

This analysis shows that the US has been involved in many issues other than criminalization and has been involved more deeply in that issue than merely urging passage of laws. Influence has extended to institutions, norm setting, and implementation. The effects have been partial and varied across countries, and, by and large, the evidence suggests that scorecard diplomacy has had meaningful effects in many countries.

SUMMARY

Does scorecard diplomacy change states' behavior? Does all this effort mean anything on the ground? Recall that the question is not whether human trafficking is diminishing, a question no current data can answer. Human trafficking is a daunting challenge to address that will require not just anti-trafficking policies but also effective ways to address crime, corruption, poverty, and inequality. The question here is about influence: Has the US been able to get governments to adopt its preferred policies? Has scorecard diplomacy influenced how governments tackle the problem?

This chapter has analyzed Step 5 in the scorecard diplomacy cycle, policy change. It has looked at several outputs and outcomes ranging from criminalization and its implementation to institutionalization and changes in how elites and laws define, discuss, and approach the problem of human trafficking.

The focus on criminalization is warranted, because it has been a primary focus of scorecard diplomacy efforts and because, while no panacea, it is associated with other meaningful efforts. The US goal has been clear: it has sought – sometimes avidly – to get countries to pass anti-TIP legislation. Furthermore, analysis shows that countries that criminalize do not simply use it as a cheap signal. Rather, on average, they continue to make improvements in other efforts to fight trafficking. In contrast, those that do not criminalize make no such efforts.

Therefore this chapter has analyzed data on criminalization of human trafficking. The relationships between inclusion in the report and tier ratings are clear. The repeated monitoring and grading seems to drive policy responses. Statistical analysis shows that if they have not already done so, countries are more likely to criminalize trafficking when they are included in the report, when they receive worse grades, and when they are downgraded.

Note that Chapter 3 already found little evidence that the US is simply assigning the ratings to make itself *appear* effective. Other things also point to a causal relationship, namely that countries tend to criminalize closer to the US reporting deadline. In several cases, countries pass laws *just in time* for the internal reporting deadline for the TIP Report and sometimes they make the link explicit.

Furthermore, the countries that were found in the previous chapter to have reacted verbally to the TIP Report are also the countries that have been most likely to criminalize trafficking, suggesting that *reaction* is also about *action*. This is significant. It suggests that the report is connected to criminalization because it illustrates that policymakers are paying attention and expressing concern that is also credibly linked with action. The case studies back up the link further, because in several countries the diplomatic interaction, the recommendations, and the wording of legislation can be identified in the chronology of the development of each case.

Finally, this chapter also examined whether scorecard diplomacy has influenced more than the passage of legislation. The case studies illustrate how efforts have targeted the content of the laws, the norms or culture around how trafficking is characterized, and whether the government acknowledges it as a problem. In some cases scorecard diplomacy has encouraged law enforcement and implementation of the law or influenced the very structure of domestic institutions used to fight trafficking such as data gathering routines or designated agencies.

All in all, this chapter has found significant evidence that US scorecard diplomacy changes government behaviors of various kinds. It appears that the surprisingly favorable opinions that NGOs and IGOs hold of scorecard diplomacy are based on actual outcomes on the ground. It is not without reason that an astonishing two-thirds of all NGOs surveyed thought that the US efforts have been important and viewed these efforts as predominantly positive.

Chapter 5 showed that countries react to being rated and especially do not like to be rated poorly. This chapter has shown that many countries take meaningful steps to improve their ratings. But who listens? Who responds? When does scorecard diplomacy work best and when does it fail? The next chapter examines these questions.

7

When Does It Work?

When assessing any policy or strategy, three questions present themselves. The first is *whether* the policy is working. Is it having any effects? Is it accomplishing its goals? The second question is: *how* it is working? What mechanisms – or active ingredients – in the policy bring about the outcomes and how do these work? The third is *when* it is working? Is the policy more or less effective in any given situation or setting? What factors condition its success? These questions help us understand the behavior of the actors involved and, more generally, how influence is exercised between states and in the international system.

So far this book has focused on the first two questions. These are important, because although some scholars have long argued that states do care about their international legitimacy or can be shamed by ad hoc denunciations, the empirical support for these claims has been absent or at best mixed. Thus, the argument that recurrent grading and monitoring of countries can influence their behavior requires a solid demonstration of the basic relationships and mechanisms. That is what this book has sought to provide up to this point.

But what about the question about *when* scorecard diplomacy works? Table 6.1 showed that scorecard diplomacy had been much more successful in some countries than others, with the influence scores ranging from a low of 2 in Zimbabwe to a high of 13 in Armenia and Indonesia.

Reassuringly – from the perspective of the validity of these scores – the countries have also varied in their policy performance, as shown in Figure 7.1, which again, uses the "3P Anti-Trafficking Policy Index" discussed in the prior chapter. Some countries made good progress, others made little, while other still, like Oman, made some progress, but then regressed.

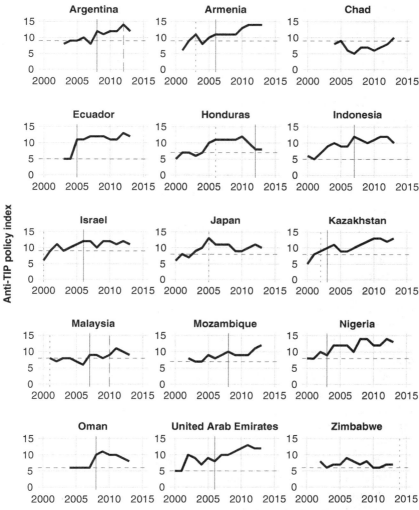

FIGURE 7.1. Variation in the 3P Anti-Trafficking Policy Index for each case study country, 2000–2013.

Dashed horizontal line indicates policy score when the country entered the TIP Report. Vertical dotted lines indicate year country passed partial anti-TIP legislation, while solid vertical lines indicate year country passed full anti-TIP legislation. Dashed lines indicate further strengthening of the law.

Source: Author's data and Cho 2015.

FIGURE 7.2. Factors that influence reputational concern and its translation into action.

Why has the influence been more effective in some cases than others? What explains variation over time within a country? By looking both at variation in the domestic environment and the policy application, this chapter complements the prior analysis of *whether* and *how* scorecard diplomacy works, with an effort to understand *when* it works.

Chapter 2 proffered a simple model of what may explain when countries are concerned about their reputation on a given issue and whether this translates into action. This model, reproduced in Figure 7.2, focused on the notions of sensitivity and exposure as key in eliciting reputational concerns in the first place, and on prioritization as crucial to translating such concerns into action.

Based on this, in the case of human trafficking, we might expect several factors to modify the effectiveness of scorecard diplomacy. This chapter codes each country case on these factors according to a simple scheme: if a factor is notable in the case study, it gets coded as present, otherwise not. Those factors that facilitate reputational concerns and the effectiveness of scorecard diplomacy are coded as +1 whereas those that obstruct it are coded as −1. If a case is not coded on a certain factor it does not mean the factor was absent, just that it played a smaller role, or that the case contained little to no information about it, which, given that the main source of the case studies is the leaked state departments cables, could simply mean that the information is missing. Thus, this scheme is basic, but it provides a manageable way to consider the forces on each case.

For overview here, but as explained further later:

Sensitivity is broken down into four factors:

- Material concerns is coded "+" (a positive influence) if the case reveals any discussion of material concerns.
- Concerns with international image is coded "+" if the case reveals expressions of concerns about how a country is perceived internationally.

- Divergent TIP norms is coded "–" (a negative influence) if domestic norms diverge markedly from international norms.
- Strained relations with the US is coded "–" if the country does not consider the US as part of a desirable in-group.

Exposure **is broken in to three factors:**

- Prominent TIP event is coded "+" if the media brings attention to a major human trafficking event.
- Active third parties is coded "+" if the case reveals a strong presence of IGOs and/or NGOs and civil society including an active media.
- US resistance to use harsh tiers is coded "–" if the US tends to soften its criticisms of the country.

Prioritization **is broken into four factors:**

- Official complicity in TIP is coded "–" if officials in the country are reported to benefit from trafficking.
- Strong interlocutors is coded "+" if the individuals within the government pay particular attention to the issue and communicate with the US.
- Competing national priorities is coded "–" if the country faces strong pressures from other agenda items such as intense conflict or drug wars.
- Government instability is coded "–" if the country faces significant periods of political instability.

The chapter analyzes these factors in two ways. First, it attempts to use statistical analysis. I say attempt because we lack good measures of all the relevant factors, and the rather bare-bones statistical analysis is already quite stressed without adding so-called interaction terms. As a result, extensive analysis using many different measures found a statistical approach using interaction terms to reveal very little. While the results were occasionally significant, which can happen just by chance, by and large, the statistical approach cannot sort out the complexity of the relationships. This is likely because, as this chapter shows, many of these factors appear to work together, so attempts to isolate them fail. Additionally, the statistical analysis focuses just on criminalization, and it's desirable to focus on more holistic outcomes. Therefore, this chapter's main focus is on comparing the presence or absence of the factors above in the 15 country cases to understand how they explain the outcomes.

Importantly, one of the factors this chapter analyzes is the execution of scorecard diplomacy itself. Reputational concerns cannot develop

if the shortcomings of governments are not consistently exposed, or
if governments think they will be shielded from criticism. Indeed, few
international reform efforts of any kind are applied consistently. Failure
to recognize this might lead to misdiagnosis of secondary factors that
condition outcomes when in fact variation may be due to inconsistent
application of the efforts. Variation in the scorecard diplomacy efforts
is therefore important to explore. This chapter does that as part of the
discussion of exposure.

This chapter now discusses these factors in greater depth and gives
examples from the cases. It ends by demonstrating the strong relationship between the influence scores from the previous chapter and an
aggregate measure of these favorability factors, which suggest that,
combined, these factors do a good job of explaining when scorecard
diplomacy matters.

* * *

OVERVIEW OF OUTCOMES

Table 7.1 summarizes how each of the country case studies fared with
respect to these factors. The case study materials, which form the basis
for these data, are available on the resources site to this book (www.cam-
bridge.org/ScorecardDiplomacy).

SENSITIVITY

Greater normative and instrumental salience will increase the likelihood
that countries are concerned about their reputation. As Chapter 2 discussed, the extent to which countries face material repercussions will
modify how sensitive they are to criticisms and reputational damage.
Whether for instrumental or normative reasons, countries may also
worry about their international image overall, which also makes them
more likely to react to all sorts of criticisms from international actors.
Two additional factors may modify the salience of norms: First, the con-
vergence between domestic and international norms. If domestic norms
differ, this will lower the domestic cost of non-compliance. Second, the
power of normative ideas is greater when they come from actors a country considers as part of a desirable group in the international community. Ideas from enemies are more easily dismissed. Thus, it likely matters
whether a country identifies with the messenger, in this case the US, or
has a strained relationship.

TABLE 7.1. *Most prominent factors modifying the success of scorecard diplomacy and their presence in the country studies*

Factors	Kazakhstan	Mozambique	Armenia	Ecuador	Israel	Nigeria	Indonesia	United Arab Emirates	Argentina	Malaysia	Oman	Japan	Honduras	Chad	Zimbabwe
Concern with material factors	+	+	+	+	+			+					+		
Concern with image	+		+		+	+		+		+	+	+			
Divergent TIP norms								–	–	–	–	–		–	
Strained relations with US									–	–					–
Prominent TIP event		+		+				+	+						
Strong interlocutors	+		+	+		+	+		+						
Active third parties	+	+	+		+	+	+		+	+					+
US resistance to use harsh tiers	–		–									–			–
Official complicity in TIP				–		–	–	–	–	–	–		–		–
Competing national priorities													–	–	–
Government instability			–		–								–		–
Favorability (scores are simple sum)	3	3	2	2	2	2	1	1	0	–1	–1	–1	–2	–2	–4
Influence ("total" scores from Table 6.1)	11	9	13	12	10	7	13	10	10	8	7	4	6	3	2

Note: "+" = Enabling factor, "–" = Obstructing factor.
Source: Country case studies by author.

Concerns About Material Factors

The theory of reputation and scorecard diplomacy acknowledges that states act both for instrumental and normative reasons, and clearly material concerns are the most direct manifestation of instrumental concerns. Indeed, it would be odd if states were not concerned about possible economic consequences of a scorecard rating. Cases like Thailand where the government worries about trade implications clearly exist. Overall, however, Chapter 5 found that policymakers rarely expressed concerns about sanctions or trade and there was no evidence that countries that get more aid were more likely to react to the TIP Report. Countries that did talk with the embassy about sanctions or other material repercussions tended to be smaller, more dependent states. Furthermore, Figure 5.6 showed that countries where aid or trade issues were discussed did not criminalize trafficking at a higher rate the following year than those for which we have no documented reactions.

Although discussions of aid or trade took up little space, they did surface and have clearly played some role. Among the 15 countries studied, economic assistance or potential trade deals were discussed in seven cases: Armenia, Mozambique, Kazakhstan, Ecuador, Israel, UAE, and Honduras. More importantly, they were flagged as facilitating influence. A former US ambassador to Armenia noted that, "[i]t was an embassy mostly about assistance. So the threat to assistance was taken very serious by us and by the Armenians."[1] Conversely, in Chad the embassy complained that the *inability* to render a credible sanctions threat undermined its efficacy. After the US waived sanctions following a Tier 3 rating in 2009, the US embassy assessed its own influence as weak, because the US offered less assistance than other donors. Sanctions, the embassy suggested, would "only limit our leverage further."[2] And indeed, Chad has made little progress and still lacks comprehensive legislation.

The cases show instances of aid and trade being at least part of the conversation and several of the countries where scorecard diplomacy was influential contained some dimension of aid or trade. Still, the evidence of the importance of sanctions or trade is mixed. Building on the previous chapter's statistical analysis of factors that influence criminalization, there is no evidence that US aid increases the likelihood of criminalization.

---

[1] Ordway interview.
[2] 09NDJAMENA137, quote from 09NDJAMENA143, which also notes "The US ranks behind France, the EU, Libya, and UN/MINURCAT in providing assistance to Chad."

Further tests (see Table A7.1 in the Results Appendix) also do not find that harsh tiers are more likely to be associated with criminalization for countries that get more US aid, even though those are the countries that might face sanctions. These findings also hold for trade, volume of foreign direct investment and US military aid. The findings do not rule out that these factors matter; additional or better data could show they do. That said, the results appear consistent with the fact that financial or economic issues were only rare topics of discussions of tiers in the cables. It is worth recalling here from Chapter 3 how frequently the US president waives the sanctions, and that countries, by and large, experience no material repercussions from Tier 3 ratings.

One model did find a significant interaction between aid and a country's inclusion in the report, suggesting that countries were more susceptible to the pressure of being included in the report the more aid they got, leading them to criminalize trafficking faster. However, this finding only holds if the model is restricted to countries that are aid eligible in the first place, as defined by the Organisation for Economic Co-operation and Development (OECD). This suggests that different countries might respond to inclusion in the report for different reasons. For countries that are not aid eligible, it's not about money or material repercussions. Perhaps it's primarily about image, standing, and status. Countries that are eligible for aid, however, are more sensitive to material pressures and respond more to being included in the report when they get more aid. Since the outcome is the same when controlling for GDP and population, this suggests there is something unique about aid-eligible countries that's not only about their GDP per capita. One would expect these countries to be most sensitive to harsher ratings that actually threaten their aid, but that's not the case. The finding only holds for inclusion in the report more generally, so it should probably be interpreted with caution.

A fair takeaway might be: some cases suggest that material factors – be they aid, trade, FDI, or military aid – make countries more susceptible to scorecard diplomacy. In particular, a subset of aid-eligible countries may worry more, and though not particularly prevalent, clearly countries consider material repercussions. As the case of Thailand shows, effects on trade can be a strong concern for countries whereas the absence of material leverage can weaken the effects of scorecard diplomacy. Material factors are likely part of the explanation for why countries care about their reputations and respond to scorecard diplomacy, but it's clearly not just all about aid, trade, or other material factors.

Concerns With Image

A country's overall concern about its image should influence how susceptible it is to the reputational threats of scorecard diplomacy.[3] After all,
this is an essential link in the scorecard diplomacy cycle and the theory of
reputation. Still, countries care about their international image to varying
degrees. It is, for example, not a central focus of North Korea's foreign
policy.

Note, however, that concern about image does not necessarily mean
that the country shares the norms of the international community, or that
democratic countries, therefore, would be more susceptible to scorecard
diplomacy. For one thing, democratic countries are more likely to perform according to these norms to begin with, so scorecard diplomacy
likely makes less of a difference. In a class of students, for example, pub-
licizing grades would likely not improve the best performers as much as
low performers, both because they already perform well, but also because
they were clearly intrinsically motivated to work hard even before the
public grading. That said, should they do poorly, they might indeed be
more horrified, but that need not translate into a general effect that high
performers are more influenced by public grading.

Rather, concern about image here refers to the fact that some countries
are just more focused on their international image, for various reasons.
Countries keen to be "in good standing" with the international community are more responsive to harsh grades. For example, Armenia and
Kazakhstan, two of the countries where the US had the most influence,
made considerable progress while they were seeking international recognition. Kazakh officials were eager to portray the country as modern and
deserving of membership in the international community and the associated clubs, such as the OSCE. As discussed more in Chapter 8, Armenia,
too, was keen to polish its image with the West in hopes of forging greater
cooperation with the EU.[4] Nigeria, likewise, hoped to improve its otherwise spotted record on human rights by becoming a model country for
how to fight human trafficking. In all these cases we see an increased
willingness to work with the US embassy.

Because it is not so straightforward as merely being about regime
types, and because multiple factors likely matter jointly, the relationship
once again cannot be established statistically. As the cases of Armenia
and Kazakhstan show, such concern is likely to be idiosyncratic and may

---

[3] Keck and Sikkink 1998, 208, Gurowitz 1999, Risse and Ropp 2013.
[4] Associated Press Worldstream 2003.

vary across time. And, ironically, some countries with poor human rights records, like Nigeria, might be more concerned about their international image, as they try to find other ways to shine on the international stage. Indeed, if anything, statistical analysis done as background for this chapter shows that non-democracies respond more to being in the TIP Report (see the three models in Table A7.5), but again, these statistics are at best suggestive.[5]

The best way to examine the role of concern for image therefore is likely the case study evidence of how often countries themselves express concern with their image and whether this links to their behavior. Several case studies suggest this is so. Furthermore, if we return to Figure 5.6, it's evident that concerns about image link to policy change. Compared to countries without a documented reaction to the TIP Report, more countries criminalized the following year if they had responded to the TIP by making efforts at face-saving, talking about their countries' image or reputations in terms like dignity or respect, or comparing themselves with others. These descriptions match well with the account in several of the case studies where those countries that express concern about their image work harder to respond to the criticisms of scorecard diplomacy.

Divergent Trafficking Norms

As Chapter 2 discussed, some countries harbor views that impede progress against human trafficking. Once again, the relationship is difficult to test statistically. One could pose that those that have committed to international norms should be more concerned with their performance. However, while countries that have ratified the international human trafficking protocol are also more likely to criminalize trafficking, statistically, scorecard diplomacy is not more likely to work for these countries. That is, the effect of tier ratings or inclusion in the report is not stronger for countries that have ratified the Palermo Protocol. However, in the case of human trafficking, this test is problematic, because scorecard diplomacy efforts have been part of pushing countries to ratify the protocol in the first place. Furthermore, again, it seems that many of the condition factors likely operate jointly.

---

[5] This does not mean that the least democratic countries are most likely to respond. As noted, China took little notice of its Tier 3 rating. As with many other international efforts to promote domestic political reforms, efforts often are most effective for countries in the middle of the democracy spectrum. Carothers 1999, 304, Kelley 2012.

Still, domestic norm divergence seems to lower receptivity to reputational concerns. What's striking is that in every case study where domestic
norms have diverged greatly, scorecard diplomacy has been diminished
and the issue has become a point of contention between the US and
domestic officials. It thus seems to be a strong factor. It's possible that the
cost of international scorn is lower when domestic actors disagree with
the premise of the criticism. For example, the US has struggled to change
Chadian mindsets about problems such as child recruitment in the army.
Furthermore, political interests worried about implications for practices
such as child herding, and child employment more generally. As a result,
although anti-trafficking legislation had been cleared by the Council of
Ministers in 2006, domestic opposition stopped it in an effort to accommodate provisions to the practice of using children as cattle herders,
because extreme poverty drives parents to essentially sell children for this
purpose, sometimes for as little as $20. These practices have made it hard
to convince politicians to reform.[6]

Even developed countries may have differing views on human trafficking. Japan's government has disagreed vehemently with the US about the
concept of human trafficking.[7] Japan has a huge commercial sex industry entangled with organized crime and once facilitated by the official
"entertainment visa."[8] The government runs what the US considers a
highly exploitative foreign trainee program.[9] The program revealed deep
disagreements about what constitutes TIP and eventually led to official
renunciation of the US definition of the problem and therefore of US criticism. The relationship got so bad that later in 2009 after the US made a
proposal for a policy change, officials warned the embassy that it would
be better for recommendations not to be seen as coming from the US,
because there was now so much resistance to US input.[10]

Similarly, in both Oman and the United Arab Emirates there was enormous resistance to the exposure and labeling of underage camel jockeys
as victims of human trafficking. Officials in these countries were accustomed to the practice. Both countries vehemently denied the charges – and
sought to hide the practice – technically acknowledging the normative

---

[6] 06NDJAMENA821, 07NDJAMENA89, 08NDJAMENA439, 09NDJAMENA230, IRIN
  2004.
[7] Onishi 2005.
[8] Kaplan and Dubro 2003, 239.
[9] Ozawa 2014.
[10] Warning from the Deputy Director of the Ministry of Foreign Affairs' International
  Organized Crime Division. See 09TOKYO2328.

prohibition; while in reality the practice was not only widespread but also culturally acceptable. The abuse was only remedied when the technological solution of robotic jockeys became available. These countries also faced cultural obstacles to a common understanding of TIP, such as the culturally and financially ingrained nature of the sponsorship system for foreign labor, normative divergences that have continued to lower the effectiveness of scorecard diplomacy.

Strained Relations With the US

As much as the status of the US enhances scorecard diplomacy, in many countries it has also been hampered by poor relations with the US. Research has shown more generally that efforts to shame countries are less effective when the countries involved don't share a common identity or norms. It's a lot easier to "dismiss the criticisms of enemies and adversaries than ... those of friends and allies."[11] If states become used to being treated like outcasts, they won't respond to criticisms.[12] In Argentina, for example, a strained US–Argentinian relationship blocked constructive cooperation on TIP before 2007. Similarly, the US embassy has had a "severely strained"[13] relationship with Zimbabwe's government, which maintained power through violence and intimidation. This forced the US to rely on international organizations such as the IOM to mediate US efforts. It's possible to observe how the effect of this varies within some countries over time. After the Unity government in 2009, the government became more responsive to a variety of actors, including the US, pressuring it on TIP legislation. In Malaysia, a rocky bilateral relationship impeded progress on TIP in the beginning, but as the relationship improved, better TIP cooperation ensued.

EXPOSURE

TIP-Related Events

Theory about agenda setting has long emphasized the importance of windows of opportunities.[14] A particular event or political setting might bring an issue to the forefront and force politicians to address it. In

---

[11] Johnston 2008.
[12] Wexler 2003. Stigma might even be turned into a virtue. Adler-Nissen 2014.
[13] o8HARARE903.
[14] Kingdon and Thurber 1984.

Mozambique, for example, legislation was helped along by a highly publicized TIP case the month before it was passed.[15] The same occurred in
Argentina. In the United Arab Emirates, an HBO documentary devas-
tated the national image and exposed human trafficking in the camel racing industry.[16] In Ecuador, political events aided US efforts in May 2005
when a sex scandal involving the Congress incentivized policymakers to
improve their image by passing the anti-TIP bill. Indeed, the embassy was
"cautiously optimistic that Congress' new vulnerability could actually
advance [US government] interests" and said they would keep pushing
for action on TIP.[17] They commended the passage of the law, saying it was
"particularly notable coming in Ecuador's exceedingly unstable political
environment."[18] Thus, TIP-related events, be they good or bad, can spur
progress.

The Importance of Strong, Reform-Minded Interlocutors

Ultimately, people drive policies. It is people who react to the tier ratings,
as evidenced in Chapter 5, and it is people who spearhead reforms. In
many countries, the US embassy has worked hard to establish relationships with such interlocutors. As a former ambassador to Kazakhstan
noted: "Good working relationships are critically important. It creates
points of collaboration. In this connection the role of locally engaged
staff members is paramount. In Kazakhstan relationships are very important. Understanding these relationships and creating them is important.
I know lots of people in different jobs. TIP is one of those areas where we
hit the jackpot, between relationships and circumstances."[19]

It's interesting that most of the cases where the US had more influence
were also cases where the embassies had strong interlocutors, whereas
the weaker cases were missing these. This suggests that this fact may be
very important in facilitating the influence of scorecard diplomacy. That
said, interlocutors may show up as important for influence for several
reasons. Maybe more zealous embassies are better at cultivating these
relationships and thus it's an effect of the embassies' efforts. Or perhaps countries more concerned with their image are also more likely to

---

[15] 08MAPUTO322.
[16] This was an Emmy and Alfred duPont award-winning documentary on the plight of
child camel jockeys in the Middle East and Ansar Burney's mission to save thousands of
children from modern day slavery. HBO 2004.
[17] 05QUITO1058.
[18] 05QUITO1267.
[19] Ordway interview.

assign the topic to an interlocutor and communicate frequently with the embassy. Or maybe it's about individual agency indeed bringing more attention to the issue in the government. It's probably a combination of the three, but the latter explanation does seem plausible, because several of the cases show variation in the efficacy of scorecard diplomacy over time, and when something leads to the loss of such a relationship, this tends to stall progress.

In Ecuador, for example, the Minister of Government, Raul Baca, acted as the Official TIP Coordinator (after US urging).[20] He sought out the embassy's involvement and invited the embassy to help start the inter-institutional commission to create a national TIP plan. The importance of his advocacy on the issue within the government became evident when political instability in 2005 led him to resign,[21] and the new office holders repeatedly changed, which disrupted progress on TIP.

Active Third Parties

It is core to the theory of scorecard diplomacy that third parties augment the message of scorecard diplomacy, thus increasing countries' concern with their international reputations. Chapter 4 paid extensive attention to the role of third parties, but when we examine the influence in the different cases, how important were third parties? It's worth noting that the basic statistical analysis from the prior chapter did not find that NGOs themselves contributed to criminalization (see Models 5.1.2 and 5.2.2). That's probably an artifact of both poor data on NGOs, and the fact that most NGOs are focused on a range of services that are not captured that well by modeling criminalization. It would be nice to show that they mattered for countries with poor ratings, but for reasons that may have more to do with the quality of the data, this also can't really be shown statistically. I'll refer the reader to the ample evidence in Chapter 4, however, for the many examples of how NGOs, IGOs, and the media amplify scorecard diplomacy. But as a former ambassador to Kazakhstan stressed, "It was a good combination of circumstances that allowed us to make progress. There was a fair amount of civil society engagement as well which really contributed to our ability to make progress."[22]

---

[20] 05QUITO2506.
[21] 04QUITO2598.
[22] Ordway interview.

US Resistance to Use Harsh Tiers

Chapter 3 discussed the common criticisms of the US TIP tiers, pointing to inaccuracies, political biases, and failures to follow through with threats of sanctions in nearly all cases, except those already under sanctions. Such variation in how scorecard diplomacy is implemented might compromise outcomes. In the 15 case studies, the resistance to assigning harsh tiers was strongest in Japan and Zimbabwe, and in their absence they responded poorly to scorecard diplomacy.

Credibility is central to the effectiveness of policy success. It is mistaken to attribute all weaknesses in outcomes to domestic conditions if policy implementation is inconsistent.[23] In the case of scorecard diplomacy several cases underscore this point. For example, as Chapter 5 showed, Thailand took it very seriously when it was dropped to Tier 3 in 2014. There was no doubt that Thailand's elites noticed and cared greatly, and that they were foremost concerned with improving the tier rating rather than addressing the problem, which shows that using tiers gets governments' attention. In stark contrast to Thailand, China did not react similarly when it was dropped to Tier 3 in 2013. Why not? Because the US applies the policy differently in these countries, and China knows it. Conditions in China are not favorable for US pressure to be effective (it lacks NGOs, aid dependency, and high media coverage of TIP), but the real reason China did not respond was because the strategy toward China was simply not credible. The drop was merely a temporary function of the new legal mandate to drop a country that had been on the Watch List too long. As the Chinese expected, the US quickly raised China to the Watch List again in 2014, despite little improvement. As one Congressional representative said: "We gave China a pass."[24] So, why should the Chinese bother?

Indeed, it seems that placing some countries on Tier 3 has become nearly taboo due to local embassy or regional office pressures.[25] A blatant, but successful, example of tier-lobbying came from the US embassy in the Netherlands in 2004.[26] As John Miller, the TIP ambassador from 2002 to 2006, explained in an interview: "The office relies on the embassies and the embassies on the internal bureaus, *but the embassy has a conflict, they report to us, but they feel a tie to the country*, they have

[23] Crawford 1997, Dunning 2004, Stone 2004, Nye 2008, 101, Kelley 2011, 2012, Ch. 7.
[24] As Rep. Smith (R-NJ) said in a Congressional hearing afterwards: "We gave China a pass." Smith 2015.
[25] Ribando 2005.
[26] 04THEHAGUE1049.

a legitimate obligation to report the view of the country they represent."[27] John Ordway, a former ambassador to Kazakhstan and Armenia, explained that the embassies, which have to balance multiple priorities, are more constrained than the singular-focused TIP Office and that creates problems: "The TIP Office is an incredible pain in the ass. They are very difficult to work with. They are an office that actually got something done. In the DOS you get the conflict between embassies that are responsible for relationships from A–Z and so they are always looking for tradeoffs."[28] Thus, as Representative Chris Smith noted in a hearing: "I know [TIP ambassador] Luis CdeBaca wages a tough fight, as did all of his predecessors, against [Deputy Chiefs of Missions], ambassadors, people in the hierarchy of the State Department, who say, don't put that country on the list."[29] Zimbabwe illustrates this contentiousness well. In 2004 the ambassador wrote Washington to "register [his] serious concern over Zimbabwe's proposed inclusion on Tier 3." While acknowledging that "the [Government of Zimbabwe]'s comprehensive maladministration has precipitated ongoing political and economic crises," he worried that a Tier 3 designation would undermine US efforts to address Zimbabwe's other substantial problems. More important, he argued, was the ongoing role the US was playing "in shaping the intellectual debate inside Zimbabwe [on democracy] and, increasingly significantly, throughout the region over pivotal issues in Zimbabwe's crisis."[30]

What is the evidence for this behavior more generally? In 2011 the US Inspector General evaluated the TIP Office. Based on surveys and interviews, the Inspector General found that the interests of the TIP Office, the local embassies, and the regional bureaus often conflict. Because some countries do not take kindly to US criticisms, local embassies and regional bureaus can get caught in the middle. While the TIP Office has a singular focus on human trafficking, embassies and regional offices must balance multiple priorities in a country. This can create "strain," as noted in the report:

As a consequence of the TVPA, J/TIP is on one side charged with doing its best to arrive at an objective yearly public assessment and ranking solely of other countries' anti-trafficking posture. On the other side are US embassies and their respective regional bureaus, responsible for advancing the full range of bilateral issues, including anti-trafficking goals … [I]t is evident there exists a circumstance

[27] Miller interview.
[28] Ordway interview.
[29] US Congress 2010.
[30] 04HARARE691_a.

created under US law that seeks to advance one policy priority by unintention-
ally putting other priorities at risk. It has caused and will continue to cause
unhelpful rancor between the United States and important partners when the
United States seeks their cooperation on both anti-trafficking and other policy
priorities.[31]

The relationship is strained further because bureaus and posts must
invest scarce resources to gain expertise on TIP issues because they think
the TIP Office "lacks the country context of embassy and desk officers."
Indeed, "some regional bureaus assert spending as many resources on TIP
issues as on all other global issues combined."[32]

All this leads to disagreements on the appropriate tier rating, either
because the embassies and regional bureaus disagree with the TIP Office
about the facts, or because they favor encouragement over punishment. The regional bureaus therefore often lobby for *milder* tiers. The
TIP Office has noted that by 2011, out of the roughly 1,500 tier ratings
given, only *once* had a regional bureau argued for a *harsher* tier rating.
One IOM interviewee who interacts with both embassies and the TIP
Office noted: "Sometimes the embassies really don't want to deal with
the [domestic] backlash about a bad rating."[33] Disagreements have been
prevalent: In 2006, 46 percent of all tier ratings led to disputes between
the TIP Office and embassies or regional bureaus, although this had
declined to 22 percent by 2011.[34] A Reuters investigation into the 2015
report uncovered even fewer disagreements – only 15 cases, or less than
8 percent. Usually the TIP Office, which lacked a permanent ambassador
at the time, lost to more lenient preferences by senior officials.[35] This contentiousness shows how hard it can be for the TIP Office to give harsh tier
ratings, and this clearly undermines countries' expectations that harsher
ratings will follow inaction. With that threat diminished, the TIP Report
influence suffers.

This tendency to grade leniently eventually led Congress to pass legislation in 2008 that prohibited countries from lingering on the Watch List
for more than two years. The message was for the Department of State
to stop using the Watch List as a soft Tier 3, because Congress realized
this undermined the report's credibility and authority. Unwillingness to

[31] Office of the US Inspector General 2012, 4.
[32] Both quotes from Office of the US Inspector General 2012, 7.
[33] Interview #3.
[34] Office of the US Inspector General 2012, 8.
[35] Szep and Spetalnick 2015.

use harsh tiers against some countries is perhaps the biggest detriment to its effectiveness.

Once a country reaches Tier 1, it can also be difficult to go back down again, although it happens. The sanctity of a Tier 1 rating might demotivate officials, who might think they are now "safe." In the global NGO survey, a few NGOs reported that governments have used favorable tier rankings as an excuse to stop working on TIP issues, stating that a common response is that "because [the country] has been ranked Tier 1, there is no need to take additional action" or pursue further anti-TIP legislation.[36] Notably, it can also work the other way around: it may be difficult to remove some countries from Tier 3. For the longest time, for example, Cuba was on Tier 3 and it was not until the opening in relations with the US that the rating was raised. When it seems impossible to raise a tier rating, countries are less likely to try. The bottom line is that for scorecard diplomacy to work, the ratings must remain true reflections of performance.

PRIORITIZATION

Official Complicity in Trafficking

Even if definitions of the problem align, official complicity in trafficking can create resistance to reforms. It's worth recalling the statistic from Chapter 3 that in 2014 police and government officials were sources of trafficking in 68 countries. This obstacle, however, does not appear to be insurmountable. While many less effective cases bore this trait, so did two of the countries where the US ended up being more influential, namely Kazakhstan and Armenia.

Argentina provides a particularly good example of how official complicity can prevent domestic concerns about reputation from translating into action. In Argentina, official complicity in the sex business and possibly trafficking, especially at the local level, became a stumbling block for progress on the TIP law. To protect the interests of corrupt officials, the proposed law included a provision that would require victims to prove that they had not initially consented. The law became hung up on this issue, with the US pressing relentlessly. Eventually the embassy's main TIP interlocutor, Anibal Fernandez, became angry at the US for insisting on the law's rewording and blamed the US for stressing the consent issue so much that it delayed other action. The IOM Country Representative

[36] Response 1387.

observed that electoral politics was making Fernandez reluctant to back
a bill that deemed adult victims' consent as irrelevant, because Fernandez
had told him "if the anti-TIP law applied to adult victims as well, the
[government] would have to go after half of all provincial governors."[37]

Other examples involve corrupt law enforcement officials. In
Indonesia, immigration officials benefitted from human trafficking on
the Indonesian–Malaysian border, impeding accurate statistic collection
and law enforcement.[38] The US repeatedly pushed for Indonesia to take
action against its corrupt police force, which was blocking implementation of anti-TIP actions. In Nigeria too, the 2005 TIP Report cited
corruption among law enforcement and immigration officials a major
impediment to anti-TIP progress. In the United Arab Emirates and Oman
the use of children as camel jockeys went all the way to the top. Similarly,
in Honduras, corruption within the immigration service "facilitated the
trafficking of tens of thousands of persons to the United States over the
past two decades," and despite US efforts to work with the IOM and
the government after the arrest of the Immigration Director in mid-2005,
the new administration made no changes and "continued to view the
Immigration Service as a patronage tool."[39] Thus official complicity in
trafficking often blocks the effectiveness of scorecard diplomacy.

Competing National Priorities and Capacity Challenges

Even if a country is willing to engage with the US, the government may
not be in a position to do so. Other competing issues such as drugs, war,
conflict, lack of resources and so forth may all thwart the best of efforts.
Not surprisingly, this factor is dominant. Almost nothing happens in the
face of it, as Table 7.1 shows.

For example, in addition to facing corruption on TIP issues among
the immigration service, Honduras is also poor, politically unstable,
and highly crime-ridden. Human trafficking has had to compete with
these other priorities. Because the fight against drugs and arms was overwhelming, rather than create dedicated action plans on human trafficking, Honduras adopted a broader national security strategy to address
terrorism, money laundering, gangs, as well as trafficking of drugs, arms,
and people. Initial efforts to pass anti-TIP legislation were embedded in
an immigration bill, which had implications for territory disputes with

[37] 07BUENOSAIRES1353.
[38] 07JAKARTA1560, 09JAKARTA378, 09JAKARTA378.
[39] 06TEGUCIGALPA1333.

neighboring countries and was bogged down by fear that decreased immigration to the US would harm remittances. Furthermore, basic funding for TIP has been a persistent challenge and it has been difficult for the government to fund shelters and other services, which has left the majority of efforts to IGOs and NGOs.[40]

Other countries have similarly faced enormous domestic instability. Chad has been overwhelmed by ethnic violence, regional instability, and the need to support the fragile peace that finally ensued in 2010. These issues diverted government attention from TIP.[41] Likewise, Zimbabwe has had to balance many competing priorities. The government-precipitated ongoing economic crises made it difficult for the US to weigh heavily on trafficking issues.[42]

Government Instability

Internal political crises and government instability can significantly undermine scorecard diplomacy, a point made also by embassy officials.[43] In Armenia, for example, the embassy noted that although the Ministerial Council to address TIP was created in December 2007, its first meeting was delayed by internal political crises.[44] In Ecuador the April 2005 political crisis and the subsequent process of re-hauling the government also detracted from the government's energy to fight trafficking, leading the embassy to redouble its efforts. The changes took a negative toll on US–Ecuador relations in general, with the embassy describing the new president as outright negatively inclined toward the US.[45] Later, in September 2010, an attempted coup again distracted the government from TIP, leading to Ecuador's demotion to Watch List in 2011. Similarly, in Honduras after the *coup d'état* of June 2009, the US halted communication with the government, limiting any TIP cooperation to NGOs until the new president was elected in January 2010. Thus, political instability debilitates scorecard diplomacy. Still, government stability fluctuates, so in most countries some progress has occurred even if the government has experienced instability.

[40] 07TEGUCIGALPA1794, 08TEGUCIGALPA165, 09TEGUCIGALPA39.
[41] 10NDJAMENA105.
[42] 04HARARE691_a.
[43] Ribando 2005.
[44] 08YEREVAN555.
[45] 05QUITO995_a, 05QUITO1018_a.

ADDING IT ALL UP

The inability to statistically isolate how individual factors explain the success of scorecard diplomacy, combined with the many examples from cases studies where their workings are evident, suggests that in addition to conditioning the effectiveness of scorecard diplomacy, these factors tend to interact with each other. There is unlikely to be a magic bullet, but also few death blows: outside of unwillingness to apply the policy consistently – which is ultimately a self-inflicted wound on the part of those implementing the policy – and conditions where countries face such high competing priorities as wars and conflict, few other factors appear to be entirely detrimental to some success.

To consider the collective usefulness of the factors summarized in the bottom two rows of Table 7.1, Figure 7.3 shows how well a simple aggregate index of the factors correlates with the basic influence score derived for each country case in the prior chapter (see Table 6.1).

The correlation is quite strong and significant, which suggests that, combined, these factors do a decent job of explaining, at least generally, when scorecard diplomacy works. It's not possible for sensitivity, exposure, or prioritization alone to effect change in a country; these

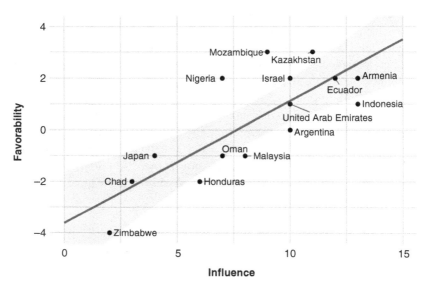

FIGURE 7.3. Correlation between influence and favorability.
N = 15. Correlation = 0.79, p = 0.00.
Source: Author's data (see Tables 6.1 and 7.1).

factors interact and scorecard diplomacy only gains traction when these all work together.

SUMMARY

To effectively elicit concerns about international reputations, scorecard diplomacy requires some conditions to be present. Countries must, first of all, be *sensitive* to criticisms, either for normative or for instrumental reasons. Second, credible actors must *expose* their performance. Finally, for concerns to translate into action, governments must be able to pay attention to, *prioritize*, and and act on the issue. Many factors influence these conditions – often simultaneously – and thus influence the effectiveness of scorecard diplomacy itself.

Factors that commonly detract from scorecard diplomacy include official complicity in trafficking, government instability, reluctance to implement scorecard diplomacy consistently, other overwhelming domestic political priorities, TIP norms that diverge from the international norms, and strained relations with the source of scorecard diplomacy, which undermines their moral authority.

Factors that commonly aid scorecard diplomacy include strong interlocutors who can spearhead reforms, countries' concern with their international image, highly active third parties like NGOs and IGOs, and prominent TIP events like high profile legal cases or scandals recounted in the media.

Does scorecard diplomacy depend on direct economic leverage? The previous chapter showed that inclusion in the report and tier ratings correlate with policy change even after accounting for factors like aid or trade. Indeed, economic factors alone explained little in the statistical analysis. That's not surprising given the finding in Chapter 3 that sanctions are usually waived so that tier ratings are unrelated to how aid flows. This chapter, furthermore, has examined whether economic leverage is necessary for scorecard diplomacy to work. The answer is negative; while scorecard diplomacy sometimes uses economic leverage, it does not depend on it. No statistical evidence suggests that countries are more responsive to tier ratings when they get more aid or trade more. So, overall, scorecard diplomacy certainly cannot be boiled down to economic factors. However, in some countries, economic leverage has facilitated scorecard diplomacy. But so much more is going on, and economic leverage is neither necessary nor sufficient.

Indeed, what is remarkable is how poorly any one given factor alone does in explaining the effectiveness of scorecard diplomacy, but how well they do when considered in *combination*. While it does seem necessary that the country is sensitive one way or the other, this could come from multiple sources and still work. And yes, exposure is necessary, but could also come in varied forms. Likewise, the country must be able to prioritize the issue, but some obstacles can be overcome. This suggests a larger point, namely that multiple factors may be present or absent, but the state of all of these matter jointly. Some factors might detract, but others might offset this. When considered jointly, however, the factors do well in explaining the outcomes.

Finally, although domestic conditions are vital and often beyond influence, much of the variation in effectiveness of scorecard diplomacy lies in its implementation. This is worth noting because this factor is indeed something that the creator controls. Case studies, interviews, and primary document analysis show that in the case of human trafficking, US scorecard diplomacy is not implemented consistently. Countries receive mixed signals, warnings that are not levied, or surprising changes in tiers. Such vacillations compromise the effectiveness of scorecard diplomacy. Furthermore, when countries are distracted by wars, conflict, and other extreme challenges, scorecard diplomacy cannot work miracles. When this is not the case, however, there are few obstacles that scorecard diplomacy cannot overcome to at least achieve some progress.

Before this book concludes, the next chapter will illustrate the dynamics of the arguments of this book with a few case studies that highlight the mechanisms, the conditions, and the effects of scorecard diplomacy and its power to elicit change through reputational concerns.

8

Country Perspectives

This book has highlighted reputational concerns as the central driver of the scorecard diplomacy cycle. The recurrent and public use of grades draws attention to government performance and allows third parties to pressure the government. The attention and pressure make governments concerned and therefore more receptive to diplomatic engagement, which in turn can facilitate policy changes. If governments are not concerned about their reputation, however, the cycle breaks down.

So far, the book has examined these steps in the cycle using multiple forms of evidence, but it has only featured snippets of the cases studies, although they have formed the backbone of the analysis. The Methods Appendix lists all the cases, explains their selection, and compares them on several dimensions. It's not feasible to summarize all the case studies here, but they are available on the book's resources site (www.cambridge. org/ScorecardDiplomacy). Nonetheless, as an end to the journey of this book, this chapter uses four cases to illustrate the core argument about reputational concerns: Armenia, Israel, Zimbabwe, and Japan. In these cases the ability of scorecard diplomacy to elicit reputational concerns has varied. How has this influenced outcomes?

As a poor country, Armenia is perhaps not a place where one might expect policy priority for human trafficking, but, nonetheless, Armenia illustrates the basic workings of scorecard diplomacy nicely, and shows how the grades activated concern and policy responses. Furthermore, the changes observed range from legal to institutional to normative behaviors. Israel is included for two reasons. First, it shows a country that, although democratic, still needed outside prodding to raise concern about human trafficking. Second, Israel's large aid relationship with the

US provides a chance to explore the relative emphasis domestic actors put on material versus image concerns. Zimbabwe is included here as a case where reputational concerns simply had no traction. It illustrates some of the main arguments about the impediments to influence and is, accordingly, rather brief. Finally, Japan, like Israel, is not necessarily a country where we'd expect strong external influences on domestic policies. Nonetheless, it demonstrates both the potency and the Achilles' heel of scorecard diplomacy, namely the consequences of inconsistency in how scorecard diplomacy is implemented.

The discussions here are snapshots of the periods when most information was available in the diplomatic cables. The initial figures uses the the the "3P Anti-Trafficking Policy Index"[1] as a rough plot of policy progress. Rather than cover every chronological detail, they highlight the core analytical points. The brief introductions provide a minimum setting; interested readers can find more in more specialized reports from IGOs and NGOs as well as the US DOS TIP Reports.

* * *

ARMENIA: TIERS AS TOOLS

With its central location to Eastern Europe, Asia and the Middle East, Armenia is a source and, to a lesser extent, destination country for men, women, and children subjected to sex and labor trafficking. Women and children are increasingly subjected to sex and labor trafficking and forced begging within Armenia. Children often work, making them vulnerable to trafficking. Official complicity in trafficking has been high. Many actors have been fighting TIP in Armenia, including UNICEF, the IOM, the OSCE, the Council of Europe, the Dutch government and the United Nations Development Programme. Figure 8.1 overviews the TIP tiers, timing of anti-TIP laws, the reign of different governments and the Anti-TIP policy index, which shows substantial progress over time along with a movement from Tier 3 to Tier 1.

The Armenian government has improved anti-TIP efforts substantially. Officials were highly motivated to improve the tier rating, and compared Armenia with other countries. When Armenia started out as a Tier 3 country in 2002, officials viewed human trafficking as a problem for donors to solve. The US pushed hard for the government to take ownership of the problem. New legislation passed in 2003 and enhanced in 2006, but it

[1] Cho et al. 2014.

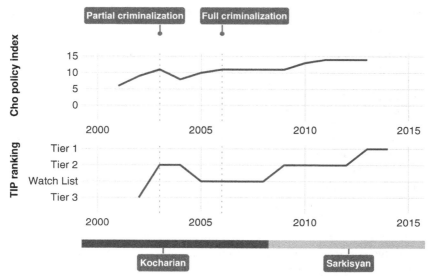

FIGURE 8.1. Overview of Armenia TIP tiers, criminalization, governments, and the 3P Anti-Trafficking Policy Index.

took longer for the government to prioritize the issue. Cooperation with ... s remained close. The willingness in 2009 of a new deputy ... to invest himself in the issue further facilitated coopera-... rmenia reached Tier 1, where it has remained since.

... Armenia demonstrates that tier ratings are useful tools, ... these ratings can drive progress, that government con-... tiers was often related to concerns about image and ... that these concerns opened up opportunities for close ... ement. This underscores the basic argument of score-... namely that reputational concerns catalyze other forms ... also shows the value of good working relationships and of indirect augmentation of scorecard pressure through collaboration with civil society and IGOs. Finally, it illustrates how the TIP Report facilitates information gathering, which can focus attention and contribute to changes in domestic practices.

From Legislation to Institution Building to Norms

US scorecard diplomacy has had a heavy hand in pushing for anti-TIP policy. In April 2003, Armenia amended its criminal code to include trafficking for sexual exploitation. The TIP Report was cataclysmic, a fact stressed by local NGOs, IGOs, and government officials.[2] An IOM official noted that

Everything began in 2001, when [the IOM] met 59 victims of trafficking, discussed their cases, and notified the Armenian government. But the government determined that there was no trafficking in Armenia and that it was too early to talk about "modern slavery" ... It was only after the US State Department's report that the government decided to take action and to work with the IOM.[3]

The US continued to play a strong background role in legislative reforms, sending a legal advisor to work on the law and offering direct – and often well-received – advice on the wording of the evolving legislation. At other times the US worked primarily through the Organization for Security and Co-operation in Europe (OSCE), which it funded to analyze the legislative gaps.[4] For several years the embassy pushed for full criminalization and stricter penalties. The eventual strengthening of penalties can be linked directly to interactions with the US about tier ratings and criticisms in the US TIP Report.[5] By funding the OSCE legislative assistance efforts and sending a resident legal advisor, the US advised on the substance of legislative reforms. Parliament amended the Criminal Code again in June 2006, following much of the US advice provided through the OSCE and other channels.[6]

The embassy continued to pressure the government to pass and fund a new action plan, and the US legal advisor played a significant role in its final formulation.[7] However, major obstacles to progress included official complicity in trafficking. In several cases the government was slow to prosecute suspected officials. The US had to push hard to get the government to allocate resources to the problem. An internal political crisis in 2008 slowed progress further.[8] Fortunately, a reliable interlocutor arose with the new Deputy Prime Minister, Armen Gevorgian, who also became chairman of the newly established Ministerial Council to Combat Trafficking and with whom the embassy had good relations.[9] He was able to magnify the message of scorecard diplomacy within the administration. Meanwhile, the embassy funded programs to strengthen

---

[2] Hovsepian 2002, BBC Summary of World Broadcasts 2004.
[3] Eghiazaryan 2005.
[4] 06YEREVAN761, 04YEREVAN1344.
[5] See for example 06YEREVAN761.
[6] 06YEREVAN960.
[7] 06YEREVAN761, 07YEREVAN106, 07YEREVAN1437.
[8] 08YEREVAN555, 09YEREVAN135.
[9] 09YEREVAN865.

law enforcement responses to trafficking, including separate grants for training in victim referral and training in investigating trafficking cases. By 2009, more vigorous prosecutions were starting and the embassy welcomed a "new level of maturity and willingness by Armenian law enforcement and the judiciary to address the trafficking issue seriously."[10]

While far from complete, progress has been remarkable. Showing sustained progress, in June 2015 a new law established standard procedures for the identification, support, protection, and reintegration of suspected and identified trafficking victims.

Scorecard diplomacy also encouraged domestic institution building. The embassy and other international actors advised the government to reorganize its administration regarding TIP policy. In October 2002, the prime minister created a government commission to address TIP and design an action plan including adding new anti-TIP provisions into the criminal code. The Commission agreed to use the anti-TIP website that the US funded. Showing the effect of the information gathering incentives of the TIP Report and the reporting requirements to the US embassy, the Commission held meetings every year to discuss the US TIP Report, which US personnel sometimes attended, and government agencies were asked to report their TIP news to the US embassy.[11] In February 2005, the Inter-Agency Anti-Trafficking Commission meeting was timed right as the embassy had to file its annual update to Washington. The participants, who included representatives from several ministries, were encouraged to send the US embassy a detailed summary of their anti-trafficking work before the TIP filing deadline. But while motivated by the TIP Report, the meeting was not just an empty show for the US. When the discussions revealed a lack of inter-agency communication, a representative of Armenian law-enforcement recommended that permanent staff be assigned under the Commission to improve its effectiveness. Embassy officials assessed that the TIP reporting requirement was "serving as a catalyst for interagency anti-TIP cooperation and ... setting the Commission up as a more effective tool in coordinating the [government] efforts on fighting TIP."[12]

Scorecard diplomacy also enabled the embassy to pressure the government to increase the commission's influence. After repeated US efforts, the commission was elevated to a council with more decision-making powers. The embassy also successfully pushed for the appointment of

[10] 09YEREVAN494.
[11] 04YEREVAN1344, 06YEREVAN214, 06YEREVAN761, *AZG Daily* 2003a.
[12] 06YEREVAN214.

a specific chairperson, and through numerous meetings with interlocutors, who on US urging took the issue to the prime minister, succeeded in getting approval of budget requests for TIP policies. The US also funded official travel to destination countries to facilitate cooperation with these countries and the creation of a training manual for the diplomatic core about how to work with victims. It also conducted an anti-trafficking seminar for judges, prosecutors, investigators, and police, and awarded other capacity-building grants.[13]

Furthermore, scorecard diplomacy contributed to a change in domestic norms and the mindset of Armenian officials. From the early years, the embassy stressed the need for Armenia to "take ownership" of the issue. Eventually, this began to happen. As the Deputy Prime Minister noted in late 2009, "mentalities" about trafficking had begun to change for the better, and US efforts had brought the issue to the fore: "it wasn't the case four years ago that trafficking was so frequently discussed in the government," he said.[14]

Armenia exemplifies how the TIP Report can spread information about practices in countries. In 2007, one of the embassy's TIP interlocutors asked the embassy for feedback on a Ministry of Foreign Affairs report comparing Armenia's policies with the reports for Azerbaijan, Turkey, and Georgia, "highlighting differences in the three countries' performance which seemed decisive in Armenia's neighbors being graded higher than Armenia" so they could target their efforts on those areas where Armenia was deficient.[15]

Tiers as Tools

The tiers meant a lot to the government and the embassy used them as a tool to spur concerns about reputation and subsequent action. For example, in February 2004 the US Deputy Chief of Mission met with the Deputy Foreign Minister Tatoul Margarian, who oversees the Interagency Commission, and stressed that Armenia's tier would depend on its arrests, investigations and other activities. The embassy continued to issue "demarches on Armenia's shaky Tier II status," and noted that they were watching the issue very closely, and repeatedly stressed what had to

---

[13] 06YEREVAN1548, 07YEREVAN1437, 08YEREVAN555, 09YEREVAN135, 06YEREVAN1548, 06YEREVAN1667, 05YEREVAN1387, 06YEREVAN895, 07YEREVAN250
[14] 04YEREVAN314, 09YEREVAN865
[15] 07YEREVAN888.

be done to retain Tier 2 status.[16] After the downgrade to the Watch List in 2005, the embassy explained privately to the Deputy Foreign Minister that it would be required to issue an interim report and would be "looking for significant progress to avoid slippage into Tier 3."[17] In 2006, the embassy continued threatening a return to a Tier 3 rating: "Post delivered a major push on trafficking in persons this week, meeting a number of senior government officials to discuss the [government]'s anti-trafficking efforts. In each meeting, we delivered a strong message: Armenia risks another year on the Tier 2 Watch List, or worse."[18] In the fall of 2006, the embassy even referred in a cable to its "anti-TIP blitz," and noted the embassy's "strong interventions with the [government]." It also speculated on the appointment of a new Deputy Prime Minister and notes that "[i]f he is appointed, we will engage with him heavily to ensure he understands the importance of his role [on TIP policy] – and the consequences to Armenia's TIP rating, should he fail to take it seriously."[19]

The Central Role of Reputational Concerns

The government was candid about its motivation to improve its tier rating. The concerns were partly rooted in material concerns. While officials never discussed assistance in any of the available cables, a former US ambassador recounted that "the threat to assistance was taken very serious by us and by the Armenians."[20] Local Armenian media speculated that the threat of sanctions could have spurred the government to create the TIP commission.[21]

Concern was more explicitly focused on Armenia's image. The head of the Armenian government's Migration and Refugees Department told local media that Armenia's Tier 3 rating in the first 2002 report was "like a cold shower" that shocked the government into action.[22] Image concern was on display as he continued, "It is clear to the world that in Armenia, not only do we understand the importance of fighting trafficking, we also take certain effective steps."[23] He noted specifically Armenia's desire for "integration into European structures." Other officials echoed this

[16] 04YEREVAN562, 04YEREVAN1344.
[17] 05YEREVAN986.
[18] 06YEREVAN1548.
[19] 07YEREVAN106.
[20] Ordway interview.
[21] No author 2003.
[22] 04YEREVAN1639
[23] No author 2015.

sentiment directly to US officials, saying that Armenia was "anxious to portray itself as an ally to UN and other International arenas in this fight,"[24] and that they hoped for US support in Armenia's efforts to join the UN Commission on Crime Prevention and Criminal Justice.

Further evidence of Armenia's concern for reputation was how the government saw the tier rating as an issue of status. Even in the early years, officials compared Armenia's rating to countries such as Azerbaijan, Russia, and Belarus.[25] When Armenia remained on the Watch List in 2006, the Deputy Foreign Minister specifically inquired why Azerbaijan had moved off the Watch List.[26] Another example was mentioned above, when, in 2007, the government drew up a detailed report to compare Armenia's report with that of Azerbaijan, Turkey, and Georgia.

Concern with image also manifested itself in officials' repeated practice of agreeing privately with the US while publicly criticizing the report. The 2006 report "touched a nerve," and the government dismissed its accuracy in public and President Kocharian called a high-level meeting to discuss the issue. Meanwhile, privately officials remained accepting and appreciative of the embassy's legal advice. The embassy commented that "[t]he deputy minister's lack of complaint behind closed doors illustrates a larger phenomenon whereby the government has criticized the TIP Report's methodology in public, but indicated in private that it takes the rating seriously."[27]

Finally, illustrating how repeated grading stimulates the "status maintenance" mechanism, Armenia has sought to keep the Tier 1 rating earned in 2013. In 2015 the media discussed the report at length, stressing that "Armenia has maintained its Tier I status for a third year in a row," and once again stressing the reputation-as-image concern, continuing: "Armenia is among just 31 countries out of 188 to have achieved Tier I status."[28]

ISRAEL: NOT REALLY ABOUT THE MONEY

Israel is primarily a destination country for men and women subjected to forced labor and sex trafficking. Low-skilled workers arrive for temporary manual jobs from Asia, Eastern Europe, and West Africa. Women

---

[24] 04YEREVAN1639
[25] 03YEREVAN1214.
[26] 06YEREVAN761
[27] 06YEREVAN836
[28] No author 2015.

from Eastern Europe, Uzbekistan, China, Ghana, and other places arrive on tourist visas to work in prostitution, but become victims of trafficking. Foreign workers sometimes pay as much as $20,000 to secure jobs, which leads to forced labor situations. Figure 8.2 overviews the basic data for Israel. While it has not made as much progress as Armenia, it now retains a Tier 1 rating.

This case illustrates many of the key mechanisms of scorecard diplomacy. The US TIP Report ratcheted government attention to human trafficking in Israel. Once the report shone the spotlight on Israel, the government convened committees and seminars to examine the issue. The attention led to policy changes that increased efforts to fight trafficking: new committees, a formal anti-TIP coordinator, comprehensive anti-trafficking legislation that included a focus on labor trafficking, and a national action plan.

Foremost, Israel illustrates how countries are not simply driven by economic concerns but by concerns about image and status. Israeli officials were strongly motivated by image concerns. Officials were ashamed that Israel was grouped with less socially desirable states and referred directly to international image and status. They expressed desire to obtain a better rating, even when sanctions were not looming.

Finally, the case also illustrates how scorecard diplomacy empowers other actors. Israeli NGOs and others used the report as an opportunity

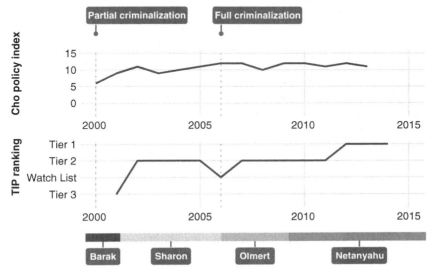

FIGURE 8.2. Overview of Israel TIP tiers, criminalization, governments, and the 3P Anti-Trafficking Policy Index.

to criticize the government. An Israeli scholar has underscored that: "[The NGOs] ... brought in the State Department to pressure the Israeli government."[29]

Progress After the Shock

Although pressures to combat TIP were present already in the late 1990s, despite criticism from organizations like Amnesty International, inaction persisted. In June 2000 the Knesset amended a 1997 prostitution law to prohibit the buying or selling of persons, or forcing a person to leave their country of residence to engage in prostitution, but a commission of inquiry into trafficking held only two sessions before its six-month mandate expired. NGOs criticized the government's lack of response.[30]

Scorecard diplomacy was key in boosting attention TIP. After the TIP Report rated Israel a Tier 3 in 2001, concrete steps followed. The Internal Security Minister held an emergency conference "on setting the matter as a top police priority."[31] The government quickly got to work on improving the rating.[32] The Knesset summoned the committee of inquiry into the trafficking of women, and the Minister of Public Security initiated a seminar on trafficking, including participants from numerous ministries, law enforcement, NGOs, and the Knesset. Many sources attribute the changes in attention to the US report.[33]

Policy changes also followed. The Attorney-General Elyalkim Rubinstein called for a crackdown on trafficking in women, charging that law enforcement officials are not doing their job.[34] In 2003, the government established the Border Police Ramon Unit to patrol along the Egypt–Israel border, and Israel passed the Criminal Organizations Bill, which facilitated the prosecution and punishment of key members of several organized TIP operations. In January 2004 in Belarus, the Israeli Police conducted the first-ever joint investigation with a foreign police force on trafficking of women.[35] Following US pressure, in February

---

[29] Efrat 2012, 218.
[30] Friedman 2001.
[31] Gilbert 2001a.
[32] Zacharia 2001.
[33] Mena Report 2002, Zacharia and Kopf 2002, Lee 2014.
[34] Marrache 2001.
[35] 05TELAVIV1679_a, 05TELAVIV1336_a, 05TELAVIV1337_a.

2004 the government opened the first shelter for trafficking victims using US funds.[36]

The government also set about changing legislation, but this took longer. Frequent elections interfered, and by 2006 there were fears that Israel would be downgraded. The embassy met with high-level officials like Foreign Minister Livni, Justice Minister Ramon, and Defense Minister Peretz, who also headed the Labor Party. Meanwhile, more than 3,000 Jews worldwide signed a petition calling for the government to stamp out the practice of human trafficking and brought this before Prime Minister Olmert to coincide with the release of the TIP Report.[37]

When the report downgraded Israel to the Watch List, the media covered it extensively. Some officials protested that Israel had made a significant effort, but the US ambassador cited legislation against labor trafficking as a *sine qua non* for an upgrade. The US also awarded an anti-trafficking award to activist Rachel Gershuni, who until then had been an informal TIP coordinator only.[38] The award led to the formalization of her role.

The demotion accelerated the issue. June 2006 was packed with meetings on the legislation with Minister of Industry, Trade, and Labor and Shas Party Chairman Eliyahu Yishai and others. The ambassador also spoke with Knesset Speaker Dalia Itzik who promised to take up TIP funding in the new budget.[39] US Attorney General Alberto Gonzales met the Israeli Minister of Justice Haim Ramon and expressed concern that Israel was "trending in the wrong direction" in its handling of trafficking issues, specifically citing the lack of legislation to outlaw labor trafficking. He also made the same point directly with Prime Minister Olmert and was assured that the bill would progress soon.[40] Yet, progress was not easy; Livni explained that political "turmoil" had impeded attention to TIP. Nonetheless, the US pushed repeatedly for attention to the legislation against labor trafficking, linking Israel's demotion to the Watch List to lack of effort on labor trafficking.[41]

July and August were equally intensive with meetings. The ambassador continued discussions with Itzik, who kept the ambassador abreast

---

[36] 07TELAVIV1672, 07TELAVIV599, and Alon 2002.
[37] 06TELAVIV1932, 06TELAVIV1984, 06TELAVIV2072.
[38] 06TELAVIV2157, 06TELAVIV2226, 06TELAVIV1652.
[39] 07TELAVIV2413.
[40] 06TELAVIV2620.
[41] 06TELAVIV2618, 06TELAVIV1923, 06TELAVIV1945, 06TELAVIV1980, 06TELAVIV2413, 06TELAVIV2784, 06TELAVIV3785, 06TELAVIV3843, 06TELAVIV2620, 06TELAVIV2621.

of Knesset anti-trafficking actions, including two new laws to strengthen enforcement and provide legal aid to trafficking victims.[42] In the fall, the ambassador met with Acting Minister of Justice Meir Sheetrit and "stressed the importance of including assistance for legal support for victims of labor trafficking in new legislation now before the Knesset."[43] To gain support across the political spectrum, the US ambassador also met with Likud leader Netanyahu, who pledged to support the legislation.[44] In October 2006 the new trafficking law passed, adding labor trafficking to the definition of trafficking.[45] NGOs noted the scorecard downgrade had spurred change. In December 2007 Israel also drafted a national plan as recommended in the TIP Report. The Knesset subcommittee on women met repeatedly to review the US TIP Report.[46]

As in any country, problems persist, but Israel has steadily improved and since 2012 has maintained Tier 1 status.

The Importance of Image, Not Just Money

When the first US TIP Report came out in 2001, Israel was one of 23 countries given the harshest rating, showing that the report did not spare allies. This shocked many in Israel as the rating garnered considerable coverage in *The Jerusalem Post*. In addition, NGOs referenced the report to address the government. For example, in 2001, Kav LaOved of the NGO Workers' Hot Line issued a statement in *The Jerusalem Post* saying, "We hope that this report will cause the Israeli authorities to understand the seriousness of the problem and begin to treat the phenomenon with the seriousness it deserves."[47] In later years, the rating continued to get media attention.[48] Thus, third parties boosted the government's exposure to poor TIP ratings. Furthermore, Israel's close relationship and identification with the US increased the normative salience of the ratings.

Israeli officials were foremost worried about Israel's international image. Although the immediate response to the initial 2001 Tier 3 was for the government to call an "[u]rgent meeting due to concern about

---

[42] 06TELAVIV2784, 06TELAVIV3482.

[43] 06TELAVIV3785.

[44] 06TELAVIV3843.

[45] 05TELAVIV1336, 05TELAVIV1337, 06TELAVIV914, 06TELAVIV915, 06TELAVIV1923, 06TELAVIV2621, 06TELAVIV3482.

[46] 07TELAVIV930, 08TELAVIV1578.

[47] Zacharia 2001.

[48] 05TELAVIV669, 06TELAVIV2072, 06TELAVIV2157, 06TELAVIV2239, 07TELAVIV1727, 07TELAVIV3314, 08TELAVIV1185, 09TELAVIV1564.

economic sanctions following the publication of the US State department report, that includes Israel in a 'blacklist' of countries that traffic in persons,"[49] this threat was not real. Indeed, in 2001, any threat of sanctions was still two years away due to the rules of the US legislation at the time, and the US president would have to make a special determination on the matter, providing yet another safeguard against sanctions coming into play. Thus, the threat of sanctions, if anything, was more stigmatizing, than financially consequential.

Indeed, interviews show it was the shame of blacklisting rather than fear of sanctions that motivated Israeli officials. For example, Zehava Gal-On, who eventually became Chair of the Knesset Subcommittee on Trafficking in Women, noted that "[t]here was no real concern about economic sanctions – it was a matter of image and our desire to be an enlightened country." Rachel Gershuni, who later became the formal TIP coordinator, compared the initial TIP Report to "fireworks," and noted, "You know how much Israelis care about how we look [in the eyes of foreigners]." When asked specifically about whether Israel's reaction was about sanctions or image, she replied, "Israelis feel isolated – [t]he world is against us. We want to belong to the enlightened nations. The threat of economic sanctions came up only in 2003, [but even before that] – we didn't want to look bad. We felt very bad about our bottom ranking."[50] This comment is noteworthy because it also points out Israel's general desire for international recognition, which makes it more sensitive to normative criticisms.

Furthermore, once Israel moved to Tier 2, concerns did not abate just because the threat of sanctions was removed.[51] Efforts were explicitly designed to move Israel to Tier 1. Officials wanted Israel to be seen as a top performer, a sentiment also often expressed in private meetings. In a meeting of the Knesset Subcommittee on Trafficking in Women, Gal-On was frustrated about Israel's record on forced labor and foreign workers and said: "It is possible that were it not for the forced labor issue *we would be in Tier 1 ... [T]he TIP Report raises the need for some new thinking by the [government]*. We will have to give thought to the question of incriminating clients of the sex industry and the issue of sex service advertising and we will be doing that in the next parliamentary session [emphasis added]."[52]

---

[49] Protocol no. 14 of the Parliamentary Inquiry Committee, cited in Efrat 2012, 204.
[50] Interviews with Galon, Gershuni, and Schonmann by Asif Efrat and cited in Efrat 2012, 204.
[51] Alon 2002.
[52] 08TELAVIV1578.

Clearly, Israel's reaction was not just about the threat of sanctions or Israel's special relationship with the US.[53] Rather, in numerous interviews, Israeli officials said they feared the report undermined Israel's quest for international legitimacy and "clashed with its self-identity."[54] Officials saw TIP as important to Israel's "society and values," as Foreign Minister Tzipi Livni told the US attorney general.[55] Similarly, the Head of the Foreign Ministry's Human Rights department said that the international repercussions of the report for Israel are "severe and steps must be taken to remove Israel from the *unflattering* category [emphasis added]."[56]

In passing the legislation, officials noted the importance of Israel being seen as conforming to global norms. Thus Law and Justice Committee Chairman Menachem Ben-Sasson said the law placed "Israel in line with the world's most enlightened nations."[57] Indeed, comparisons with other countries remained important. In 2008, during the Knesset subcommittee meeting devoted to discussing the TIP Report one NGO official questioned how Holland and Germany could be Tier 1 – ahead of Israel – given their legalization of prostitution.[58] And as Deputy Foreign Minister Danny Ayalon said in 2009 to the Knesset subcommittee analyzing the TIP Report, Israel did not want to be "lumped" with pariah states, worrying about the "troubling political implications" of receiving the same tier rating as "states like Afghanistan, Jordan, and Botswana."[59]

Politicians boasted publicly after Israel rose to Tier 1 in 2012, showing reputational value. In an article in *The Jerusalem Post*, headlined "Israel leading world in prevention and reduction of human trafficking," both the president and prime minister "took pride" in Israel's leadership on this, with Prime Minister Netanyahu connecting Israel's fight against trafficking directly to Israel's identity by invoking Moses as a forerunner of anti-slavery laws. Furthermore, showing how good ratings can become a matter of professional pride, Justice Minister Livni credited the success to the Justice Ministry and its "dedicated people" who fight this problem.[60]

---

[53] As reported in local media. See 05TELAVIV669.
[54] See Asif Efrat's chapter in his book, *Governing Guns, Preventing Plunder*, which is based on interviews done by Efrat that he shared with the author. Efrat 2012, 206.
[55] 06TELAVIV2618.
[56] Gilbert 2001a.
[57] Alon 2006.
[58] 08TELAVIV1578.
[59] 09TELAVIV1564.
[60] Cashman 2014.

ZIMBABWE: LOW SENSITIVITY TO
REPUTATIONAL COSTS

Zimbabwe is a source, transit, and destination country for men, women, and children and experiences both sex and labor trafficking. Children are subjected to forced labor in the agricultural and mining sectors. Women and girls suffer in domestic servitude. Many migrants to South Africa suffer abuse from trafficking on farms, at construction sites, in factories, and mines, and victims from elsewhere also transit through Zimbabwe to South Africa. Figure 8.3 overviews the abysmal data for Zimbabwe.

Scorecard diplomacy has had very limited success in producing anti-TIP progress in Zimbabwe. The US's poor relationship with the Zimbabwean government, combined with the governments' lack of concern for human rights abuses and the many sanctions it already faced, meant the government had little concern about its tier rating. The US embassy, faced with what it considered more important political priorities in Zimbabwe, resisted placing too much pressure on the TIP issue and fueling anti-US propaganda.

The case illustrates how the near complete lack of facilitating conditions undermines any attempts to elicit reputational concerns and bring about change. Normative salience was low, as Zimbabwe did not identify with the international norms or with the messenger. Instrumental salience was low as the country was already sanctioned. Thus, Zimbabwe was not sensitive to reputational concerns, and the result has been only minor progress.

Poor Relationships and Low Priority

Before the Unity government of 2009, there was little direct communication on TIP; even Zimbabwe's first downgrade to the Watch List in 2004 solicited little reaction. The government did not provide any information for the interim assessment and embassy staff could not secure meetings with officials, whom the embassy said were "suspicious of foreign inquiries and afraid of disclosing information that might be prejudicial to the [government] if publicized."[61] The embassy feared that too much pressure on TIP would interfere with other US priorities in Zimbabwe and that information on TIP was too anecdotal to make credible judgments.[62]

---

[61] 04HARARE1878.
[62] 04HARARE691.

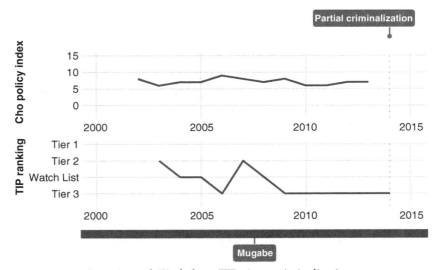

FIGURE 8.3. Overview of Zimbabwe TIP tiers, criminalization, governments, and the 3P Anti-Trafficking Policy Index.

After the drop to Tier 3 in 2006, Zimbabwe quickly rejected the report, dismissing it as "a ploy by the Americans to vilify Zimbabwe."[63] Political and economic crises, poor capacity and resources, poor data, rampant corruption, and official complicity in trafficking continually hampered scorecard diplomacy.[64]

After the Unity government in 2009, the government became more responsive to a variety of actors, including the US, pressuring it on TIP legislation.[65] South Africa encouraged Zimbabwe to pass anti-trafficking legislation in advance of the 2010 World Cup. The attorney general was surprised that "even Mozambique" had introduced anti-trafficking legislation, and began to promote its passage in Zimbabwe.[66] The US embassy supplied draft laws and helped a top official prepare briefings for the prime minister. However, other actors remained in the forefront. An IOM consultant worked with the government on the TIP law,[67] and South Africa also pushed for criminalization of TIP. The draft legislation was supposedly finalized and introduced to the Council of Ministers for

[63] Mwakalyelye 2006, *Africa News* 2006.
[64] 08HARARE1030.
[65] 09HARARE650.
[66] 09HARARE678.
[67] 09HARARE678.

debate in September 2010. Yet, while there were efforts in 2011–2012 to move the bill along, the Ministry of Justice publicly denied the existence of a trafficking problem and the bill languished. The government didn't issue temporary regulations until January 2014,[68] and parliament passed these only in March 2014.[69] The final text was unsatisfactory, however, because it defined TIP as a movement-based crime and didn't define "exploitation" properly according to international law. The act did establish a committee to draw up an action plan, but little action has followed.[70] Institution building or socialization around TIP issues has also faltered. Any institutional steps, such as the inter-ministerial task force, fell short due to lack of resources. NGOs and IGOs provide almost all services.[71] The government has persisted in denying the existence of any significant problem.

Thus, Zimbabwe has been poor ground for scorecard diplomacy. The ratings don't stoke reputational concerns, and the US has mostly supported other actors to lead the efforts. The primary actor has been the IOM,[72] supplemented by UNICEF and also many local and international NGOs. Illustrating the model of scorecard diplomacy, however, IOM efforts have often been supported by US funding.[73] Together these actors have provided the bulk of victim services, training, and awareness campaigns. The US embassy has operated in the background by cooperating with and funding the NGOs and IGOs, and helping to organize meetings between stakeholders.[74]

JAPAN: THE IMPORTANCE OF CONSISTENCY

The US has long criticized the Japanese government for its Technical Intern Training Program (TITP), which recruit migrant workers, mainly from Asia. Participants pay up to $10,000 to gain entry to the program, but then face poor working conditions and contracts that bar them from leaving. The US assesses that many are subjected to forced labor. The sex industry and the "entertainment visa" the government issued in the

---

[68] ZimSitRep_J 2014.
[69] Mbiba 2014.
[70] ZimSitRep_J 2015.
[71] 09HARARE177.
[72] 09HARARE177.
[73] 06HARARE374.
[74] 06HARARE1490.

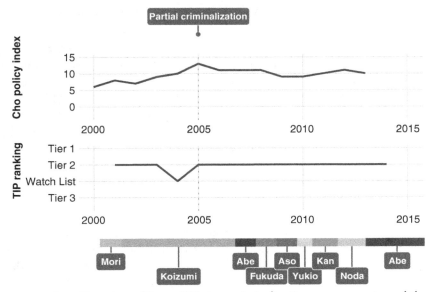

FIGURE 8.4. Overview of Japan TIP tiers, criminalization, governments, and the 3P Anti-Trafficking Policy Index.

past was also a big concern. Japan remains a destination, source, and transit country for men, women, and children subjected to sex trafficking. Traffickers use fake marriages to bring in women to the sex industry using debt bondage.[75] Figure 8.4 overviews the data for Japan, showing its stagnation since it's been stuck on Tier 2.

Japan initially associated great shame with its placement on the Tier 2 Watch List in 2004, comparing itself with other countries and asking how to improve. The rating motivated the government to fight trafficking, but when they fell short and failed to reach Tier 1 as hoped, the government became frustrated. The State Department's refusal to upgrade Japan caused tensions and eventually Japan resigned itself to a Tier 2 rating, satisfied that the US would not dare repeat a downgrade. Little progress has occurred since these early years.

The case of Japan shows that, while difficult, the US can influence even a rich peer-country, but that such relationships are vulnerable to political pressures and other factors. The case demonstrates how the clear concern of reputation led to policy changes, and, conversely, how a lack of pressure led to a lack of concern and lack of policy changes.

[75] 2016 TIP Report.

Initial Results

To see that variation in responses to ratings from one country to the other is not merely due to underlying differences in countries, it's instructive to examine how Japan's response varied with the credibility of US scorecard diplomacy over time.

Japan was first placed on the TIP Report in 2001 as a Tier 2 country. It stayed there until 2004 when for the first time the new Watch List designation was used in the report. That year Japan was the only developed nation to be placed on the Watch List, a point not lost on the media.[76] Illustrating how third parties can augment the reputational pressure of scorecard diplomacy, the drop was followed in 2005 by a similarly critical ILO report, Human Trafficking for Sexual Exploitation in Japan, highlighting Japan as a destination country with most of the victims ending up in Japan's sex and entertainment industry.[77] A newspaper headline noted, "Trafficking blots nation's repute," and linked the ILO report with the earlier US rating.[78] That summer the UN Commission on Human Rights added its criticisms.[79]

It's important to understand that in 2004 the US TIP Office dropped Japan to the Watch List despite strong political opposition from various US interests. Indeed, this move surprised many and was only possible after extensive maneuvering by the US human trafficking ambassador at the time, John Miller. In an interview Miller notes the regional bureaus were counting on the US ambassador to Japan to oppose a drop and thus protect any interference with other interests in Japan. Miller then went to Japan and invited Nancy Kassebaum, the ambassador's wife, to a meeting with local NGOs. "You couldn't listen to these NGOs without getting upset," Miller said, "and I told her what I was doing and said it would be good if we could get the embassy to support putting Japanese on the Watch List. [The US ambassador] Howard Baker to his credit actually supported the rating. It stunned the regional bureau."

Before US pressure, Japan had been skeptical of trafficking as a problem.[80] Japan had a huge commercial sex industry entangled with organized crime and facilitated by the official "entertainment visa."[81] The

---

[76] Capobianco 2013.
[77] International Labour Organization n.d.
[78] Adelstein and Shimbun 2004.
[79] Ito 2005.
[80] Onishi 2005.
[81] Kaplan and Dubro 2003, 239.

government also ran a highly exploitative foreign trainee program.[82] Thus, Japan had been numb to the Tier 2 rating until that point, even when it was one of the very few advanced industrialized countries with such a low rating. Indeed, after Japan had been rated Tier 2 in 2001, Human Rights Watch said it deserved a Tier 3 because it was refusing to acknowledge the problem.[83] The drop, however, not only stunned the US regional bureau, it also received coverage in Japan, with the *Japan Times* noting that Japan had been "blasted over human trafficking."[84] The rest of the world also took note. The *Agence France Presse* called it a "damning report."[85]

Only days after the report, Japan's justice ministry announced it would submit a bill to an extraordinary session of parliament and pass it by March, in time for the next TIP Report update.[86] Shortly after releasing the report, the embassy held a symposium jointly with the NGO Vital Voices, and the International Labour Organization that was attended by officials of the National Police Agency and the Justice Ministry.[87] Speaking at the symposium, former Justice Minister Mayumi Moriyama criticized the report for failing to account for Japan's past efforts.[88] Nonetheless, Japan soon established the Inter-Ministerial Liaison Committee and the Anti-Trafficking Task Force, which, by December 2004, produced the National Action Plan of Measures to Combat Trafficking in Persons. Out of this came revisions to Japan's Penal Code, the Law on the Control and Improvement of Amusement and Business, and the Immigration Control and Refugee Recognition Act, all in 2005.[89] Another big change that year was the tightening of eligibility criteria for Japan's entertainer visa, which the US had said was being misused for TIP. The efforts were substantial: The Director of the Ministry of Foreign Affairs's International Organized Crime Division said that he had "never seen the Japanese government undertake such a concerted effort across so many different bureaucracies and agencies."[90]

Advocates for trafficking victims attributed Japan's new impetus to acknowledge the TIP problem to scorecard diplomacy.[91] One NGO

[82] Ozawa 2014.
[83] Human Rights Watch 2001.
[84] *The Japan Times* 2004.
[85] *Agence France Presse* 2004.
[86] *Agence France Presse* 2004.
[87] *The Daily Yomiuri* 2004.
[88] Matsubara 2004.
[89] 09TOKYO1185, Capobianco 2013, 28.
[90] 09TOKYO1185_a.
[91] Onishi 2005. See also *The Japan Times* 2004a.

director said, "The NGOs are becoming more vocal ... But the primary motivation for the Japanese government is the US pressure."[92]

Concerns for Reputation

Japan's reaction was rooted in reputational concerns raised by US score-card diplomacy. In March 2003 the US anti-TIP Ambassador Miller visited Japan and was cited by the media as very critical of Japan's anti-TIP efforts and appealing to Japan's image as "leading democracy."[93] Already at that time, Japan's performance was interpreted in relation to its international peers, with the media reporting that "[a] US report on human trafficking has labeled Japan as the worst industrialized country in terms of measures aimed at preventing the trafficking of women."[94]

The drop to the Watch List was, by some accounts, interpreted as a "global humiliation."[95] It hit Japan at a time when it was keen to elevate its international status and gain "political acceptance commensurate with its growing economic power."[96] Some scholars have argued this was important as Japan was seeking to normalize its military status, to which end it also agreed to participate in the US-led war in Iraq by deploying it Self-Defense Forces, in return for US support for a Japanese seat on the UN security council.[97]

When the rating dropped, the *Japan Times* noted that, "[s]till smarting from a sharp rebuke by the US, the government is studying ways to implement sweeping changes to the Penal Code or the enactment of a new law to combat human trafficking and protect victims, government officials said Saturday."[98] A later article noted, "[t]he US report shocked Japan,"[99] a sentiment also echoed by a staff member of the Asia-Pacific Human Rights Center in Osaka, who was quoted as saying that "[t]he Japanese government was very shocked to know that they were placed on that list."[100] Japanese media described the government's actions as "efforts to be seen to be curbing human trafficking."[101]

[92] Silver 2006.
[93] Yuriko-Thomas 2004.
[94] *The Japan Times* 2004d.
[95] Capobianco 2013, 13.
[96] Katzenstein 1996, 42, Friman 2008.
[97] Shubert 2004, Williams 2005.
[98] *The Japan Times* 2004c.
[99] Johnston 2004.
[100] Silver 2006.
[101] *The Japan Times* 2004a. Most stories about the government's actions mentioned the US report as the impetus. *The Japan Times* 2004b, 2005.

When Japan changed its policies, all these actions were detailed in a glossy brochure produced by the Ministry of Foreign Affairs in English,[102] signaling that concern for reputation was a key driver for Japan.

Inconsistent Pressure

But as US resolve weakened, so did Japan's responsiveness. After Japan was raised to Tier 2, it was uncomfortable being the only OECD country at this tier. The director of the Organized Crime Division said that Japan was very disappointed with its continued Tier 2 rating and that official displeasure was expressed at much higher levels in the government this year.[103] Officials argued that worse countries were rated Tier 1 – even comparing Japan's statistics to those of a G8 country rated Tier 1, which, Japan stressed, the report criticized for suspending sentences in all but 31 percent of its trafficking convictions.[104] The Vice Foreign Minister said the Tier 2 rating was "embarrassing" and undermined domestic NGO efforts, and accused the US of "moving the goal posts."[105] US anti-TIP ambassador Mark Lagon arrived in Japan to provide the government with a formal roadmap to Tier 1 status.[106] After Lagon's visit, Japanese and US officials met to go over the roadmap, with the Japanese asking for clarifications about each of the action points in the plan, and also asking whether other Tier 1 countries met all of those.[107] During 2007 officials and the embassy had several discussions on technicalities of this sort, showing just how much attention the Japanese were paying to the US report.

Despite its reticence, Japan continued to try to follow US pressure and the recommendations in the report. In advance of the 2008 report launch, the Japanese Vice Foreign Minister mentioned that Japan was very unhappy about the previous year's TIP Report and expressed strong hope that in the new report Japan would no longer be a Tier 2 country "like Rwanda" but would gain the same status as other countries such as Canada and South Korea.[108] In 2008, after the new Tier 2 rating, the

---

[102] Japan's Actions to Combat Trafficking in Persons, A Prompt and Appropriate Response from a Humanitarian Perspective. Japanese Ministry of Foreign Affairs n.d.
[103] 07TOKYO2788.
[104] 07TOKYO3186.
[105] 07TOKYO2315, 07TOKYO2481, 07TOKYO2788, 07TOKYO5646.
[106] 07TOKYO3186.
[107] 07TOKYO3817.
[108] 08TOKYO1263.

Deputy Vice Foreign Minister called the embassy to object sharply, once again drawing comparisons with Canada and South Korea.[109]

However, local embassy officials and the TIP Office apparently disagreed about how to proceed, with the embassy urging a more "cooperative approach."[110] When this did not happen because the DOS office continued to insist on a more comprehensive anti-TIP law, Japanese officials eventually grew frustrated with US criticism and settled into the Tier 2 rating.[111] Eventually, Japan's cooperation dwindled and US efforts to provide the government with a formal roadmap to Tier 1 status faltered.[112] Since then, Japan's anti-TIP efforts have been lackluster and NGOs report having been unable to garner much attention despite the fact that the US repeatedly called out Japan in the annual TIP Report for its visiting workers' program, in 2014, for example, featuring photos in the report's introduction. Some convicted traffickers receive only fines, and the anti-trafficking legislation remains incomplete.

Yet, despite continued TIP problems in Japan, and although the US has shown in the past that scorecard diplomacy could work there, the US made no headway. The government has largely stopped reacting, and the media does not cover it much anymore either.[113] Why? Because Japan believes that the US will *not* drop it below Tier 2 again. Indeed, while Japan has continued to complain about its Tier 2 rating, the embassy has instead urged "a shift from an adversarial approach to Japan, which now is in danger of backfiring, to a cooperative approach in which the two countries spearhead a new international effort to deal with TIP."[114]

SUMMARY

The cases in this chapter illustrate the most important dynamics of scorecard diplomacy: the impetus of reputational concerns.

The case of Armenia demonstrates how a government's concern about its reputation makes it possible to use grades as tools of influence. From the beginning, the US engaged with high-level officials, who worried about the TIP tier rating and sought information about how to improve it.

[109] 08TOKYO1350.
[110] 09TOKYO1185.
[111] 09TOKYO2309, Jakiel interview.
[112] 07TOKYO3186.
[113] Author's email exchange with Aiki, Lighthouse: Center for Human Trafficking Victims, July 15, 2014.
[114] 09TOKYO1185.

Concrete results often followed discussions.[115] Interestingly, the government showed its concern with its domestic reputation by vigorously attacking the TIP Report in the media while privately cooperating. Thus, concern for reputation opened up deeper diplomatic engagement, eventually leading to meaningful policy change.

The Armenia case also shows that while the government was clearly both sensitive to and exposed to reputational concerns, several obstacles led the government to sometimes deprioritize the problem. These included extensive official complicity in trafficking, poor domestic capacity, and, in 2008, a temporary internal political crisis. These factors were offset by the arrival of a reliable interlocutor and by cooperation with IGOs, especially the OSCE and the IOM, other embassies and local NGOs.

The case of Israel speaks strongly to the idea that countries care about their reputation in terms of their status, standing, and moral legitimacy, and that these concerns are not driven purely by fear of sanctions. As a country often exposed to international criticisms, Israel's desire to project a positive image is heightened, which increases its sensitivity to reputational concerns. Indeed, Israel met all the criteria for being highly normatively sensitive: It cares greatly about its international legitimacy, its ideals align with the international standards, and it identifies with the source of the scorecard diplomacy – in this case the US. Officials responded accordingly. Although slowed by various elections and instability, Israel made steady progress. While Israel was also sensitive to material consequences, officials gave more weight to the concerns about image and reputation, than to concerns about sanctions. Indeed, the drive to earn Tier 1 – not simply stop at Tier II – demonstrated that this was not about sanctions, but about image.

If Armenia and Israel highlight the progress that is possible when scorecard diplomacy boosts reputational concerns, Zimbabwe is the counterpoint: It has not been possible to get the government's attention, nor has the embassy prioritized the issue amidst so many other problems. To try to delegitimize any reputational threats, Zimbabwe dismissed scorecard diplomacy as a political ploy. Whatever progress has occurred has been half-hearted. Clearly, scorecard diplomacy has its limits.

Finally, Japan illustrates both weakness and strength within the same case. It shows the effectiveness of scorecard diplomacy but also the necessity of consistency if scorecard diplomacy is to work. The drop to the Watch List was difficult – indeed politically momentous at the time – but it was also effective, because it showed that the US was serious and

---

[115] 08YEREVAN244.

because Japan was hugely concerned about its reputation. When the US strategy was credible, scorecard diplomacy worked in Japan. Perhaps it could still work. One former TIP Office staffer noted that even today, "[Japan] will basically declare a diplomatic emergency if there is even a whiff that they are going to fall to Tier 2 Watch List. It becomes an issue that is elevated to the secretary of state, who is then confused when a meeting supposed to talk about ballistic missiles suddenly has this TIP issue at the front of it."[116] But scorecard diplomacy will not have much effect in Japan if the US seems unwilling to turn up the pressure again due to other priorities in dealings with Japan. Such weakness undermines scorecard diplomacy, as is the case in other countries where the local embassy, the regional bureaus and the TIP Office disagree on what priority to give the fight against human trafficking.

In closing, it's worth noting that a look at the TIP tier graph for each country reveals a consistent sequencing: criminalization is often preceded by a drop in tier rating. That's not always the case of course, but it's consistent with the statistical findings in Chapter 6 that harsher tiers and downgrades are associated with faster criminalization.

Grades matter.

[116] Anonymous interview.

Conclusion

Reputation and Policy

They did not like to be cast with poisonous snakes.
– John Ordway, Ambassador to Kazakhstan 2004–2008[1]

After Germany threatened Greece with an exit from the Eurozone in the Fall 2015 bailout negotiations, Jürgen Habermas, an intellectual figurehead of European integration, accused German Chancellor Angela Merkel of "'gambling away' the efforts of previous generations to rebuild the country's postwar reputation."[2] Perhaps Merkel remembered this reaction to her hardline stance on Greece when, in response to the turmoil of the wars in northern Africa and the Middle East, she opened Germany's borders to hundreds of thousands of refugees with her "*Wir schaffen das*" – We can do it. With these words, Merkel may have boosted Germany's international reputation, but domestically her reputation suffered, and her party paid in votes.[3]

In today's information-dense world, governments must constantly worry about how their behaviors are perceived at home and abroad. Poor environmental practices can damage reputations. Thus the *Guardian* asked: "Will Australia continue to sacrifice its international reputation on the altar of coal?"[4] A violent election can undermine a country's reputation as "a safe, stable democracy with a burgeoning economy and good international ties built on commerce and tourism," as Chatham House

---

[1] Ordway interview.
[2] Oltermann 2015.
[3] Bindenagel 2016, Waters 2016.
[4] Readfearn 2015.

lamented in a report about Kenya's 2007 election.[5] Few countries are exempt from concerns about their reputation. Even China worried that its conduct in the South China Sea "could bolster international moves to counter its strategic, political and economic weight."[6] Thus China lobbied other nations heavily ahead of the South China Sea ruling by the Permanent Court of Arbitration in The Hague.[7] Indeed, some countries will go to great lengths to boost their reputations. Brazil, obsessed with its national image, took on the 2016 Olympics in a bid to show the world, in the words of then President Lula da Silva, that "Brazil has left the ranks of second-class countries and turned into a first-class country."[8] Countries and their governments thus worry about their reputation on everything from the environment and business to governance and human rights. This is not new, but it's ever more pressing in the global information society.

Because they worry, governments pay attention when others provide credible and visible information about their performance, especially if that information makes it easy to compare them with other states or track their performance over time. Countries don't like to make news with headlines that they've "tumbled down an international ranking of health services" (Ireland), "plummet[ed] in corruption ranking to among worst in EU" (Spain), "dip[ped] further in global gender equality ladder, second to last in Asean" (Malaysia),[9] or that their press freedom has "[sunk] to new lows in global index" (Hong Kong).[10] It's embarrassing that "America's high school graduates look like other countries' high school dropouts."[11] This book has shown that countries and their leaders worry about their international image or standing, they seek to save face in public, and they rush to take credit for progress. Thus, under the right conditions, countries' concern with their reputation provides an opportunity for others to influence them.

Understanding the nature of influence is the Holy Grail of international relations scholars and policymakers. In our interdependent world, states incur negative spillovers from failures of other states, be it from pollution that has no respect for borders or the flow of people crossing

---

[5] Anyimadu 2013.
[6] Townshend 2015.
[7] Reuters 2016.
[8] Cuadros 2016.
[9] Cullen 2015, *The Local* 2016, *Malay Mail Online* 2014.
[10] Kang-Chung 2015.
[11] Emanuel 2016.

those borders illegally.[12] Finding ways to get governments to deal with such problems is a mounting concern. The old tools of military intervention and sanctions are often less suited to the challenges or are too costly. The logic that states respond foremost to force or material threats might hold in some cases, but not all.[13] The nature of the challenges we face thus forces us to exercise influence more prudently.

This book has explored a subtler method of influence, namely the ability to elicit states' concern about their reputation. Some scholars who conceptualize reputation as "credibility of promises" have dismissed its effects in realms such as human rights or the environment.[14] However, I have defined reputation more broadly as the belief – by citizens, world leaders, and others – about the performance of a state or its elites and about the legitimacy, standing, or identity of the state itself within the global system and the community of states.

While once dismissed, the idea that states might respond to broad reputational concerns is gaining traction. After the creation of the League of Nations, scholars viewed the idea of the "mobilization of shame" as naive.[15] Morgenthau decried the hope in the effectiveness of "world public opinion" as misplaced.[16] Yet even these scholars acknowledged the importance of discourses, norms, and institutions. Since then, scholars increasingly recognize that social pressure can influence states, and a diverse set of theories have developed on transnational actors, shaming, international society, identity, soft power, socialization, and learning, and the broader roles of international law, norms, and institutions.[17] These share a more multidimensional understanding of power as working "in and through social relations."[18]

In this book I have argued that eliciting states' concern for their reputation can be used to influence their behavior. That said, it's important to define the scope of the argument: merely holding states publicly accountable is not a panacea. Some problems, like the Middle East conflict, are not amenable to this sort of pressure. Success depends on a combination of factors, and when a state is not sensitive on a given issue, reputations

[12] Bermeo 2015.
[13] For a discussion of the propensity of international relations to give preeminence to hard power, throughout the twentieth century and even into this one, see Baldwin 2016, Ch. 4.
[14] Mercer 1996, Downs and Jones 2002, S112.
[15] Carr 1942, 51–52.
[16] Morgenthau 1950, 197–206.
[17] Nye 1990.
[18] Barnett and Duvall 2005, 42. Baldwin discusses the many scholars who have advanced a view of power as multidimensional. Baldwin 2016.

won't matter. Provided the right conditions exist, however, eliciting reputational concerns can incentivize states and facilitate other forms of influence. From a policy perspective, appealing to reputation is a relatively low cost strategy that, dollar for dollar, pound for pound, can deliver a remarkable return on investment in terms of results for effort.

The US has exercised such reputation-driven influence through what I call *scorecard diplomacy*, which embeds recurring monitoring and grading of countries in traditional diplomacy. The introduction and Chapter 2 discussed the pathways of influence, and subsequent chapters explored the evidence. Although I've focused on human trafficking, the findings speak to the role of reputation and international relations more broadly. This concluding chapter will therefore focus on three parts.

First, it synthesizes the evidence in this book and considers some possible objections. Next, it discusses what scorecard diplomacy tells us about power and state preferences more generally. Finally, it discusses the findings from a policy perspective and provides suggestions for the use of ratings and rankings more generally.

* * *

EVIDENCE FOR THE CYCLE OF SCORECARD DIPLOMACY

This book has used various methods to examine numerous implications of the argument. What propositions have been supported and how does the evidence stack up? Figure 9.1 sorts the more than 40 findings throughout this book by the steps in the scorecard diplomacy cycle. It lists the evidence associated with each step and indicates the chapters in which the research is located, as well as the methodology used (see code below figure). The scorecard diplomacy cycle is well documented for each step, as I discuss below.

Steps 1–3: Generating Reputational Pressure

Reputational concerns arise in a credible normative environment where information engages multiple actors to pressure governments on the issue. Chapter 3 documented the international normative environment for human trafficking and showed how scorecard diplomacy generated direct and indirect pressure. Survey and interview evidence showed that other actors such as NGOs and IGOs perceived the US as highly active.

Step 1: Public monitoring and grading

- The US TIP report is issued annually and receives considerable attention **(C, Q, I/3)**
- The US specifically designed the policy to be public **(I/1)**
- No evidence of selective report inclusion or ratings **(Q/3)**

1. Public monitoring and grading
2. Ongoing diplomacy and practical assistance
3. Indirect pressure
4. Concern about current reputation and *future* ratings
5. Efforts to improve bad ratings or *maintain* good ones

Step 2: Ongoing diplomacy and practical assistance

- US diplomacy is way more visible than that of other embassies **(Q/3)**
- TIP diplomacy includes extensive meetings at high levels **(Q/3)**
- Sometimes funding is used for institution building **(C/3)**
- More grants have gone to prevention and protection than to prosecution **(Q/3)**
- Sanctions have not really been applied **(Q/3)**

Step 3: Indirect pressure

- Some NGOs use the TIP report to pressure their government **(C, I/4)**
- The US funds NGOs and IGOs to carry out programs aligned with its message **Q, C, I/4)**
- The TIP report attracts media attention **(Q/4)**
- The US facilitates wider cooperation **(C,I/4)**
- NGOs use the TIP report to talk to others **(Q/4)**
- The TIP report informs NGOs **(Q, I, C/4)**
- The TIP hero award can elevate local actors **(C/4)**

Step 4: Concern about current reputation and *future* ratings

- Countries frequently react to the report **(E/5)**
- The most common reaction is cooperation **(E/5)**
- Image-reactions are more common than economic reactions **(E/5)**
- Harsher ratings get more reactions, even if not correlated with aid **(E, Q/5)**
- Reactions to the graded TIP report are far greater than to the non-rated human rights report section on TIP **(E, Q/5)**
- More aid does not correlate with more reactions **(E, Q/5)**
- Countries tend to compare themselves with a geographic or other identity-based peer group **(E, Q/5)**
- Countries that have ratified the Palermo Protocol are more likely to have reactions **(E, Q/ 5)**
- Reactions are more likely when there is more domestic media coverage **(E, Q/5)**
- Officials object more often in public than in private **(E, Q/5)**

Step 5: Efforts to improve bad ratings or *maintain* good ones

- Law enforcement has increased since 2001 **(Q/3)**
- Countries tend to pass laws just in time for the internal reporting deadline for the TIP report **(Q/6)**
- Inclusion in report and tier status correlate with criminalization **(Q/6)**
- Countries that have documented reactions to the TIP report are more likely to criminalize **(Q/6)**
- Countries that receive TIP grants are more likely to criminalize **(Q/7)**
- Countries that criminalize show more sustained changes in prevention and protection **(Q/6)**
- IGOs and NGOs attribute effectiveness to the TIP report **(C/6)**
- NGOs attribute importance and positive influence to the US efforts **(Q/6)**
- US efforts have influenced the content of laws, norms, domestic institutions and implementation **(C/6, 8)**

  Conditioning factors **(C,Q/7)**
  - *Pros*: Strong interlocutors • Economic leverage • Concern with international image • Active third parties • TIP events
  - *Cons*: Official TIP complicity • Government instability • Differing norms • Competing political priorities • Lack of US credibility

FIGURE 9.1. The evidence of the book.
I = interviews, C = case study, S = survey, Q = quantitative analysis, E = embassy cable analysis, # = chapter in this book.

The intensity of face-to-face diplomacy was also striking given the rather low-politics nature of the issue, with embassies discussing TIP with domestic elites as much as 8–16 times per country annually, often at the level of head of state or minister or deputy minister.

Throughout, the book also offers examples of how scorecard diplomacy facilitated deeper engagement. For example, the case studies illustrated instances of diffusion of ideas when elites went abroad for training and sought to implement lessons learned when they returned. In other cases, funding helped build new domestic institutions, or the information gathering process prompted countries to delegate responsibility for data gathering to new or existing institutions, helping to create a focal point for the issue.

Chapter 4 illustrated how both NGOs and IGOs magnified the reputational pressure of scorecard diplomacy by using the TIP Report and working with the embassy. Over half of NGOs in the global survey had used the report to talk about the issue with their government and other NGOs. The chapter also illustrated how scorecard diplomacy can enlarge the base of reputational pressure by facilitating cooperation and information exchange among stakeholders. For example, in Chile, the US embassy brought together representatives from the government, the UN, NGOs, and foreign embassies to strategize about how to institutionalize practical solutions.[19] Chapter 4 also showed that the TIP Report correlates with greater media attention to the issue and that media attention peaks when the report comes out. The causal mechanism theorized to stimulate and augment pressure is thus present and functioning: strong messaging that facilitates engagement and allows other actors to increase attention and dialogue on the issue.

Step 4: Does Anyone Care? The Key Question About Concerns About Reputation

The pressure may be present, but scorecard diplomacy only works if countries care about their ratings. Because they are public, recurrent, and comparative, ratings expose government performance for more widespread criticisms from multiple actors. Still, government reactions cannot be taken for granted; the world is full of data and assessments that countries ignore.

---

[19] US Department of State and the Broadcasting Board of Governors 2012–2013, 27–28.

Not so with the TIP tiers. As seen in the examples about Israel, Jamaica, and Oman that opened this book, countries react strongly to scorecard diplomacy and care about their ratings. Sometimes countries react publicly, as seen with Thailand in Chapter 5, or Singapore's issuance of formal point-by-point rebuttals.[20] But reactions may not always be public. Indeed, US Secretary of State John Kerry has said he gets calls from ministers from around the world who complain about the tiers and the US report,[21] but these occur privately. The book therefore explored countries' reactions to the ratings through the fortuitous availability of the US embassy cables as well as media accounts and interviews.

This data showed that countries react frequently and strongly to the report and ratings with anything from anger to embarrassment to cooperation. That officials react to the *tiers* themselves is apparent from the specific discussion of the tiers, not just to the language of the report, and from the vastly greater rate at which officials react to the rated TIP Report than to the non-rated annual human rights report that devotes similar attention to the same topic. Indeed, documented reactions to the TIP Report are 25 times more common! As one IGO staffer commented, "The categorizing is really important because it gives them a benchmark."[22] The abundance, content, and intensity of reactions, something scholars are rarely able to document, demonstrate that countries care about their current and future tier ratings and that this drives them to interact with US diplomats.

Step 5: Linking Concerns to Real Outcomes

To be meaningful, scorecard diplomacy must affect behaviors. The analysis shows that countries included in the TIP Report, or that get harsher ratings, are more likely to criminalize human trafficking, and many forms of evidence suggest that scorecard diplomacy has contributed to this criminalization and other outcomes.

First, the role of the embassy can be traced in several cases, as can the US hand in formulating the content of laws. The passage of the laws is often preceded by multiple interchanges between the embassy and domestic elites about the law's content and the timing of its passage. Adaptations in trafficking laws suggest that these discussions sometimes informed domestic adaptation of definitions of trafficking in the laws and

[20] See Government of Singapore 2010.
[21] Kerry 2014.
[22] Haddin interview.

that countries have changed their understanding of the issue in ways that are being institutionalized. Furthermore, the importance of strong interlocutors in these efforts speaks to the transfer of ideas and the motivation that scorecard diplomacy can engender. The mechanisms of such learning are even documented in examples such as Armenian officials reporting that they'd combed the TIP Reports of other countries to figure out how to improve.

Some government officials were also candid that they took actions to meet a US deadline, a motivation that is also underscored by the fact that more laws get passed closer to the deadlines, although this is not statistically significant. In the global survey, NGOs also testify that the US is by far the most active embassy. A full two-thirds say it has been important in fighting human trafficking in their countries and most think that the US role has been positive. Astoundingly, hardly any NGOs said the US had played a negative role.

Some of the strongest evidence that the tier ratings contributed to change is that countries with documented reactions to their ratings were also more likely to criminalize, directly linking grades to reactions to behaviors. Research rarely includes micro-level evidence of private reactions to public criticisms of government behavior; it's difficult to do especially across several states, and thus it is often a missing link of evidence in the causal chain.[23]

Furthermore, it's not just about criminalization. The case studies examine the implementation of new laws, institution building and contributions to the local definitions and understandings of the problem. The 15 case studies produced a range of examples. While the most common influence was indeed on criminalization, the US also influenced domestic institutions and the implementation of laws in nearly as many instances. The influence was weakest on human trafficking norms, yet a moderate US influence could be traced in at least three cases and a weaker one in seven others. Thus, while most evidence exists about criminalization, perhaps because of the heavy investigational focus on this, scorecard diplomacy has influenced a broader range of outcomes. Compared to 2008, the number of prosecutions has increased by 25 percent, and convictions by 58 percent. Compared with 2003, 43 percent more victims are identified. Many countries also now have some designated national agency or commission in charge of anti-TIP efforts. The Protection Project at John Hopkins University has counted such mechanisms in 113 countries. These

---

[23] Friman 2015, 210.

efforts comport with the fact that despite claims that the US focuses too much on prosecution, its grant program favors protection and prevention programs.[24]

In sum, plentiful evidence illustrates the scorecard diplomacy cycle and shows that it has influenced state behaviors. The pressure, direct and indirect, is well documented, and detailed evidence substantiates countries' serious concern about the ratings. Finally, evidence connects the pressure with actual changes in behavior. These findings align with the observations of activists in the field. Anne Gallagher, an international lawyer and UN advisor, has commented that:

> While many factors determine how governments respond to such activity, it is the TIP reports ... that have proved to be the single greatest impetus for change ... Since 2001, I have frequently seen new laws passed, shelters established, traffickers arrested and victims rescued – solely or principally because of fear of an adverse assessment by the US. And it is not just the poor performers who are subject to influence. Even those countries that are virtually guaranteed a favourable assessment go to considerable effort each year to demonstrate their commitment to addressing trafficking.[25]

So the evidence for the argument is in, but what might be the objections?

POSSIBLE OBJECTIONS

Contributions From Other Actors and Factors

Readers might object that US scorecard diplomacy has been but one of many factors, and so attributing so much influence to it is an overstatement. IGOs and NGOs have their own programs, and some states are internally motivated to address the problem.

This book has not ignored these. The case study method provides ample opportunities to discover how multiple factors interact to bring about the outcomes. The statistical analysis also considered several other factors such as diffusion effects across regions, the share of women in parliament who might be pushing for anti-TIP policies, countries that might be predisposed to fight trafficking as evidenced by their ratification of the Palermo Protocol, aid, trade, the density of NGOs, etc. These factors indeed matter, but they do not account for the relationship between ratings and criminalization, which persists.

---

[24] For discussion, see Chapter 2.
[25] Gallagher 2014b.

Thus, the analysis has considered many other contributing factors and has stressed their importance. Other actors do not negate the effectiveness of scorecard diplomacy. Rather, they bolster the global normative environment that scorecard diplomacy invokes and facilitate action through indirect pressure and practical cooperation. Furthermore, the relationship with other actors is at times symbiotic, for example, some IGO efforts that have been credited with contributing to criminalization have received US funding.[26] The contributions of other actors thus do not undermine the importance of scorecard diplomacy, which indeed stresses the augmentation of pressure by third parties.

The Asymmetry of US Power

Another possible objection is that countries responded because the US is a dominant world actor and they do not wish to be out of favor. Thus, it's about US clout, not reputation. This argument has merit and cannot be disproved; surely it has been easier for the US than weaker states to carry this out. Indeed, most policies tend to work better in the hands of the strong. No one would argue that sanctions are a weak tool simply because they wouldn't work if Luxemburg was alone in implementing them.

Furthermore, some counterarguments are worth considering. First, if countries simply want to please the US, why care about the rating itself? Officials are often disappointed with poor ratings even if the embassy applauds the country's progress. This makes no sense if it's simply about pleasing the US. In addition, if countries seek favor with the US, it's remarkable how officials often fume at the embassy staff. Officials get angry in about one in eight cases, and in about one in ten cases they accuse the US of being arrogant, paternalistic, or even hypocritical. They also publicly denounce the US efforts. Uzbekistan's government was so upset about the 2007 Tier 3 rating that local NGOs forewarned embassy staff about the impending wrath. In Algeria in 2007, the embassy referred to the government's "rancor," which hardly indicates a desire to cozy up to the US. These critics may merely represent a sub-group that makes no

---

[26] The Council of Europe, for example, has been working to fight trafficking since 1998 when it began to host some seminars, but systematic monitoring began later than the US TIP Report. Council of Europe n.d. A focused effort in Southeastern Europe through the LARA project, launched in 2002, led to recommendations on draft legislation in seven countries, but LARA itself was funded by Sweden and the US State Department. See Council of Europe 2003, 2004.

progress, except that countries that improved also expressed anger and accusations.

Second, it's remarkable how none of the measures of US clout are significant in the statistical analysis. There is no evidence that countries with economic ties with the US – regardless of how funds are delivered, measured, or restricted – are more sensitive to being in the report or being pressured by the US. That doesn't prove that money or other unmeasured forms of "clout" do not matter, but such lack of support is not what one would expect if it were all about power.[27]

Third, the US also has disadvantages that undermine its authority. It is criticized for acting like a global policeman, for having a sizable trafficking problem, and for having no authority to author the report – all charges leveled repeatedly both by national officials seeking to dismiss US legitimacy and by academics accusing the US of unilateral overreach.[28] Furthermore, because of its political entanglements, the US implements the policy inconsistently, which weakens its impact, a subject I'll address later.

Finally, if it were only about the US flexing its muscles, why bother with this laborious – sometimes outright vexing – scorecard diplomacy? Rather, despite protests from some in the State Department, the US has deliberately used scorecard diplomacy to bolster its influence and is even seeking to copy this strategy to other areas.

WHEN DOES IT WORK?

Scorecard diplomacy has a mixed record: it only works sometimes. Much remains to be accomplished. Understanding when countries respond to reputational concerns is important. Chapter 2 argued that whether it works in a given country depends on (1) the country's *sensitivity* to reputational costs, (2) its *exposure* to criticisms, and (3) its ability to *prioritize* the issue.

The evidence in Chapter 7 aligns with these arguments. First, on sensitivity, countries were less likely to respond when they were less sensitive either because their understanding of the underlying norms and the nature of the problem differed, as in several Middle Eastern countries or in Chad or Ghana, or because they were insulated from practical

---

[27] See Tables A7.1–4 in the Results Appendix. Only US military assistance magnifies the US pressure, but this occurs only at the very highest, and most rare, levels of military aid, and so at best explains a few cases.

[28] For comments by domestic officials, see Chapter 4. For other criticisms, see for example Chuang 2005, Chacon 2005–2006, Wooditch 2011, Horning et al. 2014.

repercussions, perhaps because of their size, like China. Low sensitivity blunts reputational blows.

Exposure was also crucial. Where active third parties amplified attention and criticism, scorecard diplomacy was more successful. In Armenia, for example, plenty of NGOs and IGOs helped bolster scorecard diplomacy. In Zimbabwe, where the US had little authority or could easily be vilified, poor ratings carried less weight. When consistent and authoritative exposure was undermined because ratings were implemented inconsistently, as in Japan, scorecard diplomacy faltered. I'll return to this point shortly.

Finally, to translate reputational concerns into action, countries must be able to prioritize the issue despite domestic obstacles. As summarized in Table 7.1, these obstacles may be situations where government officials benefit from the targeted practices. For example, official complicity in trafficking is a widespread problem in nine of the case study countries and in many countries overall. Other factors include government instability, as was the case in Armenia or Zimbabwe, or strongly competing national problems, such as the drug trade or poverty in Honduras.

The caveat – and lesson – here, however, is that it is difficult to isolate the effect of a single factor. This reveals something important about our typical quest to pin down when an argument operates: *the effort to isolate singular factors that condition effectiveness may be misplaced.* Scholars are always trying to figure out the conditions under which various causal relationships work. This is because varied effects are common. Sanctions won't work in all settings, democratization efforts will work better in some cases than others, election observations might improve elections in non-violent contexts but not violent ones, etc. Naturally, we want to understand not just whether something works, but when it works. Identifying these condition factors is always hard, however. In this case it was particularly difficult, as no factor alone was significant in quantitative analysis. The reason, however, was that these factors needed to be considered as a group. It was surprising just how well they explained the effectiveness of scorecard diplomacy overall when combined into a simple aggregate measure. This tells us that whether a policy will work in a country ultimately depends on multiple factors that must be considered together. Detracting factors such as lack of active third parties might be overcome with other favorable factors such as a strong normative salience of the issue, for example. Each factor might pull in predictable directions, but not enough to make it possible to disentangle each one. Thus, these scope conditions must be considered holistically when considering when scorecard diplomacy – and likely other policies – works.

Not surprisingly, some authoritarian states seem impervious to pressure, although several non-democracies like the United Arab Emirates and Oman were highly sensitive to poor tier ratings.[29] Furthermore, just because countries are large and powerful does not preclude influence. Russia worked closely with the US after it was labeled a Tier 3 country in 2001. The DOS supported legislative drafting and the DOJ provided expertise. After legislation passed in December 2003, the Moscow director of the Angel Coalition, an anti-TIP NGO umbrella organization that helped draft the bill, told the *Moscow Times* that the TIP Report had helped motivate the legislation,[30] while a scholar noted its "enormous impact on the development of Russian law."[31] That said, the receptivity of Russia at that time again shows that it's easier to elicit reputational concerns when countries want to belong to the community of states, as Russian leaders did after the fall of the Soviet Union. The 2011 downgrade of Russia, in contrast, fell on deaf ears.

Finally, not all countries need the pressure of scorecard diplomacy, yet it would be a mistake to dismiss scorecard diplomacy as inconsequential in all democracies. Japan and Israel, for example, paid attention at times. We could also add Ireland to this category. Ireland's Justice Minister expressed "extreme displeasure" at the Tier 2 ratings in 2008 and 2009, but later Ireland passed anti-TIP legislation.[32] Even the Dutch have cared. In 2004 the US embassy – successfully – lobbied the US Secretary of State to "overrule" the TIP Office's Tier 2 recommendation, noting "the Dutch are hopping mad over this."[33] When New Zealand was first included in the report, it created a firestorm in the media.[34] An NGO staffer interviewed for this project said, "I am not sure [New Zealand's] government would have moved if not for [the US State Department]. There is incredible power in what they do."[35] Similarly, an NGO staffer from Estonia noted that the drop in the ranking "gave an extra push for the government to do something faster."[36]

---

[29] This aligns with research that finds some shaming to be counterproductive in China. Wachman 2001. That said, Johnston does find that China has been susceptible to socialization. Johnston 2008.

[30] Abdullaev 2003.

[31] Shelley 2005, 301.

[32] 09DUBLIN258.

[33] 04THEHAGUE1049.

[34] 04WELLINGTON563.

[35] Lambert interview.

[36] Vladenmaiier interview.

WHY DOES IT WORK? THE REPUTATION ARGUMENT REVISITED

Policymakers and scholars have long sought to understand why states behave as they do. Do they primarily maximize their standing relative to other states, concerned about alliances that can temper the threats of an insecure world? Or can they build trust through a set of shared norms and practices that allow them to cooperate? Do they follow international law because of positive incentives and assistance as the compliance school argues, or do they comply to avoid sanctions and punishments as the enforcement school argues?[37] In other words, is the only way to influence states by confronting them with hard, material repercussions of their actions through force or economic coercion, or can states be influenced via appeals to norms and their role in the international community? The answers matter for more than theory.

The notion that states understand languages other than coercion has become increasingly accepted and found expression in research on soft power, socialization and learning, diffusion, shaming, transnational advocacy, etc. Often, however, it's hard to document that states care about global norms or about their reputation more broadly: how do we really know that we are not simply succumbing to idealist, wishful thinking?

Image Versus Material Concerns as Driver of Reputation

Scorecard diplomacy can speak to this broadening understanding of state behaviors because it has ingredients of both schools of thought: it engages and teaches, in line with the understanding that most states will want to follow international norms and be good global citizens. It also incentivizes in the form of good grades and appeals to states' desire for legitimacy and standing. At the same time, however, it threatens with practical repercussions of bad grades. In the case of human trafficking, moreover, the unusual availability of information lets us peer into more private conversations. It's thus compelling to ask: what does scorecard diplomacy on human trafficking reveal about states' concern about material repercussions versus broader concerns about their image and standing?

The first thing this study has underscored, consistent with the developing consensus, is that these "competing" factors are in fact not competing at all, but complementary and even substitutable. Chapter 7 showed that

---

[37] For the compliance school, see Chayes and Chayes 1995. For the enforcement school, see Downs et al. 1996.

states must be sensitive to reputational concerns to respond to score-card diplomacy but that the source of this concern can vary: states could worry about losing aid, or they could worry about their "dignity," as a Malay official put it, or they could worry about both.[38] As long as they are worried about *something*, they are motivated to respond. If they are concerned neither about practical consequences nor about their reputation more broadly, scorecard diplomacy falters.

In the case of human trafficking, some states have been driven by material concerns, although this has not been as prominent as one might expect. Interviewees noted that in Kazakhstan and Armenia a large aid relationship boosted their leverage, and other embassies made similar comments. Countries not discussed herein, such as the Philippines, also testify to the power of the purse: When US ambassador Harry Thomas told top officials that the Tier 3 rating could threaten funds from the Millennium Challenge Account, action followed.[39] And Chapter 5 showed how concerned Thailand was about the sullied reputation of the fishing industry. Thus, some countries clearly worry about material con-sequences, although sanctions have rarely been meaningfully applied and were seldom discussed. If they were, usually the embassy, not the gov-ernment, initiated the discussion. Even in private embassy conversations, officials mention economic fallout much less often than one might expect if this was the overriding concern. That doesn't mean these factors don't matter, but it weighs against the exclusive narrative of the traditional logics of power. This is reinforced further by the prior point that various measures of aid, trade, military assistance and the like were not signifi-cant in statistical analysis of the effects of scorecard diplomacy, and that there is no evidence that aid recipients are more likely to react to the TIP Report in the first place, even if they get harsher tiers that might threaten that aid.

This book has argued that states care about their reputation more broadly and that they worry about their image, standing, and legitimacy. While several theories of compliance and interstate relations assume this is true, this study shows that states indeed worried about their broader reputation. Officials reacted to poor ratings by being embarrassed, trying to save face, or fretting about their or their country's image or dignity. Elites have bragged when the ratings improve. Indeed, such image-related reactions were more than three times as common as those about material

---

[38] 07KUALALUMPUR1375_a.
[39] Burkhalter interview and other anonymous sources. See also Senate 2012.

concerns. Officials also have fought to "save face" by denying the allegations or criticizing the report's integrity. Revealingly, officials were nearly twice as likely to object to the report in public than in private, where they are more conciliatory. They are also more likely to react to the report when the media is paying more attention to human trafficking. Finally, prominent TIP events like high profile legal cases or scandals also accelerate responses to poor ratings. These factors all point to concern about image, more broadly speaking, and show how it attaches itself to the state and its elites.

Quite unique to this study, officials also revealed their concern about status and relative standing in the community of states through their widespread tendency to compare their countries with other countries. This evidence is ground-breaking; few if any studies have collected such evidence before, despite persistent theoretical claims that countries are concerned about relative standing. It's striking which countries they compare themselves with (see Table 5.1). Revealing an implicit concern about identity, elites compared their countries with "peer groups," such as geographically close countries, or countries that share some other identity trait, such as Japan's reference to "other G8 countries." As the opening quote of this chapter reflected, states do "not like to be cast with poisonous snakes."

The concern for image is also evident in the fact that government officials don't just react to the report, they react specifically to harsh tiers *even* when they don't have funding or trade on the line. This was the case in the examples of reactions by democratic countries discussed earlier, and also the case with Switzerland's reaction in 2010 when the US lowered its rating to Tier 2 due to the discovery of a loophole in the prostitution law about minors, galvanizing action.[40]

---

[40] In 2010, the US dropped Switzerland to Tier 2, noting a long-standing hole in Swiss law that failed to "expressly prohibit prostitution by minors aged 16 and 17 ... leaving these children potentially vulnerable to trafficking for commercial sexual exploitation." It recommended that Switzerland should prohibit commercial sexual exploitation for all persons under 18 years. It kept Switzerland at this tier until 2013 when the law was changed. A US TIP Office staff member at the time noted that the rating made the Swiss policymakers "sit up straight in their chair," and ask why this charge was being leveled (anonymous interview). They quickly realized that they were not in conformance with several conventions, including a European Council convention on the protection of children that Switzerland signed two days after the 2010 report was released and three years after most other European nations. Later, a Swiss policymaker told the US TIP Office staff member in a side meeting that "it's really good that you did that, I am getting more attention, more staff, the issue will be elevated" (anonymous interview). This Swiss response was likely not because Switzerland felt threatened, but the Tier 2 rating motivated the government.

In sum, it's not that economic clout doesn't matter; the ability to connect scorecard diplomacy with practical consequences is not lost on the actors involved. However, the evidence also shows that states have broader reputational concerns. This speaks to the extensive literature that rests its claims on the notion that states care about their legitimacy, identity, and standing in the international community, and thus substantiates a primary assumption of how social pressure works and why international cooperation and compliance can be obtained through means other than force.

What Else Scorecard Diplomacy Teaches Us About Reputation

While states' concern about their reputation can be used to influence their behavior, not all methods of eliciting reputational concerns are equal. Reputational concerns have mostly been studied in the context of shaming, which singles states out for their transgressions and discredits their reputation. However, this book adds three dimensions to theories of reputation. First, it highlights the mechanisms of *comparisons* that elicit concerns about relative standing. It shows that states are concerned about their image relative to their peer groups, so it's not just a matter of chastising states for their bad behavior, as shaming tends to do, but of directing criticisms at their identity in a community. This relative perspective enriches our understanding of how states weigh external criticisms. For African countries that have many peer groups on Tier 2, being a Tier 2 country is less concern for alarm. For Switzerland, being the lone advanced European democracy with a Tier 2 rating was upsetting. Shame is relative to the reputation of peers.

Second, it points to the value of *iteration*. Contrary to traditional appeals to reputation through shaming, scorecard diplomacy recurs. The ongoing issuance of standardized grades allows countries and their citizens to gauge their performance over time. It may not be particularly bad to be rated Tier 2, but it may be alarming if the country has been Tier 1 for a long time. It will raise questions and call attention to slips in performance in ways that might not occur with traditional shaming which responds more ad hoc when severe thresholds are passed. This dynamic suggests that reputations can be engaged not only relative to others but also relative to oneself.

Third, this study advances a new and more dynamic explanation of why states respond to reputational pressure. The effectiveness of scorecard diplomacy suggests that assessments need not always be negative in the form of a denouncement; appeals to reputation can also be used to elicit compliant behavior through praise. Good grades can motivate states, just as they can motivate students. Favorable ratings engender a *status maintenance* effect because the reporting and monitoring recurs. Other research has emphasized the positive role of rewards, but praise differs from material rewards. Thus, this notion of the use of status and praise adds another dimension to theories of reputation; perhaps scholars should not only refer to "shaming," but also to "praising."

Finally, this study highlights the symbolic elements of reputation and how these can shape perceptions, not only of performance but also of what good performance *should* look like. For scorecard diplomacy to evoke reputational concerns, it must invoke global norms. Reputation has meaning only against some expectations. But scorecard diplomacy not only invokes norms, it also bolsters or even shapes them. Grades, ratings, and rankings are potent symbols that shape perceptions about performance, but by reducing complexity, they designate a preferred interpretation of ideal behavior as meaningful.[41]

GENERALIZABILITY AND SUSTAINABILITY

Some might object that it's hard to generalize this project to other issues. That's a fair point. This book dived deeply into human trafficking because the rich information available made it possible to move beyond the traditional correlational analysis. Whenever one focuses deeply on a narrow issue, it is wise to be cautious about generalizing. Indeed, this book makes no claim that scorecard diplomacy could be so powerful, for example, as to get North Korea to give up its nuclear ambitions, or that weaker international actors can execute this strategy with equal effects. Most likely there is no other case just like this, although the US uses a similar strategy in other issues areas such as intellectual property rights, development aid, or even terrorism.

That said, the ratings and rankings trend is growing. Beth Simmons and I have documented a sharp rise in such efforts, with over 150 such indices currently in existence[42] and new ones created every year. While some of these are stand-alone indices without much engagement, others are paired with the kind of policy engagement that resembles the US scorecard diplomacy. Some of these efforts are inconsequential, but

---

[41] For more on this issue, see Chapter 2 and Bourdieu 1989, 20.
[42] Kelley and Simmons 2014.

several are grabbing attention. Climate change activists, for example, are considering how monitoring and rating states might motivate states in ways that political institutions have failed to do. The Climate Change Performance Index by the think tank Germanwatch is one such effort, while the Climate Disclosure Leadership Index by the CDP (formerly the Carbon Disclosure Project – a global non-profit organization, founded in 2000) monitors and, like the TIP Report, grades the performance of 2,000 firms. Moreover, the international donor community now establishes formal "development goals" that are measured by key indicators – both for donors and target countries – in the hope of using similar reputational dynamics to propel changes.[43]

Research on the power of such ratings and rankings is just emerging and constitutes an exciting new area of inquiry.[44] Thus, while no other initiatives are exactly like the US TIP policy, many related efforts share its traits. Recognizing the significance of these developments, scholars have begun to explore the effectiveness of many of these efforts,[45] a sign that US scorecard diplomacy is related to a larger trend. Some interesting findings are emerging:

- The United States' Special 301 Report's "Watch List" and "Priority Watch List" designates countries with lax intellectual property rights protection, and has been found to have influenced policy in China.[46]
- Inclusion in the Aid Transparency Index by Publish What You Fund has been found to improve donor transparency.[47]
- The International Budget Partnership publishes the Open Budget Survey and an accompanying index and collaborates with civil society in many countries to improve the quality of governance.[48]
- Systematic monitoring has been found to improve election quality.[49]
- Blacklisting by the Financial Action Task Force has been linked to anti-money laundering measures around the world.[50]
- A study about the OECD's Programme on International Student Assessment (PISA) found that low educational rankings have shocked

---

[43] See the Global Development Goals Progress Index by the Center for Global Development. Center for Global Development 2011.

[44] See Chapter 2, note 24. See also Bieber and Martens 2011.

[45] Kelley and Simmons 2014, Cooley and Snyder 2015, Merry et al. 2015.

[46] Tian 2008.

[47] Honig 2016.

[48] Discussion and examples are provided in De Renzio and Masud 2011.

[49] Kelley 2012.

[50] Sharman 2008.

Germany, stimulating significant educational reforms. Other studies have also found effects.[51]

- Research on the World Bank's Doing Business Report shows that many countries implement reforms in response.[52]
- Sub-national research in Vietnam shows that indexing the performance of local government improves their governance.[53]
- A study has found that democracies increase their hostile rhetoric toward countries that are rated "not free" by Freedom House.[54]

Regardless of whether scorecard diplomacy transfers to other settings, it demonstrates a broader theoretical insight – that states care about their reputation in terms of their legitimacy and image. Such concern is unlikely unique to human trafficking. Indeed, we see similar dynamics in several of the areas mentioned above. China was so upset about its rating in the Doing Business Report that it tried to shut it down.[55] The evidence that states care about their reputation is especially valuable given the abundance of theories that assume this but lack systematic evidence.

While the rise of other ratings or rankings may mitigate concerns about generalizability, it raises questions about sustainability. An abundance of reports could lead to fatigue or selective usage. This is a real risk. That said, many assessments exist in narrow issue areas that capture the attention of select domestic reformers and networked transnational actors who focus only on the signals most relevant to them. The London-based NGO Publish What You Fund, for example, has made headway with donor agency transparency, although its Aid Transparency Index gets little media attention. Because aid agencies and other relevant stakeholders pay attention, the organization has been able to make progress with governments. Thus, even though indices and scorecards exist in several domains, the users of these may not overlap significantly, reducing the risk of saturation. Still, it's possible that with repeated exposure

[51] For research on PISA, see for example Ginsburg et al. 2005, Grek 2009, Rautalin and Alasuutari 2009, Bieber and Martens 2011.

[52] Kelley et al. 2016. For several case studies by the World Bank, see The World Bank Group 2007, 2008, 2009. For a more critical analysis, see Arruñada 2007.

[53] However, evidence suggests that provincial governments teaching to the test. See Le and Malesky 2016.

[54] Roberts and Tellez 2016.

[55] In 2013 a formal review (Independent Doing Business Report Review Panel, Independent Panel Review of the *Doing Business Report*, June 24, 2013, Washington, DC) commenced following pressure from China (*The Economist* 2013.) which was unhappy with its ranking, discussed tensions over the rankings and once again recommended that they be removed. The Bank ignored the recommendation.

across multiple issues, states' sensitivity to reputational concerns might wane. This remains to be seen and will be one topic for future research.

US TIP policy has succeeded in many aspects, but gains have not come without costs or mistakes. Based on the extensive inquiry that laid the foundation for this book, some lessons emerge. This section discusses these and offers some insights, first for US TIP policy specifically, and then for scorecards more generally.

Consistency and Credibility

The biggest weakness in a policy based on reputation is threats to its credibility and consistency. Scorecard diplomacy derives its leverage from the public ratings. They are the be all and end all; once they begin to lose credibility, their influence weakens. In general, states are less likely to respect processes and rules that lack legitimacy.[56] Actors widely perceived as biased forfeit serious recognition, a problem also recognized in election monitoring and similar efforts that rely on a reputation for effectiveness.[57] This is why much of the variation in effectiveness of scorecard diplomacy lies in its application. The TIP Report is rife with lenient tier ratings. The case studies show that when this happens, leverage fizzles. The case of Japan bears this out clearly with Japan being way more responsive when the pressure was credible. In the long run, lack of credibility diminishes the overall effectiveness of scorecard diplomacy and threatens to erode it more permanently. Once such patterns become too apparent, it may be impossible to salvage this most potent element of the policy. This is a real possibility for US TIP policy unless standards are firmly enforced. The threats to credibility come from several sources.

The first and biggest threat to credibility is **political pressures**. As Chapter 7 showed, for the TIP Office, these are enormous. The pressures occur on multiple levels: within the DOS and in the field. While the TIP Office must contend with regional offices or pressures from higher levels, embassy diplomats find themselves in a precarious situation. They are not merely conduits of neutral information to the US State Department but become targets of lobbying by local actors who seek to spin the

---

[56] Cleveland 2001, Raustiala and Slaughter 2002.
[57] Sikkink 2002, Kelley 2009, 314.

information and with whom they are simultaneously trying to accomplish other goals. In such an environment the independence of the report is difficult to maintain but of even greater importance. The more independent the office, the less blame can be laid on local diplomats. If the report is seen as malleable, lobbying will be relentless. If it is seen as independent, lobbying will be considered a waste of time. Thus, *the report and the TIP Office need greater independence and insulation from external pressures.*

Ironically, this will require commitment from the top of the US Department of State to insulate the office from such pressures, partly by tying the State Department's own hands. In the absence of a willingness to do this, the US Congress changed the law to limit the number of years in a row a country can be on the Watch List. This effort to force hard decisions has sometimes worked. Lesotho and Swaziland were among the first batch of these "auto downgrades," which led them and the local US embassies to became more engaged.[58] Thailand was similarly automatically downgraded, and the strong reaction to this was discussed in Chapter 5. In other cases, like China, the "auto downgrade" has been a temporary, ineffectual, and artificial fix to satisfy the law. The increased effectiveness in some cases has been paid for in other cases with a growing reluctance to put countries on the Watch List in the first place. On balance, therefore, the benefits of the policy remain mixed. Still, the US should continue to think about ways to ensure greater independence.

The problem of political pressures highlights the importance of strong leadership. The TIP Office wavered when it was without leadership for a year, starting in the fall of 2015. That following summer the report was not only over a month late, but the report contained some egregious ratings, as the TIP Office was powerless against the pressures upon it.[59] Some ratings were so off that 160 House and 18 Senate members wrote the Secretary of State John Kerry to protest.[60] *The anti-TIP ambassador must be a person of considerable status and authority who can command respect and keep pressure at bay. Leadership transitions should be handled expeditiously to avoid gaps in authority.*

The second threat to credibility is **accuracy and transparency**. The criteria to evaluate countries must be consistent not only between countries but also over time. This is a challenge for ratings and rankings whenever the creators wish to change the methodology or incorporate new goals.

---

[58] This insight is based on a number of interviews with people inside the US government who requested anonymity.
[59] Szep and Spetalnick 2015.
[60] Crabtree 2015, Szep and Spetalnick 2015.

In 2005, when the US increased the emphasis on labor trafficking, the cables showed that countries complained privately about the "moving goal posts." Changing the standards may be perceived as unfair, and is confusing from the perspective of norm and standard setting. Thus the embassy in Qatar reported, "[O]fficials often tell us that they don't know where our end game lies," which of course can be demoralizing. UAE's Minister of State of Foreign Affairs noted, "It appears that the US definition of human trafficking varies every year depending on the nature of debate on this issue in its domestic environment."[61] *Thus, the methodology and criteria for ratings must be clear, and if the standards need to be changed, countries need adequate instruction and time to adjust before penalties kick in.*

A third threat to credibility is the performance of the US itself. Countries will find the report more credible and be more receptive when the US convincingly demonstrates that it is making not just adequate, but outstanding efforts to address the problem. Even today the TIP report on the US laments that some state and local jurisdictions do not participate in data gathering or that some state and local officials still misunderstand what human trafficking is. Increased efforts to perform at the highest level will bolster the report's credibility, *so more attention to state and local performance in the US itself will be helpful.*

Furthermore, every effort should be made to ensure the report's accuracy. That seems self-evident, but the reality remains that gathering data of this scope remains underfunded. As it is, the staff is sizable, but embassies complain that the TIP duties burden them excessively. Despite investing so much political capital in this policy, which has strong bilateral support in the House and Senate, execution remains underfunded, although the investment needed is not that great. *If the issue is as high a political priority as the efforts suggest, the TIP Office and embassies need adequate financial resources.*

Finally, even when the policy is credible and well executed, it faces varied **receptivity**. Given limited resources, it makes sense to target efforts where the opportunities for influence are greatest. Governments facing many competing priorities will be less well positioned to act on the pressures. That said, this work has shown the value of building strong relationships with effective interlocutors, empowering NGOs, and working through IGOs. These are factors that can be controlled more than the domestic political situation. *The sweet spot lies in investing heavily*

---

[61] 09ABUDHABI626.

in these when the domestic situation is also favorable, thus optimizing chances of impact.

Downsides of Scorecard Policies

This book did not aim to assess how the policies the US has promoted have affected the scope or severity of human trafficking problems worldwide. Rather, it aimed to assess the ability of the US to use scorecard diplomacy to get states to adopt these preferred policies. These two questions cannot be entirely separated, however. It's wise to consider the possible downsides of using scorecard diplomacy to encourage policy change and what might mitigate these.

The first challenge is the **substance of responses**: in their eagerness to earn approval, some countries may rush to adopt policies that are not optimally formulated for the country's needs, a phenomenon that has also occurred in externally promoted social sector reform in Latin America.[62] One IGO interviewee stressed that the US has influenced laws around the world, but also fretted that:

I have seen countries that have literally copied and pasted from the US law. They put them in because they think that's what makes a strong law. A lot of countries have pushed to get a law in place because of the TIP Report, so sometimes that produces good results, sometimes it's too hasty. In some countries prosecutions increase as the TIP Reporting deadline draws closer. So instead of going towards bigger things it becomes: How quickly can we count numbers?[63]

The tendency to rush is exacerbated by the rather short reporting cycle. The report comes out in the summer and the deadline for updates is already April the following year.[64] After a Tier 3 rating, when an interim report is required, the time pressure is even greater. As some NGOs have protested, what can be accomplished in six months is limited.[65] This time pressure and rush to adapt highlights the need to consider the length of the reporting cycle. While there is something compelling about annual reports, this cycle may be too rushed for complex issues. Thus, *it may be beneficial to consider ways to lengthen the reporting cycle to allow for more updates after the initial deadline.*

The second challenge is when scorecards are used as **reputational decoys**. Some countries may use anti-TIP policies to earn a badge of

[62] Weyland 2009.
[63] Interview #8.
[64] Skrivánkova interview. See also 07NEWDELHI2816.
[65] 07NEWDELHI2816.

approval to cover for other abuses. Nigeria has been praised for its anti-TIP efforts, so much so that the US ambassador at large for human trafficking said in 2009 that he couldn't "talk enough about it."[66] Yet some accuse it of investing in this as a distraction from its other human rights abuses.[67] Belarus has likewise led an international campaign to brand itself positively, but in reality, the efforts were "launched to salvage the international image of Belarus and to redirect the attention of the international community away from Belarus's non-compliance on a number of other human rights regulations."[68] Some have accused Thailand of launching an aggressive anti-trafficking campaign that has "marginalized human rights and trampled on the most vulnerable."[69] Similarly, Uzbekistan has also cracked down on NGOs to silence their alternative to the government narrative.[70] Much could and should be written about such consequences on the ground. Meanwhile, *to address this, the report must consider the whole picture. When praising performance in countries with otherwise poor human rights records, officials must place human trafficking in a broader human rights context.*

The third challenge is the **grade ceiling and grade inflation**. Once countries have earned the highest grade, the pressure somewhat subsides. While countries with good grades might worry about maintaining them, they may also use an improved rating as an excuse to slack off. This is especially true if it becomes apparent that the chances of a downgrade are low. In a few cases, NGOs report that governments have used favorable tier ratings as an excuse to stop working on TIP issues, stating that a common government response is that "because [the country] has been ranked Tier 1, there is no need to take additional action" or pursue further anti-TIP legislation.[71] Indeed, although countries are supposed to maintain a pace of improvements to retain the top rating, even if this has not been so, the TIP Office has been reluctant to downgrade countries from the top tier. It turns out that the probability of a downgrade from Tier 1 is only 8.7 percent, compared to 21.7 and 16.9 percent for Tier 2 and the Watch List respectively. Once a country has earned the top grade, it's harder to move back down. But surely Tier 1 countries have room to improve? *Creating upward space on the scale might stimulate a race to*

---

[66] 08ABUJA293_a, LaFranchi 2009.
[67] Stoller and Light 2013.
[68] Zaloznaya and Hagan 2012, 353.
[69] Council on Foreign Relations 2006, Hindstrom 2015.
[70] Skrivánková interview.
[71] Response 1387.

the top. It would be pretty drastic to change the tier system now, but it's worth considering another form of distinction that countries could be motivated to earn.

Policy Insights Beyond This Case

What advice does the above discussion offer possible users of scorecards, rating and rankings more generally? Foremost: credibility is the main currency of any scorecard system. Utmost care should be given to be consistent, transparent, and politically independent. This means the following:

- Systems embedded within organizations or agencies need institutional buffers to protect the creators from pressure.
- Accuracy is the foundation for credibility. It is probably better to include fewer criteria that can be well estimated, than more than resources can support.
- If the methodology for calculating ratings or rankings change, or if the creators deliberately introduce new goals into the mix of performance outputs, it is essential to warn all the target states with enough time for them to take action before dropping them in the ratings.
- Strong leadership is required. This is especially true if the creator plans to interact extensively with the targets. Organizations would therefore do well to invest in prestigious and experienced leadership.
- Countries that create scorecards must themselves perform highly to set examples and engender legitimacy for the report.
- The optimal interval between ratings should be considered carefully. Beware of efforts to meet criteria quickly without substance.
- The dynamics of a rating scale should be weighed carefully. Sometimes few categories that stigmatize can be powerful. Other times a larger range of performance is helpful.

In addition, those who hope to evoke reputational concerns though a similar system might wish to replicate some helpful features of the US policy:

- Third party collaboration can be crucial to bolstering the message and increasing the reputational pressure. This includes media attention. Scorecards that engage other actors in bringing attention to the issue likely perform better.
- The data gathering process can be a constructive tool for dialogue and can focus attention. Many ratings and rankings merely compile

existing data. While this insulates them from political pressure, it also foregoes interaction with the targets.

- Countries are more likely to respond if the rated outcomes are actionable. Criminalization is challenging, but states know how to pass laws. They can also build shelters, run awareness campaigns, and the like. The trafficking problem as a whole, however, is intractable. If the criteria for country policies were some measure of the scope of the trafficking problem, countries would likely be discouraged. While intractable goals might be more laudable, more attainable goals might contribute to more concrete progress.

"DIPLOMATIC INDIGESTION": THE POLITICAL CHALLENGES OF SCORECARDS

By judging "the acceptability of their policies in the international sphere," scorecard diplomacy informally intrudes on states' sovereignty.[72] As a result, it incurs accusations of arrogance and perpetuates the image of the US as meddling in the affairs of other countries, acting unilaterally, imposing its own ideas on others, and having double standards.[73] Thus Congressman Chris Smith, author of the TVPA, the US anti-TIP law, has recognized the "diplomatic costs to accurate tier rankings,"[74] and former US anti-TIP ambassador Mark Lagon has noted that the ratings can cause "diplomatic indigestion."[75] Indeed, the policy has caused some backlash. Some countries threaten to cease – or have halted – cooperation with the US on trafficking, refusing to even discuss it. Japan is a case in point, India another. In 2008 India's Foreign Secretary threatened that "if the US did lower India to Tier III status, the Indian government would retaliate."[76] When it was most infuriated with its Tier 3 rating, Oman canceled several meetings on economic and military cooperation.[77] Some countries that receive poor ratings accuse the US of arrogance in an effort of what some have called counter-stigmatization.[78] Kuwait's parliament speaker grabbed headlines by calling the report "laughable" and noting

---

[72] Simmons 1998, 76. Similar reactions have occurred to the US Special 301 reports. Newby 1995, 51.
[73] See for example Williams 1988, 13.
[74] Smith 2014.
[75] Lagon and Mickelwait 2016.
[76] 08NEWDELHI126. For more on India, see also Green 2007a.
[77] 08MUSCAT425, 08MUSCAT431, 08MUSCAT527, 07MUSCAT597_a.
[78] Adler-Nissen 2014.

the old saying that "those who live in glass houses should not throw stones."[79]

The protests and high political costs of scorecard diplomacy beg the question: Is there a better alternative?

Unilateralism Versus Multilateralism: Is There an Alternative?

No institution or world forum has given the United States the right or authority to condemn or take over other nations … [The report] would be valid if it came from an organization such as the United Nations [or other multilaterals].
– The Dominican Republic newspaper*La Nation*, June 2004[80]

Some might argue that because of all the political pressures, ranking and rating is better left to more independent actors. Indeed, some countries can blunt the force of the criticisms embedded in scorecard diplomacy by delegitimizing the US, thus undermining the normative salience of the effort. On the other hand, the US has advantages such as extensive networks that provide superior access to information and policymakers, and the ability to call attention to the issue due to its status in the international community.

In the case of human trafficking, would it be better if another independent organization or a multilateral organization like the UN provided the report? Other organizations do issue reports. The Council of Europe produces something called the GRETA[81] report, but its reach is limited and it is only now getting underway. The counter-trafficking division of the IOM maintains a database. The UN Global Initiative to Fight Trafficking (UN.GIFT) issued a report in 2006 and another in 2009. These consisted of brief narratives of the problems faced and the policies in place. In 2010 the UN Office on Drugs and Crime decided that the office would publish reports every two years, with the first one in 2012. However, these reports omit many countries, and the main report focuses on global and regional analysis. Individual countries are discussed in the Appendix, which only notes basic TIP-related criminal justice statistics and states whether the country's legislation is in compliance. Additional information is sometimes included if the country has a national action plan or a dedicated national commission. The country information is thus much

---

[79] 07KUWAIT938.
[80] Cited in 04SANTODOMINGO3667.
[81] Produced by the Council of Europe Group of Experts on Action against Trafficking in Human Beings.

sparser; there are neither ratings nor negative statements that a country does not have an action plan or a national commission.

The problem is that IGOs lack both resources and political clout to execute a report similar to that of the US. So far NGO-produced alternatives have done even worse.[82] A weakness with the UNODC report is that it relies on self-reported data, whereas the US report prevents governments from controlling or hiding information. As one IGO interviewee said: "The UN organizations cannot embarrass countries in the same way. The best we can do is bring things under the ratified conventions, but that doesn't get in the newspapers."[83] Another IGO interviewee noted, "[T]he role of the UN is not to be within this field. We are here to assist states."[84] This sentiment is well supported by reactions to other attempts by the UN to use lists and other forms of shaming, as when Saudi Arabia was able to bully its way off a blacklist in the 2016 UN Report on "Children and Armed Conflict."[85]

Indeed, there is no appetite for a US-type report within the UN, as evidenced during the 2007 expert meeting on possible review. At that time the parties declared that any oversight mechanism should be:

> non-intrusive, impartial, non-adversarial, non-punitive and flexible. In addition, it should not criticize or rank states or regions but rather contribute to problem solving. It should furthermore respect the sovereignty of States ... China stressed that the data collected should not be disclosed or used for hostile interference in internal affairs. The Philippines also recommended that the information submitted should be kept confidential by the Secretariat. Only lessons learned and best practices should be made available to other States parties. Panama, along the same lines, underlined that information collected should be accessible only to the highest authorities in a State.[86]

The stated aversion to criticism and ranking is revealing. One reason for the pushback may indeed be fear of reputational pressure. This sentiment is what produced the relatively tame UNODC report now in operation. An ILO interviewee who voiced criticism about the unilateral nature of the US approach still noted that the US offers something that a member organization like the ILO cannot: "Maybe there is something to say for both approaches if they happen in tandem, which they do now. We come

---

[82] Gallagher 2014a.
[83] Noguchi interview.
[84] Anonymous, Kerry Neil.
[85] Lynch 2016.
[86] United Nations 2009, 3 and 7.

with global estimates, the US with a stick. The two together, maybe it is not too bad. There are different roads to Rome, and this offers flexibility and allows us to move together."[87]

Experts thus note that "the TIP Reports are not displacing a potentially superior alternative or performing a function that could be better discharged by the international community," and that "in the absence of an international mechanism, the US report gains more significance and importance."[88] Or as former anti-TIP ambassador John Miller said in an interview:

Groups would say: why are you doing this, why not let the UN do this. Why are you so high and mighty? The problem is *nobody* else *is* doing it. ... The answer to the question "why is the US doing it?" is: because nobody else will.[89]

THE BOTTOM LINE

The challenges facing the international community make it imperative to understand how to encourage states to act responsibly both domestically and across borders. Economic coercion and force rarely engender constructive cooperation, while international law provides a necessary normative and regulatory backbone, but usually lacks enforcement mechanisms. Meanwhile, the Internet revolution and increased mobility and communication have diversified the set of actors, loci, and forms of cooperation both within and across borders. In this landscape, understanding the nature of power and influence is as important as ever.

To this end, this book has examined a softer type of influence, namely the power of scorecards. I have argued that states respond to scorecards because they care about their reputation, and that they respond especially when such efforts are embedded in a recurring cycle of monitoring and grading coupled with diplomacy. The use of grades elicits reputational concerns particularly well because of its symbolic and comparative nature. By defining and assessing behavior against a chosen standard and evoking states' concern with how their performance is perceived both overall and relative to others, scorecard diplomacy shapes and enforces norms of behavior.

---

[87] Van de Glind interview.
[88] Mattar interview.
[89] Miller interview.

This argument has been supported by abundant evidence from the case of US efforts to fight human trafficking. The book opened by discussing the reactions from officials in Oman, Jamaica, and Israel. This book has shown that these were not isolated instances; many states have taken this policy seriously. The evidence has substantiated many of the elements of scorecard diplomacy: the ability of ratings to incentivize the government, engagement with NGOs and individual stakeholders within government, influence on legislation and other outcomes, contribution to the definition of norms embedded in legislation and the efforts to teach officials these norms via training and exchanges, the contribution to domestic institution building and data collection, as well as the facilitation and coordination of other actors such as IGOs.[90]

Furthermore, the evidence suggests that states care about their reputation, not only because they worry about material repercussions, but also because they care about their image and standing in the world. Elites worry about their own or their countries' "dignity," identify with peer countries, and shun stigmatization. They want to maintain a good grade once obtained. They seek to save face and are much more defensive in public than in private. They respond differently to reports with grades than those without, and they respond to poor grades, even if they have no apparent aid or trade on the line. These are the behaviors we would expect if countries care about international legitimacy and worry about their standing or status in international society. These reactions reference a shared set of norms and signal that states dislike being singled out for failure to adhere to these norms.

Many long-standing theories about why states cooperate or conform to international norms assume that states care about their reputation and standing in the "civilized community" of states. These are well-articulated arguments, but they've lacked a body of systematic evidence.[91] When we say states care about legitimacy or their image in the international community, what is the evidence for this? Is this something that we can understand and harness for good? To explore this question, this study has connected reputational tools like ratings with states' expressions of concerns and then with their actual behaviors, and so has provided some of the most systematic evidence to date about how reputational concerns motivate states.

---

[90] For another example of all these elements on display, see the Kazakhstan case study on the book's resources site (www.cambridge.org/ScorecardDiplomacy).
[91] A recent exception is Erickson 2015.

Human trafficking is but one of many challenges facing the world, but incremental evidence at this level of analysis is crucial to advance knowledge of how the world works. Still the case should not be overstated either. While scorecard-like efforts are rising around the world, it's worth keeping in mind that even if they reside in IGOs or NGOs, they remain controlled largely by rich industrialized countries. What is not rated and vigorously promoted through scorecard diplomacy is as revealing as what is. The US, for example, has not sought to harness state reputations about domestic police brutality or about aid to dictators. Scorecards can provide considerable "bang for the buck," but they won't shift the fundamental distribution of power in the international system.

Indeed, this study underscores how active the US remains internationally through what one might call "backstage diplomacy." Through grants and activities that empower local actors, provision of legal counsel, face-to-face diplomatic advice that often gets attention, and funding of international organizations to carry out programs aligned with its preferences, the US continues to exert influence, albeit in subtler ways. Indeed, sometimes the US mobilized other actors to diminish its own appearance of influence. Efforts to assess US influence in the world today must account for these quieter channels of influence. This book could not draw out all the interactions in the thousands of cables, but face-to-face diplomacy played a significant role by building personal relationships.[92]

Finally, while this study has shown that scorecard diplomacy can influence state behaviors, it has also shown that it requires certain conditions to succeed. Importantly, while states must be sensitive and exposed to reputational concerns, and while they must be able to prioritize them, no singular factor is necessary or sufficient for success. States may worry about their reputations for instrumental or normative reasons, but as long as they worry, there is room for influence. Furthermore, it's hard to isolate singular factors that increase or decrease the effectiveness of scorecard diplomacy. Rather, one can better understand the patterns of success by considering several factors in combination. In the real world, there are no magic bullets; multiple conditions conspire to obstruct or provide ground fertile for progress.

This work on scorecard diplomacy has drawn attention to the power of eliciting states' concern for their reputation, broadly speaking. Clearly

---

[92] This aligns with Morgenthau's argument that competent diplomacy can amplify state power. Morgenthau 1950, 105. It also supports the call for a return to a focus on the "practice" of diplomacy. Pouliot and Cornut 2015.

this is no cure-all; it may require a strong actor to wield it, and even then it may falter. But let's remember that the same is true even for sanctions or military force, which often also come up short. This book doesn't deny hard power, but it has shown that power is about more than hard capabilities; it also works in and through social relations. States care about how they are perceived, and this provides a way to incentivize them to cooperate.

Methods Appendix

The book draws on interviews with 90 people from NGOs and IGOs around the world, and US politicians and bureaucrats. These were conducted between 2012 and 2015. Most interviews were conducted via phone, but some were conducted via email and some in person. Interviews lasted from 20 minutes to over an hour, with the mode being around 45 minutes. The author also had two meetings in the US Department of State TIP Office where she met with a group of staff each time.

List of Interviewees

Unless otherwise noted, the author conducted the interview.

NGOs

1. Adhoch, Paul. CEO, Founder, and Board Member, Trace Kenya. In-person interview by Jessica Van Meir. August 7, 2014.
2. Alkalash, Linda. Founder and director, Tamkeen for Legal Aid and Human Rights, Jordan. Phone interview. November 14, 2014.
3. Altamura, Alessia. ECPAT international, Thailand. Skype interview. October 29, 2014.
4. Altschul, Monique. Fundación Mujeres en Igualdad. Argentina. In-person interview by Jessica Van Meir. July 10, 2015.
5. Araujo, Luján. Press and Communications Director, Fundación María de los Ángeles. Argentina. Email correspondence with Jessica Van Meir. October 22, 2015.

6. Buljanovic Olhagaray, Kate. Policy and Partnerships Coordinator, Child Helpline International, Netherlands. Phone interview. November 21, 2014.

7. Caminos, Viviana. Coordinator, RATT (Red Alto a la Trata y el Tráfico), Argentina. Skype interview by Jessica Van Meir. August 29, 2015.

8. Casadei, Ana Bettina. Confederación General de Trabajo and Congress. Argentina. In-person interview by Jessica Van Meir. June 30, 2015.

9. Cheeppensook, Kasira. Political science professor at Chulalongkorn University, Bangkok, Thailand. In-person interview by Pimchanok Chuaylua. January 12, 2016.

10. de Lavarene, Celhia. STOP – Stop Trafficking Of People, US. Phone interview. July 25, 2014.

11. Feingold, David. Director, Ophidian Research Institute, Thailand. Email exchange with author. March 31, 2015.

12. Ford, Carrie Pemberton. Cambridge Centre for Applied Research in Human Trafficking, United Kingdom. Phone interview. July 14, 2014.

13. Gachanja, Ruth Juliet N. Programme officer, Policy & Legislative Advocacy, The CRADLE, Kenya. In-person interview by Jessica Van Meir. July 15, 2014.

14. Gallagher, Anne. Australia-Asia Program to Combat Trafficking in Persons (AAPTIP), International Lawyer. Durham, NC. In-person interview. October 19, October 20, 2014.

15. Horowitz, Michael. Director of Hudson Institute's Project for Civil Justice Reform and Project for International Religious Liberty Monday. Major player in original passage of the TVPA. US. Phone interview. June 23, 2014.

16. Jakiel, Sarah. Chief Program Officer, Polaris Project, US. Phone interview. July 23, 2014

17. Kei, Chrisanjui. Former volunteer with Centre for Domestic Training and Development (CDTD). Nairobi, Kenya. In-person interview by Jessica Van Meir. September 30, 2014.

18. Keith, Shannon. Founder/CEO, International Princess Project, US. Phone interview. July 24, 2014.

19. Lambert, Steph. Stand Against Slavery and Justice Acts New Zealand. Phone interview. July 10, 2014.

20. Mahamoud, Omar. Project Coordinator, Friends of Suffering Humanity, Ghana. Phone interview. July 14, 2014.

21. Majdalani, Carla. Asociación Civil La Casa del Encuentro, Argentina. Skype interview by Jessica Van Meir. June 25, 2015.

22. Malinowski, Radoslaw "Radek." Founder, HAART, Nairobi, Kenya. In-person interview by Jessica Van Meir. July 30, 2014.

23. Manzo, Rosa. Director and co-founder, Fundación Quimera, Ecuador. Phone interview by Jessica Van Meir. Translated by Gonzalo Pernas Chamorro. April 2, 2015.

24. Matai, Ian. Reaching Out Romania, Romania. Phone interview. July 22, 2014.

25. Mattar, Mohamed. Executive Director, the Protection Project, Johns Hopkins University, US. Phone interview. September 24, 2015.

26. Mihaere, Peter J. Chief Executive Officer, Stand Against Slavery, New Zealand. Email correspondence. July 13, 2014.

27. Okinda, Joy. Senior Program Manager, Undugu Society. Nairobi, Kenya. In-person interview by Jessica Van Meir. August 7, 2014.

28. Otieno, Aggrey. Program Coordinator, African Network for the Prevention and Protection against Child Abuse and Neglect. Nairobi, Kenya. In-person interview by Jessica Van Meir. August 15, 2014.

29. Pongsawat, Pitch. Professor in government department of political science at Chulalongkorn University, Bangkok, Thailand. In-person interview by Pimchanok Chuaylua. January 13, 2016.

30. Prober, Roz. Beyond borders ECPAT, Canada. Phone interview. July 23, 2014.

31. Rosakova, Maia. Stellit. Durham, NC. In-person interview. August 8, 2014.

32. Rusk, Alesha. International Justice Mission, US. Phone interview. September 8, 2014.

33. Sacht, Kenny. Wipe Every Tear, Philippines. Phone interview. July 8, 2014.

34. Schmitt, Gabi. FIM – Frauenrecht ist Menschenrecht e.V. Beratungs- und Informationszentrum für Migrantinnen. Germany. Phone interview. July 15, 2014.

35. Segawa, Aiki. Lighthouse, Japan. Email exchange. July 15, 2014.

36. Skrivánkova, Klára. European Programme and Advocacy Coordinator, Anti-Slavery International, United Kingdom. In-person interview, Durham, NC. November 30, 2015.

37. Smith, Linda. Founder and President, Shared Hope International, US. Phone interview. June 20, 2014.

38. Vardaman, Samantha. Senior Director, Shared Hope International, US. Phone interview. June 26, 2014.
39. Vladenmaiier, Olena. Living for Tomorrow, Estonia. Phone interview. July 9, 2014.

IGOs

40. Garcia-Robles, Fernando. Anti-Trafficking in Persons' Coordinator, OAS. Washington, DC. Phone interview by Renata Dinamarco. January 17, 2013.
41. Haddin, Youla. Advisor on Trafficking in Persons, The Office of the High Commissioner for Human rights, Geneva. Phone interview. June 10, 2014.
42. Interview # 1. Anonymous ILO source. Phone interview. June 24, 2014.
43. Macciavello, Maria. Assistance to Vulnerable Migrant Specialist, Migrant Assistance Division, Department of Migration Management, International Organization for Migration (IOM). Geneva. Informal phone conversation. May 7, 2014.
44. Interview #3. Counter-Trafficking and Protection, International Organization for Migration (IOM), Geneva. July 15, 2014.
45. Neil, Kerry. Child Protection Specialist, UNICEF, New York, US. Phone interview. July 1, 2014.
46. Noguchi, Yoshie. Senior Legal Specialist, Child Labour, ILO, Geneva. Phone interview. June 13, 2014.
47. Rivzi, Sumbul. Senior Legal Officer, Head of Unit (Asylum & Migration), UNHCR, Geneva. June 27, 2014.
48. Rizvi, Sumbul. Senior Legal Officer, Head of Unit (Asylum & Migration), Protection Policy & Legal Advice, Pillar I – Policy & Law, Division of International Protection, UNHCR, Geneva. Phone interview. June 26, 2014.
49. Shahinian, Gulnara. Democracy Today, Former UN Special Rapporteur on Contemporary Forms of Slavery, 2008–2014. Armenia. Phone interview. November 10, 2014.
50. Van de Glind, Hans. Senior specialist and focal point for child trafficking of the ILO International Programme on the Elimination of Child Labour, ILO, Geneva. Phone interview. June 13, 2014.

Government Officials

US Government

51. Dobriansky, Paula. Former Under Secretary of State for Democracy and Global Affairs from 2001–2009. July 15, 2014.
52. Amy O'Neill Richards, Senior Advisor to the Director in the State Department's Office to Monitor and Combat Trafficking in Persons. In-person interview, Washington, DC. August 28, 2014.
53. Lagon, Mark. US TIP ambassador 2006–2009, 2007–2009 former Ambassador-at-Large, Office to Monitor and Combat Trafficking in Persons, Washington, DC. Informal conversation. February 4, 2013.
54. Miller, John. Ambassador-at-Large, Office to Monitor and Combat Trafficking in Persons, 2002–2006. Phone interview. June 18, 2014.
55. Napper, Larry. Ambassador to Kazakhstan 2001–2004. Interview College Station, Texas, via phone. February 26, 2015 and again March 3, 2015 (follow up).
56. Ordway, John. US Ambassador to Kazakhstan, 2004–2008. US Ambassador to Armenia from 2001–2004. Phone interview. March 6, 2015.
57. Princess Harriss, Senior Development Policy Officer, Department of Policy and Evaluation, Millennium Challenge Corporation. Phone interview. July 7, 2014.
58. Smith, Cindy J. Sr. Coordinator for Programs, J/TIP; US Department of State. In person interview, Washington, DC. August 15, 2014.
59. Kennelly, Nan. Principal Deputy overseeing Reports and Political Affairs. J/TIP; US Department of State. In-person interview, Washington, DC. August 15, 2014.
60. Warren, Jimmy. Senior Coordinator and Program Manager, Overseas Prosecutorial Development, Assistance, and Training (OPDAT), Criminal Division, US Department of Justice. In-person interview. October 22, 2014.
61. Taylor, Mark. Former Senior Coordinator for Reports and Political Affairs at J/TIP from 2003–2013. Phone interview. November 6, 2014.

Group meetings at the Department of State, Office to Monitor and Combat Trafficking in Persons, Washington, DC. August 15, 2014 and February 5, 2013. Attending:

62. Joe Scovitch (since January 2014), Deputy Senior Coordinator for Reports and Political Affairs, Western Hemisphere Affairs, East Asia Pacific, Africa.
63. Jane Sigmon, Senior Advisor to the Director.
64. Desirée M. Suo, Deputy Senior Coordinator, Reports and Political Affairs.
65. Soumya Silver, AF. Madagascar.
66. Aaron King, fellowship program, intern.
67. Mai Shiozaki, Senior Public Affairs Specialist.
68. Alison Friedman, Deputy Director overseeing International Programs and Public Engagement.
69. Amy Rofman, Western Hemisphere and Europe, Reports and Political Affairs.
70. Jennifer Donnelly, Western Hemisphere and Europe, Reports and Political Affairs.
71. Sara Gilmer, Western Hemisphere, Reports and Political Affairs.
72. Martha Lovejoy, Eastern and Northern Europe, Reports and Political Affairs.
73. Kendra Kreider, South East Asia and Africa, Reports and Political Affairs.
74. Julie Hicks, Near East Asia and North Africa, Reports and Political Affairs.
75. Marisa Ferri, Deputy Senior Coordinator, International Programs.
76. Ann Karl Slusarz, Public Affairs Specialist, Public Engagement.
77. Caitlin Heidenreich, Program Analyst/Student Trainee.
78. Anna Patrick, Public Engagement Staff Assistant.

Government, not US

79. Abelman, Marteen. Head of the office, Dutch national rapporteur, Holland. Phone interview. August 18, 2014.
80. Colombo, Marcelo. Head of the Prosecutor's Office for the Combatting of Trafficking and Exploitation of Persons, Argentina. Email correspondence with Jessica Van Meir. August 29, 2015.
81. Fernandez, Aníbal. Former Chief of the Cabinet of Ministers, Argentina. Phone interview by Jessica Van Meir. November 24, 2015.
82. Minayo, Lucy. Kenya National Commission on Human Rights, Senior Human Rights Officer, Kenya. Phone interview by Jessica Weiss. July 29, 2014.

83. Pineda, Nora Suyapa Urbina. Abogado, Fiscal Especial de la Niñez. president of the Commission Against Trafficking in Persons, Honduras. Phone interview by Renata Dinamarco. April 1, 2013.

84. Rodriguez, Marcela. Head of the Programa de Asesoramiento y Patrocinio para las Víctimas del Delito de Trata de Personas (Program of Advice and Sponsorship for Victims of Trafficking in Persons). Argentina. Skype interview and email with Jessica Van Meir. October 30, 2015.

85. Roujanavong, Wanchai. Director General, International Affairs Department, Office of the Attorney General of Thailand, also with ECPAT, Thailand. Phone interview. December 2, 2014.

86. Mellanen, Inkeri. Finnish advisor, National assistance system for victims of trafficking, Finland. Phone interview. November 20, 2014.

87. Encinas, Cristian. Legal Team Coordinator, National Program of Rescue and Assistance of Victims of Trafficking, Argentina. In-person interview by Jessica Van Meir. July 10, 2015.

Group interview with Prosecutor's Office for the Combatting of Trafficking and Exploitation of Persons, Argentina. In-person interview by Jessica Van Meir. July 22, 2015. Attending:

88. Victoria Sassola, prosecretaria.
89. Agustina Dangelo, jefa de despacho.
90. Octavia Botalla, official.

THE GLOBAL SURVEY

From 2012 to 2014, with the help of research assistants, I assembled a database of over 1,000 NGOs working on TIP issues around the world. During the summer and fall of 2014 over 500 NGOs working in 133 countries responded to a survey designed to understand their engagement with the US and the TIP Report, as well as their assessments of the role of the US in their countries and their own governments' performance.[1]

---

[1] See Heiss and Kelley for a complete summary of the survey results. Heiss and Kelley 2016.

Survey Methodology

With the help of Andrew Heiss, then a doctoral student at Duke, I used Qualtrics to administer the survey through the Internet. Online surveys pose several methodological challenges. First, they introduce a technology bias. Small grassroots organizations without an online presence are missing from the database and those without easy Internet access or poor English faced barriers to participate. Finally, all surveys have response bias – willingness to participate is rarely random.

We took several steps to address these problems, based on the methods and recommendations of others.[2] To encourage participation, we sent each NGO a set of three personalized email invitations, re-sent approximately every two weeks. Organizations without a working email address were contacted by phone. Each invitation included a link to the survey and an offer to complete the survey via phone, and respondents were allowed to remain anonymous. We translated the survey into Spanish and Russian and encouraged respondents to answer all free-response questions in their native language. We provided additional reminders and assistance to respondents who began the survey but did not complete it and sent links to allow organizations to resume their response. To minimize frustration that might lead respondents to quit prematurely, they were free to skip any question and could move back and forth in the survey. Additional efforts were made to reach non-responding NGOs by phone if we had very low participation from their countries.

Participation Rates and Demographics

We administered the survey to 1,103 NGOs and received responses from 480 unique organizations, yielding a participation rate of 43.5 percent. Because NGOs often work in multiple countries, we allowed respondents to answer a series of country-specific questions for up to five different countries, resulting in 561 country-organization responses. Most organizations (415, or 86.5 percent) chose to fill out the survey for just one country. Figure A1.1a shows the location of the NGO respondents' headquarters and Figure A1.1b shows their work location.

The NGOs surveyed have a nearly global reach. The majority of organizations (60 percent) are based in either Asia or Europe, roughly a quarter are based in North or South America, and fewer than 20 percent work in Africa.

---

[2] Büthe and Mattli 2011, Edwards et al. 2009.

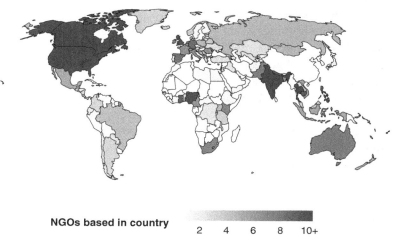

NGOs based in country

2   4   6   8   10+

FIGURE A1.1a. Country location of NGO survey respondent headquarters. Number of NGOs: 469. Number of countries: 106.

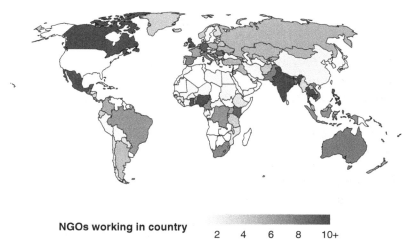

NGOs working in country

2   4   6   8   10+

FIGURE A1.1b. Country location of NGO survey respondent work. Number of countries: 125.

On average, anti-TIP NGOs spend a little over half of their time and resources focused specifically on fighting trafficking and assisting victims and an overwhelming majority (93 percent) has at least some knowledge about the TIP policies in the countries they work in. Most organizations focus on sex (85 percent) and labor (61 percent) trafficking issues; 50 percent focus on both simultaneously. A handful of organizations

(30, or 6 percent) work with human organ trafficking, and dozens of others deal with other issues such as brokered marriages, domestic servitude, illegal adoptions, and forced begging. Approximately two-thirds of NGOs serve and advocate for children and/or adult trafficking victims, and many of those who work with adults specified working especially with women and young girls.

Most organizations (83 percent) advocate for prevention and improved education about TIP issues, and nearly three-fourths assist trafficking victims by running safe houses and shelters, operating special hotlines, helping start businesses, or providing physical and emotional health care.

DOCUMENT ANALYSIS

The project drew on thousands of media accounts and hundreds of primary documents from intergovernmental organizations, the US Department of State, and other sources.

US Diplomatic Cables

The Nature of the Archive and the Prevalence of Documented Reactions to the TIP Report

The diplomatic cables archive leaked through Wikileaks in September 2011 contained about a quarter-million cables mostly from 2000 to early 2010. However, the archive is incomplete and the record is strongest in 2007–2009. One analysis of the cables estimates that the volume released constitute about 5 percent of the total between 2005 and 2010, but with considerable variation at the embassy level.[3] The coverage in the period 2001–2004, which is also part of the analysis in this book, is even lower. Figure A1.2 shows an analysis of the estimated availability by year. The estimated total cables are calculated based on an extrapolation from the number and date last available cable in any given year, which makes it possible to estimate the rate of cables in any given year up to that point and then extend this to the end of the year to arrive at a total for the year. The figure suggests that by far the best coverage occurs in 2007–2009.

---

[3] Gill and Spirling 2014.

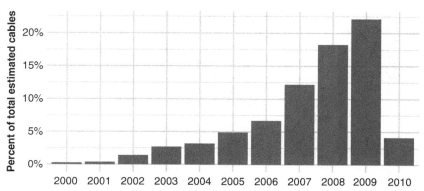

FIGURE A1.2. Observed Wikileaks US Department of State cables as a percentage of the estimated number of cables.

Identifying TIP-Related Cables

To identify cables for this project we derived an algorithm to extract all cables that discussed human trafficking, while minimizing cables about other forms of trafficking such as in drugs, ivory, wildlife, diamond, and, yes, traffic congestion! After additional manual cleaning of the data, about 8,500 relevant cables remained that discussed human trafficking in some way. These are the cables that have served as sources for the illustrations and case studies.

Analysis of Missingness

It is important to understand the pattern of cable availability. The top panel of Figure A1.3 charts the number of all available Wikileaks cables by year, while the middle panel shows the number of cables discussing TIP. The two track closely, suggesting that the availability of the TIP related cables is a function of the availability of the overall body of cables.

This same pattern holds with respect to information about how a state reacts to TIP Report. Of all the Wikileaks cables about TIP, nearly 500 documents recounted reactions by government officials to the annual TIP Reports. Some of these were repetitions of the same type of concern in the same country in the same year. It one only counts one type of reaction once per year then 481 reactions to 217 reports on 99 different countries remained.

The bottom panel of Figure A1.3 shows the total number of cables discussing a state's reaction to the TIP Report. Year 2000 is omitted because

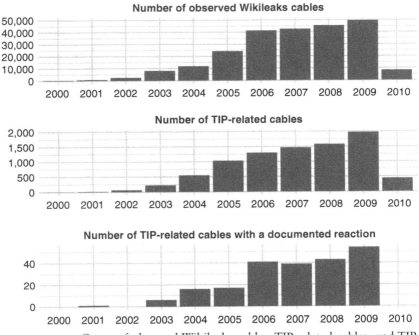

FIGURE A1.3. Count of observed Wikileaks cables, TIP-related cables, and TIP-related cables with a documented reaction.

the reports only started in 2001, and year 2010 is omitted because the archives end before the release of the 2010 report. Again, the trend tracks closely with the total number of observed cables, suggesting that whether a TIP response is present is a function of general archival availability.

Statistical analysis of the cable availability was used to analyze whether factors related to trafficking predicted the availability of cables. The dependent variable was created by first using the numbering system of the cables to calculate the total number of cables likely issued for each embassy or consulate for each year. Diplomats verified the validity of using the numbering system in this way. For each country-year, the last available cable ID number was used to calculate the rate of cables in that year to that date and then extrapolate the total for the year. For each year the actual number of available cables was then tallied for each country, based on their availability in Wikileaks. This was then used to derive the percentage of cables available for a given year for each country. The results below show no correlations with TIP factors at conventional statistical levels.

TABLE A1.1. *Percentage of estimated cables actually present*

	Model A1.1
GDP per capita (logged)	1.633***
	(0.340)
Total foreign aid (logged)	0.884***
	(0.287)
Worse total freedom	0.325***
	(0.103)
TIP tier	0.230
	(0.421)
Trafficking criminalized	−0.539
	(0.780)
Trafficking intensity in transit countries	−0.490
	(0.302)
Trafficking intensity in countries of origin	−0.178
	(0.323)
Trafficking intensity in destination countries	−0.225
	(0.276)
2000 Palermo Protocol ratification	0.286
	(0.748)
Constant	−31.380***
	(7.536)
Year fixed effects	Yes
Observations	735
R^2	0.439
Adjusted R^2	0.424
Residual Std. Error	8.175
	(df = 715)
F Statistic	29.419***
	(df = 19; 715)

Note: *p **p ***p < 0.01. Standard OLS estimates.

Coding the Cables

The documents were loaded into software for qualitative analysis, *QDA Miner*, and coding decisions were tagged in the text for retrieval and replication.[4] The complete set of cables and all codes is available at the book's resources site (www.cambridge.org/ScorecardDiplomacy).

---

[4] A full record of all statements and how they were coded is available from the author.

Coding the Reactions to the TIP Report

The cables were coded with an eye to ascertaining whether the reaction revealed concerns about a country's image or about funding. The categories were refined as the coding process unfolded. Reactions fell logically into 12 sub-categories as described in Table A1.2.

Many reports received a wide range of reactions. For example, a country might object to the content of the report, but still cooperate with the embassy. Thus countries were allowed to have multiple types of reaction in one year (indeed about 60 percent do). A reaction could also be coded as multiple types – for example, in the same statement, an official may express both anger and embarrassment. Multiple records of the same reaction were coded as just one occurrence for that report year so that if two different officials express the same reaction or the same reaction is discussed in two different cables, this reaction is simply coded as present for that country for that year.

Coding Other Items

The cables were also coded for the following: Meetings, levels of officials at meeting both US and local, US activities locally related to TIP, status of any anti-TIP law and US engagement with the law, mentions of IGOs and NGOs, diplomatic use of the tiers, for example, as sources of conditionality, discussions of funding, discussions of grant proposals, notable remarks, and several other miscellaneous tags.

Media Accounts

Reactions to Report
Stories were downloaded from LexisNexis according to the following search criteria: Stories were included if they contained the words "blacklist" OR "Watch List" OR "Watch List" OR "Tier" within the same sentence as the phrases "human trafficking" OR "Trafficking in persons." Stories were also included if they contained the terms "US" OR "U.S." OR "United States" OR "State Department" OR "Department of State" within the same paragraph as the phrase "human trafficking report" OR "Trafficking in Persons Report" OR "TIP Report" OR "report on trafficking in persons" OR "report on human trafficking." The cutoff date was the date for the search, which was September 27, 2012. This search

TABLE A1.2. *Coding scheme for the reactions to the US TIP Report documented in US Department of State cables*

Funding

Funding — Any reaction or discussion, even if not initiated by the country official, that includes mention of possible sanctions, trade implications, investment concern or other material fall out is coded as a *Funding* concern.

Image

Comparisons — Officials may make comparisons between themselves and other countries and protest at how they are grouped with specific other countries.

Public face-saving — Embassy officials note that officials make public statements that differ from private ones, usually being more accepting of the ratings in private.

Embarrassment — Officials express embarrassment or explicitly mention reputational concerns about the rating.

Negative

Anger or frustration — Officials express anger, and may even threaten the US with suspending cooperation on other issues.

US arrogance — Officials accuse the US of overreaching, perhaps criticizing the US own trafficking problem and dismissing US criticism as improper interference.

Disappointment — In discussion of ratings, officials express disappointment or other negative reactions of an unspecified nature.

Objection, moving goal posts — Officials claim the report is inaccurate or politically motivated, or they complain about the standards used in the report.

Other negative reaction — The embassy simply reports that the country reacted negatively or complained, etc.

Positive

How to improve — Countries seek specific information on how they can improve their ratings or provide US officials with plans for how they will address the shortcomings pointed out in the report.

Cooperative — Countries strike a cooperative mode, discussing ways to respond to US recommendations or ways to continue to cooperate to combat trafficking.

Appreciation — Officials express appreciation for the rating or boast about it.

is narrow; it misses many domestic news sources, or stories that refer to the trafficking report, but do not discuss tiers, for example.

This yielded 1,074 stories, 308 of which contained a government reaction to 176 separate TIP Reports. Some stories contained multiple types of reactions for a total of 326 reactions. All the reactions were coded according to the same coding scheme used for reactions to the TIP Report in the US diplomatic cables (see below).

Media Coverage of Human Trafficking in Oman

I searched LexisNexis for news stories about "Human Trafficking" or "Trafficking in Persons" during 2003–2012. These were coded by month.

Organizational Documents

Organizational websites for all major IGOs involved in the fight against human trafficking as well as major US agencies such as the Department of Justice (DOJ) and the US USAID were searched for reports on their efforts. The information was used to supplement the case studies and to understand the programs and efforts of other actors.

DATA

Data was coded specifically for this project and combined with pre-existing data. This was used for descriptive and traditional statistical analysis. Original data created included a measure of NGO presence, a dataset of public and private reactions to TIP Reports, and data on criminalization updated from a prior project of mine with Beth Simmons. Tables A1.3–4 provide a full description and summary of all the variables included in the models used in this book.

Analysis

The analysis is done on the country-year level. Models are indicated for each table.

TABLE A1.3. *Description of all variables used in statistical analysis*

Variable	Description	Source	Chapters
2000 TIP protocol ratification	An indicator (0/1) for whether a country has ratified the UN Palermo Protocol to Prevent, Suppress and Punish Trafficking in Persons Especially Women and Children, supplementing the United Nations Convention against Transnational Organized Crime	United Nations Treaty Collection (https://treaties. un.org/Pages/ViewDetails. aspx?src=TREATY&mtdsg_ no=XVIII-12-a&chapter=18)	3, 4, 5, 6, 7
Aid greater than $100 million	Dichotomous variable (0/1) indicating whether a country received more than $100 million in aid from the US.	US Overseas Loans & Grants (Greenbook)	6
Corruption	"Control of corruption captures perceptions of the extent to which public power is exercised for private gain."	Worldwide Governance Indicators project	3, 6
Coverage / Human trafficking news (logged)	The log of the number of times a country's name will appear in a news story in the LexisNexis database within 50 words of the phrase "human trafficking" (or a close cognate)	Author generated	4
Criminalization	The complete prohibition of all forms of human trafficking, including sex and labor trafficking for men and women, children and adults. Penalties must be significant, usually meaning minimum sentences of 3–5 years. Note that, because the US trafficking report comes out annually in June, to avoid sequencing errors in our inference, a country is coded as having fully criminalized in a given year only if it had done so prior to the issuance of the report in June. Dates usually refer to the actual enactment of the legislation, but in cases where that information is not available, the month of passage of the legislation is used. If no date could be established, the country was coded as having fully criminalized that year (equivalent to an assumption that it criminalized before the report came out, thus biasing any systematic error against a finding of an effect of the report on criminalization).	UN Global Report on Trafficking, 2009. US TIP Reports, International Organization of Migration (IOM) database and other sources	3, 4, 5, 6, 7

(*continued*)

TABLE A1.3. (*continued*)

Variable	Description	Source	Chapters
FDI from US (logged)	Total amount of foreign direct investment (FDI) from the US.	Bilateral FDI statistics, UN Conference on Trade and Development (http://unctad.org/en/Pages/DIAE/FDI%20Statistics/FDI-Statistics-Bilateral.aspx)	7
First demotion (t−1)	Dichotomous variable (0/1) coded 1 in a year that a country is placed either on the Watch List or rated a Tier 3 (without first having been on the Watch List) for the first time.	TIP Report	6, 7
First demotion (t−2)	Dichotomous variable (0/1) coded 1 in a year that a country is placed either on the Watch List or rated a Tier 3 (without first having been on the Watch List) for the first time.	TIP Report	6, 7
First demotion (t−3)	Dichotomous variable (0/1) coded 1 in a year that a country is placed either on the Watch List or rated a Tier 3 (without first having been on the Watch List) for the first time.	TIP Report	6, 7
GDP (logged)	GDP in current US dollars	World Bank indicators	3
GDP per capita (logged)	GDP / Total Population (logged) in current US dollars	World Bank indicators	4, 5, 6
Has BIT with US	Dichotomous variable (0/1) indicating whether a country has signed a bilateral investment treaty (BIT) with the US.	Office of the United States Trade Representative (https://ustr.gov/trade-agreements/bilateral-investment-treaties)	7
Imports to US (logged)	Total value of imports to the US for a given country.	IMF (http://data.imf.org/regular.aspx?key=61013712)	7

In report	Dichotomous variable indicating whether a country is included in the report.	TIP Report	4, 6, 7
Missing information	A count of number of variables for which information is missing in a given year for: Freedom House civil liberties, the International Country Risk Guide corruption score, Erik Voeten's UN Affinity voting data, and four variables from the World Bank: Net Overseas Development Assistance (ODA), Intentional homicides, health expenditures, and GDP. The variable also counts the three variables from the UN incidence data on TIP, adding a one for each of these variables where the UN did not find any information.	Author generated based on included variables and their sources	3, 6, 7
NGO density	A count of number of total times the annual US State Department TIP Report for a given country mentions the word NGO, divided by the number of reports in the data. Thus, it captures average number of NGO mentions per report for a given country and it is a constant for each country. The data is extended backwards to years before a country was included in the report.	TIP report, variable generated by author	3, 6
Reaction	Indicator of whether a country had any reaction to the report in a given year.	Author generated from Wikileaks cables	5, 6
Regional density of criminalization	A measure capturing the percentage of countries in a region that have criminalized trafficking.	Generated based on the criminalization variable	3, 6, 7
Rule of law	"Rule of law captures perceptions of the extent to which agents have confidence in and abide by the rules of society."	Worldwide Governance Indicators project	3
Share of total trade with US	Share of a country's total trade (imports plus exports) that is with the US.	International Monetary Fund, Direction of Trade Statistics	5
Share of women in parliament	Share of voting seats in the lower house of national parliaments held by women (percentage of total seats), as of the last day of the listed year.	Women in National Parliaments, statistical archive. www.ipu.org/ wmn-e/classif- arc.htm, accessed February 2012	6, 7

(continued)

Variable	Description	Source	Chapters
Tier 1	Dichotomous variable (0/1) indicating whether the US has rated a country as Tier 1.	TIP Report	6
Tier 2	Dichotomous variable (0/1) indicating whether the US has rated a country as Tier 2.	TIP Report	5, 6
Tier 3	Dichotomous variable (0/1) indicating whether the US has rated a country as Tier 3.	TIP Report	5, 6
Total population (logged)	The log of total population.	World Bank indicators	3, 4, 5, 6
Total population (logged)	The log of total population.	World Bank indicators	3
Total reactions	Count of non-media reactions in Wikileaks cables.	Author generated from Wikileaks cables	6
Trafficking intensity in countries of origin	Incidence of reporting of trafficking persons in origin countries. 1=very low; 2=low; 3=medium; 4=high; 5=very high.	2006 UNODC TIP Report, Appendix 5: Incidence of reporting of (destination/origin/transit) countries. The incidence from the 2006 report is extended to all years in the analysis.	3, 4, 6
Trafficking intensity in destination countries	Incidence of reporting of trafficking persons in destination countries. 1=very low; 2=low; 3=medium; 4=high; 5=very high.	2006 UNODC TIP Report, Appendix 5: Incidence of reporting of (destination/origin/transit) countries. The incidence from the 2006 report is extended to all years in the analysis.	3, 4, 6

Variable	Description	Source	
Trafficking intensity in transit countries	Incidence of reporting of trafficking persons in transit countries. 1=very low; 2=low; 3=medium; 4=high; 5=very high.	2006 UNODC TIP Report, Appendix 5: Incidence of reporting of (destination/origin/transit) countries. The incidence from the 2006 report is extended to all years in the analysis.	3, 4, 6
US aid (logged)	The log of Total Aid from the US constant 2010 $US. We add 1 before taking the log so that the value for no aid is 0.	US Overseas Loans & Grants (Greenbook)	3, 5, 6, 7
US aid as share of total aid (logged)	Proportion of foreign aid from the US out of all received aid.	AidData (http://aiddata.org)	7
US military aid (logged)	Total military aid provided by the US.	Security Assistance Monitor (www.securityassistance.org/data/country/military/country/1996/2017/is_all/Global)	7
US pressure	Dichotomous variable (0/1) indicating whether the US has placed the country on the Watch List or rated the country Tier 3.	TIP Report	3, 5, 7
Watchlist	Dichotomous variable (0/1) indicating whether the US has placed a country on the Tier 2 Watch List, which means that it may drop to Tier 3 the following year.	TIP Report	5, 6
Worse civil liberties	Freedom House Civil Liberties; 1 to 7 scale, with 1 representing the best civil liberties and 7 the worst.	Freedom House (www.freedomhouse.org/reports)	3, 4, 6, 7
Worse total freedom	Sum of Freedom House political rights and civil liberties scores. 2 to 14 scale, with 2 representing the best total freedom and 7 the worst.	Freedom House (www.freedomhouse.org/reports)	5, 6

TABLE A1.4a. *Summary of continuous variables used in statistical analysis*

Variable	Mean	Median	Standard deviation	Min	Max
Corruption	−0.057	−0.31	0.98	0.0	2.4
Coverage / Human trafficking news (logged)	3.333	3.53	1.57	0.0	7.7
FDI from US (logged)	8.039	0.00	9.57	0.0	25.4
GDP (logged)	23.376	23.20	2.35	18.0	30.1
GDP per capita (logged)	7.723	7.66	1.57	4.4	10.9
Imports to US (logged)	19.010	19.58	4.62	0.0	26.7
Missing information	2.545	2.00	1.63	0.0	7.0
NGO density	2.901	2.89	1.43	0.0	9.1
Rule of law	−0.099	−0.34	0.97	0.0	2.0
Total population (logged)	15.653	15.85	1.99	10.7	21.0
Total reactions	0.360	0.00	1.05	0.0	10.0
Trafficking intensity in countries of origin	2.350	3.00	1.56	0.0	5.0
Trafficking intensity in destination countries	2.251	2.00	1.45	0.0	5.0
Trafficking intensity in transit countries	1.395	1.00	1.49	0.0	5.0
US aid (logged)	13.910	16.47	6.57	0.0	22.9
US military aid (logged)	11.818	13.58	6.01	0.0	23.0
Worse civil liberties	3.353	3.00	1.80	1.0	7.0
Worse total freedom	6.807	6.00	3.88	2.0	14.0

Statistical Packages

All statistical analysis and the figures in this manuscript was done with the following software and with the able assistance of Andrew Heiss.

Hlavac, Marek. 2015. *stargazer: Well-Formatted Regression and Summary Statistics Tables*. http://CRAN.R-project.org/package= stargazer. Version 5.2.

R Core Team. 2016. *R: A language and environment for statistical computing*. Vienna, Austria: R Foundation for Statistical Computing. www.r-project.org. Version 3.3.0.

Wickham, Hadley. 2009. *ggplot2: Elegant Graphics for Data Analysis*. Springer New York. http://had.co.nz/ggplot2/book. Version 2.1.0.

TABLE A1.4b. *Summary of binary variables used in statistical analysis*

Variable	Mean proportion	Standard deviation
2000 TIP protocol ratification	0.42	0.49
Aid greater than $100 million	0.20	0.40
Criminalization	0.36	0.48
First demotion (t–1)	0.09	0.28
First demotion (t–2)	0.08	0.27
First demotion (t–3)	0.07	0.25
Has BIT with US	0.27	0.44
In report	0.74	0.44
Reaction	0.16	0.37
Regional density of criminalization	0.30	0.30
Share of total trade with US	0.12	0.14
Share of women in parliament	0.15	0.10
Tier 1	0.12	0.32
Tier 2	0.37	0.48
Tier 3	0.08	0.28
US aid as share of GDP (logged)	0.02	0.06
US aid as share of total aid (logged)	0.10	0.16
US pressure	0.24	0.43
US trade as share of GDP (logged)	0.09	0.11
Watchlist	0.16	0.37

CASE STUDIES

Drawing on the interviews and the document analysis, over 15 case studies were crafted to systematically examine evidence for the steps in the scorecard diplomacy cycle to analyze the likelihood of causality between US efforts and observed outcomes.

The cases serve to examine whether scorecard diplomacy sometimes works as purported, whether its possible to figure out some factors that facilitate or hinder it, and to illustrate some of the core mechanisms by probing the occurrence of some of the interaction on the ground. The cases are not selected to test the overall effectiveness of scorecard diplomacy by demonstrating a strong correlation between US efforts and progress.

The case studies are extraordinarily rich due to the availability of the embassy cables, but the availability of information is very uneven over time. This makes it difficult to draw inferences about what happens during times when there is less information and thus to compare countries to themselves over time. The strategy is to focus primarily on the times when information is rich. Thus, the focus usually wanes by early 2010. The information contains variation in outcomes: at times embassies report progress and at other times stagnation, or setbacks. What can be learned about these episodes? How do they fit with the arguments about scorecard diplomacy, and what do they tell us about which other factors are important?

Case Selection

The cases studies are of countries and consider the activities of multiple stakeholders at the international, national, and local levels. Countries were chosen based on and limited by a several factors. First and foremost, because the main source for the information is the diplomatic cables and because the subset of cables released was very uneven across countries, it was important to choose cases that were relative information rich, that is, cases with more cables about trafficking. This likely biases the cases towards countries where the US has been more active, although variation remains. It's also worth noting that the measure of engagement, namely the share of overall diplomatic cables that are on the subject of trafficking, does not differ statistically between the cases and non-cases. See Table A1.6 for this and other comparison statistics. Second, because legislation has been such a major part of US efforts, it was useful to choose several cases where there were cables when legislation was being discussed in various countries. Another important factor was variation in tier ratings across the cases. Finally, it was useful to have some variation in region and regime type to see whether any differences were apparent.

Table A1.5 overviews the basic characteristics of the chosen cases, including the level of US effort, the range of tiers they received in the years they were included in the report, as well as a measure of how often on average that the US TIP Reports mentioned NGOs or IGOs for each of these countries. It also shows the level and year of criminalization.

Comparison of Case Study Country Attributes with Non-Case Study Countries

A comparison of policy progress in the case studies versus the rest of the sample is useful. As seen in Table A1.6, the case studies are similar to the non-country cases in most regards, including the perceived level and type of trafficking problem in the early 2000s and the engagement of IGOs and NGOs with the US embassy and TIP. They are similar on other important things such as GDP per capita, population size and aid. The case studies do have a higher level of US engagement as measured in

TABLE A1.5. Overview of case study attributes

	Total TIP documents (% of all available cables for country)	Year of first documents (first year of TIP Report)	Range of TIP tiers (WL: Watch List)	Level of criminalization* (years)	NGO activity** mean = 2.90 range 0–9	Main IGOs** (activity level) mean= 0.81 range 0–4
Argentina	194 (9%)	2004 (2004)	2–WL	Full (2008) Strengthened (2012)	4.5	0.75
Armenia	92 (5%)	2003 (2002)	2–3	Partial (2003) Full (2006)	4.6	0.5
Chad	43 (5%)	2005 (2005)	2–3	None	3	3.85
Ecuador	115 (8%)	2004 (2004)	2–3	Full (2005)	2	0.75
Honduras	131 (7%)	2002 (2001)	2–WL	Partial (2006) Full (2012)	4.63	0.63
Indonesia	151 (5%)	2006# (2001)	2–3	Partial (pre study) Full (2007)	4	0.63
Israel	82 (2%)	2004 (2001)	2–3	Partial (2000) Full (2006)	4.36	0.09
Japan	70 (1%)	2006 (2001)	2–WL	Partial (2005)	3.72	2
Kazakhstan	94 (5%)	2006 (2001)	2–3	Partial (2002) Full (2003)	4.27	0.45
Malaysia	133 (13%)	2006 (2001)	2–3	Partial (2001) Full (2007) Strengthened (2010)	2.81	0.27
Mozambique	93 (10%)	2003 (2003)	2–WL	Full (2008)	4.22	0.66
Nigeria	179 (6%)	2001 (2001)	1–WL	Full (2003)	2	.45
Oman	163 (10%)	2004 (2005)	2–3	Full (2008)	.28	.71
UAE	179 (6%)	2003 (2001)	1–3	Full (2006)	1.45	1
Zimbabwe	38 (1%)	2003 (2002)	2–3	Partial (2014)	3.55	2.44

* Partial indicates some covering laws that did not fully meet the UN Trafficking protocol criteria
** Based on authors data calculated on average mentions in the annual TIP Reports.
# One in 2003.

TABLE A1.6. *Comparison of case study countries and other countries in years they are included in the TIP Report*

Statistic	Case study countries	Other countries	Difference	Significant difference at p = 0.05
US TIP effort (% of cables mentioning TIP)	0.063	0.0402	0.0228	Yes, more engaged
Tier	2.24	2.02	0.219	Yes, higher tiers
Incidence (transit)	0.933	1.5	−0.563	No
Incidence (origin)	2.2	2.4	−0.195	No
Incidence (destination)	2.4	2.27	0.129	No
Count of NGOs	3.3	2.88	0.413	No
Count of IGOs	1.02	0.802	0.213	No
TIP media coverage	113	89.5	23.1	Yes, more coverage
GDP per capita (constant 2000 dollars)	$8,677	$6,973	$1,704	No
Population	48M	45M	3,620,624	No
Corruption	2.13	2.62	−0.485	Yes, more corrupt
Political rights	3.98	3.44	0.542	Yes, less democratic
Aid (OECD)	$14.5	$230	−$215	No
Aid (US)	$121	$96	$24.8	No
Ratification of 2000 Palermo Protocol	0.8	0.791	0.00915	No

the percent of US cables devoted to the trafficking issue, and also slightly worse tiers, and more news coverage of TIP issues. In general, they are slightly "worse" countries in terms of democracy and corruption, which likely explains the higher engagement – the US clearly does not engage as much with countries consistently rated Tier 1, for example, but it made no sense to included such countries in the case studies. While the chosen cases get more total news coverage, they don't get more per capita. Similarly, they get more aid, but not per capita. The fact that the cases are

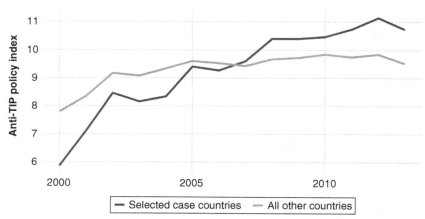

FIGURE A1.4. Average 3P anti-TIP policy index for 15 case study countries compared to all other countries.

more corrupt and less democratic might actually make them less amenable to pressure.

How do the selected cases fare in terms of improvements compared to the non-selected cases? Figure A1.4 relies on data from the "3P Anti-Trafficking Policy Index"[5] and shows that the countries sampled have overall had greater improvements than the non-sampled countries, partly because they were significantly worse to begin with and because several of the non-sampled countries just started out very high and had little room for improvement. This is consistent with the above and with the desire to be able to learn about the active ingredients of scorecard diplomacy. However, the non-sampled countries have also improved. Thus the chosen cases over-represent improvements, but do not misrepresent the general trend.

Case Study Methodology

The embassy cables for each country case were loaded into a software program for qualitative analysis called *QDA Miner*. The cases were read and coded with respect to types of events. Two graduate and two undergraduate students assisted in the coding. Everything was double coded. The coding was very heavily supervised in weekly group meetings and I went over every single case. The codes were not intended for

[5] Cho 2015. See discussion in Chapter 6.

quantitative analysis but to help with the case study analysis. The list of things noted was long, but included things such as:

- Meetings between US and in-country stakeholders, and the level of these officials involved (head of state, ministerial level, other government officials, and NGOs or IGOs).
- Types of US engagement in the country (practical assistance, funding programs, pushing for legislation, etc.).
- Progress on TIP legislation including comments on the implementation of the legislation, wording, updates on political obstacles and so forth.
- Reactions to the reports (as discussed in Chapter 5).
- Things of note, such as whether embassy officials were making claims about the effectiveness of US efforts, arguing for certain tier ratings, making use of conditionality or instructing officials on improvements that would need to be made to reach certain tier ratings, etc.
- The presence and activity of other stakeholders like IGOs and NGOs.

A synopsis was drawn up of the coding categories for each case. Next, the case was filled in as much as possible with other sources, including reports from the UN and other IGOs and NGOs, as well as media accounts and in some instances interviews. The next step was to write up chronologies. Although often long, the chronologies contained uneven information across time due to the variation in the availability of embassy cables and other sources. Nonetheless, during certain periods the cases were often much more detailed than would normally be obtained with standard case study materials due to the confidential nature of the cables. After the chronologies were completed, a longer case study was written, which was then condensed to a shorter version (which is available on the book's resources site, www.cambridge.org/ScorecardDiplomacy). Examples from the case studies are discussed in context in the throughout the book.

To understand the likelihood that the US brought about the observed outcomes, that is, to draw any causal inference between US actions and policy outcomes, the case studies paid attention to three things in particular: (1) **Sequencing**, which is important for causal inference.[6] (2) **Congruence:** The substance of US recommendations must relate to the actions taken by a government. (3) **Testimony:** How the actors involved attribute causality to various outcomes.

---

[6] Grzymala-Busse 2010.

Results Appendix

CHAPTER 3

TABLE A3.1. *Time to a country's inclusion in the annual US TIP Report*

	Time to inclusion in report Model 3.1.1
Total population (logged)	1.008
	(0.071)
Missing information	0.789***
	(0.070)
NGO density	1.083
	(0.057)
Worse civil liberties	1.155**
	(0.073)
Regional density of criminalization	1.586
	(0.875)
2000 Palermo Protocol ratification	1.045
	(0.264)
Trafficking intensity in countries of origin	1.138*
	(0.080)
Trafficking intensity in transit countries	1.251***
	(0.078)
Trafficking intensity in destination countries	1.247***
	(0.095)

(continued)

TABLE A3.1. (*continued*)

	Time to inclusion in report Model 3.1.1
Number of countries	146
Number of inclusions	145
Observations	384

Notes: $^*p<0.1$; $^{**}p<0.05$; $^{***}p<0.01$.

Robust standard errors in parentheses. All explanatory variables are lagged one period unless otherwise noted.

Cox Proportional Hazard models.

TABLE A3.2. *Correlates of shaming in the annual US TIP Report*

	US pressure	
	Model 3.2.1	Model 3.2.2
Worse civil liberties	1.720***	1.766***
	(0.094)	(0.102)
US aid (logged)	1.063***	1.069***
	(0.017)	(0.017)
GDP (logged)	1.637***	1.540***
	(0.117)	(0.109)
Total population (logged)	0.607***	0.643***
	(0.050)	(0.053)
2000 Palermo Protocol ratification	2.606***	2.636***
	(0.353)	(0.359)
NGO density	1.188***	1.194***
	(0.058)	(0.059)
Corruption	0.568***	
	(0.081)	
Rule of law		0.698**
		(0.099)
Constant	0.0001***	0.0002***
	(0.0001)	(0.0002)
Pseudo R-squared	0.1641	0.1591
Observations	1,846	1,846

Notes: $^*p<0.1$; $^{**}p<0.05$; $^{***}p<0.01$.

Logit models; odds ratios reported. Standard errors in parentheses. All explanatory variables are lagged one period.

CHAPTER 4

TABLE A4.1. *Determinants of receiving increased coverage of TIP issues*

	Logged coverage	
	Model 4.1.1	Model 4.1.2
In report	0.396***	0.301***
	(0.091)	(0.088)
First year in report	0.030	0.073
	(0.059)	(0.064)
Coverage (lagged)	0.208***	0.215***
	(0.029)	(0.032)
Worse civil liberties	0.103***	0.119***
	(0.044)	(0.045)
GDP per capita (logged)	0.262*	0.205
	(0.200)	(0.191)
2000 Palermo Protocol ratification	0.033	0.014
	(0.052)	(0.053)
Population (logged)	2.821***	2.891***
	(6.053)	(6.479)
Trafficking intensity in countries of origin		−1.626***
		(0.054)
Trafficking intensity in transit countries		0.217*
		(0.159)
Trafficking intensity in destination countries		−3.090***
		(0.023)
Constant	−53.320***	−35.524***
	(0.000)	(0.000)
Year fixed effects	Yes	Yes
Country fixed effects	Yes	Yes
Observations	1,748	1,478

Notes: *$p < 0.1$; **$p < 0.05$; ***$p < 0.01$.

All explanatory variables are lagged one period unless otherwise noted.
Standard OLS models.

CHAPTER 5

TABLE A5.1. *Determinants of observing a reaction to the TIP Report in Wikileaks cables*

	Reaction in cables		
	Model 5.1.1	Model 5.1.2	Model 5.1.3
Tier 2	1.179	1.167	2.154[**]
	(0.303)	(0.311)	(0.647)
US pressure (Watch List or Tier 3)	3.901[***]	4.146[***]	
	(0.964)	(2.044)	
Watch List			5.861[***]
			(1.879)
Tier 3			4.116[***]
			(1.500)
US aid (logged)	1.009	1.011	1.033
	(0.015)	(0.020)	(0.022)
US aid (logged) × US pressure		0.996	
		(0.031)	
GDP per capita (logged)			1.353[***]
			(0.115)
Population (logged)			0.894
			(0.066)
Share of total trade with US			1.754
			(0.988)
Worse total freedom			1.099[***]
			(0.031)
2000 Palermo Protocol ratification			2.097[***]
			(0.385)
Human trafficking news (logged)			1.723[***]
			(0.190)
Constant	0.090[***]	0.089[***]	0.001[***]
	(0.023)	(0.026)	(0.002)
Pseudo R-squared	0.0583	0.0584	0.1564
Observations	1,356	1,356	1,118

Notes: [*]p<0.1; [**]p<0.05; [***]p<0.01.

Logit models; odds ratios reported. Standard errors in parentheses. All explanatory variables are lagged one period.

CHAPTER 6

TABLE A6.1. *Time to TIP criminalization*

	Time to TIP criminalization		
	Model 6.1.1	Model 6.1.2	Model 6.1.3
In report	6.213[***] (3.812)	3.815[***] (1.342)	4.149[***] (1.429)
Share of women in parliament	1.022[**] (0.009)	1.022[***] (0.009)	1.018[**] (0.008)
Worse civil liberties	0.892 (0.087)	0.906 (0.090)	0.866[**] (0.056)
Regional density of criminalization	5.597[***] (3.370)	3.535[**] (1.988)	4.672[***] (2.394)
2000 Palermo Protocol ratification	1.959[**] (0.536)	1.883[**] (0.513)	2.030[***] (0.505)
Missing information (t–2)	1.192 (0.156)	1.165 (0.124)	1.203[**] (0.098)
Trafficking intensity in countries of origin	0.935 (0.090)		
Trafficking intensity in transit countries	1.160 (0.135)		
Trafficking intensity in destination countries	0.951 (0.112)		
Total population (logged)		0.947 (0.081)	
NGO density		1.133 (0.090)	
GDP per capita (logged)		1.111 (0.128)	
Corruption		1.029 (0.223)	
US aid (logged)			0.974 (0.016)
Number of countries	136	149	152
Number of criminalizations	95	99	107
Observations	1,251	1,307	1,392

Notes: [*]p<0.1; [**]p<0.05; [***]p<0.01.

Robust standard errors in parentheses. All explanatory variables are lagged one period unless otherwise noted.

Cox Proportional Hazard models.

TABLE A6.2. *Time to TIP criminalization*

	Time to TIP criminalization		
	Model 6.2.1	Model 6.2.2	Model 6.2.3
Tier 1	4.965*** (3.083)	2.790** (1.282)	
Tier 2	2.625* (1.328)	1.660 (0.612)	
Watch list	8.518*** (4.348)	5.069*** (1.900)	
Tier 3	12.299*** (6.489)	9.669*** (3.697)	
In report			3.478*** (1.247)
First demotion (t–3)			2.249** (0.754)
First demotion (t–2)			1.790* (0.552)
First demotion (t–1)			1.281 (0.378)
Share of women in parliament	1.024*** (0.010)	1.026*** (0.009)	1.024*** (0.008)
Worse civil liberties	0.789** (0.083)	0.813** (0.084)	0.816*** (0.051)
Regional density of criminalization	5.239*** (3.157)	4.352** (2.640)	5.765*** (2.875)
2000 Palermo Protocol ratification	1.969** (0.577)	2.150*** (0.597)	1.688** (0.414)
Missing information	1.143 (0.143)	1.043 (0.111)	1.207** (0.098)
Trafficking intensity in countries of origin	1.012 (0.100)		
Trafficking intensity in transit countries	1.129 (0.132)		
Trafficking intensity in destination countries	0.910 (0.105)		
Total population (logged)		0.954 (0.089)	
NGO density		1.096 (0.084)	
US aid (logged)		0.965 (0.025)	

	Time to TIP criminalization		
	Model 6.2.1	Model 6.2.2	Model 6.2.3
GDP per capita (logged)		0.893 (0.116)	
Corruption		1.123 (0.275)	
Number of countries	136	149	152
Number of criminalizations	95	99	107
Observations	1,251	1,307	1,392

Notes: *p < 0.1; **p < 0.05; ***p < 0.01.

Robust standard errors in parentheses. All explanatory variables are lagged one period unless otherwise noted.

Cox Proportional Hazard models.

TABLE A6.3. *Determinants of TIP criminalization for countries in the report*

	Criminalization	
	Model 6.3.1	Model 6.3.2
Reactions (no media)	1.732* (0.526)	
Total reactions (no media)		1.196** (0.099)
Share of women in parliament	1.028** (0.012)	1.030** (0.012)
Worse total freedom (political rights + civil liberties)	0.938* (0.033)	0.940* (0.033)
2000 Palermo Protocol ratification	1.359 (0.362)	1.354 (0.360)
Big aid	1.206 (0.359)	1.236 (0.369)
Regional density of criminalization	7.857*** (4.652)	8.005*** (4.718)
Constant	0.040*** (0.027)	0.038*** (0.026)
Year fixed effects	Yes	Yes
Pseudo R-squared	0.0962	0.0981
Observations	758	758

Notes: *p < 0.1; **p < 0.05; ***p < 0.01.

Logit models; odds ratios reported. Robust standard errors in parentheses. All explanatory variables are lagged one period.

TABLE A6.4. *The effect of TIP-specific funding on criminalization*

	Time to TIP criminalization
	Model 6.4.1
Total US funding for TIP (logged)	1.040**
	(0.020)
Share of women in parliament	1.024***
	(0.009)
Worse total freedom (political rights + civil liberties)	0.936**
	(0.026)
2000 TIP protocol ratification	2.370***
	(0.567)
Regional density of criminalization	6.565***
	(3.115)
Missing information	1.163*
	(0.092)
Number of countries	149
Number of criminalizations	103
Observations	1,085

Notes: *p **p ***p < 0.01.

Robust standard errors in parentheses. All explanatory variables are lagged one period unless otherwise noted.
Cox Proportional Hazard models.

TABLE A6.5 *Coding of US influence on the passage of legislation*

Country (coding)	US influence on passage of legislation
Argentina (2)	US pushed heavily for legislation through numerous meetings and tier pressure. Some NGOs credit US efforts.
Armenia (3)	US pushed heavily for legislation through numerous meetings and tier pressure. Comprehensive legislation passed in 2006. US credited with big role by NGOs, IGOs, and politicians.
Chad (1)	US applied pressure through downgrades. Chad has not able to pass specific anti-TIP legislation.
Ecuador (2)	The US pushed strongly for passage of anti-TIP legislation, which passed in 2005. The US contributed to progress, though not always as quickly as desired.
Honduras (2)	The US stressed the importance of legislation with top officials. Progress was slow and only partial success came in 2005.

TABLE A6.5. (*continued*)

Country (coding)	US influence on passage of legislation
Indonesia (3)	The US pushed along comprehensive Indonesian anti-TIP legislation and often brought up progress on the legislation as an incentive for tier improvement. The bill passed in 2007 right before the embassy TIP reporting to Washington.
Israel (3)	The US TIP Report ratcheted government attention to human trafficking, and the US played a strong role in changing legislation. The 2006 TIP Report downgraded Israel to the Watch List, and the ambassador cited legislation against labor trafficking as a *sine qua non* for an upgrade. June 2006 was packed with meetings on the legislation, which passed in October.
Japan (3)	After the 2004 downgrade, Japan was "shocked." Action on several fronts followed, including tightening of the eligibility for the misused entertainer visa, and 2005 passage of anti-TIP legislation, although this legislation was not entirely to US satisfaction. Commentators attributed Japan's actions to American pressure.
Kazakhstan (3)	The US embassy was heavily involved in pushing for legislation and engaged on a high political level. Legislation were enacted in March 2006 in time for the annual TIP Report update.
Malaysia (2)	Malaysia's Tier 3 ranking on the 2007 TIP Report was one of the primary factors leading the government to pass an anti-TIP law.
Mozambique (3)	US technical assistance and diplomatic engagement was crucial to moving the law along in the legislative process. When by 2007 the law had not progressed the US dropped Mozambique to the Watch List, and embassy pressure was key in moving the issue on the agenda. The law was passed on April 10 that year, just in time to be included in the 2008 TIP Report.
Nigeria (1)	The US applied pressure already from the first TIP Report in 2001, but the law was also advocated heavily by domestic NGOs. The Senate passed the law in February 2003 and it became law in July that year.
Oman (3)	US applied heavy pressure including successive Tier 3 ratings in 2007–2008, which infuriated top Oman officials and led to a crisis in the relationship. Nonetheless, this produced action in Oman resulting in the November 2008 passage of the new law criminalizing human trafficking.

(*continued*)

Country (coding)	US influence on passage of legislation
UAE (3)	The US pushed heavily for criminalization of the use of underage camel jockeys and TIP, but was blinded in 2002–2003 by fake signals of compliance. The drop to the Watch List in 2004 expedited enactment of the camel jockey law explicitly stating that their effort to meet the TIP Reporting deadline. In November 2006, the government enacted comprehensive anti-TIP law.
Zimbabwe (1)	Before 2009 the US had little effective interaction. After the Unity government, the US mostly supported the IOM to work with the government on the law. Not until March 2014 – right before the TIP reporting deadline – did the law pass.

Source: Case studies available at the book's resources site (www.cambridge.org/Scorecard Diplomacy).

TABLE A6.6. *Coding of US influence on content of law*

Country (coding)	US influence on content of law
Argentina (3)	Offered input into content of law, pushing for issue around consent of victims. First law in 2008 included US opposed consent clause. 2012 amendment eliminated it.
Armenia (3)	US offered input into content of law, pushing for stricter penalties and full criminalization. Legislative assistance offered through the OSCE and resident legal advisor.
Chad (1)	Organized and funded, though UNODC, a technical workshop on the draft law that brought together all stakeholders including government, civil society and IGOs.
Ecuador (3)	The American Bar Association (ABA) contributed significantly to the wording of the legislation. The embassy commented directly on the wording as the law was being drawn up.
Honduras (2)	The US provided sample legislation. When 2005 law did not include labor trafficking, US pressed for this until 2012 when it was adopted, but US was still not entirely happy with wording.

TABLE A6.6. (*continued*)

Country (coding)	US influence on content of law
Indonesia (3)	A US-funded technical advisor worked with the parliamentary committee on the legislation. As the legislation moved along the US submitted comments on the language, which led to a significantly expanded definition of human trafficking including US efforts to include debt bondage.
Israel (3)	As part of the pressure for new legislation, the US shaped how trafficking was defined, effectively broadening the law to include labor trafficking.
Japan (1)	Japanese officials asked for specific examples of trafficking crimes that the US does not believe are criminalized by Japanese law.
Kazakhstan (3)	Embassy met with officials in detailed meetings about the content of the legislation and monitored it very closely. The US, along with the IOM and OSCE, attended the inter-agency TIP working group and was involved in the discussion of the draft amendments.
Malaysia (1)	The embassy advised drafters in the attorney general's office by providing them with US anti-trafficking legislation as well as references to other countries' laws.
Mozambique (3)	After ministerial-level meetings, US-paid legal consultants were included on the team drafting the legislation. The US was asked to provide model legislation and remained active in the drafting process.
Nigeria (0)	The US did not offer much input on the wording as far as the documents tell.
Oman (3)	The US was also heavily involved with the drafting of TIP legislation. The US funded an international expert to work with Oman on legislation. The Ministry of Foreign Affairs requested and received examples of anti-TIP legislation from the US embassy, and worked closely with Oman's anti-trafficking committee.
UAE (3)	The embassy provided officials with a model anti-TIP law and discussed its definitions. The US stressed the importance of defining the TIP issue more broadly and treating TIP victims as victims rather than criminals.
Zimbabwe (2)	The US embassy supplied draft laws and helped a top official prepare briefings for the prime minister, but overall had little direct access.

Source: Case studies available at the book's resources site (www.cambridge.org/Scorecard Diplomacy).

TABLE A6.7. *Coding of US influence on implementation*

Country (coding)	US influence on implementation
Argentina (2)	Pressure to address official complicity in trafficking. Together with IOM worked with government to train judges and officials, provided technical assistance.
Armenia (3)	Pressure to address official complicity in trafficking and increasing prosecutions. Several grants to support the strengthening of law enforcement and victim referral. Anti-trafficking seminar for judges, prosecutors, investigators, and police.
Chad (0)	Implementation low.
Ecuador (2)	The US constantly pushed for implementation. It funded education programs and training programs, including shelters and a child protection police unit. USAID met with over 40 US and Ecuadorian government officials, civil society, and international donors to assess the needs.
Honduras (0)	Implementation low.
Indonesia (3)	US focused on implementation and tied the tier rating to implementation issues. The US worked with closely and successfully with police, funded public awareness campaigns, and traveled to the field to assess implementation needs.
Israel (1)	In December 2007 Israel followed US recommendation to create a national plan. Israel has not required a lot of US assistance in implementation.
Japan (0)	US has been uninvolved with implementation.
Kazakhstan (1)	Despite passage of the law, the US placed Kazakhstan on the Watch List because its poor efforts to prosecute and convict traffickers. The US has had ongoing dialogues about implementation issues, but gained only mild traction.
Malaysia (1)	The US played got the government to investigate allegations of trafficking of Burmese refugees to the Thai border by immigration officials, actions that slowed the flow, according to the UNHCR. The US provided training and brought in experts to talk to officials on implementing the new law. Overall, however, US had little impact on implementation on labor trafficking.
Mozambique (1)	It took a long time for implementation of the law to start. The US urged this matter repeatedly. By 2011, the regulations were still not in place but the government prosecuted and Mozambique convicted trafficking offenders for the first time, increased prevention efforts, and trained local officials about legal remedies provided under new law.

TABLE A6.7. (*continued*)

Country (coding)	US influence on implementation
Nigeria (2)	The US played a strong role in promoting implementation. It increased attention to official complicity in TIP, and worked closely with NAPTIP, the government's anti-TIP agency, encouraging arrests, prosecutions, and convictions, which increased. It funded an IOM addition of an anti-TIP training module to the basic training curriculum for new police recruits.
Oman (0)	Implementation has been lagging. The US report laments the "modest effort," "minimal progress," or even "no discernible" efforts across some areas of performance.
UAE (1)	When the UAE failed to enforce the camel jockey law, the US dropped the UAE to Tier 3 in 2005. Working with the government and UNICEF progress resulted, until the issue was essentially resolved. In 2009 the US demoted the UAE to push for progress on labor issues. This has been modest, although the UAE is still recognized as being further along on TIP issues than others in the region.
Zimbabwe (0)	Too soon to assess influence of latest efforts, but none before.

Source: Case studies available at the book's resources site (www.cambridge.org/Scorecard Diplomacy).

TABLE A6.8. *Coding of US influence on institutions*

Country (coding)	US influence on institutions
Argentina (2)	The US successfully lobbied the government to formalize its inter-agency TIP coordination process and appoint a focal point to direct TIP-related activities. It also influenced the creation of the Trafficking Prevention and Assistance program.
Armenia (3)	The US advised the government to reorganize the domestic administration and oversight of TIP policy and when the government created a TIP commission, the embassy pushed to give the commission clout, and eventually was successful in getting its work moved to the Council level and successfully pushed for a specific person as chair. Embassy officials observed that the TIP reporting requirement catalyzed inter-agency anti-TIP cooperation and bolstered the status of the commission.

(*continued*)

Country (coding)	US influence on institutions
Chad (1)	The 2009 downgrade prompted Chad to form an inter-ministerial committee able to undertake the initiatives recommended by the US Action Plan, but nothing much came of it. It was not until 2014 that as a response to US pressure, a permanent inter-ministerial committee got up and running.
Ecuador (3)	The US funded shelters and the child protection police unit DINAPEN within the Ministry of the Interior. The attorney general followed an embassy suggestion to assign special TIP prosecutors. The embassy also successfully pressed for specific persons for appointments and positions within the government. The Ministry of Government invited the embassy to help start the inter-institutional commission.
Honduras (2)	The 2007 report continued the US embassy's frustration with the difficulty of extracting highly decentralized [TIP data] and contributed to the creation of a nationwide system to track all forms of criminal complaints, including TIP, although data continued to be a challenge. The inter-institutional commission consistently discusses the US TIP Report.
Indonesia (3)	The US was heavily involved with capacity building. It helped establish medical centers to treat TIP victims specifically, work that continued into 2007, leading to a fully functional hospital with psychological treatment options. US police training led to the creation of local anti-TIP units in big cities such as Jakarta. USAID funded a TIP shelter that worked with the police to offer victim services.
Israel (2)	The US influenced domestic institutions by promoting and funding domestic shelters, prompting the government to created new committees that directly examined the annual TIP Report, and even influencing the choice of the official anti-TIP coordinator.
Japan (0)	None found.
Kazakhstan (2)	The US helped build domestic TIP infrastructure. The biggest effort was the creation of the anti-TIP center in Karaganda to train police and security officers, and hold roundtables to discuss TIP issues. The US Bureau of International Narcotics and Law Enforcement Affairs supported its operation and influenced course content.

TABLE A6.8. (*continued*)

Country (coding)	US influence on institutions
Malaysia (2)	The US provided funding and pushed for the building of shelters, served as an important advisor and liaison between anti-TIP actors, and provided well-received training. The US pushed the government to work more closely with NGOs.
Mozambique (1)	The US supported construction of the Moamba Reception Center for TIP victims. US also contributed to informal institutions by leading a regular forum for civil society, government, and the diplomatic corps to discuss trafficking issues.
Nigeria (3)	The US helped develop a national action plan, worked closely with NAPTIP, the government's anti-TIP agency, and the American Bar Association headed the creation of a TIP database system.
Oman (0)	None found.
UAE (1)	The US report promoted statistics gathering.
Zimbabwe (0)	None found.

Source: Case studies available at the book's resources site (www.cambridge.org/Scorecard Diplomacy).

TABLE A6.9. *Coding of US influence on norms and practices*

Country (coding)	US influence on norms and practices
Argentina (1)	The US pushed to define trafficking to not exclude cases where victims had initially consented. NGOs spearheaded this. The US also educated judges on victim treatment.
Armenia (1)	Armenia has used the TIP Report to systematically examine the policy solutions of other countries.
Chad (0)	None found.
Ecuador (2)	Through repeated meetings, US officials sought to educate government officials about the nature and scope of TIP. The US embassy engaged with government officials to understand the difference between TIP and smuggling.

(*continued*)

TABLE A6.9. (*continued*)

Country (coding)	US influence on norms and practices
Honduras (0)	None found.
Indonesia (1)	Local officials agreed extensive training had improved police dealings with TIP victims.
Israel (1)	A Knesset subcommittee noted that "[T]he TIP Report raises the need for some new thinking by the [government]" on the question of incriminating clients of the sex industry and the issue of sex service advertising.
Japan (0)	None found.
Kazakhstan (2)	The US directed educational trips abroad for officials, who applied the lessons they learned when they came home. The US trained religious leaders in trafficking issues to promote local tolerance for returning victims of sex trafficking.
Malaysia (2)	The US helped Malaysia acknowledge the problem, and helped some officials understand that trafficking could not be voluntary. Scorecard diplomacy also influenced the government's understanding of labor trafficking. In 2010 the government made its first labor trafficking arrests, and amended the Anti-TIP Act to include labor or services obtained through coercion to the definition of trafficking. Training on treatment of victims also facilitated understanding problems of detention facilities.
Mozambique (1)	The Moamba Reception Center for TIP victims was influenced by visits by officials to "safe houses" in the US.
Nigeria (1)	US officials met with police commissioners who lacked a basic understanding of TIP, and the embassy explained the distinctions between trafficker and victim, trafficking and smuggling, and so on.
Oman (1)	The US contributed to the traditional use of children as camel jockeys becoming taboo.
UAE (2)	The US contributed to the making the traditional use of children as camel jockeys taboo. The US embassy also sought to socialize officials into their view of labor trafficking, about which officials were in denial, but success has been modest at best. TIP has become a more openly acknowledged problem.
Zimbabwe (0)	None found.

Source: Case studies available at the book's resources site (www.cambridge.org/Scorecard Diplomacy).

CHAPTER 7

TABLE A7.1. *Time to TIP criminalization: presence in report (aid)*

	Model 7.1.1	Model 7.1.2	Model 7.1.3	Model 7.1.4	Model 7.1.5	Model 7.1.6
			Time to TIP criminalization			
In report	2.462*	3.651***	3.757***	0.340	3.744***	4.201***
	(1.251)	(1.330)	(1.476)	(0.372)	(1.452)	(1.923)
Share of women in parliament	1.018**	1.019**	1.020**	1.005	1.009	1.010
	(0.008)	(0.008)	(0.008)	(0.009)	(0.009)	(0.009)
Worse civil liberties	0.864**	0.838***	0.841***	0.869*	0.904	0.892
	(0.057)	(0.053)	(0.053)	(0.065)	(0.064)	(0.064)
Regional density of criminalization	5.037***	5.181***	5.213***	5.782***	4.541**	4.751***
	(2.638)	(2.639)	(2.692)	(3.082)	(2.520)	(2.609)
2000 Palermo Protocol ratification	1.991***	1.872***	1.855***	1.869**	1.924**	1.847**
	(0.499)	(0.450)	(0.439)	(0.517)	(0.550)	(0.513)
Missing information (t–2)	1.213**	1.228**	1.236***	1.276***	1.203**	1.217**
	(0.100)	(0.100)	(0.099)	(0.111)	(0.104)	(0.103)
US aid (logged)	0.936**			0.976		
	(0.030)			(0.039)		
US aid × In report	1.053			1.174**		
	(0.038)			(0.077)		

(continued)

TABLE A7.1. (*continued*)

	Time to TIP criminalization					
	Model 7.1.1	Model 7.1.2	Model 7.1.3	Model 7.1.4	Model 7.1.5	Model 7.1.6
US aid as share of GDP (logged)	0.988 (0.012)	0.988 (0.012)			0.993 (0.007)	0.993 (0.007)
US aid as share of GDP × In report	1.011 (0.013)	1.011 (0.013)			1.007 (0.008)	
US aid as share of total aid (logged)			0.289 (0.432)			0.998 (1.488)
US aid as share of total aid (logged) × In report			2.660 (4.330)			1.355 (2.211)
Number of countries	152	150	152	132	130	132
Number of criminalizations	107	105	107	86	84	86
OECD DAC[1] eligible countries only	No	No	No	Yes	Yes	Yes
Observations	1,392	1,373	1,392	1,275	1,257	1,275

Notes: [*] $p < 0.1$; [**] $p < 0.05$; [***] $p < 0.01$.
Robust standard errors in parentheses. All explanatory variables are lagged one period unless otherwise noted.
Cox Proportional Hazard models.
[1] Development Assistance Committee.

TABLE A7.2. *Time to TIP criminalization: presence in report (trade)*

	Time to TIP criminalization				
	Model 7.2.1	Model 7.2.2	Model 7.2.3	Model 7.2.4	Model 7.2.5
In report	2.673** (1.224)	4.683*** (1.777)	7.587** (6.532)	4.634*** (2.049)	9.050 (13.324)
Share of women in parliament	1.021*** (0.008)	1.019** (0.008)	1.019* (0.008)	1.020** (0.008)	1.019** (0.008)
Worse civil liberties	0.876** (0.055)	0.832*** (0.053)	0.833*** (0.051)	0.825*** (0.054)	0.838*** (0.054)
Regional density of criminalization	6.060*** (3.052)	5.311*** (2.623)	5.199*** (2.690)	5.400*** (2.768)	5.265*** (2.633)
2000 Palermo Protocol ratification	1.818** (0.449)	1.828** (0.442)	1.846** (0.484)	1.797** (0.422)	1.849** (0.444)
Missing information (t–2)	1.169* (0.098)	1.244** (0.099)	1.234*** (0.098)	1.224** (0.099)	1.255*** (0.108)
US trade as share of GDP (logged)	0.126 (0.385)				
US trade as share of GDP (logged) × US pressure	10.119 (32.085)				
Has BIT with US		1.640 (0.961)			

(continued)

TABLE A7.2. (*continued*)

	Time to TIP criminalization				
	Model 7.2.1	Model 7.2.2	Model 7.2.3	Model 7.2.4	Model 7.2.5
Has BIT with US × ln report		0.599 (0.380)			
US military aid (logged)			1.047 (0.057)		
US military aid (logged) × ln report			0.951 (0.056)		
FDI from US (logged)				1.002 (0.034)	
FDI from US (logged) × ln report				0.988 (0.035)	
Imports to US (logged)					1.050 (0.080)
Imports to US (logged) × ln report					0.960 (0.073)
Number of countries	140	152	152	152	152
Number of criminalizations	101	107	107	107	107
Observations	1,270	1,392	1,392	1,392	1,392

Notes: *p<0.1; **p<0.05; ***p<0.01.
Robust standard errors in parentheses. All explanatory variables are lagged one period unless otherwise noted.
Cox Proportional Hazard models.

TABLE A7.3. *Time to TIP criminalization: US pressure (aid)*

	Time to TIP criminalization					
	Model 7.3.1	Model 7.3.2	Model 7.3.3	Model 7.3.4	Model 7.3.5	Model 7.3.6
US pressure	1.140	3.254***	3.994***	2.190	3.555***	4.850***
	(1.128)	(0.741)	(0.880)	(2.942)	(0.880)	(1.244)
Share of women in parliament	1.021**	1.025***	1.026***	1.012	1.013	1.016
	(0.009)	(0.009)	(0.008)	(0.010)	(0.010)	(0.010)
Worse civil liberties	0.823***	0.784***	0.804***	0.816***	0.840**	0.851**
	(0.057)	(0.054)	(0.054)	(0.062)	(0.064)	(0.063)
Regional density of criminalization	6.335***	7.212***	7.217***	5.742***	5.489***	5.891***
	(3.076)	(3.593)	(3.652)	(2.963)	(2.885)	(3.099)
2000 Palermo Protocol ratification	2.164***	1.900***	1.907***	1.906**	2.078***	2.039**
	(0.564)	(0.462)	(0.461)	(0.531)	(0.584)	(0.569)
Missing information (t–2)	1.079	1.087	1.097	1.150*	1.069	1.072
	(0.085)	(0.084)	(0.084)	(0.097)	(0.090)	(0.090)
US aid (logged)	0.960**			1.070		
	(0.018)			(0.061)		
US aid × US pressure	1.074			1.030		
	(0.064)			(0.082)		

(continued)

TABLE A7.3. (continued)

	Time to TIP criminalization					
	Model 7.3.1	Model 7.3.2	Model 7.3.3	Model 7.3.4	Model 7.3.5	Model 7.3.6
US aid as share of GDP (logged)		0.998 (0.003)			0.999 (0.003)	
US aid as share of GDP × US pressure		1.012 (0.008)			1.009 (0.008)	
US aid as share of total aid (logged)			0.831 (0.537)			3.196 (2.408)
US aid as share of total aid (logged) × US pressure			0.231 (0.303)			0.070* (0.095)
Number of countries	152	150	152	132	130	132
Number of criminalizations	107	105	107	86	84	86
OECD DAC eligible countries only	No	No	No	Yes	Yes	Yes
Observations	1,392	1,373	1,392	1,275	1,257	1,275

Notes: *p<0.1; **p<0.05; ***p<0.01.
Robust standard errors in parentheses. All explanatory variables are lagged one period unless otherwise noted.
Cox Proportional Hazard models.

TABLE A7.4. *Time to TIP criminalization: US pressure (trade)*

	Time to TIP criminalization				
	Model 7.4.1	Model 7.4.2	Model 7.4.3	Model 7.4.4	Model 7.4.5
US pressure	2.798***	3.381***	1.389	4.212***	3.996
	(0.747)	(0.861)	(0.813)	(1.318)	(4.882)
Share of women in parliament	1.028***	1.026***	1.025***	1.027***	1.026***
	(0.009)	(0.009)	(0.008)	(0.009)	(0.008)
Worse civil liberties	0.828***	0.790***	0.813***	0.780***	0.796***
	(0.056)	(0.053)	(0.052)	(0.053)	(0.055)
Regional density of criminalization	7.143***	6.794***	7.147***	7.131***	7.035***
	(3.570)	(3.337)	(3.494)	(3.615)	(3.568)
2000 Palermo Protocol ratification	1.781**	1.825**	1.922**	1.852**	1.869**
	(0.456)	(0.455)	(0.511)	(0.449)	(0.464)
Missing information (t−2)	1.061	1.106	1.096	1.068	1.111
	(0.088)	(0.085)	(0.083)	(0.084)	(0.095)
US trade as share of GDP (logged)	0.143				
	(0.247)				
US trade as share of GDP (logged) × US pressure	10.612				
	(22.155)				
Has BIT with US		1.039			
		(0.345)			

(continued)

TABLE A7.4. (*continued*)

Time to TIP criminalization

	Model 7.4.1	Model 7.4.2	Model 7.4.3	Model 7.4.4	Model 7.4.5
Has BIT with US × US pressure		1.132 (0.459)			
US military aid (logged)			0.972 (0.022)		
US military aid (logged) × US pressure			1.073* (0.043)		
FDI from US (logged)				0.996 (0.014)	
FDI from US (logged) × US pressure				0.984 (0.020)	
Imports to US (logged)					1.014 (0.060)
Imports to US (logged) × US pressure					0.993 (0.061)
Number of countries	140	152	152	152	152
Number of criminalizations	101	107	107	107	107
Observations	1,270	1,392	1,392	1,392	1,392

Notes: $^*p<0.1$; $^{**}p<0.05$; $^{***}p<0.01$.
Robust standard errors in parentheses. All explanatory variables are lagged one period unless otherwise noted.
Cox Proportional Hazard models.

TABLE A7.5. *Determinants of criminalization – effects of democracy interacted with scorecard diplomacy treatments*

	Criminalization		
	Model 7.5.1 Presence in TIP Report	Model 7.5.2 Lower tier ratings	Model 7.5.3 Downgrading
Worse democracy (Freedom House civil liberties)	0.360**	0.735***	0.770***
	(0.144)	(0.075)	(0.070)
In TIP Report	0.634		
	(0.474)		
Lowest tier		3.827**	
		(2.285)	
First demotion (t–3)			0.387
			(0.412)
First demotion (t–2)			1.954
			(1.736)
First demotion (t–1)			3.735*
			(2.948)
Share of women in parliament	1.024**	1.032***	1.032***
	(0.011)	(0.011)	(0.012)
2000 Palermo Protocol ratification	1.980***	1.877**	1.800**
	(0.515)	(0.492)	(0.474)
Regional density of criminalization	8.528***	10.298***	9.072***
	(4.904)	(5.918)	(5.123)

(continued)

TABLE A7.5. (*continued*)

	Criminalization		
	Model 7.5.1 Presence in TIP Report	Model 7.5.2 Lower tier ratings	Model 7.5.3 Downgrading
Missing info	1.237** (0.112)	1.120 (0.094)	1.098 (0.091)
Worse democracy × In TIP Report	2.471** (1.007)		
Worse democracy × Lowest tier		1.056 (0.161)	
Worse democracy × First demotion (t−3)			1.693** (0.390)
Worse democracy × First demotion (t−2)			1.091 (0.237)
Worse democracy × First demotion (t−1)			0.853 (0.179)
Constant	0.091*** (0.075)	0.049*** (0.027)	0.053*** (0.029)
Year fixed effects	Yes	Yes	Yes
Pseudo R-squared	0.1512	0.1591	0.1422
Observations	1,031	1,031	1,031

Notes: $p < 0.1$; $p < 0.05$; $p < 0.01$.
Logit models; odds ratios reported. Standard errors in parentheses. All explanatory variables are lagged one period.

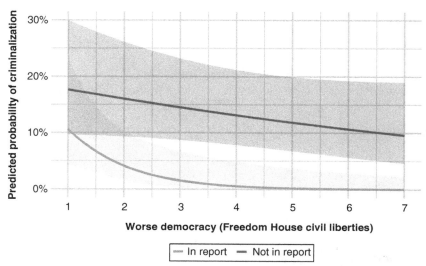

FIGURE A7.1. Predicted probability of criminalization across different levels of democracy, given presence in the annual TIP Report (Model 7.5.1).

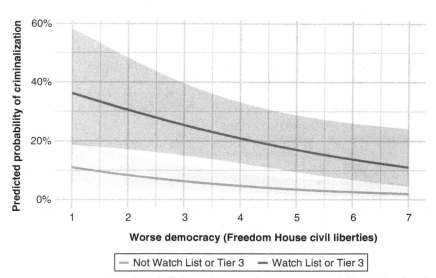

FIGURE A7.2. Predicted probability of criminalization across different levels of democracy, given assignment to the lowest TIP tier (Model 7.5.2).

References

Abbott, Kenneth, and Duncan Snidal. 2000. "Hard and soft law in international governance." *International Organization* 54 (3): 421–456.

Abdullaev, Nabi. 2003. "Bill makes human trafficking a crime." *The Moscow Times*, February 19, 2003. Accessed February 4, 2016. www.themoscowtimes.com/sitemap/free/2003/2/article/bill-makes-human-trafficking-a-crime/240267.html.

Ad Hoc Committee on the Elaboration of a Convention against Transnational Organized Crime. 1999. Revised Draft Protocol to Prevent, Suppress and Punish Trafficking in Women and Children, Supplementing the United Nations Convention against Transnational Organized Crime. New York: United Nations General Assembly.

Adair, John G. 1984. "The Hawthorne effect: A reconsideration of the methodological artifact." *Journal of Applied Psychology* 69 (2): 334–345. doi: 10.1037/0021-9010.69.2.334.

Adelstein, Jake, and Yomiuri Shimbun. 2004. "Trafficking blots nation's repute." *The Daily Yomiuri*, November 23, 2004, 4.

Adler, Emanuel. 1992. "The emergence of cooperation: National epistemic communities and the international evolution of the idea of nuclear arms control." *International Organization* 46 (1): 101–145.

Adler-Nissen, Rebecca. 2014. "Stigma management in international relations: Transgressive identities, norms, and order in international society." *International Organization* 68 (1): 143–176.

Africa News. 2006. "Zimbabwe; govt denies human trafficking reports." Last Modified November 23, 2006. Accessed December 19, 2016. http://allafrica.com/stories/200611270333.html.

Agence France Presse. 2004. "Japan vows to fight human trafficking after damning US report." June 15, 2004. Accessed through Lexis Nexis Academic.

Alon, Gideon. 2002. "Report: 3,000 women a year trapped in sex slave industry." *Haaretz*, December 8, 2002. Accessed June 20, 2016. www.haaretz.com/report-3-000-women-a-year-trapped-in-sex-slave-industry-1.26034.

2006. "Human traffickers to be sentenced to 16–20 years in prison." *Haaretz*, October 17, 2006. Accessed January 5, 2016. www.haaretz.com/news/human-traffickers-to-be-sentenced-to-16-20-years-in-prison-1.201598

Alt, James E., Randall L. Calvert, and Brian D. Humes. 1988. "Reputation and hegemonic stability: A game-theoretic analysis." *American Political Science Review* 82 (2): 445–466.

Alter, Karen J. 2014. *The New Terrain of International Law: Courts, Politics, Rights*. Princeton University Press.

American Political Science Association. 2009. "US standing in the world: Causes, consequences, and the future." Accessed December 21, 2016. www.apsanet.org/Portals/54/APSA%20Files/publications/APSA_USStanding_short_Final.pdf.

Andreas, Peter, and Kelly Greenhill. 2010. *Sex, Drugs, and Body Counts: The Politics of Numbers in Global Crime and Conflict*. Cornell University Press.

Anyimadu, Adjoa. 2013. "Kenya's elections: Rebuilding reputation." Last Modified February 22, 2013. www.chathamhouse.org/media/comment/view/189549.

Apodaca, Clair. 2007. "The whole world could be watching: Human rights and the media." *Journal of Human Rights* 6 (2): 147–164.

Arruñada, Benito. 2007. "Pitfalls to avoid when measuring institutions: Is 'Doing Business' damaging business?" *Journal of Comparative Economics* 35 (4): 729–747.

Asbarez.com. 2015. "Armenia maintains 'Tier 1' status in the 2015 Trafficking in Persons Report." July 1, 2015. Accessed August 12, 2016. http://asbarez.com/138159/armenia-maintains-tier-1-status-in-the-2015-trafficking-in-persons-report/.

Associated Press Worldstream. 2003. "Armenia appeals for closer ties to EU." Last Modified December 4, 2003. Accessed January 5, 2016. www.azatutyun.am/content/article/1572712.html.

AZG Daily. 2003a. "British Embassy launches project to raise awareness about people trafficking and smuggling." March 4, 2003. Accessed December 21, 2016. www.azg.am/wap/?nl=EN&id=2003030402&Base_PUB=0.

2003b. "Servants of black business." March 26, 2003. Accessed August 12, 2016. www.azg.am/EN/2003032604.

Baesler, J., and J. Burgoon. 1994. "The temporal effects of story and statistical evidence on belief change." *Communication Research* 21 (5): 582–602.

Baldwin, David. 1985. *Economic Statecraft*. Princeton University Press.

2016. *Power and International Relations: A Conceptual Approach*. Princeton University Press.

Bandura, Romina. 2008. "A survey of composite indices measuring country performance: 2008 update." New York: United Nations Development Programme, Office of Development Studies (UNDP/ODS Working Paper).

Barkin, Samuel, and Bruce Cronin. 1994. "The state and the nation: Changing norms and rules of sovereignty in international relations." *International Organization* 48: 107–130.

Barnett, Michael N. 1998. *Dialogues in Arab Politics: Negotiations in Regional Order*. Columbia University Press.

Barnett, Michael, and Raymond Duvall. 2005. "Power in international politics." *International Organization* 59 (1): 39–75.

Barnett, Michael, and Martha Finnemore. 2004. *Rules for the World: International Organizations in Global Politics*. Cornell University Press.

Barry, Colin, Chad Clay, and Michael Flynn. 2012. "Avoiding the spotlight: Human rights shaming and foreign direct investment." *International Studies Quarterly* 57 (3): 532–544. doi: 10.1111/isqu.12039.

Batson, C. D. 1987. "Prosocial motivation: Is it ever truly altruistic?" *Advances in Experimental Social Psychology* 20: 65–122.

BBC Monitoring Latin America. 2011. "Text from the Caribbean Media Corporation: Bahamian inter-ministerial committee to examine US report on human trafficking." BBC. Accessed December 17, 2015. https://wikileaks.org/gifiles/docs/76/762006_us-the-bahamas-bahamian-inter-ministerial-committee-to.html.

BBC Summary of World Broadcasts. 2004. "Armenian official upbeat on fight against human trafficking." Last Modified June 18, 2004. Accessed January 5, 2016. www.armeniandiaspora.com/showthread.php?5411-Armenian-official-upbeat-on-fight-against-human-trafficking.

Bermeo, Sarah. 2015. "Foreign aid and development: Throwing off the shadow of the past." October 29, 2015. Available at SSRN: http://ssrn.com/abstract=2683664 or http://dx.doi.org/10.2139/ssrn.2683664.

Bertone, Andrea Marie. 2008. "Human trafficking on the international and domestic agendas: Examining the role of transnational advocacy networks between Thailand and United States." Dissertation. Edited by College Park University of Maryland.

Bieber, Tonia, and Kerstin Martens. 2011. "The OECD PISA study as a soft power in education? Lessons from Switzerland and the US." *European Journal of Education* 46 (1): 101–116. doi: 10.1111/j.1465-3435.2010.01462.x.

Bindenagel, J. D. 2016. "Merkel's 'we can do it!' Perhaps not!" Last Modified January 21, 2016. Accessed December 21, 2016. www.theglobalist.com/merkel-germany-immigration-politics-europe/.

Blader, Steven, and Ya-Ru Chen. 2012. "Differentiating the effects of status and power: A justice perspective." *Journal of Personality and Social Psychology* 102 (5): 994.

Bourdieu, Pierre. 1989. "Social space and symbolic power." *Sociological Theory* 7 (1): 14–25.

Brooks, Sarah M., Raphael Cunha, and Layna Mosley. 2015. "Categories, creditworthiness, and contagion: How investors' shortcuts affect sovereign debt markets." *International Studies Quarterly* 59 (3): 587–601. doi: 10.1111/isqu.12173.

Broome, André, and Joel Quirk. 2015. "Governing the world at a distance: The practice of global benchmarking." *Review of International Studies* 41 (Special Issue 5): 819–841. doi: 10.1017/S0260210515000340.

Buchanan, Allen. 2003. *Justice, Legitimacy, and Self-Determination: Moral Foundations for International Law*. Oxford University Press.

Bull, Hedley. 1977. *The Anarchical Society: A Study of Order in World Politics*. Columbia University Press.

Butcher, Kate. 2003. "Confusion between prostitution and sex trafficking." *The Lancet* 361 (9373): 1983.

Büthe, Tim. 2012. "Beyond supply and demand: A political-economic conceptual model." In *Governance by Indicators: Global Power through Classification and Rankings*, edited by Kevin Davis, Angelina Fisher, Benedict Kingsbury, and Sally Engle Merry, 29–51. Oxford University Press.

Büthe, Tim, and Walter Mattli. 2011. *The New Global Rulers: The Privatization of Regulation in the World Economy*. Princeton University Press.

Capobianco, Paul. 2013. "Human trafficking in Japan: Legislative policy, implications for migration, and cultural relativism." Dissertation. Languages, Literatures, and Culture, Seton Hall University.

Carothers, Thomas. 1999. *Aiding Democracy Abroad: The Learning Curve*. Carnegie Endowment for International Peace.

Carr, Edward H. 1942. *The Twenty Years Crisis: An Introduction to the Study of International Relations*. Macmillan.

Cashman, Greer. 2014. "Israel leading world in prevention and reduction of human trafficking." *Jerusalem Post*, December 2, 2014. Accessed December 21, 2016. www.jpost.com/Israel-News/Politics-And-Diplomacy/Israel-leading-world-in-prevention-and-reduction-of-human-trafficking-383473.

Center for Global Development. 2011. "MDG Progress Index: Gauging country-level achievements." Accessed December 21, 2016. www.cgdev.org/page/mdg-progress-index-gauging-country-level-achievements.

Chacon, Jennifer. 2005–2006. "Misery and myopia: Understanding the failures of US efforts to stop human trafficking." *Fordham L. Rev.* 74: 2977–3040.

Charoensuthipan, Penchan. 2014a. "Ministry hopes to impress US: Proof of anti-trafficking measures." *Bangkok Post*, December 29, 2014. Accessed December 21, 2016. www.bangkokpost.com/news/general/452736/ministry-hopes-to-impress-us.

2014b. "Rogue trawlers to face more scrutiny at sea: Government to deploy database, trackers to keep eye on fishing boats." *Bangkok Post*, December 29, 2014. Accessed December 21, 2016. www.bangkokpost.com/print/452761/.

Chayes, Abram, and Antonia Handler Chayes. 1993. "On compliance." *International Organization* 47 (2): 175–205.

1995. *The New Sovereignty: Compliance with International Regulatory Agreements*. Harvard University Press.

Checkel, Jeffrey. 1998. "Review: The constructivist turn in international relations theory." *World Politics* 50 (2): 324–348.

2001. "Why comply? Social learning and European identity change." *International Organization* 55 (3): 553–588.

2005. "International institutions and socialization in Europe: Introduction and framework." *International Organization* 59 (4): 801–826.

Cho, Seo-Young. 2015. "Evaluating policies against human trafficking worldwide: An overview and review of the 3P index." *Journal of Human Trafficking* 1 (1): 86–99.

Cho, Seo-Young, and Krishna Chaitanya Vadlamannati. 2012. "Compliance with the anti-trafficking protocol." *European Journal of Political Economy* 28 (2): 249–265. doi: http://dx.doi.org/10.1016/j.ejpoleco.2011.12.003.

Cho, Seo-Young, Axel Dreher, and Eric Neumayer. 2014. "Determinants of anti-trafficking policies: Evidence from a new index." *The Scandinavian Journal of Economics* 116 (2): 429–454. doi: 10.1111/sjoe.12055.

Chuang, Janie. 2005. "The United States as global sheriff: Using unilateral sanctions to combat human trafficking." *Michigan Journal of International Law* 27: 437–437.

2006. "Beyond a snapshot: Preventing human trafficking in the global economy." *Indiana Journal of Global Legal Studies* 13 (1): 137–163.

2012. "The use of indicators to measure government responses to human trafficking." In *Governance by Indicators: Global Power through Classification and Rankings*, edited by Kevin Davis, Angelina Fisher, Benedict Kingsbury, and Sally Engle Merry, 317–344. Oxford University Press.

2013. "Exploitation creep and the unmaking of human trafficking law." Unpublished paper, American University, Washington, DC.

2015. "Exploitation creep and the unmaking of human trafficking law." *The American Journal of International Law* 108 (4): 609–649.

Chwieroth, Jeffrey M. 2009. *Capital Ideas: The IMF and the Rise of Financial Liberalization*. Princeton University Press.

Clark, Ian. 2005. *Legitimacy in International Society*. Oxford University Press.

Cleveland, Sarah. 2001. "Norm internalization and U.S. economic sanctions." *Yale J. Int'l Law* 26 (1): 1–103.

Clinton, William J. 1998. Memorandum for the Secretary of State, the Attorney General, the Administrator of the Agency for International Development, the Director of the United States Information Agency, Subject: Steps to Combat Violence Against Women and Trafficking in Women and Girls.

Collier, Paul. 1997. "The failure of conditionality." In *Perspectives on Aid and Development*, edited by C. Gwyn and J. Nelson, 51–77. Johns Hopkins University Press.

Collins, Stephen D. 2009. "Can America finance freedom? Assessing US democracy promotion via economic statecraft." *Foreign Policy Analysis* 5 (4): 367–389.

Cook, Fay Lomax, Tom R. Tyler, Edward G. Goetz, Margaret T. Gordon, David Protess, Donna R. Leff, and Harvey L. Molotch. 1983. "Media and agenda setting: Effects on the public, interest group leaders, policy makers, and policy." *Public Opinion Quarterly* 47 (1): 16–35.

Cooley, Alexander. 2015. "The emerging politics of international rankings and ratings: A framework for analysis." In *Ranking the World: Grading States as a Tool of Global Governance*, edited by Alexander Cooley and Jack Snyder, 1–38. Cambridge University Press.

Cooley, Alexander, and Jack Snyder. 2015. *Ranking the World: Grading States as a Tool of Global Governances*. Rutgers University Press.

Corrales, Javier. 2006. "Political obstacles to expanding and improving schooling in developing countries." In *Educating all Children: A Global Agenda*, edited by J. E. Cohen, D. Elliot Bloom, and M. B. Malin, 231–299. American Academy of Arts and Science.

Council of Europe. 2003. Criminal Law Reform on Trafficking in Human Beings in South-Eastern Europe. Strasbourg.

2004. LARA Project – Trafficking in Human Beings: Criminal Law Reform in South-eastern Europe, Final Project Report. Strasbourg.

Council of Europe. n.d. Action against Trafficking in Human Beings. Accessed December 21, 2016. www.coe.int/t/dghl/monitoring/trafficking/Docs/activities/Historical_en.asp#TopOfPage.

Council on Foreign Relations. 2006. "Women and foreign policy symposium: Human trafficking – an overview, May 3, 2006." Accessed December 21, 2016. www.cfr.org/human-rights/symposium-human-trafficking-session-1-human-trafficking-overview-rush-transcript-federal-news-service-inc/p10653.

Crabtree, Susan. 2015. "Senators blast State Dept. for playing politics with human-rights rankings." *Washington Examiner*, August 4, 2015. Accessed February 4, 2016. www.washingtonexaminer.com/senators-blast-state-dept.-for-playing-politics-with-human-rights-rankings/article/2569508.

Crawford, Gordon. 1997. "Foreign aid and political conditionality: Issues of effectiveness and consistency." *Democratization* 4 (3): 69–108.

Crescenzi, Mark J. C. 2007. "Reputation and interstate conflict." *American Journal of Political Science* 51 (2): 382–396.

Crescenzi, Mark J. C., Jacob D. Kathman, and Stephen B. Long. 2007. "Reputation, history, and war." *Journal of Peace Research* 44 (6): 651–667.

Cuadros, Alex. 2016. "Why Brazilians are so obsessed with the Ryan Lochte story." *The New Yorker*, August 18, 2016.

Cullen, Paul. 2015. "Ireland falls in international health service rankings." *The Irish Times*, January 27, 2016. Accessed December 21, 2016. www.irishtimes.com/news/health/ireland-falls-in-international-health-service-rankings-1.2080281.

Dafoe, Allan, Jonathan Renshon, and Paul Huth. 2014. "Reputation and status as motives for war." *Annual Review of Political Science* 17 (1): 371–393. doi: 10.1146/annurev-polisci-071112-213421.

Dahl, Robert. 1957. "The concept of power." *Behavioral Science* 2 (3): 201–215.

The Daily Yomiuri. 2004. "Government must act on human trafficking." Last Modified June 24, 2004. Accessed December 21, 2016. https://article.wn.com/view/2004/06/24/Govt_must_act_on_human_trafficking/.

David-Barrett, Elizabeth, and Ken Okamura. 2013. "The transparency paradox: Why corrupt countries join the extractive industries transparency initiative." APSA Annual Conference, Chicago.

Davis, Kevin, Benedict Kingsbury, and Sally Engle Merry. 2012a. "Indicators as a technology of global governance." *Law & Society Review* 46 (1): 71–104. doi: 10.1111/j.1540-5893.2012.00473.x.

Davis, Kevin E., Angelina Fisher, Benedict Kingsbury, and Sally Engle Merry, eds. 2012b. *Governance by Indicators: Global Power through Classification and Rankings*. Oxford University Press.

De Renzio, Paolo, and Harika Masud. 2011. "Measuring and promoting budget transparency: The Open Budget Index as a research and advocacy tool." *Governance* 24 (3): 607–616. doi: 10.1111/j.1468-0491.2011.01539.x.

Deitelhoff, Nicole. 2009. "The discursive process of legalization: Charting islands of persuasion in the ICC case." *International Organization* 63 (1): 33–65.

DeStefano, Anthony. 2007. *The War on Human Trafficking: US Policy Assessed.* Rutgers University Press.

Deutsch, Karl Wolfgang. 1963. *The Nerves of Government.* Free Press of Glencoe.

DiMaggio, Paul J., and Walter W. Powell. 1983. "The iron cage revisited: Institutional isomorphism and collective rationality in organizational fields." *American Sociological Review* 27 (2): 147–160.

Doezema, Jo. 2002. "Who gets to choose? Coercion, consent, and the UN Trafficking Protocol." *Gender & Development* 10 (1): 20–27.

Downs, George, David Rocke, and Peter Barsoom. 1996. "Is the good new about compliance good news about cooperation?" *International Organization* 50 (3): 379–406.

Downs, George, and Michael Jones. 2002. "Reputation, compliance, and international law." *The Journal of Legal Studies* 31 (S1): S95–S114.

Drezner, Daniel. 2003. "The hidden hand of economic coercion." *International Organization* 57 (3): 643–659. doi: 10.1017/S0020818303573052.

Dunning, Thad. 2004. "Conditioning the effects of aid: Cold War politics, donor credibility, and democracy in Africa." *International Organization* 58 (2): 409–423.

Dür, Andreas, Leonardo Baccini, and Manfred Elsig. 2014. "The design of international trade agreements: Introducing a new dataset." *The Review of International Organizations* 9 (3): 353–375.

Eagleton-Pierce, Matthew. 2013. *Symbolic Power in the World Trade Organization.* Oxford University Press.

The Economist. 2013. "Stand up for 'Doing Business'." May 25, 2013.

———. 2014. "Half a peg downward." June 20, 2016. Accessed December 21, 2016. www.economist.com/blogs/banyan/2014/06/human-trafficking.

Edwards, Phillip J., Ian Roberts, Mike J. Clarke, Carolyn DiGuiseppi, Reinhard Wentz, Irene Kwan, Rachel Cooper, Lambert M. Felix, and Sarah Pratap. 2009. "Methods to increase response to postal and electronic questionnaires (Review)." *Cochrane Database of Systematic Reviews* 3: 1–12.

Efrat, Asif. 2009. "Toward internationally regulated goods: Controlling the trade in small arms and light weapons." *Fordham Int'l LJ* 32 (5): 1466–1523.

———. 2012. *Governing Guns, Preventing Plunder: International Cooperation against Illicit Trade.* Oxford University Press.

Eghiazaryan, Aghavni. 2005. "Anti-trafficking efforts in Armenia." HETQ. Last Modified December 12, 2005. Accessed December 22, 2015. http://hetq.am/eng/news/9526/anti-trafficking-efforts-in-armenia.html.

Elklit, Jørgen, and Andrew Reynolds. 2002. "The impact of election administration on the legitimacy of emerging democracies: A new comparative politics research agenda." *Commonwealth & Comparative Politics* 40 (2): 86.

Emanuel, Gabrielle. 2016. "America's high school graduates look like other countries' high school dropouts." National Public Radio.

Erickson, Jennifer. 2015. *Dangerous Trade: Arms Exports, Human Rights, and International Reputation.* Columbia University Press.

Ermita, Eduardo. 2009. RP's Bid for MCA Compact Partner Status–Opening Remarks at Government of Philippines-hosted event at the Willard Hotel in Washington, DC, July 1, 2009.

Espeland, Wendy, and Michael Sauder. 2007. "Rankings and reactivity: How public measures recreate social worlds." *American Journal of Sociology* 113 (1): 1–40. doi: 10.1086/517897.

Espeland, Wendy Nelson, and Mitchell L. Stevens. 1998. "Commensuration as a social process." *Annual Review of Sociology* 24: 313–343.

Fearon, James. 1994. "Domestic political audiences and the escalation of international disputes." *American Political Science Review* 88 (3): 577–592.

Ferghana Information Agency. 2015. "Cotton Campaign urges signing petition damning Uzbekistan for forced labour." December 11, 2015. Accessed 19 January 2016. http://enews.fergananews.com/news.php?id=3094.

Fernquest, Jon. 2014. "2 Thais arrested for human trafficking." Accessed December 21, 2016. www.bangkokpost.com/learning/learning-from-news/437561/2-thais-arrested-for-human-trafficking.

Festinger, Leon. 1962. *A Theory of Cognitive Dissonance*. Vol. 2. Stanford University Press.

Finkel, Steven, Anibal Pérez-Liñán, Mitchell Seligson, and Dinorah Azpuru. 2006. "Effects of US foreign assistance on democracy building: Results of a cross-national quantitative study." In *Final Report, Prepared for USAID*. USAID.

Finnemore, Martha. 1996. *National Interests in International Society*. Cornell University Press.

Finnemore, Martha, and Kathryn Sikkink. 1998. "International norm dynamics and political change." *International Organization* 52 (4): 887–917.

Foester, Amy. 2009. "Contested bodies." *International Feminist Journal of Politics & Society* 11 (2): 151–173.

Foot, Kirsten A., Amoshaun Toft, and Nina Cesare. 2015. "Developments in anti-trafficking efforts: 2008–2011." *Journal of Human Trafficking* 1 (2): 136–155.

Foucault, Michel. 1995. *Discipline & Punish: The Birth of the Prison*. Vintage.

Franck, Thomas. 1990. *The Power of Legitimacy Among Nations*. Oxford University Press.

Franklin, James 2008. "Shame on you: The impact of human rights criticism on political repression in Latin America." *International Studies Quarterly* 52 (1): 187–211. doi: 10.1111/j.1468-2478.2007.00496.x.

Fredette, Kalen. 2009. "Revisiting the UN Protocol on Human Trafficking: Striking balances for more effective legislation." *Cardozo J. Int'l & Comp. L.* 17: 101.

Friedman, Allison. 2013. Public Comment at Duke Round Table, October 23, 2013. Duke University.

Friedman, Ina. 2001. "Victoria's, and Israel's, ugly secret." *The Jerusalem Report*. Last Modified March 12, 2001. Accessed December 21, 2016. http://theawarenesscenter.blogspot.com/2004/01/victorias-and-israels-ugly-secret.html.

Friman, H. Richard. 2015. "Conclusion: Exploring the politics of leverage." In *The Politics of Leverage in International Relations: Name, Shame, and Sanction*, edited by Richard Friman, 201–218. Palgrave Macmillan.

Friman, Richard. 2008. "Shades of compliance: Human trafficking and the politics of name and shame." Annual Meeting of the International Studies Association, San Francisco, CA, March 26–29.

Gallagher, Anne. 2001. "Human rights and the new UN protocols on trafficking and migrant smuggling: A preliminary analysis." *Human Rights Quarterly* 23 (4): 975–1004.

Gallagher, Anne T. 2011. "Improving the effectiveness of the international law of human trafficking: A vision for the future of the US Trafficking in Persons reports." *Human Rights Review* 12 (3): 381–400.

Gallagher, Anne. 2014a. "The global slavery index is based on flawed data: Why does no one say so?" *Guardian*, November 28, 2014. Accessed December 21, 2016. www.theguardian.com/global-development/poverty-matters/2014/nov/28/global-slavery-index-walk-free-human-trafficking-anne-gallagher.

2014b. "The trafficking watchlist may be flawed, but it's the best measure we have." *Guardian*, June 27, 2014. Accessed December 21, 2016. www.theguardian.com/global-development/poverty-matters/2014/jun/27/human-trafficking-watchlist-report.

Gallagher, Anne T. 2015. "Two cheers for the trafficking protocol." *Anti-Trafficking Review* 4: 14–32.

Gallagher, Anne, and Paul Holmes. 2008. "Developing an effective criminal justice response to human trafficking lessons from the front line." *International Criminal Justice Review* 18 (3): 318–343.

GAO. 2006. Human Trafficking. Better Data, Strategy, and Reporting Needed to Enhance U.S. Antitrafficking Efforts Abroad. Report to the Chairman, Committee on the Judiciary and the Chairman, Committee on International Relations, House of Representatives.

Garcia, Gabriel. 2006. "The State Department Human Trafficking Report: Raw ideology rather than bona fide research." Council on Hemispheric Affairs. Last Modified June 28, 2006. Accessed January 13, 2016. www.coha.org/the-state-department-human-trafficking-report-raw-ideology-rather-than-bona-fide-research/.

Garriga, Ana. 2016. "Human rights regimes, reputation, and foreign direct investment." *International Studies Quarterly* 60 (1): 160–172. doi: 10.1093/isq/sqw006.

George, Alexander L., and Timothy J. McKeown. 1985. "Case studies and theories of organizational decision making." *Advances in Information Processing in Organizations* 2 (1): 21–58.

Gilbert, Nina. 2001a. "Coalition MKs losing restraint." *Jerusalem Post*, July 19, 2001.

2001b. "Sex traffic victims won't be jailed." *Jerusalem Post*, July 24, 2001.

Gill, Michael, and Arthur Spirling. 2014. "Estimating the severity of the WikiLeaks United States diplomatic cables disclosure." *Political Analysis* 23 (2): 299–305.

Gilley, Bruce. 2013. *The Right to Rule: How States Win and Lose Legitimacy.* Columbia University Press.

Gilpin, Robert. 1981. *War and Change in World Politics.* Cambridge University Press.

Ginsburg, Alan, Geneise Cooke, Steve Leinwand, Jay Noell, and Elizabeth Pollock. 2005. "Reassessing US international mathematics performance: New findings from the 2003 TIMSS and PISA." *American Institutes for Research.*

Global Alliance Against Traffic in Women. 2007. Collateral Damage: The Impact of Anti-Trafficking Measures on Human Rights around the World. Bangkok, Thailand.

Goldstein, Judith, and Robert Keohane. 1993. *Ideas and Foreign Policy: Beliefs, Institutions, and Political Change.* Cornell University Press.

Government of Singapore. 2010. Singapore's Detailed Response to the Allegations in the 2010 US State Department's Trafficking in Persons Report.

Grant, Ruth W., and Robert O. Keohane. 2005. "Accountability and abuses of power in world politics." *American Political Science Review* 99 (1): 29–43.

Gray, Julia. 2013. *The Company States Keep: International Economic Organizations and Investor Perceptions.* Cambridge University Press.

Green, Eric. 2007a. "Public awareness of human trafficking increasing, Rice says." USINFO.

2007b. "State Department: NGO groups key in battle against human trafficking." US Fed News Service.

Greene, Jennifer, and Charles McClintock. 1985. "Triangulation in evaluation: Design and analysis issues." *Evaluation Review* 9 (5): 523–545. doi: 10.1177/0193841x8500900501.

Grek, Sotiria. 2009. "Governing by numbers: The PISA 'effect' in Europe." *Journal of Education Policy* 24 (1): 23–37.

Grobe, Christian. 2010. "The power of words: Argumentative persuasion in international negotiations." *European Journal of International Relations* 16 (1): 5–29.

Grzymala-Busse, Anna. 2010. "Time will tell? Temporality and the analysis of causal mechanisms and processes." *Comparative Political Studies* 44 (9): 1267–1297.

Gurowitz, Amy. 1999. "Mobilizing international norms: Domestic actors, immigrants, and the Japanese state." *World Politics* 51 (3): 413–445.

Guzman, Andrew. 2002. "A compliance-based theory of international law." *California Law Review* 90 (6): 1823.

Haas, Peter M. 1992. "Introduction: Epistemic communities and international policy coordination." *International Organization* 46 (1): 1–35.

Haas, Peter M., Robert O. Keohane, and Marc A. Levy. 1993. Institutions for the Earth: Sources of Effective International Environmental Protection. MIT Press.

Hafner-Burton, Emilie. 2005. "Trading human rights: How preferential trade agreements influence government repression." *International Organization* 59 (3): 593–629.

Hansen, Hans Krause. 2011. "The power of performance indices in the global politics of anti-corruption." *Journal of International Relations and Development* 15.

Hansen, Hans Krause, and Arthur Mühlen-Schulte. 2012. "The power of numbers in global governance." *Journal of International Relations and Development* 15 (4): 455–465.

Harsanyi, John C. 1966. "A bargaining model for social status in informal groups and formal organizations." *Behavioral Science* 11 (5): 357–369.

Harsanyi, John. 1971. "The dimension and measurement of social power." In *Power in Economics*, edited by Kurt Rothschild, 77–96. Penguin Books.

Hathaway, James C. 2008. "The human rights quagmire of human trafficking." *Va. J. Int'l L.* 49: 1.

Hawkins, Darren. 2002. *International Human Rights and Authoritarian Rule in Chile: Human Rights in International Perspective*. Vol. 6. University of Nebraska Press.

———. 2004. "Explaining costly international institutions: Persuasion and enforceable human rights norms." *International Studies Quarterly* 48 (4): 779–804. doi: 10.1111/j.0020-8833.2004.00325.x.

HBO. 2004. *Child Camel Jockeys in the Middle East- Ansar Burney*. HBO documentary, edited by HBO Real Sports Studio.

Heiss, Andrew, and Judith Kelley. 2016. From the trenches: A global survey of the Anti-TIP NGOs sector and its views of US efforts. Manuscript. Duke University.

Hendrix, Cullen S., and Wendy H. Wong. 2013. "When is the pen truly mighty? regime type and the efficacy of naming and shaming in curbing human rights abuses." *British Journal of Political Science* 43 (3): 651–672.

Hindstrom, Hanna. 2015. "How American anti-trafficking policy is failing Asian migrants." *Democracy Lab*. Accessed February 4, 2016. http://foreignpolicy.com/2015/08/17/how-american-anti-trafficking-policy-is-failing-asian-migrants-thailand-burma-rohingya/.

Holmes, Marcus. 2013. "The force of face-to-face diplomacy: Mirror neurons and the problem of intentions." *International Organization* 67 (4): 829–861.

Honig, Dan. 2016. Seeing is Believing: The Normative Drivers of Agency Response to the Aid Transparency Index. Prepared for presentation at IO/WCFIA Conference on Assessment Power in World Politics, Cambridge, MA, May 6–7, 2016.

Hopf, Ted. 2010. "The logic of habit in International Relations." *European Journal of International Relations* 16 (4): 539–561. doi: 10.1177/1354066110363502.

Horning, Amber, Christopher Thomas, Alana M. Henninger, and Anthony Marcus. 2014. "The Trafficking in Persons Report: A game of risk." *International Journal of Comparative and Applied Criminal Justice* 38 (3): 257–280.

Hovsepian, Marlena. 2002. "Fighting human trafficking." *Armenian Daily*. Last Modified November 19, 2002. Accessed December 21, 2016. www.azg.am/wap/?nl=EN&id=2002111901&Base_PUB=0.

Hufbauer, Gary, Jeffrey Schott, and Kimberly Elliott. 1990. *Economic Sanctions Reconsidered*. Institute for International Economics.

Hugh-Jones, David. 2013. "Reputation and cooperation in defense." *Journal of Conflict Resolution* 57 (2): 327–355.

Human Rights Watch. 2001. U.S. State Department Trafficking Report a "Mixed Bag." Accessed December 21, 2016. www.hrw.org/legacy/english/docs/2001/07/12/usint124.htm.

———. 2003. "Letter to Colin Powell on the Trafficking in Persons Report 2003." Accessed February 8, 2016. www.hrw.org/news/2003/06/26/letter-colin-powell-trafficking-persons-report-2003.

Hurd, Ian. 1999. "Legitimacy and authority in world politics." *International Organization* 53 (2): 379–408.

2008. *After Anarchy: Legitimacy and Power in the United Nations Security Council.* Princeton University Press.

Hyde, Susan. 2011. *The Pseudo-Democrat's Dilemma: Why Election Monitoring Became an International Norm.* Cornell University Press.

Hyland, Kelly E. 2001. "The impact of the Protocol to Prevent, Suppress and Punish Trafficking in Persons, Especially Women and Children." *Human Rights Brief* 8 (2): 12.

Ikenberry, G. John, and Charles A. Kupchan. 1990. "Socialization and hegemonic power." *International Organization* 44 (3): 283–315.

International Labour Organization. 2012. *ILO Global Estimate of Forced Labour 2012: Results and Methodology.* Geneva.

2014. *Profits and Poverty: The Economics of Forced Labour.* Geneva.

n.d. "Forced labour, human trafficking and slavery." Accessed December 21, 2016. www.ilo.org/global/topics/forced-labour/lang–en/index.htm.

International Organization for Migration. 2010. *Legal Review on Trafficking in Persons in the Caribbean.* 2nd edition. Geneva.

IRIN. 2004. "CHAD: Children sold into slavery for the price of a calf." December 21, 2004. Accessed January 6, 2016. www.irinnews.org/report/52490/chad-children-sold-into-slavery-for-the-price-of-a-calf.

Isarabhakdi, Vijavat. 2014. "Thailand's efforts to fight trafficking." *New York Times*, July 3, 2014, Letters to the editor. Accessed December 21, 2016. www.nytimes.com/2014/07/04/opinion/thailands-efforts-to-fight-trafficking.html.

Ito, Masami. 2005. "Tokyo still weak on human-trafficking: UN investigator." *The Japan Times*, July 14, 2005. Accessed December 21, 2016. www.japantimes.co.jp/news/2005/07/14/national/tokyo-still-weak-on-human-trafficking-u-n-investigator/#.V9wIK5MrKNZ.

Jackson, Patrick Thaddeus. 2002. "Rethinking Weber: Towards a non-individualist sociology of world politics." *International Review of Sociology* 12 (3): 439–468.

Jackson, Robert H. 1993. "The weight of ideas in decolonization: Normative change in international relations." In *Ideas and Foreign Policy: Beliefs, Institutions, and Political Change*, edited by J. Goldstein and R. Keohane, 111–138. Cornell University Press.

Jacobson, Harold K., and Edith Brown Weiss. 1997. "Compliance with international environmental accords." In *International Governance on Environmental Issues*, edited by Mats Rolén, Helen Sjöberg, and Uno Svedin, 78–110. Springer.

Jacoby, Wade. 2004. *The Enlargement of the European Union and NATO: Ordering from the Menu in Central Europe.* Cambridge University Press.

Jamaican Information Service. 2007. Press Statement from the National Anti-Trafficking in Persons Task Force, June 13. Jamaica.

Jamaican Ministry of National Security. 2012. The National Task Force Against Trafficking In Persons. Press Release No. 2713. Accessed February 17, 2017. http://go-jamaica.com/pressrelease/item.php?id=2211.

The Japan Times. 2004. "Japan blasted over human trafficking." June 16, 2004. Accessed December 21, 2016. www.japantimes.co.jp/2004/06/16/announcements/japan-blasted-over-human-trafficking/#.V6NdX1f91-p.

2004a. "Costly crackdown." December 7, 2004. Accessed December 21, 2016. www.japantimes.co.jp/community/2004/12/07/issues/costly-crackdown/#.V9wP45MrKNZ.

2004b. "Entertainers face visa crackdown as ministry targets prostitution." August 27, 2004. Accessed December 21, 2016. www.japantimes.co.jp/news/2004/08/27/national/entertainers-face-visa-crackdown-as-ministry-targets-prostitution/#.V9w6W5MrKNZ.

2004c. "Legal changes eyed to combat trafficking of human beings." July 4, 2004. Accessed January 5, 2016. www.japantimes.co.jp/2004/09/23/announcements/human-trafficking-woes-fail-to-gain-recognition/#.VjzdxoT93ms.

2004d. "NPA claims 83 women trafficked in for sex in 2003." March 26, 2004. Accessed December 21, 2016. www.japantimes.co.jp/news/2004/03/26/national/npa-claims-83-women-trafficked-in-for-sex-in-03/#.WGKGEbGZOu4.

2005. "Trafficking victims to get residency." January 19, 2005. Accessed December 21, 2016. www.japantimes.co.jp/news/2005/01/19/national/trafficking-victims-to-get-residency/#.V9w5_5MrKNZ.

Japanese Ministry of Foreign Affairs. n.d. *Japan's Actions to Combat Trafficking in Persons*. Japan.

Jervis, Robert. 1989. *The Logic of Images in International Relations*. Columbia University Press.

Jikkham, Patsara. 2014. "PM orders trafficking crackdown." Accessed December 21, 2016. www.bangkokpost.com/news/general/452003/pm-orders-trafficking-crackdown.

2015a. "PM vows to get tough on trafficking." *Bangkok Post*, April 4, 2015. Accessed December 21, 2015. http://m.bangkokpost.com/news/517923.

2015b. "Prayut threatens to punish journos." *Bangkok Post*, March 26, 2015. Accessed December 22, 2015. www.bangkokpost.com/archive/prayut-threatens-to-punish-journos%20Prayut%20threatens%20to%20punish%20journos.%2026%20March%202015,%20Bangkok%20Post/508311.

Jitcharoenkul, Prangthong, Manop Thip-osod, and Patsara Jikkham. 2015. "Trafficking: 'All US demands met'." *Bangkok Post*, April 1, 2015. Accessed December 21, 2015. www.bangkokpost.com/archive/trafficking-all-us-demands-met/514075.

Johnston, Alastair Iain. 2001. "Treating international institutions as social environments." *International Studies Quarterly* 45 (4): 487–515. doi: 10.1111/0020-8833.00212.

2008. *Social States: China in International Institutions, 1980–2000*. Princeton University Press.

Johnston, Eric. 2004. "Human trafficking woes fail to gain recognition." *The Japan Times*, September 23, 2004. Accessed December 21, 2016. www.japantimes.co.jp/2004/09/23/announcements/human-trafficking-woes-fail-to-gain-recognition/#.WFsSC7GZP1I.

Kalantarian, Karine. 2006. "Law enforcement officials cleared of human trafficking." HETQ. Last Modified March 6, 2006. Accessed December 21, 2016. http://hetq.am/eng/news/10052/law-enforcement-officials-cleared-of-human-trafficking.html.

Kang-Chung, N. G. 2015. "Hong Kong press freedom sinks to new low in global index." *South China Morning Post*. Last Modified February 13, 2015. Accessed December 21, 2016. www.scmp.com/news/hong-kong/article/1711311/hong-kong-press-freedom-sinks-new-low-global-index.

Kaplan, David, and Alec Dubro. 2003. *The Yakuza: Japan's Criminal Underworld*. University of California Press.

Kapstein, Ethan B. 2006. "The new global slave trade." *Foreign Affairs* 85: 103.

Katzenstein, Peter J. 1996. *Cultural Norms and National Security: Police and Military in Postwar Japan*. Cambridge University Press.

Katzenstein, Peter J., and Robert Owen Keohane. 2007. *Anti-Americanisms in World Politics*. Cornell University Press.

Keck, Margaret E., and Kathryn Sikkink. 1998. *Activists Beyond Borders: Advocacy Networks in International Politics*. Cornell University Press.

Kelley, Judith. 2004a. *Ethnic Politics in Europe: The Power of Norms and Incentives*. Princeton University Press.

2004b. "International actors on the domestic scene: Membership conditionality and socialization by international institutions." *International Organization* 58 (3): 425.

2007. "Who keeps international commitments and why? The International Criminal Court and bilateral nonsurrender agreements." *American Political Science Review* 101 (3): 573–589.

2009. "D minus elections: The politics and norms of international election observation." *International Organization* 63 (4): 765–787.

2011. "Do international election monitors influence opposition boycotts?" *Comparative Political Studies* 44 (11): 1527–1556.

2012. *Monitoring Democracy: When International Election Observation Works and Why It Often Fails*. Princeton University Press.

Kelley, Judith, and Beth Simmons. 2014. "The power of performance indicators: Rankings, ratings and reactivity in international relations." Paper prepared for the annual meeting of the American Political Science Association, August 27–September 1, 2014, Washington, DC.

2015. "Politics by number: Indicators as social pressure in international relations." *American Journal of Political Science* 59 (1): 55–70.

2016. "Global assessment power in the twenty-first century." Manuscript under review.

Kelley, Judith, Beth Simmons, and Rush Doshi. 2016. "The power of ranking: The ease of doing business indicator as a form of social pressure." Prepared for presentation at IO/WCFIA Conference on Assessment Power in World Politics, Cambridge, MA, May 6–7, 2016.

Kelly, Annie. 2013. "How NGOs are using the Trafficking in Persons report: The US diplomatic tool used to engage governments on trafficking can also be effective in helping campaign for change." *Guardian*. Accessed December 21,

2016. www.theguardian.com/global-development-professionals-network/2013/jun/21/ngos-using-trafficking-persons-report

2015. "Uzbekistan accused of brutal crackdown on activists investigating forced labour." *Guardian*, October 21, 2015. Accessed January 19, 2016. www.theguardian.com/global-development/2015/oct/21/uzbekistan-forced-labour-cotton-harvest-violent-crackdown-activists.

Kelman, Herbert C. 1958. "Compliance, identification, and internalization: Three processes of attitude change." *The Journal of Conflict Resolution* 2 (1): 51–60.

Keohane, Robert O. 1984. *After Hegemony: Cooperation and Discord in the World Political Economy*. Princeton University Press.

Keohane, Robert O. 1998. "When does international law come home." *Houston Law Review* 35: 699.

Keohane, Robert O., and Joseph S. Nye, Jr. 1998. "Power and interdependence in the information age." *Foreign Affairs* September/October issue: 81–94.

Kerry, John. 2014. Remarks at the Release of the 2014 Trafficking in Persons Report, June 20, 2014.

Kessler, Glenn. 2015. "Why you should be wary of statistics on 'modern slavery' and 'trafficking'." *Washington Post*, April 24, 2015. Accessed December 17, 2015. www.washingtonpost.com/blogs/fact-checker/wp/2015/04/24/why-you-should-be-wary-of-statistics-on-modern-slavery-and-trafficking/.

Killick, Tony. 1997. "Principals, agents and the failings of conditionality." *Journal of International Development* 9 (4): 483–495.

Kim, Moonhawk. 2012. "Ex ante due diligence: Formation of PTAs and protection of labor rights1." *International Studies Quarterly* 56 (4): 704–719.

Kingdon, John W., and James A. Thurber. 1984. *Agendas, Alternatives, and Public Policies*. Vol. 45. Little, Brown.

Klotz, Audie. 1995. "Norms reconstituting interests: Global racial equality and U.S. sanctions against South Africa." *International Organization* 49 (3): 451–478.

Kratochwil, Friedrich, and John Gerard Ruggie. 1986. "International organization: A state of the art on an art of the state." *International Organization* 40 (4): 753–775.

Krebs, Ronald, and Patrick Jackson. 2007. "Twisting tongues and twisting arms: The power of political rhetoric." *European Journal of International Relations* 13 (1): 35–66.

Kreps, David M., and Robert Wilson. 1982. "Reputation and imperfect information." *Journal of Economic Theory* 27 (2): 253–279.

Kuppusamy, Baradan. 2007. "RIGHTS-MALAYSIA: Human trafficking charges stick – activists." IPS (Latin America). Last Modified June 15, 2007. Accessed December 22, 2016. www.ipsnews.net/2007/06/rights-malaysia-human-trafficking-charges-stick-activists/.

LaFranchi, Howard. 2009. "Economic downturn fuels human trafficking." [Web]. *The Christian Science Monitor*. Last Modified June 17, 2009. Accessed January 6, 2016. www.csmonitor.com/USA/2009/0617/p02s07-usgn.html.

Lagon, Mark. 2010. U.S. Spotlight on Human Trafficking: Taking Stock of What Has Worked. Committee on Foreign Affairs (2nd Session, 111th Congress ed.).

2014. Illicit Fishing and Human Trafficking: Harming Business, Natural Resources, and Vulnerable People. Legislative Hearing on H.R. 69, The Illegal, Unreported and Unregulated Fishing Enforcement Act of 2013 (Bordallo); H.R. 2646, The REFI Pacific Act; and The Pirate Fishing Elimination Act.

Lagon, Mark, and Laila Mickelwait. 2016. "The U.S. government turns a blind eye to policies that fuel sex trafficking." *Washington Post*. Accessed February 4, 2016. www.washingtonpost.com/opinions/the-us-government-turns-a-blind-eye-to-policies-that-fuel-sex-trafficking/2016/02/01/959352e2-c6c6-11e5-a4aa-f25866baodc6_story.html?hpid=hp_no-name_opinion-card-c%3Ahomepage%2Fstory.

Larson, James, and Christine Callahan. 1990. "Performance monitoring: How it affects work productivity." *Journal of Applied Psychology* 75 (5): 530–538.

Lasswell, Harold. 1958. *Politics: Who Gets What, When, How*. Meridian Books.

Lawrence, Felicity and Kate Hodal. 2014. "Thai government condemned in annual US human trafficking report." *Guardian*, June 20, 2014. Accessed December 21, 2015. www.theguardian.com/global-development/2014/jun/20/thai-government-us-human-trafficking-report.

Layne, Christopher. 2012. "This time it's real: The end of unipolarity and the Pax Americana." *International Studies Quarterly* 56 (1): 203–213. doi: 10.1111/j.1468-2478.2011.00704.x.

Le, Anh, and Edmund Malesky. 2016. "Do subnational governance indices lead to improved governance? Evidence from field experiment in Vietnam." Prepared for presentation at IO/WCFIA Conference on Assessment Power in World Politics, Cambridge, MA, May 6–7, 2016.

Lebovic, James, and Erik Voeten. 2006. "The politics of shame: The condemnation of country human rights practices in the UNCHR." *International Studies Quarterly* 50 (4): 861–888.

Lebovic, J. H., and E. Voeten. 2009. "The cost of shame: International organizations and foreign aid in the punishing of human rights violators." *Journal of Peace Research* 46 (1): 79–97.

Lee, Vered. 2014. "Human trafficking to Israel has been beaten: Let's now tackle prostitution." *Haaretz*, March 17, 2014. Accessed December 22, 2016. www.haaretz.com/opinion/.premium-1.580160.

Legro, Jeffrey W. 1997. "Which norms matter? Revisiting the 'failure' of internationalism." *International Organization* 51 (1): 31–63. doi: 10.1162/002081897550294.

Lerum, Kari, Kiesha McCurtis, Penelope Saunders, and Stéphanie Wahab. 2012. "Using human rights to hold the US accountable for its anti-sex trafficking agenda: The universal periodic review and new directions for US policy." *Anti-Trafficking Review* 1: 80–103.

Levy, Jack. 1994. "Learning and foreign policy: Sweeping a conceptual minefield." *International Organization* 48 (2): 279–312.

Levy, Jack S., and William R. Thompson. 2011. *Causes of War*. John Wiley & Sons.

Linos, Katerina. 2013. *The Democratic Foundations of Policy Diffusion*. Oxford University Press.

The Local. 2016. "Spain plummets in corruption ranking to among worst in EU." Last Modified January 27, 2016. Accessed December 21, 2016. www.thelocal.es/20160127/spain-one-of-europes-most-corrupt-countries.

Locke, Richard M. 2013. *The Promise and Limits of Private Power: Promoting Labor Standards in a Global Economy*. Cambridge University Press.

Löwenheim, Oded. 2008. "Examining the state: A Foucauldian perspective on international 'governance indicators'." *Third World Quarterly* 29 (2): 255–274. doi: 10.1080/01436590701806814.

Lumsdaine, David Halloran. 1993. *Moral Vision in International Politics: The Foreign Aid Regime, 1949–1989*. Princeton University Press.

Lutz, Ellen, and Kathryn Sikkink. 2000. "International human rights law and practice in Latin America." *International Organization* 54 (3): 633–659.

Lynch, Colum. 2016. "Saudi Arabia threatened to break relations with U.N. over human rights criticism in Yemen." *Foreign Policy*, June 7, 2016.

Maguire, Amy. 2016. "Title." *The Conversation*, August 24, 2016. Accessed December 21, 2016. http://theconversation.com/why-does-international-condemnation-on-human-rights-mean-so-little-to-australia-53814.

Malay Mail Online. 2014. "Malaysia dips further in global gender equality ladder, second to last in ASEAN." Last Modified October 29. Accessed December 21, 2016. www.themalaymailonline.com/malaysia/article/malaysia-dips-further-in-global-gender-equality-ladder-second-to-last-in-as.

Manners, Ian. 2002. "Normative power Europe: A contradiction in terms?" *Journal of Common Market Studies* 40: 235–258.

Marinov, Nikolay. 2005. "Do economic sanctions destabilize country leaders?" *American Journal of Political Science* 49 (3): 564–576.

Marrache, Marion. 2001. "A-G calls for crackdown on trafficking in women." *The Jerusalem Post*, August 1, 2001. Accessed December 21, 2016. http://theawarenesscenter.blogspot.com/2001/08/a-g-calls-for-crackdown-on-trafficking.html.

Masenior, Nicole Franck, and Chris Beyrer. 2007. "The US anti-prostitution pledge: First Amendment challenges and public health priorities." *PLoS Medicine* 4 (7): e207. doi: 10.1371/journal.pmed.0040207.

Matsubara, Hiroshi. 2004. "Cooperation key to war on human trafficking." *The Japan Times*, June 26, 2004. Accessed December 21, 2016. www.japantimes.co.jp/2004/06/26/announcements/cooperation-key-to-war-on-human-trafficking/#.V6jvHFf91-0.

Mbiba, Lloyd. 2014. "Zim passes new human trafficking bill." Last Modified March 10, 2014. Accessed December 21, 2016. www.dailynews.co.zw/articles/2014/03/10/zim-passes-new-human-trafficking-bill.

McCauley, Kevin. 2014. "H&K promotes Thailand's human rights push." Last Modified February 13, 2014. Accessed December 21, 2015. www.odwyerpr.com/story/public/1894/2014-02-13/hk-promotes-thailands-human-rights-push.html.

Mena Report. 2002. "Israel's thriving sex industry records one billion dollars a year." Last Modified December 9, 2002. Accessed December 21, 2016. www.albawaba.com/business/israel%E2%80%99s-thriving-sex-industry-records-one-billion-dollars-year-0.

Mercer, Jonathan. 1996. *Reputation and International Politics*. Cornell University Press.

Merry, Sally Engle. 2011. "Measuring the world: Indicators, human rights, and global governance: With CA comment by John M. Conley." *Current Anthropology* 52 (S3): S83–S95. doi: 10.1086/657241.

Merry, Sally Engle, Kevin E. Davis, and Benedict Kingsbury. 2015. *The Quiet Power of Indicators: Measuring Governance, Corruption, and Rule of Law.* Cambridge University Press.

Mertus, Julie, and Andrea Bertone. 2007. "Combating trafficking: International efforts and their ramifications." In *Human Trafficking, Human Security, and the Balkans*, edited by Richard Friman and Simon Reich, 40–16. University of Pittsburgh Press.

Meyer, John W., and Brian Rowan. 1977. "Institutionalized organizations: Formal structure as myth and ceremony." *American Journal of Sociology* 83: 340–363.

Millennium Challenge Corporation. 2008. Congressional Notification of Transmittal Sheet. Attachement 1: Relevant Background on Moldova, July 2, 2008.

Ministry of Foreign Affairs of the Kingdom of Thailand. 2014. Thailand's Anti-Trafficking Progress Exceeds U.S. State Department Criteria For Upgrade. Press Release No. 159/2557.

Monks, James, and Ronald G. Ehrenberg. 1999. "U.S. News & World Report's College Rankings: Why they do matter." *Change: The Magazine of Higher Learning* 31 (6): 42–51.

Morgenthau, Hans. 1950. *Politics among Nations: The Struggle for Peace and Power.* 4th edition. Knopf.

Mullainathan, Sendhil, Jens Ludwig, and Jeffrey R. Kling. 2011. "Mechanism experiments and policy evaluations." *Journal of Economic Perspectives* 25 (3): 17–38.

Mutz, Diana C. 1998. *Impersonal Influence: How Perceptions of Mass Collectives Affect Political Attitudes.* Cambridge University Press.

Mwakalyelye, Ndimyake. 2006. VOA News: Harare rejects U.S. Human Trafficking Allegations US Fed News. Accessed July 27, 2012. www.zimbabwesituation.com/old/jun8_2006.html#Z21.

Nance, M. 2015. "Naming and shaming in financial regulation: Explaining variation in the Financial Action Task Force on Money Laundering." In *The Politics of Leverage in International Relations: Name, Shame, and Sanction*, edited by Richard Friman, 123–142. Palgrave Macmillan.

Nathan, Debbie. 2005. "Oversexed." *The Nation*, August 29 – September 5.

The Nation. 2015. "Thailand remains on bottom of TIP report." Accessed February 17, 2017. www.nationmultimedia.com/news/national/aec/30265366.

Neubauer, Chuck. 2012. "Top human traffickers need not fear Obama." *The Washington Times*, July 29, 2012. Accessed December 17, 2015. www.washingtontimes.com/news/2012/jul/29/the-failure-of-the-white-house-to-enforce-threaten/?page=all.

Neumann, Iver B. 2007. "'A speech that the entire ministry may Stand for,' or: Why diplomats never produce anything new." *International Political Sociology* 1 (2): 183–200.

Newby, Kim. 1995. "The effectiveness of Special 301 in creating long term copyright protection for US companies overseas." *Syracuse J. Int'l L. & Com.* 21: 29.

Newton, Kennety, and Pippa Norris. 2000. "Confidence in public institutions: Faith, culture or performance?" In *Disaffected Democracies: What's Troubling the Trilateral Countries*, edited by Susan Pharr and Robert Putnam, 52–73. Princeton University Press.

No to Trafficking. 2009. "DOJ orders inventory of human trafficking cases, seeks help of High Court." Last Modified June 24, 2009. Accessed December 17, 2015. http://trafficking.org.ph/v5/index.php?option=com_content&task=vi ew&id=2766&Itemid=56.

Nye, Joseph S., Jr. 1990. "Soft power." *Foreign Policy* 80: 153–171. doi: 10.2307/ 1148580.

Nye, Joseph S. 2004. *Soft Power: The Means to Success in World Politics*. 1st edition. Public Affairs.

2008. "Public diplomacy and soft power." *The ANNALS of the American Academy of Political and Social Science* 616 (1): 94–109. doi: 10.1177/ 0002716207311699.

2010. "The future of American power." *Foreign Affairs* 89 (6): 2–12.

Office of Inspector General. 2010. Survey of the Millennium Challenge Corporation's Policies and Procedures to Address U.S. Government Anti-Trafficking Policy.

2011. Review of the Millennium Challenge Corporation's Approach to Addressing and Deterring Trafficking in Persons. Washington, DC.

Office of the Inspector General. 2012. Inspection of the Office to Monitor and Combat Trafficking in Persons.

Office of the US Inspector General. 2012. Inspection of the Office to Monitor and Combat Trafficking in Persons, Report Number ISP-I-12–37, June 2012. United States Department of State.

Öhler, Hannes, Peter Nunnenkamp, and Axel Dreher. 2012. "Does conditionality work? A test for an innovative US aid scheme." *European Economic Review* 56 (1): 138–153. doi: http://dx.doi.org/10.1016/j.euroecorev.2011.05.003.

Oldfield, John R. 1998. *Popular Politics and British Anti-Slavery: The Mobilisation of Public Opinion Against the Slave Trade, 1787–1807*. Vol. 6. Psychology Press.

Ollus, Natalia. 2008. The United Nations Protocol to Prevent, Suppress and Punish Trafficking in Persons, Especially Women and Children: A Tool for Criminal Justice Personnel. *Resource Material Series No. 62*, 16–30. Accessed December 21, 2016. www.unafei.or.jp/english/pdf/RS_No62/No62_07VE_ Ollus2.pdf.

Oltermann, Philip. 2015. "Merkel 'gambling away' Germany's reputation over Greece, says Habermas." *Guardian*, July 16, 2016. Accessed December 21, 2016. www.theguardian.com/business/2015/jul/16/merkel-gambling-away-germanys-reputation-over-greece-says-habermas.

Onishi, Norimitsu. 2005. "Japan, easygoing til now, plans sex traffic crackdown." *New York Times*, February 16, 2005, 1, A. Accessed January 6, 2016. www. nytimes.com/2005/02/16/world/asia/japan-easygoing-till-now-plans-sex-traffic-crackdown.html?_r=0.

OSCE. 2008. Human Trafficking Manual for Journalists. Accessed January 6, 2016. www.osce.org/serbia/36212?download=true.

Ozawa, Harumi. 2014. "Japan sanctioning mass 'slave labor' by duping foreign trainees, observers say." *The Japan Times*, Last Modified November 23, 2014. Accessed January 6, 2016. www.japantimes.co.jp/news/2014/11/23/ national/japan-sanctioning-mass-slave-labor-via-foreign-trainee-program/ #.Vp5t1jb91-p.

Parks, Bradley C. 2014. "Brokering Development Policy Change: The Parallel Pursuit of Millennium Challenge Account Resources and Reform." In *Dissertation*, edited by The London School of Economics and Political Science. June 2014.

Parks, Bradley C., and Zachary J. Rice. 2013. "Does the 'MCC effect' exist? Results from the 2012 MCA Stakeholder Survey." Report, Center for Global Development. Accessed December 22, 2016. www.cgdev.org/publication/ does-"mcc-effect"-exist-results-2012-mca-stakeholder-survey.

Parks, Bradley, Zachary Rice, and Samantha Custer. 2015. The Marketplace of Ideas for Policy Change: Who Do Developing World Leaders Listen To and Why? William and Mary College: AidData Report. Accessed December 22, 2016. http://aiddata.org/sites/default/files/marketplaceofideas_fullreport.pdf.

Peterson, Timothy M. 2013. "Sending a message: The reputation effect of US sanction threat behavior." *International Studies Quarterly* 57 (4): 672–682.

Phillips, Janet. 2008. "People trafficking: An update on Australia's response, Research Paper no. 5 2008–09." *Australian Parliamentary Library*: 5.

Pierson, Paul. 1993. "When effect becomes cause: Policy feedback and political change." *World Politics* 45 (4): 595–628. doi: 10.2307/2950710.

Pouliot, Vincent, and Jérémie Cornut. 2015. "Practice theory and the study of diplomacy: A research agenda." *Cooperation and Conflict*: 0010836715574913.

Price, Richard. 1998. "Reversing the gun sights: Transnational civil society targets land mines." *International Organization* 52 (3): 613–644.

Protection Project. 2014. The Protection Project Review of the Trafficking in Persons Report.

Ragin, Charles C. 2000. *Fuzzy-Set Social Science*. University of Chicago Press.

Raustiala, Kal, and Anne-Marie Slaughter. 2002. "International law, international relations and compliance." In *Handbook of International Relations*, edited by W. Carlsnaes, T. Risse, and B. Simmons, 583–358. Sage Publications.

Rautalin, Marjaana, and Pertti Alasuutari. 2009. "The uses of the national PISA results by Finnish officials in central government." *Journal of Education Policy* 24 (5): 539–556. doi: 10.1080/02680930903131267.

Readfearn, Graham. 2015. "Will Australia continue to sacrifice its international reputation on the alter of coal." *Guardian*, June 5, 2015. Accessed December 27, 2016. www.theguardian.com/environment/planet-oz/2015/jun/05/will-australia-continue-to-sacrifice-its-international-reputation-on-the-alter-of-coal.

Renshon, Jonathan. 2016. "Status deficits and war." *International Organization* 70 (3): 513–550.

Renshon, Jonathan, Allan Dafoe, and Paul Huth. Forthcoming. "To whom do reputations adhere: Experimental evidence on influence-specific reputation." *American Journal of Political Science*.

Reus-Smit, Christian. 2007. "International crises of legitimacy." *International Politics* 44 (2): 157–174.

Reuters. 2015. "Thailand toughens trafficking law with death penalty, steep fines." Last Modified March 26, 2015. Accessed December 21, 2015. www.reuters.com/article/us-thailand-trafficking-idUSKBN0MM10V20150326.

———. 2016. "China risks damaging international reputation if it rejects tribunal ruling on South China Sea disputes, US warns." *South China Morning Post*. Last Modified April 29, 2016. Accessed December 27, 2016. www.scmp.com/news/china/diplomacy-defence/article/1939925/china-risks-damaging-international-reputation-if-it.

Ribando, Clare. 2005. "Trafficking in persons in Latin America and the Caribbean." In *CRS Report for Congress*. United States Government.

Richards, Kathy. 2004. "The trafficking of migrant workers: What are the links between labour trafficking and corruption?" *International Migration* 42 (5): 147–168.

Ridgeway, Cecilia. 2013. "Why status matters for inequality." *American Sociological Review* 79 (1): 1–16. doi: 10.1177/0003122413515997.

Rieh, Soo Young. 2002. "Judgment of information quality and cognitive authority in the Web." *Journal of the American Society for Information Science and Technology* 53 (2): 145–161.

Risse, Thomas. 2000. "Let's argue! Communicative action in world politics." *International Organization* 54 (1): 1–39.

Risse, Thomas, and Steve Ropp. 2013. "Introduction and overview." In *The Persistent Power of Human Rights: From Commitment to Compliance*, edited by Thomas Risse, Steve Ropp, and Kathryn Sikkink, 1–25. Cambridge University Press.

Risse, Thomas, and Kathryn Sikkink 1999. "The socialization of international human rights norms into domestic practice: Introduction." In *The Power of Human Rights: International Norms and Domestic Change*, edited by Thomas Risse, Steve C. Ropp, and Kathryn Sikkink, 1–38. Cambridge University Press.

Risse, Thomas, and Kathryn Sikkink. 2013. "Conclusions." In *The Persistent Power of Human Rights: From Commitment to Compliance*, edited by Thomas Risse, Steve Ropp, and Kathryn Sikkink, 275–295. Cambridge University Press.

Risse, Thomas, Steven Ropp, and Kathryn Sikkink. 1999. The Power of Human Rights: *International Norms and Domestic Change*. Cambridge University Press.

Roberts, Jordan, and Juan Tellez. 2016. "Freedom House's Scarlet Letter: Negative assessments and verbal conflict." Prepared for presentation at IO/WCFIA Conference on Assessment Power in World Politics, Cambridge, MA, May 6–7, 2016.

Robson, Keith. 1992. "Accounting numbers as 'inscription': Action at a distance and the development of accounting." *Accounting, Organizations and Society* 17 (7): 685–708.

Rosenau, James N. 1986. "Before cooperation: Hegemons, regimes, and habit-driven actors in world politics." *International Organization* 40 (4): 849–894.

Rosenberg, Matthew, and Joe Cochrane. 2015. "Key shift on Malaysia before Trans-Pacific Partnership deal." *New York Times*, July 27, 2015. Accessed

December 17, 2015. www.nytimes.com/2015/07/28/world/asia/thailands-low-ranking-in-human-trafficking-report-could-hamper-trade-deal.html.

Rutten, Rosanne. 2006. "Shame and worker activism: Emotional dynamics in face-to-face encounters." *Qualitative Sociology* 29 (3): 353–372.

Sartori, Anne. 2002. "The might of the pen: A reputational theory of communication in international disputes." *International Organization* 56 (1): 121–149.

Schachter, Oscar. 1991. *International Law in Theory and Practice*. Vol. 13. Martinus Nijhoff Publishers.

Scheff, Thomas J., and Suzanne M. Retzinger. 2000. "Shame as the master emotion of everyday life." *Journal of Mundane Behavior* 1 (3): 303–324.

Schelling, Thomas. 1980. *The Strategy of Conflict*. Harvard University Press.

Schimmelfennig, Frank. 2001. "The community trap: Liberal norms, rhetorical action, and the Eastern enlargement of the European Union." *International Organization* 55 (1): 47–80.

Schimmelfennig, Frank, Stefan Engert, and Heiko Knobel. 2003. "Costs, commitment and compliance: The impact of EU democratic conditionality on Latvia, Slovakia and Turkey." *Journal of Common Market Studies* 41 (3): 495–518.

Scott, James M., and Carie A. Steele. 2011. "Sponsoring democracy: The United States and democracy aid to the developing world, 1988–20011." *International Studies Quarterly* 55 (1): 47–69.

Sen, Amartya. 1999. *Development as Freedom*. Oxford University Press.

Shannon, Vaughn. 2000. "Norms are what states make of them: The political psychology of norm violation." *International Studies Quarterly* 44 (2): 293–316.

Sharman, Jason C. 2007. "Rationalist and constructivist perspectives on reputation." *Political Studies* 55 (1): 20–37.

2008. "Power and discourse in policy diffusion: Anti-money laundering in developing states." *International Studies Quarterly* 52 (3): 635–656.

Shelley, Louise. 2005. "Russia's law against trade in people: A response to international pressure and domestic coalitions." In *Public Policy and Law in Russia: In Search of a Unified Legal and Political Space*, edited by F. F. J. M. Feldbrugge, D. D. Barry, and R. S. Sharlet, 291–305. Martinus Nijhoff Publishers.

Shubert, Atika. 2004. "Japan pushes for UN Council seat." *CNN.com*, September 22, 2004. Accessed January 19, 2016. http://edition.cnn.com/2004/US/09/22/un.reforms/index.html.

Sikkink, Kathryn. 1993. "Human rights, principled issue-networks, and sovereignty in Latin America." *International Organization* 47 (3): 411–441.

2002. "Restructuring world politics: The limits and assymmetries of soft power." In *Restructuring World Politics: Transnational Social Movements, Networks, and Norms*, edited by Sanjeev Khagram, James Riker, and Kathryn Sikkink, 301–319. University of Minnesota Press.

Sil, Rudra, and Peter J. Katzenstein. 2010. *Beyond Paradigms: Analytic Eclecticism in the Study of World Politics*. Palgrave Macmillan.

Silver, Steve. 2006. "The trafficking scourge." *The Japan Times*, August 15, 2006. Accessed December 21, 2016. www.japantimes.co.jp/community/2006/08/15/issues/the-trafficking-scourge/#.VjzeYIT93ms.

Simmons, Beth. 1998. "Compliance with international agreements." *Annual Review of Political Science* 1 (1): 75–93.

2000. "International law and state behavior: Commitment and compliance in international monetary affairs." *American Political Science Review* 94 (4): 819–835.

2009. *Mobilizing for Human Rights: International Law in Domestic Politics*. Cambridge University Press.

2010. "Treaty compliance and violation." *Annual Review of Political Science* 13 (1): 273–296. doi: 10.1146/annurev.polisci.12.040907.132713.

Sinclair, Timothy. 2005. *The New Masters of Capital: American Bond Rating Agencies and the Politics of Creditworthiness*. Cornell University Press.

Skocpol, Theda. 1995. *Protecting Soldiers and Mothers*. Harvard University Press.

Smith, Chris. 2014. Effective Accountability: Tier Rankings and the TIP Report: Hearing before the House of Representatives, 113th Congress 2 (2014). Statement of Rep. Chris Smith, Chairman, Subcommittee on Africa, Global Health, Global Human Rights, and International Organizations, April 29, 2014.

2015. Accountability and Transformation: Tier Rankings in the Fight Against Human Trafficking. Subcommittee on Africa, Global Health, Global Human Rights and International Organizations.

Sri Lanka Ministry of Defence. 2011. US State Department Elevates Sri Lanka's Status on Human Trafficking Enforcement. Sri Lanka Ministry of Defence.

Stoller, Julia, and Jaclyn Light. 2013. Are Nigeria's Human Trafficking Efforts Paternalistic? An Interview with Stacey Vanderhurst. Brown Human Rights Report.

Stone, Randall. 2004. "The political economy of IMF lending in Africa." *American Political Science Review* 98 (4): 577–591.

Sychov, Alyaksandr. 2009. "Human trafficking: A call for global action." *Global Strategy Journal* 22 (14): 1–11.

Szep, Jason, and Matt Spetalnick. 2015. "Special report: State Department watered down human trafficking report." *Reuters*, August 3, 2015. Accessed December 21, 2016. www.reuters.com/article/us-usa-humantrafficking-disputes-special-idUSKCN0Q821Y20150804.

Tallberg, Jonas, and Michael Zürn. 2015. The Legitimacy and Legitimation of International Organizations. Manuscript.

Thai Anti-Human Trafficking Action. 2014. Thailand's Trafficking in Persons Country Report, 2014.

n.d. "News and updates." Accessed December 21, 2015. www.thaianti-humantraffickingaction.org/Home/?cat=1.

Thomas, Daniel. 2001. *The Helsinki Effect: International Norms, Human Rights, and the Demise of Communism*. Princeton University Press.

Tian, Dexin. 2008. "The USTR Special 301 Reports: An analysis of the US hegemonic pressure upon the organizational change in China's IPR regime." *Chinese Journal of Communication* 1 (2): 224–241.

Tibaijuka, Anna. 2005. Report of the Fact-finding Mission to Zimbabwe to assess the Scope and Impact of Operation Murambatsvina by the Special Envoy on Human Settlements Issues in Zimbabwe. United Nations.

Tomz, Michael. 2007a. "Domestic audience costs in international relations: An experimental approach." *International Organization* 61 (4): 821–840. doi: 10.1017/S0020818307070282.

2007b. *Reputation and International Cooperation: Sovereign Debt across Three Centuries*. Princeton University Press.

Townshend, Ashley. 2015. "China may fear reputation damage more than military threats over South China Sea." *Guardian*, August 28, 2015. Accessed December 21, 2016. www.theguardian.com/commentisfree/2015/aug/29/china-may-fear-reputation-damage-more-than-military-threats-over-south-china-sea.

Tumnukasetchai, Piyanut, and Petchanet Pratruangkrai. 2014. "Anxious wait for TIP report – The Nation." Accessed December 21, 2016. www.nationmultimedia.com/national/Anxious-wait-for-TIP-report-30236691.html.

Tyldum, Guri, and Anette Brunovskis. 2005. "Describing the unobserved: Methodological challenges in empirical studies on human trafficking." *International Migration* 43 (1–2): 17–34. doi: 10.1111/j.0020-7985.2005.00310.x.

United Nations. 2000. United Nations Convention Against Transnational Organized Crime (with protocols). New York.

2009. Conference of the Parties to the United Nations Convention against Transnational Organized Crime, "Report on the Meeting of Experts on Possible Mechanisms to Review Implementation of the United Nations Convention against Transnational Organized Crime held in Vienna on 30 September 2009." UN Doc. CTOC/COP/WG.1/2009/3, October 14, 2009.

The United States Department of Justice. 2012. "About the Office of Overseas Prosecutorial Development, Assistance and Training." Accessed December 17, 2015. www.justice.gov/criminal/opdat/about/.

United States House of Representatives. 2010. Committee on Foreign Affairs. *U.S. Spotlight on Human Trafficking: Taking Stock of What Has Worked*. 2nd Session, 111th Congress. September 30.

United States Senate Committee on Foreign Relations. 2016. Cardin Introduces Major Anti-Corruption Legislation: Accountability Mechanism Styled After Trafficking in Persons Report. Accessed February 17, 2017. www.foreign.senate.gov/press/ranking/release/cardin-introduces-major-anti-corruption-legislation-?

UNODC. 2006. Measures to Combat Trafficking in Human Beings in Benin, Nigeria, and Togo. Accessed February 17, 2017. www.unodc.org/documents/human-trafficking/ht_research_report_nigeria.pdf.

2009. UNODC Report on Human Trafficking Exposes Modern Form of Slavery. Accessed February 17, 2017. www.unodc.org/unodc/en/frontpage/unodc-report-on-human-trafficking-exposes-modern-form-of-slavery-.html.

2014. Global Report on Trafficking in Persons (United Nations publication, Sales No. E.14.V.10). Accessed February 17, 2017. www.unodc.org/documents/data-and-analysis/glotip/GLOTIP_2014_full_report.pdf.

2015. "Chad strengthens legislation against human trafficking thanks to UNODC support." Accessed December 20, 2015. www.unodc.org/westandcentralafrica/en/chad–anti-human-trafficking-law–25-26-march-2015.html.

US Congress. 2000. The Trafficking Victims Protection Act, P.L. 106–386. United States Government.

2002. Foreign Government Complicity in Human Trafficking: A Review of the State Department's "2002 Trafficking in Persons Report." Hearing before the Commitee on International Relations, House of Representatives, 107th Congress, June 19, 2002.

2005. Trafficking Victims Protection Reauthorization Act of 2005, H.R.972. United States Government.

2010. Hearing before the Commission on Security & Cooperation in Europe: U.S. Helsinki Commission. A Decade of The Trafficking in Persons Report. July 14, 2010. Accessed December 27, 2016. www.csce.gov/international-impact/events/decade-trafficking-persons-report.

2014. Effective Accountability: Tier Rankings in the Fight Against Human Trafficking. Hearing before the Subcommittee on Africa, Global Health, Global Human Rights, and International Organizations, April 29, 2014. Edited by the Committee on Foreign Affairs.

US Department of State. 2012–2013. Request for Information for the 2015 Trafficking in Persons Report.

2015. Annual Report on Trafficking in Persons.

US Department of State and the Broadcasting Board of Governors. 2012–2013. Semiannual Report to the Congress, October 1, 2012 to March 31, 2013. Office of Inspector General.

US Department of State Office to Monitor and Combat Trafficking in Persons. 2010. USG TIP Projects with Funds Obligated in Fiscal Year 2010.

US Senate. 2012. The Next Ten Years in the Fight Against Human Trafficking: Attacking the Problme with the Right Tools. Hearning before the Committee on Foreign Relations, July 17, 2012. Edited by United States Senate.

US State Department. 2002. Exhibition against Trafficking of Women Opens in Yerevan; Dept. of State, USAID, American Bar Assoc. among supporters.

Vachudova, Milada Anna. 2005. *Europe Undivided Democracy, Leverage, and Integration after Communism.* Oxford University Press.

Varela, Cecilia Inés. 2012. Del Tráfico De Las Mujeres Al Tráfico De Las Políticas. Apuntes Para Una Historia Del Movimiento Anti-Trata En La Argentina (1998–2008), Revista Publicar, Colegio de graduados de antropología, año X, número XII, Nro 12, 2012. Accessed December 27, 2016. http://ppct.cai-cyt.gov.ar/index.php/publicar/issue/view/196/showToc ISSN impreso 0327-6627 – ISSN en línea 2250-7671.

Von Bogdandy, Armin, and Matthias Goldmann. 2008. "The exercise of international public authority through national policy assessment." *Int'l Org. L. Rev.* 5: 241.

Wachman, Alan M. 2001. "Does the diplomacy of shame promote human rights in China?" *Third World Quarterly* 22 (2): 257–281. doi: 10.2307/3993410.

Walter, Barbara F. 2009. *Reputation and Civil War: Why Separatist Conflicts are so Violent.* Cambridge University Press.

Waters, Angela. 2016. "Chancellor Merkel's party suffers loss in home state over migrant policy." *USA Today*, September 4, 2016. Accessed September 5,

2016. www.usatoday.com/story/news/world/2016/09/04/merkels-migrant-policy-focus-vote-german-chancellors-home-state/89863102/.

Weber, Max. 1968 [1925]. *Economy and Society: An Outline of Interpretive Sociology*. Vol. 1. Bedminster Press.

Weiss, Edith, and Harold Jacobson, eds. 2000. *Engaging Countries: Strengthening Compliance with International Environmental Accords*. The MIT Press.

Weitzer, Ronald. 2005. "The growing moral panic over prostitution and sex trafficking." *The Criminologist* 30 (5): 1–5.

Wendt, Alexander. 1999. *Social Theory of International Politics*. Cambridge University Press.

Wexler, Lesley. 2003. "The international deployment of shame, second-best responses, and norm entrepreneurship: The campaign to ban landmines and the landmine ban treaty." *Arizona Journal of International and Comparative Law* 20: 561–606.

Weyland, Kurt. 2009. *Bounded Rationality and Policy Diffusion: Social Sector Reform in Latin America*. Princeton University Press.

Williams, Ian. 2005. Security Council Reform Debate Highlights Challenges Facing UN. Accessed December 27, 2016. http://fpif.org/security_council_reform_debate_highlights_challenges_facing_un/.

Williams, William Appleman. 1988. *The Tragedy of American Diplomacy*. W. W. Norton & Company.

Wooditch, Alese. 2010. "The efficacy of the trafficking in persons report: A review of the evidence." *Criminal Justice Policy Review* 22 (4): 471–493.

The World Bank Group. 2007. Celebrating Reform 2007. Doing Business Case Studies. The World Bank.

2008. Celebrating Reform 2008. Doing Business Case Studies. The World Bank.

2009. Celebrating Reform 2009. Doing Business Case Studies. The World Bank.

Wyler, Liana. 2013. Trafficking in Persons: International Dimensions and Foreign Policy Issues for Congress. Congressional Research Service.

Wyler, Liana, Alison Siskin, and Clare Ribando. 2009. Trafficking in Persons: U.S. Policy and Issues for Congress. Congressional Research Service.

Yalch, Richard, and Rebecca Elmore-Yalch. 1984. "The effect of numbers on the route to persuasion." *Journal of Consumer Research* 11 (1): 522–527. doi: 10.2307/2489139.

Young, Oran R. 1979. *Compliance and Public Authority: A Theory with International Applications*. Resources for the Future.

1992. "The effectiveness of international institutions: Hard cases and critical variables." In *Governance without Government: Order and Change in World Politics*, edited by James Rosenau and Ernst-Otto Czempiel, 160–194. Cambridge University Press.

Yuriko-Thomas, Lisa. 2004. "Japan criticized over poor effort to prevent human trafficking." *The Japan Times*, March 20, 2004. Accessed December 27, 2016. www.japantimes.co.jp/news/2004/03/20/national/japan-criticized-over-poor-effort-to-prevent-human-trafficking/#.V9wzKZMrKNZ.

Zacharia, Janine. 2001. "US: Israel among states lax on human trafficking." *The Jerusalem Post*, July 13, 2001.

Zacharia, Janine, and Shula Kopf. 2002. "US report shows Israel clamping down on trafficking in women." *The Jerusalem Post*, June 6, 2002.

Zaloznaya, Marina, and John Hagan. 2012. "Fighting human trafficking or instituting authoritarian control." In *Governance by Indicators: Global Power through Classification and Rankings*, edited by Kevin Davis, Angelina Fisher, Benedict Kingsbury, and Sally Engle Merry, 344–364. Oxford University Press.

Zhu, Yuchao. 2011. "'Performance legitimacy' and China's political adaptation strategy." *Journal of Chinese Political Science* 16 (2): 123–140.

ZimSitRep_J. 2014. "Anti-trafficking in persons regulations gazetted." Last Modified January 9, 2014. Accessed December 21, 2016. www.zimbabwesituation.com/news/zimsit_bill-watch-12014-8th-january-anti-trafficking-persons-regulations-gazetted/.

———. 2015. "President establishes anti-trafficking committee." Last Modified January 14, 2015. Accessed December 21, 2016. www.zimbabwesituation.com/news/zimsit_w_president-establishes-anti-trafficking-committee-the-herald/.

Index